VOLUME SIX

ADVANCES IN TRANSPORT POLICY AND PLANNING

Standard Transport Appraisal Methods

VOLUME SIX

ADVANCES IN TRANSPORT POLICY AND PLANNING

Standard Transport Appraisal Methods

Edited by

NIEK MOUTER
Faculty of Technology, Policy and Management, Engineering Systems and Services Department, Transport and Logistics Group, Delft, Netherlands

ELSEVIER

ACADEMIC PRESS
An imprint of Elsevier

Academic Press is an imprint of Elsevier
50 Hampshire Street, 5th Floor, Cambridge, MA 02139, United States
525 B Street, Suite 1650, San Diego, CA 92101, United States
The Boulevard, Langford Lane, Kidlington, Oxford OX5 1GB, United Kingdom
125 London Wall, London, EC2Y 5AS, United Kingdom

First edition 2020

ISBN: 978-0-12-820821-2
ISSN: 2543-0009

For information on all Academic Press publications
visit our website at https://www.elsevier.com/books-and-journals

Publisher: Zoe Kruze
Acquisitions Editor: Sam Mahfoudh
Editorial Project Manager: Shellie Bryant
Production Project Manager: James Selvam
Cover Designer: Alan Studholme

Typeset by SPi Global, India

Contents

Contributors

Henrik Andersson
Toulouse School of Economics, University of Toulouse Capitole, Toulouse, France

Rosa M. Arce-Ruiz
Transport Research Centre—TRANSyT—Universidad Politécnica Madrid, Madrid, Spain

Amor Ariza-Álvarez
Transport Research Centre—TRANSyT—Universidad Politécnica Madrid, Madrid, Spain

Aldo Arranz-López
Transport Research Centre—TRANSyT—Universidad Politécnica Madrid, Madrid, Spain

Marco Dean
Bartlett School of Planning, University College London, London, United Kingdom

Gerard de Jong
Significance, The Hague, The Netherlands; ITS, University of Leeds, Leeds, United Kingdom

Carl Koopmans
Department of Spatial Economics, Vrije Universiteit Amsterdam, School of Business and Economics; SEO Amsterdam Economics, Amsterdam, Netherlands

Marco Kouwenhoven
Significance, The Hague; Delft University of Technology, Delft, The Netherlands

Niek Mouter
Faculty of Technology, Policy and Management, Engineering Systems and Services Department, Transport and Logistics group, Delft, Netherlands

Petter Næss
Department of Urban and Regional Planning, Norwegian University of Life Sciences, Ås, Norway

Csaba G. Pogonyi
Imperial College London, London, United Kingdom

Julio A. Soria-Lara
Transport Research Centre—TRANSyT—Universidad Politécnica Madrid; Institute of Economics, Geography, and Demography, Spanish National Research Council (CSIC), Madrid, Spain

Rob van Nes
Transport & Planning, Faculty of Civil Engineering and Geosciences, Delft University of Technology, Delft, Netherlands

José Manuel Vassallo
Professor of Transport Economics and Planning, Transport Research Centre (TRANSyT), Universidad Politécnica de Madrid, Madrid, Spain

Preface

For many reasons, governments are involved in transport policy and planning. For instance, governments finance transport infrastructure projects and deploy policies to restrict transport-related negative external effects. Government decisions on transport policy and planning almost always involve a trade-off between negative and positive effects accruing from the policy option(s). For instance, the development of a new motorway leads to travel time savings for road users and can improve traffic safety, but at the same time such a motorway can also increase noise pollution for residents and result in the encroachment of landscapes. Moreover, transport projects are generally accompanied with high construction costs. It is up to politicians to judge whether the positive impacts of transport projects and policies can legitimate the negative impacts. Hence, they frequently want to receive systematic information regarding the positive and negative effects of the transport policy options that are considered. Several appraisal methods are deployed by governments for this purpose dominant examples being cost–benefit analysis (CBA) and multicriteria analysis (MCA). For these appraisal methods excellent handbooks are available. For instance, Boardman et al. (2018) produced a very comprehensive handbook for CBA and Dodgson et al. (2009) is an example of a much-used manual for MCA. However, to the best of my knowledge, an up-to-date structured overview of the literature regarding these appraisal methods in the context of transport policy and planning is missing in the literature.

This book volume aims to review the literature about three standard appraisal methods being CBA, MCA, and environmental impact assessment (EIA). Examples of important target groups of this book volume are (graduation) students and PhD students who quickly want to get a grip on new developments, past developments, or knowledge gaps with regard to these appraisal methods and more experienced scholars who quickly want to catch up with the state-of-the-art of a particular transport appraisal method. Moreover, this book volume can be useful for practitioners who want to update their knowledge with regard to the appraisal studies they commission/apply and, finally, this book is meant for teachers of courses who want to educate students in the state-of-the-art of different appraisal methods. To directly reveal my hidden agenda for accepting the invitation of Prof. Bert van Wee, the Series Editor-In-Chief, to edit this book volume: I was one of these teachers who was in need of a structured overview of the literature regarding appraisal methods. At Delft University of Technology I am teaching the course "Advanced Evaluation Methods for Transport Policy Decision-Making" at the MSc level. In this course, students get acquainted with the research frontier of various appraisal methods and they should also be able to critically reflect on the underlying assumptions and the merits of the appraisal methods that are part of the course. I hope that this book volume can support them in meeting these objectives and of course I hope that also students from other universities can grasp these benefits.

The most important topic for the review chapters concerns a description/discussion of the state-of-the-art of the method. What are new developments and new insights? Most of the chapters also discuss the use and application of the method. For which purposes do practitioners use the method and how do they evaluate the merits of the method (what are the main pros and cons)? The chapters all end with a discussion of future research challenges. What are the main gaps in the literature? What are the main challenges and important directions for further research?

1. Overview of the book chapters

This book consists of nine chapters. The first three chapters are dedicated to cost–benefit analysis which is the dominant method of transportation project appraisal (Naess, 2020). Koopmans and Mouter (2020) (Chapter 1) aim to provide an up-to-date overview of recent literature regarding the application and the development of CBA in the context of transport policy and planning. For me it was a great pleasure to write this chapter together with Carl—who is also known in the Netherlands as "Mister CBA." Although we already work for years on quite similar topics, we never found the chance to collaborate and this was a very good occasion to join forces. In this chapter various research challenges are identified. First of all, pinpointing how the outcomes of a CBA can be interpreted turns out to be surprisingly hard. Some scholars claim that CBA measures the social welfare effect of transport projects, whereas other scholars argue that it is more appropriate to adopt a descriptive interpretation of CBA, namely that it only measures aggregate net willingness-to-pay and nothing more. The chapter also reviews the development in the literature toward directly measuring welfare impacts in a more direct way through self-reported well-being questionnaires (SRWB). Koopmans and Mouter (2020) discuss four caveats of valuing impacts of government projects through this approach that might be interesting to alleviate in further research projects.

Changes in travel time and accident risk are often the main impacts of transport projects. In a CBA, these impacts are transferred into monetary terms through generic price tags called the value of travel time (VTT) and the value of a statistical life (VSL). Because these money metrics can have a decisive effect on the outcomes of a CBA I decided to solicit separate chapters that review the literature on these two metrics. Luckily, three very experienced scholars (Gerard de Jong, Marco Kouwenhoven, and Henrik Andersson) were willing to write chapters which cover interesting new developments regarding the VTT and the VOSL. De Jong and Kouwenhoven (2020) (Chapter 2) explain that the first empirical studies to estimate the VTT used data on choices that travelers actually made (revealed preference data, RP), but in the 1980s studies began to use data on hypothetical route choices (stated preference data, SP). De Jong and Kouwenhoven (2020) review differences and similarities between (particularly European) empirical studies that aim to estimate the VTT. They also pay attention to the VTT for business travel, the VTT in freight transport, and the VTT reliability being the monetary value that is attached to reductions in the variability of travel time. Finally, they define a number of research challenges. They observe that the available passenger VTT studies almost exclusively refer to car drivers and recommend an extension to under-researched modes (car-passenger, bicycle, walking, or even Mobility as a Service). Furthermore, they signal that the introduction of the automated vehicle will probably severely impact the value that individuals attach to travel time savings and they provide various directions for further research to study this topic (note that this topic is also covered in a previous book volume of this series, Milakis et al., 2020). In Chapter 3, Andersson (2020) explains that RP methods and SP methods are also deployed for measuring how much society would be willing to spend to prevent one unidentified death (the VSL). He also describes the theoretical economic model behind the VSL concept. Andersson (2020) provides various examples of market behavior (RP) which can be used to elicit preferences for safety (purchase of seat belts, bicycle helmets, and cars) and also reviews some pros and cons of using RP or SP data for estimating the VSL.

Chapter 4 reviews the literature on transport models (Van Nes and De Jong, 2020). Transport models may seem an unusual topic in a book on appraisal methods, as they are not appraisal methods themselves. However, the reason why a chapter is dedicated to this topic is that transport models are the backbone for appraisal methods through providing crucial input such as the calculation of time gains and cost savings and changes in the use of the different travel modes, which have an impact on overall user benefits, emissions and safety, among other things. Van Nes and De Jong (2020) discuss a range of important topics in their chapter. They start with an overview of the overall setup of transport models. Both aggregate and disaggregate model approaches are considered. Furthermore, a description is given of practical issues when building and using these models in practice, with special attention for quality control (e.g., audits, guidelines, standardization, and protocols). The chapter concludes with a reflection on the value and limitations of transport modeling and an overview of new modeling developments. Van Nes and De Jong (2020) explain that transport models are being improved for all kinds of reasons and they make a distinction between improvements that result from developments in the transport system itself (Mobility as a Service, automated driving and a growing interest in environmentally friendly modes such as cycling), new requirements from practice (new assessment criteria become important, such as reliability of travel times, demand management, and traffic management), and scientific developments (the availability of new data sources and simulation-based modeling).

Empirical evidence shows that transportation projects tend to have a positive impact on the economy. Hence, it is not a surprise that policy makers often have high expectations about economic benefits of transportation. However, in many occasions policy makers receive a disappointing message from analysts who explain to them that the additional economic benefits are not as high as they anticipated because a large part is already captured in the direct user benefits. Of course, the wider economic benefits that are additional to direct user benefits should be incorporated in the appraisal of transport projects, and in Chapter 5 Pogonyi (2020) reviews the literature about the wider economic benefits of transportation. His chapter particularly focuses on agglomeration benefits and provides a theoretical discussion of how several agglomeration benefits (e.g., learning, sharing, and matching) might materialize. Moreover, Pogonyi (2020) reviews a range of studies that aim to provide causal estimates for the impact of transport projects on wider economic benefits. Furthermore, this chapter shows how findings from the literature on wider economic benefits are used in transport project appraisal. In addition, Pogonyi (2020) highlights some possible directions for further research such as the agglomeration losses of transport investments (e.g., displacement of economic activity and sprawl) and the impact of the availability of highly disaggregate microdata that provides opportunities to apply advanced quasi-experimental methodologies.

Chapter 6 (Dean, 2020) reviews the literature concerning the appraisal method multicriteria analysis (MCA). MCA is a standard appraisal method in the toolbox of practitioners who aspire to provide systematic information to elected officials concerning the merits of a transport project. I am really pleased that Marco Dean was willing to dedicate a lot of time and energy to reviewing the literature about MCA and writing this chapter. The chapter shows that MCA comprises various classes of methods, techniques, and tools (with different degrees of complexity) which explicitly consider multiple objectives and criteria (or attributes) in decision-making problems. This chapter provides a comprehensive overview of the different MCA methods available in the transport domain which illustrates the current state-of-the-art in the use of MCA in the transport sector and discusses the potential advantages and limitations of the appraisal method. The chapter highlights that a fundamental disconnection exists between theory and transport assessment practice, with several methods proposed in the academic literature (e.g., sophisticated MCA methods based on advanced mathematical principles) which are rarely employed in real-world applications.

Chapter 7 (Mouter et al., 2020) compares CBA and MCA. The chapter establishes that the root of all the differences between CBA and MCA is that the welfare economics provides strict procedures for conducting a CBA, whereas MCA methods are not based on this theory which gives MCA analysts a relatively large degree of freedom when conducting the appraisal. The authors identify five inherent differences between the two methods: (1) a CBA investigates how citizens and firms that are affected by a transport project experience the impacts of the project, whereas a MCA is based on the judgments of experts and/or stakeholders who might not experience any impacts of a transport project themselves; (2) a CBA only includes the impacts that affect the welfare of individuals, whereas MCA analysts have the full freedom to include every possible impact in their studies; (3) CBA measures a project's societal value by making impacts of transport projects comparable in monetary terms using the notion of individuals' willingness to pay. The aggregation of impacts/criteria in a MCA can be partly based on translating impacts/criteria into monetary terms, but the aggregation is also based on at least one other weighting method (e.g., scoring or ranking); (4) CBA inherently accounts for the fact that social impacts of transport projects occur over a number of periods by discounting future impacts of the project, whereas the time dimension is rarely included in a

MCA; (5) the final indicators of a CBA (e.g., the net present value or the benefit–cost ratio) communicate very clearly and are therefore easy to use in the media and the public/political debate. The interpretation of the outcome of a MCA is relatively unclear.

Chapter 8 (Soria-Lara et al., 2020) reviews the literature on the environmental impact assessment (EIA), the third standard appraisal method that is covered in this book. EIA essentially refers to the evaluation of the likely effects of major projects (and other actions) that significantly affect the environment. It provides decision-makers with an indication of the environmental consequences of their actions. A key difference between EIA and the other two appraisal methods covered in this book (CBA and MCA) is that in many countries conducting an EIA for an infrastructure project with any environmental consequences is mandatory by law. Julio Soria-Lara and his co-authors cover a wide range of topics in their chapter. They focus on new developments regarding EIA and identify potential research gaps. They explore the technical developments in project and baseline information, the identification and evaluation of environmental impacts, the use of impact prediction methods, and the techniques to compare project alternatives. The chapter also describes various process-related barriers such as EIA timing, transparency, stakeholders' involvement in early EIA stages, and public participation. Based on this review, a set of further research issues are discussed in the context of EIA for transport projects.

As said, I think that it is really important for students to be able to critically reflect on the underlying assumptions of appraisal methods and not only learn how they work. Petter Naess is a professor in the field of transport who reflected on basically every assumption and implication of CBA and I am therefore very pleased that he was willing to summarize many of these reflections in Chapter 9 (Naess, 2020). He also provides suggestions for what could be done to avoid the shortcomings identified. Naess emphasizes that the criteria for project evaluation should be explicit rather than concealed in the minds of the individual planners and decision-makers. Moreover, he stresses that the decisions on proposed projects should be informed by impact analyses that do not give privilege to effects that can easily be quantified.

An observation in various chapters is that the academic literature seems to focus on the refinement of the technicalities of the appraisal methods, while there is limited attention for the extent to which appraisal methods provide useful information for key user groups such as civil servants and elected officials (e.g., Dean, 2020; Koopmans and Mouter, 2020). Koopmans and

Mouter (2020) observe that most research efforts tend to focus on improving the quantitative predictions provided by CBAs rather than making CBA analyses more useful for political decision-making. Dean (2020) could not find any studies which investigate the opinions of politicians, government officials, civil servants, and other transport decision-makers regarding the perceived pros and cons of multicriteria tools and techniques. Soria-Lara et al. (2020) conclude that the connection of EIA with real-life policymaking can be substantially improved as EIA studies are often conducted when key decisions on alternatives have already been made and EIA implementation in transport planning is often a series of disconnected steps where experts and stakeholders participate separately with zero feedback between them. These findings line up with the conclusion of Marsden and Reardon (2017) that most of the transport literature does not engage with real-world transport policy and focuses on quantitative analysis alone. Hence, I think that one important lesson that can be learned from this book volume is that more research time of academics should be allocated toward investigating how (outcomes of) appraisal methods are experienced by practitioners and what measures should be taken to further improve the usefulness of appraisal studies for key user groups.

References

Andersson, H., 2020. The value of statistical life. In: Mouter, N. (Ed.), Standard Transport Appraisal Methods. Advances in Transport Policy and Planning, vol. 6. Elsevier, Amsterdam, pp. 75–99 (Chapter 3).

Boardman, A.E., Greenberg, D.H., Vining, A.R., Weimer, D.L., 2018. Cost-Benefit Analysis Concepts and Practice. Prentice Hall, New Jersey.

De Jong, G., Kouwenhoven, M., 2020. Value of travel time and travel time reliability. In: Mouter, N. (Ed.), Standard Transport Appraisal Methods. Advances in Transport Policy and Planning, vol. 6. Elsevier, Amsterdam, pp. 43–74 (Chapter 2).

Dean, M., 2020. Multi-criteria analysis. In: Mouter, N. (Ed.), Standard Transport Appraisal Methods. Advances in Transport Policy and Planning, vol. 6. Elsevier, Amsterdam, pp. 165–224 (Chapter 6).

Dodgson, J.S., Spackman, M., Pearman, A., Phillips, L.D., 2009. Multi-Criteria Analysis: A Manual. Department for Communities and Local Government, London.

Koopmans, C.C., Mouter, N., 2020. Cost-benefit analysis. In: Mouter, N. (Ed.), Standard Transport Appraisal Methods. Advances in Transport Policy and Planning, vol. 6. Elsevier, Amsterdam, pp. 1–42 (Chapter 1).

Marsden, G., Reardon, L., 2017. Questions of governance: rethinking the study of transportation policy. Transp. Res. A Policy Pract. 101, 238–251.

Milakis, D., Thomopoulos, N., van Wee, B. (Eds.), 2020. Policy Implications of Autonomous Vehicles. Elsevier, The Netherlands, pp. 149–162.

Mouter, N., Dean, M., Koopmans, C., Vassallo, J.M., 2020. Comparing cost-benefit analysis and multi-criteria analysis. In: Mouter, N. (Ed.), Standard Transport Appraisal Methods. Advances in Transport Policy and Planning, vol. 6. Elsevier, Amsterdam, pp. 225–254 (Chapter 7).

Naess, P., 2020. Project appraisal methods: Tools for optimizing or for informed political debate? In: Mouter, N. (Ed.), Standard Transport Appraisal Methods. Advances in Transport Policy and Planning, vol. 6. Elsevier, Amsterdam, pp. 287–318 (Chapter 9).
Pogonyi, C.G., 2020. The wider economic benefits of transportation. In: Mouter, N. (Ed.), Standard Transport Appraisal Methods. Advances in Transport Policy and Planning, vol. 6. Elsevier, Amsterdam, pp. 129–164 (Chapter 5).
Soria-Lara, J.A., Arce-Ruiz, R.M., Arranz-Lopez, A., Ariza-Alvarez, A., 2020. Environmental Impact Assessment for transport projects: A review of technical and process-related issues. In: Mouter, N. (Ed.), Standard Transport Appraisal Methods. Advances in Transport Policy and Planning, vol. 6. Elsevier, Amsterdam, pp. 255–285 (Chapter 8).
Van Nes, R., De Jong, G., 2020. Transport models. In: Mouter, N. (Ed.), Standard Transport Appraisal Methods. Advances in Transport Policy and Planning, vol. 6. Elsevier, Amsterdam, pp. 101-128 (Chapter 4).

CHAPTER ONE

Cost-benefit analysis

Carl Koopmans[a,b,*] and Niek Mouter[c]
[a]Department of Spatial Economics, Vrije Universiteit Amsterdam, School of Business and Economics, Amsterdam, Netherlands
[b]SEO Amsterdam Economics, Amsterdam, Netherlands
[c]Faculty of Technology, Policy and Management, Engineering Systems and Services Department, Transport and Logistics group, Delft, Netherlands
*Corresponding author: e-mail address: c.koopmans@seo.nl

Contents

Advances in Transport Policy and Planning, Volume 6
ISSN 2543-0009
https://doi.org/10.1016/bs.atpp.2020.07.005

Abstract

Cost-Benefit Analysis (CBA) measures a project's societal value by quantifying the project's societal effects and making costs and benefits comparable in monetary terms. CBA is the most widely applied tool for the appraisal of transport projects. This chapter aims to provide an up-to-date overview of recent literature regarding the application and the development of CBA in the context of Transport Policy and Planning. We describe the history of CBA and its foundations in welfare economics. We review literature on recent developments and debates regarding the method as well as the literature on the implementation of CBA in practice. Finally, we describe research challenges related to CBA: which questions regarding applying CBA for Transport Policy and Planning need to be answered in future research?

Keywords: Cost-benefit analysis, Benefit-cost analysis, Transport project, Transport appraisal, Transport infrastructure, Evaluation decision-making

Comparing the advantages and disadvantages of a potential decision is something we all do, all the time. We choose between foodstuffs, schools, jobs, transport modes, etcetera. We may choose because of positive or negative feelings about particular choice options, but we may also try to compare the pros and cons. Cost-benefit analysis[a] tries to do this in a systematic and consistent way, based on economic theory. In essence, Cost-Benefit Analysis (CBA) measures a project's societal value by quantifying the project's societal effects and making costs and benefits comparable in monetary terms. CBA measures the monetary value of the effects of a policy through the willingness-to-pay (WTP) of those who are affected (see, e.g., Boadway, 2006). For a positive effect, the WTP is the maximum amount which a person is prepared to pay for it. For negative effects, the willingness-to-pay is negative (then often called willingness-to-accept). Finally, transport projects are typically intertemporal in nature, so the benefits and costs occur over a number of periods (e.g., Boadway, 2006). To account for this, impacts are presented as present values, implying that—even after a correction for inflation—it is, for example, better to have one euro or dollar now than in 10 years' time. The discount rate is used to express this valuation. Often, present values are aggregated into a final indicator such as the net present value (NPV) or the benefit-cost ratio (BCR).

CBA is often used when considering investment decisions, both by firms and governments. Typically, firms will look mainly at their own costs and benefits, while government decisions may consider positive and negative effects for many (or all) people and firms in their jurisdiction. Because of this

[a] Cost-benefit analysis is sometimes called benefit-cost analysis.

broad scope, Cost-Benefit Analysis for government decisions is often called Social Cost-Benefit Analysis.

This chapters aims to provide an up-to-date overview of recent literature regarding the application and the development of CBA in the context of Transport Policy and Planning to allow the reader to get up to speed quickly and efficiently to advance their own research. To grasp recent developments, we started our review of the literature with selecting articles published in the period 2015–2019 in some of the main journals which publish research on the development and use of CBA for transport policies: Economics of Transportation, Journal of Transport Economics and Policy, Research in Transportation Economics, Journal of Benefit Cost-Analysis and Transportation Research Part A. In our review we also included various books published in the last decade which codify and synthesize advances in the literature regarding CBA. Relevant references that were found in the academic papers and books were also included (snowballing). For specific subjects (e.g., the history of CBA) we searched for papers by specific authors (e.g., Jules Dupuit).

Section 1 introduces the method: its foundation in welfare economics, its history, and its relation to other methods. Section 2 describes the state-of-the-art of the method: recent developments of the method that followed from our literature review are addressed in this section. In Section 3 literature regarding the implementation of CBA in practice is described, including its relation with decision-making on infrastructure projects. Finally, Section 4 describes research challenges related to CBA: which questions need to be answered in the future?

1. The CBA method

1.1 History of CBA

A systematic process for decision-making was described in the 18th century by Benjamin Franklin (1772). He made a list of pros and a list of cons, and then stroke out pros and cons of equal importance. Sometimes this would imply striking out two or three pros against one con (or vice versa). In the end, only pros or cons are left, and the best choice is clear. Franklin writes: *"And tho' the Weight of Reasons cannot be taken with the Precision of Algebraic Quantities, yet when each is thus considered separately and comparatively ... I think I can judge better."*

In such a rationalized decision process, determining the relative importance of the pros and cons is crucial. There are many ways to do this, most of which fall into two main types: multi-criteria analysis (MCA) and CBA. Both methods work by quantifying impacts and choosing weights (Franklin's "Algebraic Quantities") for each impact. In MCA, the weights are chosen by the analyst, politicians, civil servants or others. In CBA, preferences of individual citizens are the basis of the appraisal (Sen, 1979). Franklin applies simplified MCA by determining the importance of pros and cons himself, without numbers. In CBA, the importance of pros and cons of a project is determined by the number of euros (or dollars) society (people and firms in a country, or a group of countries, or the world) is willing to pay for these impacts.

In this chapter, we concentrate on CBA. MCA is treated in chapter "multicriteria analysis" by Dean. Apart from multi-criteria analysis and social cost-benefit analysis, there are methods which focus on specific types of impacts, such as environmental impact assessment (see chapter "Environmental impact assessment for transport projects: a review of technical and process-related issues" by Soria-Lara et al.) and economic impact analysis (treated briefly in this chapter).

Cost-benefit analysis was largely invented by Jules Dupuit in the 1840s. Dupuit was Chief Engineer for the City of Paris and later Inspector-general of the French Corps des Pont et Chaussées (the state-run organization responsible for roads and bridges). He contributed to economic discussions by introducing, among other things, willingness-to-pay and the consumer surplus (which he called relative utility). A telling quote of Dupuit is *"The only utility is that which people are willing to pay for"*. He presented the demand curve and many of its properties. And he described "thought experiments" of the costs and benefits of toll bridges (Talvitie, 2018). Also, he presented numerical examples of the calculation of costs and benefits of a canal (Dupuit, 1844).

Extensive real-world application of CBA started with the US Flood Control Act of 1936, which made CBA mandatory for flood control projects. In 1950, guidelines were published. After 1960, the use of CBA became mandatory in the United States, Canada and the United Kingdom for certain policies and projects. Around 1970 the OECD, the UN and the World Bank formally adopted CBA. In the United States, application of the efficiency criterion was required from 1980 onward for all regulations with a substantial impact (Mishan and Quah, 2007, p. 243–244). Almost all Western countries now have rules which state that CBA should be performed for regulatory changes. In most Western countries, government agencies have produced CBA guidelines (Boardman et al., 2018).

1.2 Welfare

Welfare economics provides the theoretical foundations for CBA (Boadway and Bruce, 1984). Welfare economics investigates the social desirability of alternative economic situations (e.g., comparing the situation with a government project and the situation without a government project). The theory is mainly used in public economics, the analysis of government decisions on the economy of a country. Such decisions include taxation and government spending, but also regulation (e.g., environmental regulation). Typical issues in welfare economics are the optimal level of taxes and the desirability of different types of spending (e.g., health care, social security benefits and transport infrastructure).

To analyze the social desirability of government policies, the concept of the social welfare function is used (Bergson, 1938; extended by Samuelson, 1947). A social welfare function is a formal representation of the value judgments regarding the emphasis society should place on the interests of different citizens and it can be used to provide a ranking, or ordering, of different economic situations (Beckerman, 2011; Nyborg, 2014). Public policy decisions frequently have to take account of values that lie outside the range of values that individuals take into account in their private market activities (Beckerman, 2011). Hence, at least in principle, the social welfare function also includes external effects, defined as impacts which do not affect the individual welfare of consumers or the production costs of producers. These include, for example, the equity of any effects on the distribution of gains and losses, including the distributions across time and space (Beckerman, 2011). Such external effects are usually not included in common indicators of the state of an economy such as GDP or unemployment.

The welfare of society is usually seen as a logical construction from the welfare (or utility) of individuals (Beckerman, 2011). Hence, the ranking of economic situations is based on an aggregation of individual utility functions. Since individuals' utility cannot be observed directly it is assumed that utility can be inferred from choices individuals make when faced with alternative situations (Beckerman, 2011). Welfare economics assumes that individuals' utility of both consumption goods and effects of government projects can be inferred from choices individuals make within their budget constraint (Fuguitt and Wilcox, 1999). Specifically, the utility individuals derive from consumption goods and effects of government projects can be measured through the amount of money individuals are willing to pay from their after-tax income in (hypothetical) markets. The willingness-to-pay can be derived from behavior in markets or from surveys. These methods are treated in Section 1.2.

However, aggregating across individuals to come up with a measure of social welfare is problematic as numerous controversial assumptions have to be made. First and foremost, one needs to make an ethical decision when specifying the social welfare function by providing a definition of "welfare." Beckerman (2011) notes that there is scope for a wide variety of views as to what constitutes the welfare of society. If one is "utilitarian," what matters is the impact of a policy on aggregate utility, if one is "egalitarian," what matters is the likely effect on overall equality, if one is "prioritarian," what matters is the likely effect on the worst off and if one is a "libertarian," what matters is the degree of restraint on the free choices of individuals. Moreover, Harsanyi (1955, p.309) notes that: "everybody will have a social welfare function on his own, different from that of everybody else, except to the extent to which different individuals' value judgments happen to coincide with one another." Hence, there is no way of proving that one conception of welfare is superior to another as there can hardly be a more value-loaded concept than the term "welfare" (Beckerman, 2011). This makes every specification of the social welfare function controversial.

Second, when evaluating economic states using a social welfare function one implicitly assumes that it is possible to compare the utility impacts across individuals. Arrow's impossibility theorem proved that if one persists with preference functions that are ordinal and not comparable across individuals, a social welfare function that represents aggregate welfare of individuals on the basis of individual preference ordering does not exist (unless in case one is prepared to violate some very compelling axioms of social choice). Hence, the assumption of interpersonal comparability of cardinal utility functions is essential in order to postulate a social welfare function in terms of individual utilities (Beckerman, 2011). Some economists believe in the possibility of interpersonal comparability of utility (e.g., Bronsteen, 2013), but there are also many economists who believe that one cannot make scientifically valid comparisons between different people's utilities. Binmore (2005, p. 116) illustrates this debate as follows: "traditional economists suffer from a severe case of schizophrenia on the subject of interpersonal comparisons of utility. In classes on welfare economics, the idea that we can compare how much utility different people are getting is so taken for granted that nobody feels the need to explain how this is possible. But in the class next door, students of microeconomics are simultaneously taught that interpersonal comparison of utility is so obviously a laughable impossibility that nobody needs to give the reasons why." A third group of economists argues that it should be assumed that individuals are able to make *rough* interpersonal comparisons between utilities. Beckerman (2011), for instance, argues that parents continually make judgments about whether the benefits to one child outweigh the burdens or disappointments imposed on another child or the parents themselves.

1.3 Pareto improvements and the Hicks-Kaldor criterion

One way for welfare economics to escape from the controversial assumptions listed above is the positioning of CBA as an instrument which searches for "*Pareto improvements*": changes which will improve the utility of at least one person, without reducing the utility of any person. Such changes will increase social welfare. However, in practice, government policies will hardly ever be able to satisfy this criterion. For instance, when considering new transport infrastructure, taxpayers will pay the costs, and quite probably there will be negative external effects, e.g., noise or CO_2 emissions.

A more practical concept is the *Kaldor-Hicks criterion*, which relaxes the Pareto conditions by adding the possibility of compensation (Hicks, 1939; Kaldor, 1939). The Kaldor-Hicks criterion asserts that a policy (or other change) can be considered as welfare-increasing if those who benefit can compensate those who suffer from it, creating a Pareto improvement after compensation. Standard CBAs are generally based on the Kaldor-Hicks criterion. According to the Kaldor-Hicks criterion, the compensation does not actually have to take place: it is enough that it is theoretically possible. This implies that there is only a potential Pareto improvement, and not necessarily an actual Pareto improvement. CBA assesses whether the Kaldor-Hicks-criterion is satisfied by expressing all the positive and negative effects of a policy in monetary terms and adding them up. If the sum is positive, those who benefit can theoretically compensate those who suffer. The consequence of using the Kaldor-Hicks criterion is that CBA recommends projects where the sum of gains outweigh the sum of losses, both expressed in monetary terms, so that winners can potentially compensate the losers.

The main issue with the Kaldor-Hicks criterion is that full compensation is typically not possible even in theory (Hammond, 1979). First, it is questionable whether a democratic government can just take money from the individuals who gain from a policy and give it to the individuals who lose from the policy to compensate them. If the transfer is not mandated by the general tax system, doing so may be in conflict with citizens' constitutional property rights or other laws (Nyborg, 2014). A possibly even bigger problem is to identify losers and winners, as well as the magnitude of their loss or gain: this requires private information on, e.g., individuals' preferences. If an individual knows that her reported WTP is being used to make her actually pay (or receive compensation), she has every incentive to misreport her WTP (Nyborg, 2014). Moreover, there is the problem that compensation will result in transaction costs. Taking gains from gainers and transfer it to losers will arguably result in high administrative costs. Therefore, it is not at all evident that one can infer from a CBA with a positive net present value that the gainers will be able to compensate the losers and have some gains left after compensation.

In addition, the Kaldor-Hicks criterion assumes that the WTP of each individual is equally important. This is a controversial assumption because aggregating WTPs implies that CBA "treats as equivalent a rich man's dollar gained and a poor man's dollar lost" (Persky, 2001). As in reality losers are in many cases not fully compensated, the analyst is back at square one because he implicitly has to make an interpersonal comparison between the utility gains of the gainers and the utility losses of the losers (Beckerman, 2011). The Kaldor-Hicks criterion makes the implicit assumption that the marginal utility of income is equal across individuals. Interpersonal comparisons of utility therefore enter CBA via the rear door. If marginal utility of income is equal between individuals this implies that people with a low marginal utility of income are benefitted, which are generally people with a high level of income and wealth (Nyborg, 2014).

1.4 Total net willingness to pay

In sum, economists have to make controversial assumptions when measuring the welfare generated by a government project either through a social welfare function or through the Kaldor-Hicks criterion. Nyborg (2014) explains that this can be avoided when adopting a more descriptive interpretation of CBA being total net willingness to pay, i.e., how much the population in sum claims to be willing to pay to realize the impacts of the project less its actual costs (Nyborg, 2014). In her view, using names such as net benefits, net social value, welfare effects or efficiency is unfortunate, and serves to confuse rather than convey the precise meaning of the final indicator(s) of a CBA study.

1.5 CBA versus other methods

Economic impact analysis (EIA) is a widely used tool to assess the economic effects of decisions taken by governments or organizations. Typically, a

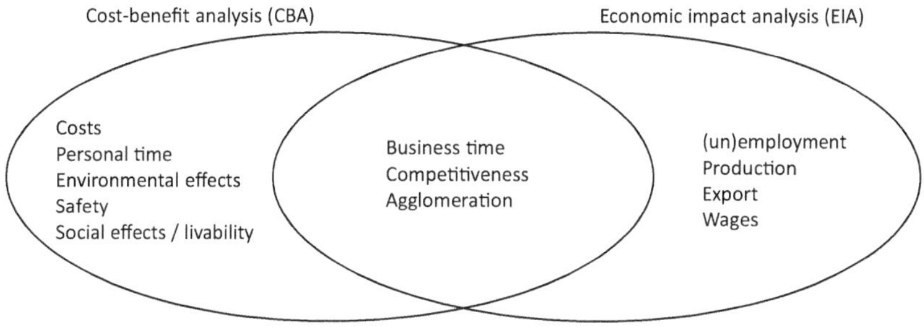

Source: Adapted version of Figure 2 in Weisbrod et al. (2016)

Fig. 1 Different elements in CBA and economic impact analysis. *Source: adapted version of Fig. 2 in Weisbrod, G., Mulley, C., & Hensher, D. (2016). Recognising the complementary contributions of cost benefit analysis and economic impact analysis to an understanding of the worth of public transport investment: a case study of bus rapid transit in Sydney, Australia. Res. Transp. Econ., 59, 450–461.*

range of economic impacts is computed, such as effects on competitiveness, GDP, (un)employment, profits and wages (see Fig. 1). In EIA, these effects are not weighted or added as in CBA and MCA, other than computing effects on total GDP or total (un)employment. Instead, the economic impacts are presented separately. Effects on private households are usually not included in EIA, other than unemployment. Methods often used in EIA are input-output analysis, land use models, regional economic models, and macroeconomic models including computable general equilibrium models (Weisbrod, 2008).

EIA is not grounded in welfare economics. Welfare indicators such as GDP are included in EIA, but this does not reflect the full set of effects as defined in welfare economics. For instance, external effects are usually not a part of EIA. Also, the costs of government investments and the economic impacts that follow from these costs, are often not a part of EIA's in practice. On the other hand, EIA pays more attention to specific economic effects which are not presented explicitly in CBA's, such as effects on employment and export.

Several alternative methods to assess the impacts of transport projects are described in other chapters:

- Multi-criteria analysis (chapter "Multicriteria analysis" by Dean)
- Environmental Impact Assessment (chapter "Environmental impact assessment for transport projects: a review of technical and process-related issues" by Soria-Lara et al.)

2. State-of-the-art of the method

This section describes state-of-the-art innovations, insights and academic debates with respect to applying CBA for transport projects. We structured this section along several topics that were addressed in various papers that we extracted from our literature review: costs, risk and uncertainty, valuation methods, discounting and wider economic benefits. Finally, we present critical comments on CBA made in recent literature.

2.1 Costs

In CBA, the costs often receive limited attention. Most effort is usually put into quantifying benefits. However, every dollar or euro of costs has the same impact on the net balance as a dollar or euro of benefits. Another reason to pay attention to "costs" is the risk of cost overruns.

Pickrell (1990) showed that the capital costs were higher than the estimated costs in all but one of ten rail transit projects in the United States, the overrun being between minus 11% and plus 83%. Operating expenses were exceeded by minus 10% to plus 205%. Flyvbjerg et al. (2002) analyzed cost overruns in a sample of 258 transport infrastructure projects, 242 of which are in Europe and North America. The construction costs were underestimated in 86% of the projects. For all projects together, the actual costs were on average 28% higher than the estimated costs. This difference is statistically significant. Recently, Flyvbjerg's (e.g. Flyvbjerg et al., 2002; Flyvbjerg, 2008) methods were criticized by Love and Ahiaga-Dagbui (2018). They point at the strong heterogeneity of the dataset used, spanning 20 countries and 88 years (1910–1998). Odeck and Kjerkreit (2019) assessed cost overruns for a specific country (Norway) and conclude that construction costs were underestimated by only 9% on average for 27 Norwegian infrastructure projects. Flyvbjerg et al. (2018) stress that the research aimed at using all available data, checking for possible non-representiveness. Love and Ahiaga-Dagbui (2018) suggest replacing the cost estimate made at the time of the decision to build with a later, more accurate estimate. Flyvbjerg et al. (2018) note that they wanted to check how well-informed decision-makers were when they decided to invest.

Flyvbjerg et al. (2002) offer several possible explanations for cost overruns, concluding that "strategic misrepresentation" (lying) is the most probable cause. Political pressure from proponents of the projects seems to bias cost estimates downward. Another cause may be "optimism bias"

(Flyvbjerg, 2008). Love and Ahiaga-Dagbui (2018) note that the conclusion that strategic misrepresentation is the most plausible cause, is not supported by empirical research. Flyvbjerg et al. (2018) point to research in behavioral science, which shows the importance of human bias. Furthermore, they state that principal-agent theory shows that lying about cost can be rational. Also, they note that, if only "honest errors" were the cause, the cost inaccuracies would be random, which is not the case. However, Eliasson and Fosgerau (2013) show that the cause of cost overruns and benefit shortfalls may be selection bias: if there is randomness in the prediction of net payoffs of projects, projects which show large net payoffs are more likely to be selected than similar projects which show smaller payoffs. Nicolaisen (2012) points to possible "availability bias" in the projects selected in Flyvbjerg's studies. That is, the finding of the meta-analyses of Flyvbjerg and co-workers that transport projects systematically suffer from cost overruns, might be caused by transport projects suffering from large costs overruns having a higher probability of being evaluated ex-post.

To remedy "strategic misrepresentation" and "optimism bias," Flyvbjerg (2008) suggests "reference class forecasting": using previous costs of similar projects to estimate the costs of a new project. This would replace the "inside view" of a group of planners preparing the project with an "outside view" of the real world. The result would be an uplift of the estimated costs by 15–40% (aiming at a 50% probability of cost overrun, i.e., the median of the cost distribution). Eliasson and Fosgerau (2013) note however that general uplift factors will not affect project selection (implicitly assuming that the selection process is based on net benefits). However, if projects can be divided in classes with different uplifts, project selection may be influenced. Odeck and Kjerkreit (2019) assume that the cause of less optimism bias in Norway may be the Norwegian Quality Assurance regime. Under this regime, cost estimates for large projects are scrutinized by external consultants appointed by the Ministry of Finance. This may be an example of a best practice.

2.2 Risk and uncertainty

Transport infrastructure projects involve substantial risks of cost overruns and demand shortfalls. As cost overruns have already been treated above, we focus on demand risks in this section. In ten rail transit projects in the United States analyzed by Pickrell (1990), the ridership was 28–83% lower than expected. Flyvbjerg et al. (2002) showed that passenger forecasts were overestimated by more than 20% in 84% of the rail projects in a large sample of projects from Western countries. The average overestimation was 106%. For road projects, passenger forecasts were on average overestimated by only 8.7%, but the over- or underestimation is larger than 20% in 50% of the cases. Flyvbjerg et al. (2002) stress that risks resulting from inaccurate forecasts are typically ignored or underestimated. Odeck and Kjerkreit (2019) conclude that traffic volumes and accident cost reductions are underestimated in the ex ante evaluation of Norwegian transport projects, making ex ante CBA's too pessimistic. They stress the importance of improving traffic forecasts. Nicolaisen and Driscoll (2014) performed a review of ex post studies of demand forecasts for transport infrastructure projects. They conclude that the accuracy of these forecasts is poor: there are both biases (the differences between forecasts and actual traffic have non-zero means) and imprecision (these differences have large standard deviations). Vickerman (2017) also stresses that traffic forecasts are often inaccurate.

Asplund and Eliasson (2016) try to answer the question whether uncertainty leads to unclear CBA results and useless CBA's. Adding uncertainty to CBA results in datasets of Norwegian and Swedish infrastructure projects, they show that the results are affected more by uncertainty with respect to investment costs and transport demand, than by uncertainties in valuations and effects. However, they also conclude that selecting projects based on CBA which includes uncertainty, still strongly increases the social return of transport investment compared to randomly selecting projects.

According to Nicolaisen and Driscoll (2014), the most important causes of poor transport demand predictions in their review are inaccurate forecasts of exogenous variables such as economic growth, car ownership and migration. It is not clear from the review whether the specification of the transport models used also plays a role.

Miller and Szimba (2015) offer a list of methods to address risk and uncertainty: sensitivity analysis, scenario analysis, Monte Carlo Simulation, Quantified Optimism Bias (i.e., uplift factors for costs, as described above) and qualitative approaches. They show that all these methods are used in CBA's in practice. Sensitivity analysis and scenario analysis are widely applied. Monte Carlo simulation is used frequently, and Quantified Optimism Bias and qualitative approaches are used rarely. Miller and Szimba (2015) describe several best practices in dealing with risk and uncertainty. Examples are taking account of interdependencies between projects, identifying other policy measures which could help reach the same goals as transport infrastructure, and a list of possible risks which should be checked. Hartgen (2013) suggests two ways of dealing with inaccurate forecasts. The first (hubris) involves improvement of predictions by monitoring performance, better data and models, and reducing optimism bias. The second (humility) is to openly quantify and present the inherent uncertainty in demand forecasts.

Other authors look into the way uncertainty is presented in CBA's. Mouter et al. (2015) use a conceptual psychological framework to analyze how CBA results may be received by different types of decision-makers. They conclude that it is important to present uncertainties, but that this may not be received well by certain types of individuals. Remedies may be increasing personal accountability of decision-makers and a clear presentation of CBA results. Wangsness et al. (2015) analyze what CBA guidelines from 19 countries say about uncertainty. Almost all guidelines advise to use sensitivity analysis to assess uncertainty. 7 of the 19 guidelines advise to highlight uncertainty in the summary table of the CBA. Wangsness et al. (2015) recommend that best-case and worst-case outcomes are presented in the summary table, along with a most likely estimate.

2.3 Valuation methods

In CBA, ideally prices are directly inferred from market behavior. However, in many cases such prices are not available. This is the case in particular for the value of travel time savings and of external effects. These external effects may be substantial. For instance, Gössling et al. (2019) estimate that the external costs of car use are €0.11 per kilometer.

Several methods are used to monetize these effects. These methods can be distinguished in five types:

- *Damage costs*
- *Revealed preference* (based on behavior or prices in markets)
- *Stated preference* (answers given in surveys)
- *Mitigation costs* (costs made to reduce or eliminate negative effects)
- *Costs associated with meeting a target set by politicians*

In some cases, damage costs can be computed directly. For instance, if the amount of fish caught in a river falls, and this can be attributed to pollution, the reduction in revenues for fishermen can be computed. It is important to distinguish this method from the mitigation cost approach below. The difference is that the mitigation cost involves a decision to take mitigating measures, while the damage cost method does not need such a decision.

An important revealed preference method is *Hedonic pricing*, in which effects of, e.g., noise or amenities on property prices are used. For instance, the value of replacing a highway through a city with a tunnel, may be computed by comparing house prices before and after the tunnel is built (e.g., Tijm et al., 2019). *Natural experiments* may reveal the choices people make between time and money. An example is the choice between pay-lanes (without congestion) and free lanes (longer travel time) on a highway (e.g., Small et al., 2005). A third revealed preference method is the *Travel cost method*, in which the costs are measured which are spent to travel to an attractive location (e.g., a nature park). These costs include both financial outlays (e.g., admission fees, gasoline) and time spent (through the value of travel time). These costs can be considered as a lower bound for the benefits derived from visiting the location (when the benefits are lower than the costs, the trip would not have been made).

Stated preference methods also come in different shapes. The *Contingent Valuation Method* (CVM) uses surveys to ask people directly, in open-ended questions, what money value they attach to effects they (may) experience. This can be either their willingness-to-pay (WTP): the money they would pay to avoid a negative effect, or their willingness-to-accept (WTA): the money they would need to receive to compensate a negative effect. Another stated preference method uses S*tated choice experiments* (some authors consider this as a specific type of CVM, e.g., Carson and Czajkowski, 2014). Using this method, the respondents in a survey choose between different options, including financial changes. From their choices, the average value they attach to an effect can be derived. An example would be a choice between preservation of a nature reserve and a reduction of taxes, using different values for the size of the tax reduction. From the answers given, the tax reduction can be computed which is, on average, equivalent to the preservation of the nature reserve. CVM may elicit the value of a fixed set of changes, while choice experiments can provide marginal values for individual attributes of a choice (Johnston et al., 2017).

Mitigation cost methods may compute the costs of reducing a negative effect, e.g., using the costs of sound barriers along a highway as a proxy for the value of the negative welfare effect of highway noise. We note that this is not a measurement of the negative welfare effect itself, but of something that may or may not be related to the negative welfare effect. For instance, using this method the value of negative welfare effect does not directly depend on the number of people who suffer from it. The decision to mitigate will itself have costs and benefits (the money value of a reduction of effects), which are not necessarily equal to each other.

Studies may measure the costs associated with meeting a target set by politicians. It is doubtful whether this may still be called CBA as defined above.

However, such studies do provide useful information on the considerations of politicians. Welfare economists in principle adopt the postulation of "non-paternalism" which implies that individuals are conceived to be the best judge of their own welfare. Hence, the citizens and firms that are affected by the policy (either directly or through externalities such as through noise pollution) are the sole objects who have standing in a CBA study and their preferences are respected. In principle, preferences of experts, stakeholders and policy makers about the impacts of the transport project do not play any role in the analysis. However, in practice, impacts of government policies are sometimes monetized based on judgments of policy makers.

For instance, the impact of government projects on CO_2 emissions is generally rooted in pledges of policy makers instead of stated or revealed preferences of individual citizens (e.g., Isacs et al., 2016). Because individual preferences and markets such as the EU Emission Trading System (ETS) suffer from many distortions (e.g., incomplete markets, free rider effects, etc.), many CBA practices decided to ground CO_2 prices in other approaches such as the marginal abatement cost approach (e.g., Aalbers et al., 2016; Isacs et al., 2016). This method values the reduction of CO_2 emissions based on a fixed level of abatement targets defined by government agencies and calculates the costs associated with the reduction of CO_2 emissions to meet these targets (Bruyn et al., 2010; Mandell, 2011). Some authors classify the avoidance cost method as political willingness to pay (Ahlroth et al., 2011). Although this valuation method departs from the traditional valuation paradigm of CBA it can be regarded as a practical method for the monetization of CO_2 emissions. The Netherlands is one example of a CBA practice which values the impact of government projects on CO_2 emissions based on governmental pledges regarding CO_2 abatement levels.

The table below shows which methods are most often used in CBA practice to monetize often-found costs and benefits in CBAs of transport projects. The table contains all the methods described above. The impacts in the table are discussed in more detail in other chapters (Table 1).

2.4 Discussions on contingent valuation

In the literature, the pros and cons of using the *Contingent Valuation Method* (CVM) are prominently discussed. Opponents point at hypothetical bias: what people say in response to a hypothetical question is not necessarily what they do. Also, they identify an "embedding effect": the value measured is

Table 1 Methods used in CBA and chapters in which these are treated.

Cost or benefit	Often-used monetization method(s)	Chapter in this book	Selected sources on monetization
Travel time savings	Stated choice experiments Natural experiments	2	Wardman et al. (2016), Small (2012), Batley et al. (2019)
Death, injuries (e.g., from traffic accidents)	Hedonic prices (wages for dangerous jobs) Stated choice experiments	3	Viscusi (2018), De Blaeij et al. (2003)
CO_2	Damage costs Mitigation costs Cost of meeting targets	9, 10	Nordhaus (2017), Kuik et al. (2009), Aalbers et al. (2016), Isacs et al. (2016)
Local emissions (e.g., particulate matter, NO_x)	Damage costs (e.g., health losses and deaths)	9, 10	OECD (2014), Section 2.4, European Commission (2019), chapter 4, Chay and Greenstone (2005)
Noise	Damage costs (e.g., health losses) Hedonic prices (house prices) Stated choice experiments	9, 10	European Commission (2019), chapter 6, Defra (2014), Dekkers and van der Straaten (2009), Bristow et al. (2015)
Effects on nature and landscapes	Hedonic prices (house prices) Travel cost method Mitigation costs	9, 10	Kumar (2011), Oueslati and Salanié (2011)

different when it is measured on its own, or embedded as a part of a more inclusive package (Hausman, 2012).[b] Another objection is the absence of a meaningful budget constraint (Arrow et al., 1993). Proponents stress that, although CVM is not perfect, the alternative to using CVM in practice may be to use a zero value, which would be worse (Carson, 2012). Choice experiments seem to offer a better alternative to (regular) CVM, being closer to economic theory (Carson and Czajkowski, 2014).

[b] Note that this issue might also emerge in Revealed Preference studies.

In the last decade, much progress has been made in the Stated Preference literature. Based on an extensive review of the literature, Johnston et al. (2017) present 23 recommendations for performing CVM in practice. One of the fields where progress was made is avoiding hypothetical bias. Carson and Groves (2007) suggested that ensuring that respondents believe that their choices in a survey might have consequences in real-life (consequentiality) can reduce the discrepancy between respondents' stated behavior and revealed behavior. Herriges et al. (2010) distinguishes between payment consequentiality and policy consequentiality. Payment consequentiality means that respondents believe that their choices in the questionnaire might have real *financial* consequences and policy consequentiality implies that participants in a questionnaire believe that their choices might affect government policies which can result in real-life consequences for themselves and others. Carson et al. (2014) find that consequential SP choices encourage truthful preference revelation. Zawojska and Czajkowski (2015) indeed find that no significant discrepancy between stated and revealed values exists when studies adhere to consequentiality. This finding also encouraged transport economists to include real-life impacts for respondents in their questionnaires (e.g., Fayyaz et al., 2018; Hultkrantz and Savsin, 2018; Krčál et al., 2019). For instance, respondents in the Fayyaz's value of travel time savings study were asked to make route choices which really affected their travel time and travel cost in a drive simulator. Strikingly, Krčál et al. (2019) find that the value of time obtained from *hypothetical* route choice experiments are 30% lower than the value of time from the same experiments which have real consequences for individuals. This contrasts the upward bias which is generally found in stated preference studies. Their conclusion is that participants in the real experiments have a higher value of time because, unlike the participants in the hypothetical experiments, they take scheduling constraints into account.

CVM studies show strong differences between the willingness-to-pay (WTP) to not experience a negative effect and the willingness-to-accept (WTA): the money needed to compensate the same effect. In most cases, WTA is larger than WTP. The difference is larger for public goods than for private goods. The framing of the question matters: a loss is valued higher than an equivalent gain (Tunçel and Hammitt, 2014). The effect of framing is explored further below, as part of a section on behavioral economics. Hammitt (2015) points out that WTP and WTA use different starting points for estimating the compensation in the Kaldor-Hicks test (the situation without the effect and with the effect, respectively). He advocates comparing the gains and losses for different groups, instead of adding these up using a (Kaldor-Hicks) compensation test. Knetsch (2015) states: "Current [CBA] practice, which rarely takes such reference dependence into account, is therefore likely to substantially understate the value and importance of projects, policies, and programs that reduce losses." However, Viscusi (2015) warns: "While there is experimental and empirical evidence that reference point effects may be influential, there often remains a considerable gap between these findings and having firm empirical evidence that would warrant abandoning the standard WTP values as the default benefit measure."

2.5 Discounting

In CBA, costs and benefits which occur over several years must be made comparable to each other. This is done by discounting, which amounts to reducing future benefits and costs. The overarching rationale for discounting is that most people (and public authorities, and private corporations) do not value future costs and benefits as highly as present costs and benefits (Beckerman, 2011). Approaches to choosing social discount rates (discount rates applied to public projects) can be distinguished into two categories: the descriptive approach and the prescriptive approach (e.g., Arrow et al., 1995; Baum, 2009).

The descriptive approach selects discount rates that reflect the real-world market behavior of people today. It implicitly assumes that the "individual discount rate" that individuals apply to personal benefits and costs equals the "social discount rate" that should be applied to social benefits and costs (Howard, 2013). When performing a CBA for a government project, the descriptive approach sets the social discount rate equal to the rate of return money would receive had it not been used in the project (Mouter, 2018). As such, the risk-free discount rate is assumed to be equal to some measure of the real rate of return on investment in the private sector. Hence, this approach is also known as the "opportunity cost of capital approach" (Nordhaus, 2007). In case the discount rate is not selected based on market rates, analysts adopting a descriptive approach analyze the rate at which individuals are willing to trade future consumption with consumption today, also known as the "consumption behavior approach." In this case, the discount rate can be expressed through the so-called Ramsey (1928) model which was designed to assess tradeoffs between present and future consumption:

$$r = \delta + \gamma g$$

In this equation, r is the real discount rate, δ reflects the rate of pure time preference which is also called "the rate of impatience" (individuals' preference for consumption now, rather than in the future, with an unchanging level of consumption over time), γ reflects the diminishing marginal utility of consumption and g is the relative consumption growth per capita.

The prescriptive approach to discounting derives social discount rates from fundamental ethical views, even if the resulting rates do not match market rates (e.g., Dasgupta, 2008; Stern, 2008). A first argument employed by prescriptivists to criticize the "opportunity cost of capital" approach is that standing is only granted to individuals who participate in financial markets (Baum, 2009). In the descriptive approach, people today may value the stakes of the next generation, but it is also plausible that individuals may only optimize consumption over one's own lifetime and not consider future generations in their market behavior (Mouter, 2018). As a result, prescriptivists argue that the social discount rate for government projects affecting future generations can only be established based on ethical considerations about the way future project effects should (ethically) be valued compared to present project effects. Prescriptivists generally also use the Ramsey equation to structure their argument, but they claim that parameters δ and γ should be based on value judgments instead of empirical observations (e.g., Stern, 2008). In their view, determining the pure rate of time preference (p) is a normative rather than an empirical question: "how much should future well-being count, relative to current well-being, in the social welfare function?" Proponents of sustainability tend to set δ equal to zero or close to zero, as a sustainability goal suggests that future generations are equally important as present generations (apart from a very small risk of extinction of mankind). From a normative point of view, the variable γ in the Ramsey equation can be interpreted as a measure of society's relative aversion to intertemporal inequality (e.g., Gollier, 2012a; Goulder and Williams, 2012). The more weight society gives to equality between generations, the higher the value of the parameter (Arrow et al., 1995).

Discount rates proposed by prescriptivists are generally lower than discount rates proposed by descriptivists. For instance, Stern (2008), being a prescriptivist, recommends $\delta = 0.1\%$, $g = 1.3\%$ and $\gamma = 1$, advising a discount rate of 1.4%. Nordhaus (2007), being a descriptivist, strongly argues that market rates of interest would imply $\delta = 2.7\%$, which would lead to a discount rate of 4%.

Mouter (2018) reviews some of the main arguments invoked by prescriptivists and descriptivists. He observes that there is also a prescriptive approach which argues that the social discount rate should be based on social discount rates of citizens' rather than ethical views of scholars. For instance, Sagoff (1988) argues that the social discount rate should be grounded in public discount rates instead of private discount rates, because individuals may not discount impacts that accumulate for themselves in the same fashion as impacts that accrue for others, or society as a whole. Stern (2008) asserts that in imperfect economies (suffering from, among others, externalities and missing markets), the social value of a unit of private consumption/investment may be different from the social value of a unit of public investment. According to Stern, it is a serious mistake to argue that the social discount rate should be anchored by importing one of the many private rates of return on the markets. Finally, Beckerman (2011) states that it cannot be assumed that the market interest rate faced by private firms or corporations equals the discount rate that ought to be used in social policy. We are aware of only one study which empirically studies whether individuals' personal discount rates differ from their social discount rate (Howard, 2013). Howard (2013) concludes that individuals discount social payments at a lower rate than personal payments, based on a comparison of individuals' discount rates for monetary payments that accrue to the individual with monetary payments that benefit society more generally.

Apart from determining the risk-free discount rate (i.e., the risk-free discount rate in year 1), the time structure of the discount rate also needs to be determined. Among a significant number of scholars in the field there is strong consensus that the risk-free discount rate should decline over time (e.g., Arrow et al., 2014; Atkinson and Mourato, 2008; Boardman et al., 2018). The most important rationale for a declining risk-free discount rate is that the large uncertainty associated with aggregate consumption in the distant future (parameter "g" in the Ramsey equation) should induce the prudent representative agent to use lower rates to discount more distant cash flows (Gollier, 2012b, 2013). Turró and Penyalver (2019), for instance, argue if sustainability considerations are included in setting the discount rate, a declining discount rate for very long periods (>30 years) may offer a useful approach.

Moreover, the literature provides arguments to adjust the discount rate for risks via a risk premium (Mouter, 2018). The main argument in existing literature (e.g., Damodaram, 2008; Gollier, 2012a) for discounting risky project effects with a higher discount rate is grounded in the observation that people are risk averse and therefore prefer certain, rather than uncertain, future effects.

As addressed the literature on the selection of discount rates offers widely differing recommendations regarding which discount rate should be used which is also reflected in the divergence between discount rates applied in practice. Koopmans and Rietveld (2013) compared discount rates used in 14 mainly Western countries. They conclude that these rates vary considerably among countries, and that there is a downward trend over time. This trend reflects falling interest rates. Mackie et al. (2014) show that the discount rates used in seven Western countries vary from 3% to 8%. The United Kingdom uses a discount rate of 3.5% which falls to 2.5% for periods of more than 75 years (Treasury, 2018).

Mouter (2018) reviews how the CBA Guidelines in five European countries translate the different recommendations from the literature into their selection of discount rates. Mouter (2018) concluded that these countries attempt to substantiate their discount rates using academic studies and empirical evidence in markets (descriptive approach). However, the discount rates chosen appeared also to be based on practical, political-administrative and judgmental arguments. Furthermore, he observes that both the political-administrative arguments and judgmental arguments are not—or are poorly—communicated in the guidelines of the five countries. This makes it difficult for the user of the CBA to decide whether s/he agrees with the reasonableness of the judgments. He proposes four solutions to the transparency of discounting policies:

(1) practices who adopt a descriptive approach should make it clear why they have adopted a descriptive, instead of a prescriptive approach.

(2) when analysts choose to adopt a descriptive approach when selecting a social discount rate it is important to make the arguments explicit that underpin the choice between using public discount rates (how does society think that the government should discount the impacts of public investments) or private discount rates (based on market behavior);

(3) when countries choose to determine the social discount rate based on private discount rates, it is recommended that they clearly communicate why one particular market rate has been selected from the multiple market rates that are available;

(4) guidelines should provide specific underpinnings, in case components of the discounting policy are based on discretionary decisions made without any specific references to empirical evidence and/or ethical considerations.

Apart from these recommendations to increase the transparency of discounting policies scholars argue that it is important to conduct sensitivity analyses on the normative judgments in the discounting policy and to inform CBA users about alternative CBA outcomes based on these sensitivity analyses (e.g., Boadway, 2006; Kaplow et al., 2010; Nordhaus, 2007; Stern, 2008). This allows CBA users to consider CBA outcomes which coincide with their own belief system (Mouter, 2018).

2.6 Wider economics benefits

Transport projects are often claimed to provide new jobs and reduce unemployment. A reduction in unemployment would then be a benefit in addition to transport benefits such as time savings for travelers. Additional jobs may be created for building the project, but also later when the infrastructure is used if the project increases employment, e.g., by attracting firms. Employment benefits may be computed by multiplying the reduction in unemployment with the benefits generated by an unemployed person who becomes employed. Apart from unemployment changes, transport infrastructure projects may change the wage level. If the demand for labor goes up, its price (i.e., the wage level) may increase, creating benefits for existing workers. However, this is not an additional social benefit, but a transfer from employers to workers. Therefore, we focus on unemployment effects.

The size of the reduction of unemployment is not necessarily equal to the number of workers employed as a result of the project. A part of these workers will be previously unemployed workers, and another part will be previously employed workers, creating job vacancies. Some of these vacancies may be filled by unemployed workers, and other vacancies will not be filled. At a high level of unemployment, most of the workers hired will be from the ranks of the unemployed. At a relatively low level of unemployment, most workers hired will be previously employed (Boardman et al., 2018, p. 150). This implies that the net effect on unemployment needs to be estimated on a case-by-case basis, taking account of the level of unemployment in the economic sectors involved.

Benefits of newly employed workers can be computed as the value of the production created by the additional worker (labor productivity) minus the opportunity costs. In the literature, the opportunity costs of labor have been discussed for a long time (e.g., Harberger, 1971). These opportunity costs are the lost value of what these workers would have done if they had not been employed as a result of the infrastructure project. For unemployed workers, the opportunity costs are the lost value of leisure time.

For previously employed workers, it is the lost value (labor productivity) of their previous job.

Recently, Masur and Posner (2012) have argued that there are additional benefits of reducing unemployment, such as a higher wage (i.e., productivity) in the long run, lower mortality, higher homeownership, more health insurance (in the United States), and a higher level of subjective well-being. Haveman and Weimer (2015) add other factors to this list: recruiting costs, job search costs, effects on family and friends of the unemployed person, and better health/lower health costs. They present a numerical example which shows that including other factors may strongly affect employment benefits. We note that these new developments offer opportunities to both improve CBA and bring CBA closer to the importance of unemployment reduction felt by many people.

Wider economic effects are often not included in CBA's because this may lead to double counting with transport benefits. For instance, transport improvements may increase land values. The value of time savings and the impact on land prices are in effect alternative measures of the same benefit. However, not including wider economic effects is only valid if the markets in which these effects occur, are perfectly competitive. Which is usually not the case (Vickerman, 2017). In competitive markets, any transport cost reduction will be reflected in lower prices because of fierce competition. Moreover, wider economic effects have an impact on the distribution of cost and benefits in society. Vickerman (2017) notes that the best approach to estimate (additional) wider economic benefits is to use empirical models based on New Economic Geography, Graham (2007) being an example. However, he also stresses that these models have limitations. Results are not easily transferable to other projects. There may be discontinuities (tipping points) in behavior, for instance where changes in transport costs cause a firm to relocate. Chapter "The wider economic benefits of transportation" by Pogony of this book provides a more in-depth discussion of including wider economic benefits in transport appraisal.

2.7 Critiques on CBA

Academics have different attitudes toward CBA. Some scholars advocate that politicians should assign a considerable weight to CBA in their decisions (e.g., Eliasson et al., 2015; Sunstein, 2002), whereas other scholars severely criticize the method (e.g., Ackerman and Heinzerling, 2004; Kelman, 1981; Sagoff, 1988). Sen (2000, p. 931) illustrates this controversy within academia as follows: "the discipline of cost-benefit analysis—if discipline it is—has fearless champions as well as resolute detractors. It is, partly, a battle of giants, for there are heavyweight intellectuals on both sides." Overviews regarding critiques raised against CBA are provided by Ackerman and Heinzerling (2004) and Sagoff (1988). Naess (2006) and Van Wee (2012) summarize critiques that refer to applying CBA for the appraisal of transport policies and projects. It is beyond the scope of this chapter to provide an exhaustive overview of all critiques raised against CBA. Hence, in this chapter we confine ourselves to a discussion of one critique which recently resulted into a lively discussion in various branches of the literature. This particular critique targets the assumption in CBA that the welfare of a government policy can be estimated through individuals' private willingness to pay in the context of private consumer choices. The above-mentioned assumption is criticized on two grounds. First of all, scholars contest the extent to which consumers' choices provide an accurate measure of welfare (e.g., Bernheim, 2016; Shogren and Thunström, 2016; Sunstein, 2016). Second, scholars dispute the extent to which the preferences individuals hold in a private consumer context provide valuable information for the evaluation of the impacts of a transport project that emerge from a collective government decision (e.g., Sen, 1995, 2000).

Sunstein (2016) explains that people might make (systematic) "hedonic forecasting errors" in the sense that they might be willing to pay for goods that do not have substantial positive effects on their welfare (and might be unwilling to pay for goods that would have substantial positive effects). There is consensus among academics that economists should not instruct policy makers to mimic errors made by consumers (Shogren and Thunström, 2016). Viscusi and Gayer (2016) therefore advise analysts to correct these actions relative to the choices that consumers would make had they been fully informed and fully rational. On the other hand, Bernheim (2016) observes that an increasing number of scholars advocates measuring welfare impacts in a more direct way through self-reported well-being questionnaires (henceforth: SRWB) than through observing people's choices. A typical happiness survey question asks the respondent to rate his or her happiness with life on scales such as from 0 to 10, 1 to 10, or 1 to 7. Sunstein (2016) illustrates that the "willingness to pay from consumer choices" approach and SRWB approach can result in largely divergent conclusions with regard to the assessment of a regulatory policy which is associated with huge costs and substantial positive employment effects. Sunstein (2016) explains that the CBA for this project was negative, but that happiness research draws different conclusions. Sunstein (2016) refers to a study of Bronsteen (2013) which shows that losing one's job has severe impact on one's happiness (even after people find new employment) whereas the monetary costs resulting from the new regulations has a nearly irrelevant influence one people's happiness. Hence, notwithstanding the negative CBA, this regulation may be implemented when one analyzes it from a happiness perspective (Sunstein, 2016).

Authors such as Sunstein (2016) and Bernheim (2016) recognize the importance of happiness research, but at the same time they point at various reasons why SRWB cannot be used as anything like a substitute for private WTP based CBA. First, SRWB research is still in its infancy and research does not provide enough information for computing the welfare effects of *specific* government projects (Sunstein, 2016). A second problem involves linguistics (Bernheim, 2016). Bernheim (2016) explains that people construe common words and phrases according to their own experiential associations which makes it difficult to pin down whether individuals have the same thing in mind when answering the SRWB questions. Bernheim (2016, P. 25) illustrates his point with the following example wherein choice and self-reported well-being conflict: "While attending a party, Norma says she would be happier drinking wine than soda, but she nevertheless chooses soda. She explains this apparent conflict by noting that she is better off drinking soda because she has to drive home." Bernheim explains that Norma construes the word "happy" in a very narrow way leaving out relevant dimensions that influence her well-being which, in this case, would be measured more accurately through her revealed choice. The two issues with SRWB mentioned above might be alleviated in further research projects. However, an objection which might be more difficult to rectify, concerns the critique on the consequentiality of respondents' answers in SRWB questionnaires. Likewise, in SP surveys which fail to include consequentiality, there are no consequences for participants in SRWB questionnaires when they give incorrect answers which results in a high risk of hypothetical bias (Bernheim, 2016). Finally, it should be noted that the SRWB method assumes that happiness can be measured cardinally in a way that is comparable across people. Section 1 already explained why this is a controversial assumption.

The second category of critique boils down to the observation that choices are strongly affected by context. Scholars criticize the common practice in CBA to transform preferences obtained in one context to another context. Bernheim (2016) explains that behavioral economic research shows that preferences are not monolithic, stable and coherent. In his view, it is much more plausible to assume that preferences are "constructed" or "discovered." The theory of constructed preferences contents that individuals do not possess a set of "true" or "stable" preferences, but that they instead aggregate the many diverse aspects of an experience only when called upon to do so for a given purpose, such as making a choice or answering a question about their wellbeing (Bernheim, 2016). As a result, the various dimensions of an individual's subjective experience may be sensitive to context. For example, circumstances may render one aspect of experience more psychologically salient than another.

Transport CBA already recognizes the importance of context by using different standard numbers for the valuation of travel time savings in different contexts (Mouter, 2016). For instance, in the Netherlands the value of travel time savings for business trips differs from the value of time for commuting and leisure trips (KiM, 2013). However, perhaps the most relevant contextual variable that is ignored in standard CBA is the fact that impacts of government projects are evaluated in a non-representative context (e.g., Ackerman and Heinzerling, 2004; Sen, 1995, 2000). For instance, the value individuals attach to travel time in the context of a government decision are inferred from the value they attach to this impact in the context of a (hypothetical) private route choice. Hence, travel time savings are evaluated in another context than the one in which these benefits actually occur (Mouter and Chorus, 2016). Valuing impacts of a government project through observing their consumer choices ignores that people may place a value on the way collective decisions are made (Weimer, 2017). Mouter et al. (2019) assert that this critique can be alleviated through conducting valuation experiments in which respondents receive information about the context in which the effects will actually accrue (in most cases a government decision, see Mouter et al., 2019 for such a valuation experiment). Empirical research conducted in a transport context indeed shows that individuals make substantially different choices when making the decision in the context of a government decision while being informed about the overall effects compared to a context in which they make a private consumer choice (e.g., Mouter et al., 2017).

3. Application of CBA in practice

3.1 Formal role of CBA

The formal role of CBA differs between countries. In practices such as Chile, the United Kingdom and the Netherlands, CBA provides information for decision-making about the extent to which funding is approved for a specific transport project (Gómez-Lobo, 2012; Mouter et al., 2013). On the other hand, CBA is formally used in practices such as Sweden and Norway to rank large numbers of transport investments against each other (Eliasson et al., 2015). In these countries, CBA is primarily used for choosing investments from a shortlist of suggested investments given a total available budget.

Apart from the formal role of CBA, there are differences in implementation. In the US, the federal government uses CBA extensively. Individual states increasingly apply CBA, but they do not always use rigorous methods (White and VanLandingham, 2015). Andersson (2018) notes that CBA is less well-established in Europe compared to the US. Since 1994, many CBA guidelines have been written in European countries and by the EU, but guidelines do not imply that CBA's are accurate, fully accepted and implemented in planning decisions (Andersson, 2018).

3.2 Impact of CBA on decision making

Several researchers tried to uncover the extent to which CBA actually affects decision-making on transport projects by investigating the statistical relationship between results of CBA studies and political decisions on investments in transport infrastructure (e.g., Annema et al., 2017; Eliasson et al., 2015; Odeck, 2010). The broad picture is that these studies show that there is no significant statistical relation between the monetized effect estimations in CBA studies and political decisions. The exception is the Swedish Transport Administration's selection in the construction of the Investment Plans 2010–2021 and 2018–2029, which seemed to be strongly affected by CBA results (Bondemark et al., 2020; Eliasson et al., 2015). However, decisions of Swedish politicians were only weakly affected by these recommendations, and only for small projects (Eliasson et al., 2015).

Furthermore, several studies have analyzed how politicians use CBA in the context of transport investment decisions by interviewing politicians (Mouter, 2017a, b; Nyborg, 1998; Sager and Ravlum, 2005; Sager and Sørensen, 2011). These studies establish that CBA is at best one of the factors that influences politicians' judgments. None of the politicians interviewed in these studies stated that they solely base their judgment on the results of CBA studies. When politicians use CBA in forming their viewpoint, it is most likely that the results affect their opinion about the desirability of different alternatives of a specific transport project (Mouter, 2017a). Nyborg (1998) observes that in Norway, politicians use CBA as a screening device to pick projects requiring closer political attention, but few seemed to use it to rank projects.

3.3 Opportunistic and symbolic use

It is more likely that politicians use a CBA as ammunition in discussions with other politicians than as an input for their desirability judgment of transport projects (Mouter, 2017a; Nyborg, 1998). When the CBA does not support a politician's opinion, she will criticize the CBA, and she will emphasize the importance of CBA when the results support her opinion (even when she did not used CBA as input for her viewpoint). The literature also identifies that politicians use CBA to make themselves and their decisions look more rational, which is also called "symbolic use" (Mouter, 2017a; Sager and Ravlum, 2005). The institutionalization of CBA has symbolic value for politicians, since the search for and processing of information may itself send out signals that will enhance the status of the political body. In Norway, for instance, researchers observed that the main function of CBA was to legitimize the Norwegian Transport Plan and the political process related to it (Sager and Sørensen, 2011). Politicians must be able to show the public that the output of expert analysis was available to them when they made their decisions, so it can be credibly stated that expert advice was considered as part of the policymaking.

3.4 Barriers hampering the impact of CBA on political viewpoints

The scientific studies in which politicians were interviewed about their use of CBA identified several barriers which need to be rectified to increase politicians' use of CBA when forming their judgments. A first barrier which limits the use of CBA by politicians concerns their trust in the impartiality of the results (Mouter, 2017a). Politicians do not seem to think that results of CBAs are deliberately manipulated, but they have the idea that CBA analysts implicitly and even unconsciously make political choices while carrying out a CBA which influences (the communication of) the results (Mouter, 2017a; Nicolaisen, 2012). For instance, politicians believe that in cases in which analysts can make a choice between multiple assumptions which all are defendable, they can be tempted to choose the assumption that best fits the interests of the institution that commissions the CBA (Mouter, 2017a).

A second barrier is that politicians often receive the CBA too late in the process to (substantially) influence their viewpoint (Mouter, 2017a). Generally, key decisions regarding transport projects are made in the early stage of the policy cycle. In this phase, it is highly likely that decision makers merely receive information about the transport project and the problem it needs to resolve from lobbyists or from a first-hand look during a site visit. Decision makers are presented with CBA results at the end stage of policy preparation. In the Netherlands, it sometimes even happens that Members of Parliament receive a CBA study a few days before the decisive parliamentary debate regarding the transport project (Mouter, 2017a). In those cases, it is highly unlikely that a CBA would have any impact on political decisions.

A third barrier is that politicians assign a relatively low weight to the results of a CBA in their judgments because they contest CBA's normative premises (Mouter, 2017a; Nyborg, 1998). They find that projects which coincide with their own belief system score relatively poorly in CBAs. An example of a normative decision concerns the individuals that are (not) included in the analysis which is also known as the question of "standing." CBA generally adopts a "welfarist" approach to social evaluation which means that the preferences of individual citizens form the basis of a CBA (Sen, 1979). This implies that costs and benefits for animals, and nature in general, only count when humans value them (Baum, 2009). This normative choice might not be in line with the belief system of politicians from Green Parties. Another normative decision concerns the weighting of the preferences of different individuals when establishing the social welfare effect of the project. Standard CBA adopts a utilitarian framework (every man counts for one and not more than one) which implies that individuals' willingness to pay is aggregated. This might not align with the beliefs of politicians who put more (or less) emphasis on the well-being of a certain group within society (e.g., left-wing parties putting a higher emphasis on impacts on low-income people compared to rich individuals).

The literature does not provide conclusive evidence about the extent to which low understanding of CBA by politicians might be a reason for the low influence on political decisions. Annema et al. (2017) for instance argue that "low understanding" might be a plausible explanation for the absence of correlation between CBA results and political decisions. However, Mouter et al. (2017a) and Nyborg (1998) observed that the politicians they interviewed seemed to have a good understanding about the method. For instance, Nyborg (1998, p. 393) writes: "a lack of understanding may be one possible explanation why politicians hardly used cost-benefit ratios for ranking projects. In our survey, we did not explicitly try to test whether respondents' understanding of the cost-benefit methodology was satisfactory, and the interviews do not provide a sufficient basis for firm claims about this. Still, after discussing project evaluation with most respondents for nearly two hours (with approximately half of the time allocated to cost-benefit analysis), we could not identify any respondents who had clearly misunderstood major features of the method. A few respondents demonstrated a considerable insight, including both one of those who were most positive (a Conservative) and one of those who did not find cost-benefit analysis useful at all (Socialist Left Party). We could not see any indications that the most skeptical respondents had a poorer understanding than the others."

3.5 What explains the positive attitude of politicians toward CBA?

Although the results of a CBA do not seem to substantially impact decision-making in a political environment, academic studies universally find that politicians and civil servants have a positive attitude toward the institutionalization of the method (Beukers et al., 2012; Mouter, 2017b; Mouter et al., 2013; Nyborg, 1998). The institutionalization of CBA can bring several benefits to decision-making on transport projects. The literature distinguishes at least eight categories of positive features of CBA.

First, CBA is based on a rigorous theoretical framework being welfare economics that allows for the trade-off between money and social impacts. The principles of welfare economics provide CBA researchers and users with a very clear frame of reference when reflecting on the impacts of policy measures that should (not) be included in a CBA, and how these impacts could be measured and monetized.

Second, CBA enhances the attention given to citizens' interests in the political process. Two important postulates underlying welfare economics and CBA are "individualism" and "non-paternalism." In combination, these postulates assert that the welfare impacts of individual members of society resulting from the project form the basis for establishing the societal welfare effect (individualism) and individuals are conceived to be the best judge of their own welfare (non-paternalism). Because impacts for citizens and firms—and not the interests of stakeholders, academics or policy makers—, are the focal point of a CBA analysis, the instrument is also known as the "taxpayers only model of representation at the political negotiation table" (Mackie et al., 2014).

Third, CBA can be an antidote to overcome cognitive limitations and biases from causing policymakers to neglect vital aspects of proposed policies (Mackie et al., 2014). This is also known as "the cognitive argument for CBA" (Sunstein, 2000). Politicians may face hundreds of projects, and it is simply not possible to completely process all these options. In such situations, humans are bound to use simple heuristics. Appraisal tools such as CBA make it easier for politicians to structure information and remember and consider all or most aspects of a suggested project. Politicians think that this is advantageous because it can prevent them from forgetting to consider important consequences for citizens and firms in the decision-making process (Mouter, 2017b).

Fourth, CBA is considered to be a useful building block for forming an opinion regarding public projects because the method provides insights into the order of magnitude of positive and negative impacts of a project by translating these effects into money. This provides guidance when making decisions. When the societal costs of a project are (substantially) higher than the benefits this can alarm politicians to not support a project. Fifth, due to standardization and the fact that the final indicators of a CBA (e.g., the benefit-cost ratio) communicate very clearly, CBA makes projects comparable. Sixth, CBA can enhance the sharpness of political debates and the underpinning of political decisions (Mouter, 2017b). That is, politicians have found a need to argue in a more precise way about why they want a project despite a negative CBA, or why they don't want a project despite a positive CBA. For instance, with regard to the negative CBA results of light rapid transit (LRT) it was found that decision makers made great efforts to emphasize and inscribe the strategic values of the projects, not included in the CBAs, into diagrams, reports, maps, etc., in order to visualize and make these values "real" for decision makers (Nicolaisen et al., 2017). Seventh, civil servants use CBAs to optimize infrastructure projects in the early phases of their planning process. Finally, CBA can act as a filter (gatekeeper) to prevent weak projects proceeding very far through the planning process. For instance, civil servants from higher tier governments use a negative CBA as an argument in discussions with civil servants from lower tier governments to clarify that it would be better not to have any high expectations about receiving a national contribution for the project because of the poor CBA score (Mouter, 2017b). Hence, in this process, many projects are terminated before they even reach national executives.

4. Future research challenges

This section discusses future research challenges. What are the main challenges and important directions for further research?

4.1 What does CBA actually measure?

First of all, pinpointing how we may interpret this measure turns out to be surprisingly hard. When CBA is seen as measuring social welfare—either through postulating a social welfare function or through the Kaldor-Hicks criterion—one must accept some controversial assumptions. An alternative approach is to go for the more descriptive interpretation of CBA, namely that it only measures aggregate net willingness-to-pay) and nothing more. The question is whether using aggregate WTP as a measure of social welfare is warranted. Critics of CBA in theoretical welfare economics tend toward answering no. They would favor alternative approaches that are more explicit about the normative assumptions made and believe that any criterion for social welfare is bound to be controversial. Advocates of CBA tend to emphasize the benefits of that procedure compared to alternatives in the policy process, e.g., weighting effects in other ways or only quantifying all relevant effects without weighting. We recommend organizing an academic symposium in which the pros and cons of all three approaches are further fleshed out.

4.2 Improving the accuracy of estimations

A first set of issues occurs in estimating transport benefits. As noted above, traffic forecasts are uncertain, to a large extent because exogenous factors such as migration are hard to predict. Also, the time period assessed is sometimes too short to see the full benefits. Moreover, improving the accuracy of investment costs of infrastructure remain an unsolved issue. Using reference class forecasting as advised by Flyvbjerg (2008) may partly solve the problem of systematic underestimation of costs. However, even if investment costs are estimated without systematic bias using uplift factors (a zero mean of the differences between estimates and actual costs), there may still be large differences between estimates and results (a large standard deviation of the differences). Also, a tendency to select projects with too low estimates of investment costs as described by Eliasson and Fosgerau (2013) may remain. A more comprehensive solution may be to create institutions which encourage better cost estimates (Odeck and Kjerkreit, 2019). A major research challenge would be to assess which set of institutions may be best at reducing errors in estimating investment costs. Further research may also focus on a sharper view of the causes of cost overruns, showing to what extent selection bias and availability bias affect cost estimates and cost overruns.

4.3 Risk and uncertainty

As noted above, risk and uncertainty in CBA results are still a substantial problem, despite the host of methods that are applied to compute the size of the variation that may occur in practice (Miller and Szimba, 2015; Nicolaisen and Driscoll, 2014). The way forward may consist of better predictions if possible and accepting and presenting risk and uncertainty where this is unavoidable. Both strands would require further research. Improving predictions would include carrying out ex post CBA's more often, comparing results to ex ante estimates and using the outcomes to improve ex ante CBA's of future projects. Dudley et al. (2019) point out that it is important to include uncertainties in CBA and to learn from experience. Better ways to present risks may arise from further study of the ways civil servants and politicians react to different formats for presentation of CBA results, building on research by Mouter et al. (2015) and Wangsness et al. (2015). Further research may focus on the uncertainty in exogenous factors and the impact of this uncertainty on transport demand predictions. Also, more research is needed on presenting uncertainty in CBA results: how do decision makers perceive different types of information such as point estimates combined with sensitivity analysis, best-case and worst case results (with or without a most likely point estimate), and confidence intervals?

4.4 Discount rate

We think that the debate between descriptivists and prescriptivists about setting the discount rate cannot (and should not) be fully resolved through further research as the difference between the two positions is in part based on ethical views. However, research may shed more light on the merits of both approaches in actual practice. We are aware of only one study that explicitly investigates individuals' discount impacts accruing from public investments (social discount rates; Howard, 2013), whereas numerous prescriptivist scholars ground their recommendations about the social discount rate on their own ethical reflections. Analyzing citizens' preferences regarding the way a government should discount future impacts of government projects might be an interesting avenue for research. Empirical studies can, for instance, explore how individuals trade reduction in travel time or improved traffic safety accruing from a government project in a year from now against similar impacts at a later point in time (e.g., 5 years from now or 10 years from now). Furthermore, academics who aspire to conduct research that would better equip practitioners to design discounting policies in the face of varying recommendations from the literature are encouraged to investigate how the choices they make can be made more transparent. Finally, it is worth investigating the extent to which it is practically feasible to conduct sensitivity analyses on the normative judgments in the discounting policy.

4.5 Wider economic benefits

Public investments may lead to "crowding out" of private investments; this is usually not included in CBA's. Focusing on the valuation of travel time, Vickerman (2017) notes that business travel time saved is valued about three times as high as leisure time saved. This value may be overestimated given the increasing possibilities for mobile communication. Vickerman (2017) adds that measuring connectivity (between firms and individuals) instead of accessibility (total travel costs) may improve the estimation of benefits, but also that the connectivity approach has not been implemented adequately yet.

4.6 Improving the use of CBA in policy making

In the sections above, it was noted that CBA has a (very) limited impact on decision-making about transport infrastructure investment in Europe. Numerous reasons are covered in the literature: (1) CBA's sometimes are carried out too late in the decision-making process to have a strong impact; (2) politicians not fully trust the impartiality of the studies; (3) politicians do not agree with the normative assumptions underlying CBA; (4) politicians have a hard time understanding the results of a CBA. An interesting observation regarding the fourth reason is that academics which interviewed politicians observed that they had quite a good understanding about the method. In terms of research we observe that most studies focus on improving the quantitative predictions provided by CBAs rather than making CBA analyses more useful for political decision-making. This lines up with the findings of Marsden and Reardon (2017) who established that the majority of the studies on transport policy are one-step removed from understanding the real-world complexities of policy-making as most of the literature does not engage with real world transport policy and focused on quantitative analysis alone. At best, scholars recommend increasing politicians' understanding of CBA by presenting these quantitative analysis in a better way to make them more accessible for politicians. Marsden and Reardon (2017) assert that the distance between transportation policy research and real-world transport policy making implies that the field is not advancing our understanding of options and opportunities to intervene and improve policy processes. In line with Marsden and Reardon (2017) we argue that research on transport CBA should not only be about providing better information and tools to aid policy makers, but also about developing a body of knowledge that understands why transport decisions come to be made in the way they are and to comprehend how CBAs can be better institutionalized and further developed to positively influence these decision-making processes. Mouter (2017a), for instance, notes that if scholars aspire to increase the usefulness of CBA for politicians it is important to further investigate solutions for improving the institutional design of CBA to safeguard the early publication of CBA and the trust in CBA's impartiality instead of allocating resources to research areas which are widely studied at present (e.g., Value of Time, Value of Statistical Life) as none of the politicians argued that they would assign more value to CBA if, for example, the Value of Time was calculated in a more sophisticated way.

4.7 Further developing well-being research

Various scholars argue that consumers' choice might be erroneous (e.g., they might be willing to pay for goods that do not have substantial positive effects on their welfare and might be unwilling to pay for goods that would have substantial positive effects). Hence, an increasing number of scholars advocates measuring welfare impacts in a more direct way through self-reported well-being questionnaires (henceforth: SRWB) than through observing people's choices. One the other hand, many scholars assert that as yet self-reported well-being questionnaires (henceforth: SRWB) do not provide a substitute for willingness to pay based valuation of impacts of government projects as many caveats remain: (1) SRWB research does not provide enough information for computing the welfare effects of *specific* government projects; (2) individuals construe common words and phrases according to their own experiential associations which makes it difficult to pin down whether individuals have the same thing in mind when answering the SRWB questions; (3) there are no consequences for participants in SRWB questionnaires when they give incorrect answers which results in a high risk of hypothetical bias; (4) SRWB assumes that happiness can be measured cardinally in a way that is comparable across people. We believe that it is interesting to conduct future research projects which aspire to alleviate these caveats. For example, anchoring vignettes (hypothetical persons or situations) have been used to assess comparability of answers across individuals (e.g., Kapteyn et al., 2010; León et al., 2013). This field of research is still small, and would be worth expanding.

4.8 Incorporating CBA in broader assessment frameworks

In the previous section, it was shown that politicians tend to assess projects using other criteria than welfare measured through willingness-to-pay. They often focus on employment and output (GDP) instead of consumer surplus (Vickerman, 2017). This may cause them to prefer Economic Impact Analysis (EIA) over CBA. As CBA is more comprehensive, this would in our view lead to a loss of information. Andersson (2018) notes that CBA is a powerful tool, but it should not be the only basis for decision-making. Mackie et al. (2014) note that all the seven Western countries they assess, include CBA in a more comprehensive framework which includes non-monetized benefits. Moreover, the willingness-to-pay measured in CBA is not the only metric for welfare, as described above. In our view, the "best of both worlds" may be approached by not only presenting CBA results in terms of costs and benefits, but also as effects on employment, GDP, the distribution of welfare between groups and over time, and other impacts politicians find important (see, e.g., Weisbrod et al., 2016). A drawback of this "mixed approach" may be that politicians will sometimes prioritize projects based on other criteria than net benefits. However, in the end politicians need to make decisions. It may be argued that they are entitled to choose the criteria they deem important.

The challenges described above are hard to solve, but they offer opportunities for very interesting and socially relevant research. If researchers are able to further improve CBA and bring the results closer to the needs of decision-makers, we anticipate that this will result in better informed decisions which ultimately lead to a better transport infrastructure.

References

Aalbers, R., Renes, G., Romijn, G., 2016. WLO- klimaatscenario's en de waardering van CO_2 uitstoot in MKBA's. Centraal Planbureau (CPB), The Hague, Netherlands.

Ackerman, F., Heinzerling, L., 2004. Priceless: On Knowing the Price of Everything and the Value of Nothing. The New Press, New York.

Ahlroth, S., Nilsson, M., Finnveden, G., Hjelm, O., Hochschorner, E., 2011. Weighting and valuation in selected environmental systems analysis tools e suggestions for further developments. J. Clean. Prod. 19, 145–156. https://doi.org/10.1016/j.jclepro.2010.04.016.

Andersson, H., 2018. Application of BCA in Europe–experiences and challenges. J. Benefit-Cost Anal. 9 (1), 84–96.

Annema, J.A., Frenken, K., Koopmans, C.C., Kroesen, M., 2017. Relating cost-benefit analysis results with transport project decisions in the Netherlands. Lett. Spat. Resour. Sci. 10 (1), 109–127.

Arrow, K.J., Cline, W.R., Maler, K.G., Munasinghe, H., Squitiere, R., Stiglitz, J.E., 1995. Intergenerational equity and rate of the discount rate in long-term social investment. In: IEA World Congress, 1995.

Arrow, K.J., Cropper, M.L., Gollier, C., Groom, B., Heal, G.M., Newell, R.G., Nordhaus, W.D., Pindyck, R.S., Pizer, W.A., Portney, P.R., Sterner, T., Tol, R.J.S., Weitzman, M.L., 2014. Should governments use a declining discount rate in project analysis? Rev. Environ. Econ. Policy 8 (2), 145–163.

Arrow, K., Solow, R., Portney, P.R., Leamer, E.E., Radner, R., Schuman, H., 1993. Report of the NOAA panel on contingent valuation. Fed. Regist. 58 (10), 4601–4614.

Asplund, D., Eliasson, J., 2016. Does uncertainty make cost-benefit analyses pointless? Transp. Res. A Policy Pract. 92, 195–205.

Atkinson, G., Mourato, S., 2008. Environmental cost-benefit analysis. Annu. Rev. Env. Resour. 33, 317–344.

Batley, R., Bates, J., Bliemer, M., Börjesson, M., Bourdon, J., Cabral, M.O., Chintakayala, P.K., Choudhury, C., Daly, A., Dekker, T., Drivyla, E., Fowkes, T., Hess, S., Heywood, C., Johnson, D., Laird, J., Mackie, P., Parkin, J., Sanders, S., Sheldon, R., Wardman, M., Worsley, T., 2019. New appraisal values of travel time saving and reliability in Great Britain. Transportation 46 (3), 583–621.

Baum, S.D., 2009. Description, prescription and the choice of discount rates. Ecol. Econ. 69 (1), 197–205.

Beckerman, W., 2011. Economics as Applied Ethics. Value Judgments in Welfare Economics. Palgrave Macmillan.

Bergson, A., 1938. A reformulation of certain aspects of welfare economics. Q. J. Econ. 52 (2), 310–334.

Bernheim, B., 2016. The good, the bad, and the ugly: a unified approach to behavioral welfare economics. J. Benefit-Cost Anal. 7 (1), 12–68.

Beukers, E., Bertolini, L., Te Brömmelstroet, M., 2012. Why cost benefit analysis is perceived as a problematic tool for assessment of transport plans: a process perspective. Transp. Res. A Policy Pract. 46 (1), 68–78.

Binmore, K., 2005. Natural Justice. Oxford University Press.

Boadway, R., 2006. Principles of cost-benefit analysis. Public Policy Rev. 2 (1), 1–44.

Boadway, R.W., Bruce, N., 1984. Welfare economics. B. Blackwell, New York.

Boardman, A.E., Greenberg, D.H., Vining, A.R., Weimer, D.L., 2018. Cost-Benefit Analysis: Concepts and Practice, fifth ed. Cambridge University Press.

Bondemark, A., Sundbergh, P., Tornberg, P., Brundell-Freij, K., 2020. Do impact assessments influence transport plans? The case of Sweden. Transp. Res. A Policy Pract. 134, 52–64.

Bristow, A.L., Wardman, M., Chintakayala, V.P.K., 2015. International meta-analysis of stated preference studies of transportation noise nuisance. Transportation 42 (1), 71–100.

Bronsteen, J., 2013. Well-being analysis vs. cost-benefit analysis. Duke Law J. 62, 1603–1689.

Carson, R.T., 2012. Contingent valuation: a practical alternative when prices aren't available. J. Econ. Perspect. 26 (4), 27–42.

Carson, R.T., Czajkowski, M., 2014. The discrete choice experiment approach to environmental contingent valuation. In: Hess, S., Daly, A. (Eds.), Handbook of Choice Modelling. Edward Elgar Publishing.

Carson, R.T., Groves, T., 2007. Incentive and informational properties of preference questions. Environ. Resource Econ. 37, 181–200.

Carson, R.T., Groves, T., List, J.A., 2014. Consequentiality: a theoretical and experimental exploration of a single binary choice. J. Assoc. Environ. Resour. Econ. 1 (1/2), 171–207.
Chay, K.Y., Greenstone, M., 2005. Does air quality matter? Evidence from the housing market. J. Polit. Econ. 113 (2), 376–424.
Damodaram, A., 2008. Strategic Risk Taking. A framework for Risk Management. Wharton School Publishing.
Dasgupta, P., 2008. Discounting climate change. J. Risk Uncertain. 37, 141–169.
De Blaeij, A., Florax, R.J., Rietveld, P., Verhoef, E., 2003. The value of statistical life in road safety: a meta-analysis. Accid. Anal. Prev. 35 (6), 973–986.
De Bruyn, S., Korteland, M., Davidson, M., Bles, M., 2010. Shadow Prices Handbook Valuation and Weighting of Emissions and Environmental Impacts (March). pp. 1–140. Retrieved from http://www.ce.nl/?go=home.downloadPub&id=1032&file=7788_defMainReportMaKMV_1271765427.pdf.
Defra, 2014. Environmental Noise: Valuing Impacts on: Sleep Disturbance, Annoyance, Hypertension, Productivity and Quiet. Department for Environment Food & Rural Affairs, London.
Dekkers, J.E.C., van der Straaten, J.W., 2009. Monetary valuation of aircraft noise: a hedonic analysis around Amsterdam airport. Ecol. Econ. 68 (11), 2850–2858.
Dudley, S.E., Pérez, D.R., Mannix, B.F., Carrigan, C., 2019. Dynamic benefit-cost analysis for uncertain futures. J. Benefit-Cost Anal. 10 (2), 206–225.
Dupuit, J., 1844. De la mesure de l'utilité des travaux publics. Ann. Ponts Chaussees 166, 332–375.
Eliasson, J., Börjesson, M., Odeck, J., Welde, M., 2015. Does benefit-cost efficiency influence transport investment decisions? JTEP 49, 377–396.
Eliasson, J., Fosgerau, M., 2013. Cost overruns and demand shortfalls–deception or selection? Transp. Res. B Methodol. 57, 105–113.
European Commission, 2019. Handbook on the External Costs of Transport: Version 2019. European Commission, Brussels, Belgium.
Fayyaz, M., Bliemer, M., Beck, M., 2018. Route choice behaviour in stated choice experiments with and without consequences route choice behaviour in stated choice experiments with and without consequences. In: IATBR 2018, Santa Barbara.
Flyvbjerg, B., 2008. Curbing optimism bias and strategic misrepresentation in planning: reference class forecasting in practice. Eur. Plan. Stud. 16 (1), 3–21.
Flyvbjerg, B., Ansar, A., Budzier, A., Buhl, S., Cantarelli, C., Garbuio, M., Molin, E., 2018. Five things you should know about cost overrun. Transp. Res. A Policy Pract. 118, 174–190.
Flyvbjerg, B., Holm, M.S., Buhl, S., 2002. Underestimating costs in public works projects: error or lie? J. Am. Plann. Assoc. 68 (3), 279–295.
Franklin, B., 1772. Letter to Joseph Priestley. https://founders.archives.gov/documents/Franklin/01-19-02-0200.
Fuguitt, D., Wilcox, S., 1999. Cost-Benefit Analysis for Public Sector Decision-Makers. Greenwood Publishing Group.
Gollier, C., 2012a. Pricing the Planet's Future: The Economics of Discounting in an Uncertain World. Princeton University Press, Princeton, NJ.
Gollier, C., 2012b. Term Structure of Discount Rates for Risky Investments. Preliminary Draft.
Gollier, C., 2013. Pricing the planet's Future: The Economics of Discounting in an Uncertain World. Princeton University Press.
Gómez-Lobo, A., 2012. Institutional safeguards for cost benefit analysis: lessons from the Chilean national investment system. J. Benefit-Cost Anal. 3 (1), 1–30.
Gössling, S., Choid, A., Dekkere, K., Metzlerf, D., 2019. The social cost of automobility, cycling and walking in the European Union. Ecol. Econ. 158, 65–74.

Goulder, L.H., Williams, R.C., 2012. The Choice of Discount Rate for Climate Change Policy Evaluation. Discussion paper resources for the future.

Graham, D.J., 2007. Agglomeration, productivity and transport investment. JTEP 41 (3), 317–343.

Hammitt, J.K., 2015. Implications of the WTP–WTA disparity for benefit–cost analysis. J. Benefit-Cost Anal. 6 (1), 207–216.

Hammond, P.J., 1979. Straightforward individual incentive compatibility in large economies. Rev. Econ. Stud. 46, 263–282.

Harberger, A.C., 1971. On measuring the social opportunity cost of labour. Int. Labour Rev. 103, 559.

Harsanyi, J.C., 1955. Cardinal welfare, individualistic ethics and interpersonal comparisons of utility. J. Polit. Econ. 63 (4), 309–321.

Hartgen, D.T., 2013. Hubris or humility? Accuracy issues for the next 50 years of travel demand modeling. Transportation 40 (6), 1133–1157.

Hausman, J., 2012. Contingent valuation: from dubious to hopeless. J. Econ. Perspect. 26 (4), 43–56.

Haveman, R.H., Weimer, D.L., 2015. Public policy induced changes in employment: valuation issues for benefit-cost analysis. J. Benefit-Cost Anal. 6 (1), 112–153.

Herriges, J., Kling, C., Liu, C.C., Tobias, J., 2010. What are the consequences of consequentiality? J. Environ. Econ. Manag. 59, 67–81.

Hicks, J., 1939. The foundations of welfare economics. Econ. J. 49 (196), 696–712.

Howard, G., 2013. Discounting for personal and social payments: patience for others, impatience for ourselves. J. Environ. Econ. Manag. 66, 583–597.

Hultkrantz, L., Savsin, S., 2018. Is 'referencing' a remedy to hypothetical bias in value of time elicitation? Evidence from economic experiments. Transportation 45 (6), 1827–1847.

Isacs, L., Oran Finnveden, G., Dahllöf, L., Håkansson, C., Petersson, L., Steen, B., Wikstr, A., 2016. Choosing a monetary value of greenhouse gases in assessment tools: a comprehensive review. J. Clean. Prod. 127, 37–48. https://doi.org/10.1016/j.jclepro.2016.03.163.

Johnston, R.J., Boyle, K.J., Adamowicz, W., Bennett, J., Brouwer, R., Cameron, T.A., Hanemann, W.M., Hanley, N., Ryan, M., Scarpa, R., Tourangeau, R., Vossler, C.A., 2017. Contemporary guidance for stated preference studies. J. Assoc. Environ. Resour. Econ. 4 (2), 319–405.

Kaldor, N., 1939. Welfare propositions of economics and interpersonal comparisons of utility. Econ. J. 49 (195), 549–552.

Kaplow, L., Moyer, E., Weisbach, D.A., 2010. The social evaluation of intergenerational policies and its application to integrated assessment models of climate change. B.E. J. Econ. Anal. Policy Symp. 10 (2), 7.

Kapteyn, A., Smith, J.P., Van Soest, A., 2010. Life satisfaction. In: Diener, E., Helliwell, J.E., Kahneman, D. (Eds.), International Differences in Subjective Well Being. Oxford University Press, Oxford, pp. 70–104.

Kelman, S., 1981. Cost benefit analysis: an ethical critique. In: Donaldson, T., Werhane, P.H., Cording, M. (Eds.), Ethical Issues in Business: A Philosophical Approach. Prentice Hall, Upper Saddle River, pp. 559–564.

KiM, 2013. The Social Value of Shorter and more Reliable Travel Times. KiM Netherlands Institute for Transport Policy Analysis, The Hague.

Knetsch, J., 2015. The curiously continuing saga of choosing the measure of welfare changes. J. Benefit-Cost Anal. 6 (1), 217–225. https://doi.org/10.1017/bca.2015.4.

Koopmans, C., Rietveld, P., 2013. 14. Long-term impacts of mega-projects: the discount rate. In: Priemus, H., van Wee, B. (Eds.), International Handbook on Mega-Projects. Edward Elgar Publishing, p. 313.

Krčál, O., Peer, S., Staněk, R., Karlínová, B., 2019. Real consequences matter: why hypothetical biases in the valuation of time persist even in controlled lab experiments. Econ. Transp. 20, 100138.
Kuik, O., Brander, L., Tol, R.S., 2009. Marginal abatement costs of greenhouse gas emissions: a meta-analysis. Energy Policy 37 (4), 1395–1403.
Kumar, P., 2011. The Economics of Ecosystems and Biodiversity: Ecological and Economic Foundations. Routledge.
León, C.J., Araña, J.E., de León, J., 2013. Valuing the social cost of corruption using subjective well being data and the technique of vignettes. Appl. Econ. 45 (27), 3863–3870.
Love, P.E., Ahiaga-Dagbui, D.D., 2018. Debunking fake news in a post-truth era: the plausible untruths of cost underestimation in transport infrastructure projects. Transp. Res. A Policy Pract. 113, 357–368.
Mackie, P., Worsley, T., Eliasson, J., 2014. Transport appraisal revisited. Res. Transp. Econ. 47, 3–18.
Mandell, S., 2011. Carbon emission values in cost benefit analyses. Transp. Policy 18 (6), 888–892.
Marsden, G., Reardon, L., 2017. Questions of governance: rethinking the study of transportation policy. Transp. Res. A Policy Pract. 101, 238–251.
Masur, J.S., Posner, E.A., 2012. Regulation, unemployment, and cost-benefit analysis. Va. Law Rev. 98, 579.
Miller, M., Szimba, E., 2015. How to avoid unrealistic appraisal results? A concept to reflect the occurrence of risk in the appraisal of transport infrastructure projects. Res. Transp. Econ. 49, 65–75.
Mishan, E.J., Quah, E., 2007. Cost-benefit analysis, fifth ed. 1, Routledge, pp. 243–244. Appendix.
Mouter, N., 2016. Value of time: to differentiate or not to differentiate? Transp. Res. Rec. 2597, 82–89. Transportation Research Board, Washington.
Mouter, N., 2017a. Dutch politicians' use of cost–benefit analysis. Transportation 44 (5), 1127–1145.
Mouter, N., 2017b. Dutch politicians' attitudes towards cost-benefit analysis. Transp. Policy 54, 1–10.
Mouter, N., 2018. A critical assessment of discounting policies for transport cost-benefit analysis in five European practices. Eur. J. Transp. Infrastruct. Res. 18, 4.
Mouter, N., Annema, J.A., van Wee, B., 2013. Attitudes towards the role of cost–benefit analysis in the decision-making process for spatial-infrastructure projects: a dutch case study. Transp. Res. A Policy Pract. 58, 1–14.
Mouter, N., Chorus, C.G., 2016. Value of time: a citizen perspective. Transp. Res. A 91, 317–329.
Mouter, N., Holleman, M., Calvert, S., Annema, J.A., 2015. Towards improved handling of uncertainty in cost-benefit analysis: addressing the 'price-quality' and 'communication' dilemmas. Eur. J. Transp. Infrastruct. Res. 15, 3.
Mouter, N., Koster, P.R., Dekker, T., 2019. An introduction to participatory value evaluation. In: Working paper Tinbergen Institute 19-024/V.
Mouter, N., van Cranenburgh, S., van Wee, G.P., 2017. Do individuals have different preferences as consumer and citizen? The trade-off between travel time and safety. Transp. Res. A 106, 333–349.
Naess, P., 2006. Cost-benefit analysis of transportation investments. Neither critical nor realistic. J. Crit. Realism 5 (1), 32–60.
Nicolaisen, M.S., 2012. Forecasts: Fact or Fiction?: Uncertainty and Inaccuracy in Transport Project Evaluation. (Doctoral Dissertation, Department of Development and Planning, Aalborg University).

Nicolaisen, M.S., Driscoll, P.A., 2014. Ex-post evaluations of demand forecast accuracy: a literature review. Transp. Rev. 34 (4), 540–557.

Nicolaisen, M.S., Olesen, M., Olesen, K., 2017. Vision vs. evaluation–case studies of light rail planning in Denmark. Eur. J. of Spatial Dev. 65, 1–26.

Nordhaus, W.D., 2007. A review of the stern review on the economics of climate change. J. Econ. Lit. 45 (3), 686–702.

Nordhaus, W.D., 2017. Revisiting the social cost of carbon. Proc. Natl. Acad. Sci. 114 (7), 1518–1523.

Nyborg, K., 1998. Some Norwegian politicians' use of cost-benefit analysis. Public Choice 95 (3–4), 381–401.

Nyborg, K., 2014. Project evaluation with democratic decision-making: what does cost-benefit analysis really measure? Ecol. Econ. 105, 124–131.

Odeck, J., 2010. What determines decision-makers' preferences for road investments? Evidence from the Norwegian road sector. Transp. Rev. 30 (4), 473–494.

Odeck, J., Kjerkreit, A., 2019. The accuracy of benefit-cost analyses (BCAs) in transportation: an ex-post evaluation of road projects. Transp. Res. A Policy Pract. 120, 277–294.

OECD, 2014. The Costs of Air Pollution: Health Impact of Road Transport. OECD, Paris.

Oueslati, W., Salanié, J., 2011. Landscape valuation and planning. J. Environ. Plan. Manag. 54 (1), 1–6.

Persky, J., 2001. Cost-benefit analysis and the classical creed. J. Econ. Perspect. 15 (4), 199–208.

Pickrell, D.H., 1990. Urban Rail Transit Projects: Forecast Versus Actual Ridership and Costs. US Department of Transportation (October 1989).

Ramsey, F.P., 1928. A mathematical theory of saving. Econ. J. 38 (152), 543–559.

Sager, T., Ravlum, I.A., 2005. The political relevance of planners' analysis: the case of a parliamentary standing committee. Plan. Theory 4 (1), 33–65.

Sager, T., Sørensen, C.H., 2011. Planning analysis and political steering with new public management. Eur. Plan. Stud. 19 (2), 217–241.

Sagoff, M., 1988. The Economy of the Earth: Philosophy, Law, and the Environment. Cambridge University Press.

Samuelson, P.A., 1947. Foundations of Economic Analysis. Harvard University Press, Cambridge.

Sen, A., 1979. Utilitarianism and welfarism. J. Philos. 76, 463–489.

Sen, A.K., 1995. Environmental evaluation and social choice: contingent valuation and the market analogy. Jpn. Econ. Rev. 46 (1), 23–37.

Sen, A.K., 2000. The discipline of cost-benefit analysis. J. Leg. Stud. 29 (2), 931–952.

Shogren, J.F., Thunström, L., 2016. Do we need a new behavioral benchmark for BCA? J. Benefit-Cost Anal. 7 (1), 92–106.

Small, K.A., 2012. Valuation of travel time. Econ. Transp. 1 (1–2), 2–14.

Small, K.A., Winston, C., Yan, J., 2005. Uncovering the distribution of motorists' preferences for travel time and reliability. Econometrica 73 (4), 1367–1382.

Stern, N., 2008. Chapter 2, annex 2A "ethical frameworks and Intertemporal equity". In: The Economics of Climate Change: The Stern Review. Cambridge University Press.

Sunstein, C.R., 2000. Cognition and cost-benefit analysis. J. Leg. Stud. 29 (S2), 1059–1103.

Sunstein, C.R., 2002. The Cost-Benefit State: The Future of Regulatory Protection. American Bar Foundation, Chicago.

Sunstein, C.R., 2016. Cost-benefit analysis, Who's your daddy? J. Benefit-Cost Anal. 7 (1), 107–120.

Talvitie, A., 2018. Jules Dupuit and benefit-cost analysis: making past to be the present. Transp. Policy 70, 14–21.

Tijm, J., Michielsen, T.O., van Maarseveen, R., Zwaneveld, P., 2019. How large are the non-travel time effects of urban highway tunneling? Evidence from Maastricht, the Netherlands. Transp. Res. A Policy Pract. 130, 570–592.

Treasury, 2018. The Green Book. Appraisal and Evaluation in Central Government. Treasury, London.

Tunçel, T., Hammitt, J.K., 2014. A new meta-analysis on the WTP/WTA disparity. J. Environ. Econ. Manag. 68 (1), 175–187.

Turró, M., Penyalver, D., 2019. Hunting white elephants on the road. A practical procedure to detect harmful projects of transport infrastructure. Res. Transp. Econ. 75, 3–20.

Van Wee, B., 2012. How suitable is CBA for the ex-ante evaluation of transport projects and policies? A discussion from the perspective of ethics. Transp. Policy 19 (1), 1–7.

Vickerman, R., 2017. Beyond cost-benefit analysis: the search for a comprehensive evaluation of transport investment. Res. Transp. Econ. 63, 5–12.

Viscusi, W.K., 2015. Reference-dependence effects in benefit assessment: beyond the WTA–WTP dichotomy and WTA–WTP ratios. J. Benefit-Cost Anal. 6 (1), 187–206.

Viscusi, W.K., 2018. Best estimate selection bias in the value of a statistical life. J. Benefit-Cost Anal. 9 (2), 205–246.

Viscusi, W.K., Gayer, T., 2016. Rational benefit assessment for an irrational world: toward a behavioral transfer test. J. Benefit-Cost Anal. 7 (1), 69–91.

Wangsness, P.B., Rødseth, K.L., Minken, H., 2015. Handling and Presenting Uncertainty in Cost-Benefit Analysis. (TØI Report 1443/2015).

Wardman, M., Chintakayala, V.P.K., de Jong, G., 2016. Values of travel time in Europe: review and meta-analysis. Transp. Res. A Policy Pract. 94, 93–111.

Weimer, D.L., 2017. Behavioral Economics for Cost-Benefit Analysis: Benefit Validity when Sovereign Consumers Seem to Make Mistakes. Cambridge University Press.

Weisbrod, G., 2008. Models to predict the economic development impact of transportation projects: historical experience and new applications. Ann. Reg. Sci. 42 (3), 519–543.

Weisbrod, G., Mulley, C., Hensher, D., 2016. Recognising the complementary contributions of cost benefit analysis and economic impact analysis to an understanding of the worth of public transport investment: a case study of bus rapid transit in Sydney, Australia. Res. Transp. Econ. 59, 450–461.

White, D., VanLandingham, G., 2015. Benefit-cost analysis in the states: status, impact, and challenges. J. Benefit-Cost Anal. 6 (2), 369–399.

Zawojska, E., Czajkowski, M., 2015. Re-examining empirical evidence on contingent valuation–Importance of incentive compatibility. (Working paper).

CHAPTER TWO

Value of travel time and travel time reliability

Gerard de Jong[a,b,*] and Marco Kouwenhoven[a,c]
[a]Significance, The Hague, The Netherlands
[b]ITS, University of Leeds, Leeds, United Kingdom
[c]Delft University of Technology, Delft, The Netherlands
[*]Corresponding author: e-mail address: dejong@significance.nl

Contents

Abstract

The value of travel time is an important input to cost-benefit analysis of transport projects. Time gains are often one of the main benefits of transport projects, but they need to be converted from hours and minutes to money units, using a value of travel time. Many countries around the world have official values of travel time (by travel purpose, often also by mode) for this conversion. Only a few countries also include travel

Advances in Transport Policy and Planning, Volume 6
ISSN 2543-0009
https://doi.org/10.1016/bs.atpp.2020.07.010

time reliability benefits in project appraisal, partly because of lack of values of travel time reliability, but mainly because of a lack of forecasting models that include travel time reliability. This chapter describes methods used for deriving the value of travel time and reliability and briefly discusses how to forecast time and reliability changes. Finally, some selected outcomes and suggestions for future research are presented. In this chapter, we focus on national value of travel time (and reliability) studies, that have been carried out especially in Europe, and that have been feeding into official appraisal guidelines.

Keywords: Value of travel time, Value of travel time savings, Value of reliability, Value of travel time reliability, Value of travel time variability, Stated preference, Revealed preference, Discrete choice, Logit model

1. Introduction

1.1 What is the value of travel time and what is it used for in practice?

The value of travel time (VTT) is the amount of money at which a change in travel time can be compensated. Travel time is regarded as a disutility and reducing travel time increases utility and vice versa. The amount of money that is required to keep utility constant then is the VTT. The focus in practice is on reducing travel time, because the value of time is often used as input to cost-benefit analysis (CBA) of infrastructure investment projects. The time savings that result from these projects are converted into money units by invoking one or more standard values of travel time, so that these can be compared to other costs and benefits in money units. The same values are sometimes also used to calculate the societal costs of time losses. Since the VTT applies both to travel time savings and travel time losses, we prefer to speak of the value of travel time (VTT) rather than the value of travel time savings (VTTS). We will show that time savings may be valued differently from time losses, and using 'value of travel time savings' as a general term may lead to confusion.

VTT is relevant both in passenger and freight transport. In the latter case VTT stands for 'value of transport time.' In this chapter, we will mainly look into the VTT for passenger transport, but touch upon freight in a few places.

Apart from the use of VTT in CBA, the VTT is sometimes also used as an input to forecasting models. Some of these transport models have their own estimated coefficients for transport time and cost (and therefore their own implied values of travel time might differ from the ones used in CBA), but other models use the national VTT to combine transport time and cost into a single explanatory variable, called 'generalized cost' or 'generalized time.' In the context of CBA, the VTT should reflect the monetary rate that society is willing to pay for time savings or willing to accept for time losses. For forecasting models, the VTT used should reflect the behavior of the decision-makers that is modeled (e.g., that of the travelers).

1.2 What is the value of travel time reliability?

Infrastructure projects might lead to travel time savings, but also to reductions in the variability of travel time, and therefore to travel time reliability benefits. The monetary unit value that society attaches to these savings is the value of travel time variability (VTTR), where there are several possibilities for defining a unit of reliability.

Many countries use a VTT in project appraisal, and for most projects this is the biggest benefit component, but only few practical appraisal systems include reliability benefits. Use of the VTTR as an input to forecasting models (to compute a generalized cost measure that also includes reliability) is even more uncommon.

1.3 Theoretical foundations of the VTT

The VTT that is used in CBA can be derived from micro-economic theory (see Jara-Diaz, 2008; McFadden, 1981). A particularly insightful derivation was proposed by DeSerpa (1971) and Evans (1972). The final result for the VTT to be used in appraisal from that model is:

$$\mathrm{VTT} = \mu/\lambda - (\partial U/\partial T_{\mathrm{travel}})/\lambda \qquad (1)$$

where

VTT = value of travel time for use in appraisal
U = utility
T_{travel} = travel time
μ = Lagrangian multiplier of the time constraint
λ = Lagrangian multiplier of the money budget constraint (marginal utility of income)

Eq. (1) implies that the VTT can be written as the difference between two monetary factors:

- the opportunity value of time: the utility that could be attained if the travel time was used for some other activity at the origin or destination (e.g., for working).

- the utility created while traveling (compared to some reference activity), e.g., by relaxing, reading a book or a newspaper, writing messages on a smartphone/laptop or watching a movie on a tablet.

The first component is likely to increase over time. But the second component tells us that technological changes that make travel time more productive or—more generally speaking—more worthwhile, may lead to a reduction in the VTT. The VTT therefore does not necessarily increase over the years, and certainly not at the same rate as real income. Investments in for instance Wi-Fi connections in trains may lead to a lower need for society to invest in travel time reductions. Of course, in such a situation the increase in utility related to activities during the journey should be included in another benefit component of the CBA.

The micro-economic derivation of the VTT mentioned above does not consider the VTTR. However, the VTTR can be based on scheduling theory, as will be discussed in Section 3.

1.4 Existing reviews

Besides a review of the underlying theory that was already mentioned (Jara-Diaz, 2008), several reviews of the VTT, and a few on the VTTR, are already available.

Passenger transport

- Gunn (2008): introduction to VTT and some of its history;
- Small (2012): conceptual overview, identification of knowledge gaps;
- Carrion and Levinson (2012): review on VTTR;
- Mackie et al. (2014): overview of appraisal methods in selected countries, including VTT used;
- Wardman et al. (2016): European meta-analysis of passenger VTT (building on earlier meta-analyses).

Freight transport

- de Jong (2008): review of measurement methods and results on the freight transport VTT;
- Feo-Valero et al. (2011): review of the VTT literature for freight;
- Vierth (2013): definition and use of VTT and VTTR for freight in selected countries;
- Binsuwadan et al. (2019): international meta-analysis for freight VTT;
- de Jong (2020): introduction to freight VTT.

1.5 Short history

The concept of a VTT already appeared in the work of Dupuit, published in 1844 and 1849, who is considered the grandfather of CBA (Bruzelius, 1979). He worked out the toll that was minimally required to make travelers shift from stage-coach to train.

Measurement of the VTT as we define it today, for use in the CBA of transport projects, probably started in the UK in the 1960s. A graphical approach was applied by Beesley (1965) and early quantitative models were estimated by Quarmby (1967) and Dalvi and Lee (1969). In these early years, the VTT for project appraisal in the UK was assumed to be some fixed fraction of the wage rate, with different fractions for different purposes (in some countries this still is how the VTT is set).

The first empirical studies used data on choices that travelers actually made, such as mode choice (revealed preference data, RP), but in the 1980s studies began to use data on hypothetical choices (stated preference data, SP).

An important landmark was the first national VTT study in the UK, carried out by MVA, ITS Leeds and TSU Oxford (MVA et al., 1987). This was followed by national VTT studies in other countries in Europe: The Netherlands (1988), Sweden (1994), Norway (1994–6), Switzerland (2003), Denmark (2004) and Germany (2012–13). In a number of these countries there have been one or more follow-up national studies to update the VTT and/or to extend the investigation to the VTTR: UK (1994, 2014–15), The Netherlands (1997, 2009/2011, 2020), Sweden (2007/2008) and Norway (2009, 2018–19). These are all national passenger VTT studies and the newer ones also include the VTTR. National freight VTT (and VTTR) studies have also been carried out in the UK (1994), The Netherlands (1992, 2003–4, 2010), Norway (2009, 2018–19) and Germany (2012–13). Also in Australia, New Zealand, the US and Japan specific VTT and VTTR studies have taken place, sometimes also in the form of a national study.

1.6 Overview of the chapter

In the remainder of this chapter, we will review the VTT and VTTR by focusing on the above-mentioned national studies, in terms of the methods used and the outcomes obtained. There are many other studies that have also produced a VTT and VTTR: the meta-analysis for passengers of Wardman et al. (2016) included values from 389 studies all carried out in Europe in the period 1963–2011. The meta-analysis on the freight VTT of Binsuwadan et al. (2019) uses 56 studies from around the world. Nevertheless, the national studies are the source of the officially recommended VTT (and VTTR) in the respective countries and, together with the various meta-analyses, have been influential for values used elsewhere.

In order to include travel time and reliability changes in a CBA of a transport project, two pieces of information are required:

- A set of VTT and VTTR (e.g., by travel purpose, or by travel purpose and mode, possibly also by trip length, income and geography (Börjesson and Eliasson, 2014, 2019); and for freight transport if affected by the project);
- Forecasts of the travel times and reliability levels with and without the project (e.g., by mode and purpose); this also includes predicting the impact of infrastructure projects on reliability.

We call the former the 'P-side' (P of price) and the latter the 'Q-side' (Q of quantity).

The P-side usually comes in the form of standard values, often nationally recommended values, although a project-specific VTT is also possible. The forecasts for the Q-side come from applications of transport models. Many countries have the tools to forecast future levels of travel times, but only very few have forecasting models that include reliability. In the following sections, both sides will be discussed, but with an emphasis on the P-side. Methods to determine the VTT will be reviewed in Section 2 and those for VTTR in Section 3. In Section 4 some selected outcomes for both VTT and VTTR will be presented. The forecasting models for the Q-side for time and reliability will briefly be discussed in Section 5. Finally, Section 6 contains our view on the future research challenges.

2. Methods used to determine the VTT (P-side)

2.1 Cost savings vs SP and RP models

The earliest VTT studies were based on the cost savings approach (CSA), which tries to find the cost of the input factors that will be saved when transport time is saved. A reduction in travel time could release time for use in production, and the opportunity costs would then be the wage costs. This approach does not properly account for the worthwhile use of travel time by the traveler that was discussed in Section 1, which is considered a major drawback of this method. The CSA approach is nowadays used mostly for business travel, and we will come back to the use of this method and other methods for business travel (the 'Hensher equation,' willingness-to-pay) when discussing the business VTT in Section 5.

The alternative approach for determining the VTT is to do a modeling study. This could be either an Revealed preference (RP) study (usually about mode choice, but possibly also mode-destination choice or route choice), an Stated Preference (SP) study (usually about route choice) or a combined RP/SP study. RP-based VTT are usually the by-product of the development of a national or regional freight transport forecasting models.

In RP studies, researchers often encounter two related problems. First, it is difficult to determine which non-chosen alternatives were available in practice and if so what the travel time and cost for these were. Second, there often is a high degree of correlation between transport time and cost, which makes it difficult to estimate both coefficients independently. Often this results in a non-significant coefficient for either of these attributes. In an SP experiment, the researcher can control the attribute levels and their correlation, so these problems can be avoided/reduced. SP studies have been very popular in VTT research since the late 1980s, where the first national VTT studies in the UK and The Netherlands showed that both data types gave similar values, but with more precision and at lower cost for the SP data. One of the disadvantages of SP is that its unexplained variance does not have to coincide with the unexplained variance on real data. This is relevant for forecasting, but not for VTT research, because in such studies one usually only needs the ratio of the time to the cost coefficient (and everything else cancels out).

SP is however not without problems when carried out for establishing the VTT. One of the main problems is that the VTT is not the same for all persons, and even not the same for all trips of one person. The (national) VTT used for valuation should be an appropriate average (i.e., over all persons, over all trips, or over all minutes traveled). However, some SP surveys (and especially the earlier ones) were not very sensitive for trips and persons with a very high VTT (Kouwenhoven and van Cranenburgh, 2019). This may have led to a downward bias in the average VTT. To a large extent, this problem has been solved in more recent SP surveys that include choice tasks that are especially designed to detect high VTT (Börjesson et al., 2012).

A second problem is that SP suffers from 'hypothetical bias': responses that have no consequences for the respondents might differ from responses in actual choice situations on things that have consequences for the decision-makers (Hensher, 2010). Studies that compare SP and RP for the same respondents and choice problems have found differences in the resulting VTT, with SP values being clearly lower than RP values (Hultkrantz and Savsin, 2018; Krčál et al., 2019). Situating the choice experiment in a context that the respondent actually experienced and offering time and cost changes relative to the experienced values (the reference values) may not be sufficient to obtain the required values (see the discussion in Section 2.2).

2.2 SP experiments with reference-based choice situations

Many of the recent national VTT SP surveys used predominantly so-called reference-based questions. This means that the SP choices are always framed around the current travel time and cost. This type of SP-choice is developed following prospect theory (Kahneman and Tversky, 1979, 1992) which says that:

- the valuation of an attribute depends on the current value of that attribute, i.e., it depends on the reference alternative (the situation as observed now): reference dependence
- there will be a difference in the valuation of gains and losses in an attribute: losses are valued more negatively: loss aversion
- there will be a difference in the valuation at different values of an attribute (e.g., between a short and a long transport) and for time changes of a different size: size dependence (a particular manifestation of this might be the VTT for small time savings; this issue is discussed in Welch and Williams, 1997 and Daly et al., 2014).

The researcher can try to control for the influence of the latter effect by explicitly modeling the dependence of the VTT and VTTR on these factors. The reference dependence and the gains/losses effects can be taken into account by following the framework by De Borger and Fosgerau (2008): for SP surveys with two alternatives and two attributes (time and cost) per choice situation, which is a format that has been used in many national VTT and VTTR studies (often in combination with other experiments in the same interview), four flavors of reference-based choice situations exist (also see Fig. 1):

- Willingness-To-Pay (WTP): a choice between the reference trip and a faster and more expensive trip;
- Willingness-To-Accept (WTA): a choice between the reference trip and a slower and cheaper trip;

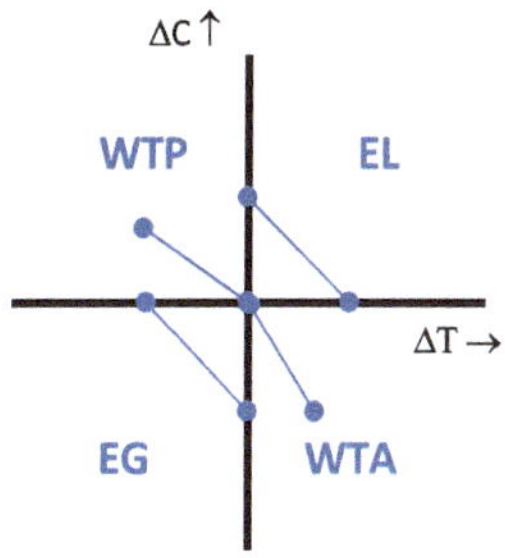

Fig. 1 Cost and time differences presented in the SP.

- Equivalent Gain (EG): a choice between a reference trip that is faster and a reference trip that is cheaper;
- Equivalent Loss (EL): a choice between a reference trip that is slower and a reference trip that is more expensive.

The loss aversion hypothesis states that gains are valued less per unit than losses. Therefore, it should be that the WTP is smaller than the value for EG and EL, and these values are again smaller than the WTA: WTP < EG, EL < WTA. Under certain conditions a reference-free VTT can be obtained by taking the geometric average of WTP and WTA (or equivalently, the geometric mean of EG and EL) (De Borger and Fosgerau, 2008). This was confirmed in several empirical studies.

However, these and other studies have shown that even with this formulation a dependence of the VTTS on the time and cost changes offered in the SP relative to the reference levels can remain (e.g., Fosgerau, 2017). This implies that the resulting VTTS will depend on the design of the SP. Though not all is well understood, this problem is recognized as a fundamental problem which seemingly cannot be solved by more clever designs. This has led some researchers to look at RP data again (e.g., Varela et al., 2018) or joint SP-RP data for measuring the VTT.

2.3 Model specification

Below, we briefly show some of the most popular model specifications. Since these models explain the choice between discrete alternatives (e.g., modes for RP or the alternatives offered in an SP), we are in the realm of discrete choice models. For models that are built for the sole purpose of deriving monetary valuations, the mixed logit specification is nowadays the prevalent type of model. In the mixed logit model, the behavioral coefficients (like time and cost coefficients) can vary stochastically between respondents, and/or alternatives can be correlated in many ways (Train, 2002).

Among models that are estimated for use as forecasting models, the more standard multinomial and nested logit models are dominant. This is caused by the fact that forecasting models are run many times after they have been estimated (and this would take very long with mixed logit because of the repeated simulation that is required for mixed logit) whereas for a monetary valuation just doing model estimation is sufficient.

Regardless whether one uses mixed, nested or multinomial logit models, the researcher also has to specify the observed part of the utility function (as well as make an assumption on the unobserved or random part). The form that was used in all earlier studies and that is still used as a starting point for recent studies is the linear additive model in *utility space* or *preference space.* These models have a simple utility function with linear cost and a time terms (and possibly other observed terms; as well as an additive random error term):

$$U = \beta_C \cdot C + \beta_T \cdot T + \ldots \tag{2}$$

where

β_C = Cost coefficient (to be estimated)

C = Travel or transport cost

β_T = Time coefficient (to be estimated)

T = Travel or transport time

The VTT can be calculated by dividing the time coefficient by the cost coefficient.

This function in preference space is mathematically equivalent to the following model in *willingness-to-pay (WTP) space,* where the VTT is estimated directly.

$$U = \beta_C \cdot (C + VTT \cdot T) + \cdots \tag{3}$$

Using logarithmic utilities weights the information of all respondents in a different way than standard utility functions do. Some authors have found that this utility specification improves the model fit (Kouwenhoven and van Cranenburgh, 2019):

$$U = \mu \cdot log(C + VTT.T)\ldots \tag{4}$$

where

μ = scale parameter

Over the last 15 years, the Random Valuation (RV) specification has been used for binary choice experiments with only time and cost as attributes in most (national) studies. In this specification, the choice alternatives are re-ordered in such a way that the first alternative is always the slow and cheap option, and the second option is the fast and expensive option. In that case, the utilities can be specified as follows:

$$\begin{aligned} U(slowest) &= \mu \cdot BVTT \\ U(fastest) &= \mu \cdot VTT \end{aligned} \tag{5}$$

where

BVTT = Boundary value of time of the choice situation $= -(C_1 - C_2)/(T_1 - T_2)$

The latest Danish, Norwegian, Swedish and UK national VTT surveys used this specification where additionally the utilities were specified using logarithms. This was done since they discovered that their SP observations were better reproduced when the error-terms were multiplicative rather than additive (e.g., Börjesson and Eliasson, 2014; Börjesson et al., 2012; Fosgerau, 2006). In other words: the size of the error-terms depended on the time and cost levels.

$$\begin{aligned} U(slowest) &= \mu \cdot log(BVTT) \\ U(fastest) &= \mu \cdot log(VTT) \end{aligned} \tag{6}$$

Several authors have found that this last specification outperforms the other specifications for VTT-datasets, i.e., this specification results in the best model fit (Kouwenhoven and van Cranenburgh, 2019; Ojeda-Cabral et al., 2016).

2.4 The national VTT studies in Europe

Table 1 provides an overview of the methods used in the national VTT (and sometimes also VTTR) studies carried out in Europe since 1988. We focus on Europe here, because in several European countries, one or more national VTT (and VTTR) studies have been carried out which have fed into the current national appraisal guidelines, and there has been a lot of interaction between the various national studies within Europe. But national appraisal guidelines with recommended VTT and VTTR can also be found outside Europe, e.g., in New Zealand.

All these national studies primarily or exclusively rely on SP data. The table contains information on the following aspects of the methodology:

- The methods used to recruit respondents to provide information about a trip they really made and take part in SP experiments that relate to these trips;

Table 1 Overview of the methods used in European national passenger VTT (and VTTR) studies.

Study	Reference	Recruitment method	Survey method	Modes	SP experiments	Choice models estimated
Netherlands 1988	Hague Consulting Group (1990)	En-route	Paper-based, mailback	Car, train and local PT	Time vs cost	MNL with interactions
Sweden 1994	Dillén and Algers (1998)	Number plates, population register	Paper-based, mailback	Car, bus, train	Time vs cost Time vs cost vs frequency	MNL with interactions
Norway 1994–96	Ramjerdi et al. (1997)	En-route and phone	Personal interviews	Car, bus, train, air	Time vs cost vs automatic traffic control, frequency or delay	MNL with interactions
UK 1995	Accent and Hague Consulting Group (1999), Mackie et al. (2003)	En-route	Paper-based, mailback	Road transport: all purposes	Time vs cost Time vs cost vs delay, scheduling, road type or toll	MNL with interactions; Mackie et al. (2003): power-law dependence on base levels
Netherlands 1997	Hague Consulting Group (1998)	En-route	Paper-based, mailback	Car, train and local PT; all purposes	Time vs cost	MNL with interactions
Switzerland 2003	Axhausen et al. (2006)	From another survey (KEP2)	Paper-based, mailback	Car, bus and train	Time vs costs vs headway or congestion	MNL with interactions; power-law dependence on base levels
Denmark 2004	Fosgerau et al. (2007)	Internet panel and phone panel	Personal interview or web survey	Car and public transport	Most results based on time vs cost	Non-parametric models, multiplicative error models, sign and size effects, mixed logit

Sweden 2007–8	Börjesson and Eliasson (2014)	Number plates, population register and on-board	Phone or web survey	Car, bus, train	Time vs cost	Non-parametric models, multiplicative error models, sign and size effects, mixed logit
Norway 2009	Ramjerdi and Flügel (2010)	Internet panel	Web survey	Car, bus, train, air	Time vs cost Time vs cost vs reliability, seat or congested	Non-parametric models, multiplicative error models, nonlinear probability weighting, mixed logit
Netherlands 2009/2011	Significance et al. (2013)	Internet panel and en-route	Web survey	Car, train, local PT, air, recreational navigation	Time vs cost Time vs cost vs reliability	Power-law dependence on base levels, interactions, panel latent class models
Germany 2012–13	Axhausen et al. (2014)	Phone and internet panel	Paper-based, mailback or web survey	Car, public transport, walking, cycling, air	Time, cost, reliability, transfers, frequency, residence and job location	MNL with interactions, power-law dependence on base levels
UK 2014–15	Batley et al. (2019)	En-route and phone	Web and phone survey	Car, bus, rail, other PT, walking, cycling	Time vs cost Time vs cost vs reliability, crowding, frequency or congested	Multiplicative error models, sign and size effects, mixed logit
Norway 2018–19	Flügel et al. (2019)	En-route, email register and internet panel	Web survey	Car, bus, train, cycling, air	Time vs cost Time vs cost vs reliability, crowding or congested	Multiplicative error models, sign and size effects, mixed logit

- The survey method: the method used to ask the questions and register the responses (e.g., web survey);
- The transport modes studied in a particular study (and for which a VTT is provided);
- Type of experiment and choice of attributes;
- Types of models estimated (e.g., multinomial logit (MNL) with interaction effects for the influence of observed attributes of the person and the trip, or mixed logit models).

Recruitment of respondents from a commercial internet panel has led to problems in some studies (see Flügel et al., 2019; Kouwenhoven et al., 2014), notably in the third Dutch (2009–11) and the third Norwegian (2018–19) study implausibly low VTTs were obtained from models estimated on these data, which was probably caused by self-selection of low VTT persons (within each population segment) into the internet panel.

In terms of method for doing the interviews, internet survey is the preferred method nowadays, although sometimes coupled with other interview methods to accommodate groups of the population that do not (often) use internet.

With respect to the transport modes, the car was included in all the national studies in Table 1, and various means of public transport in almost all. Walking and cycling are included in some of the more recent studies (now also in the ongoing fourth national Dutch study), which may show a shift in transport policy focus toward the non-motorized modes.

Many of the national studies include two-alternative/two attributes (time vs cost) experiments, but also more complicated experiments, especially to include reliability (see Section 4). The use of the binary format has recently been criticized (Hess et al., 2020) for missing relevant attributes, though the problems with the binary format may also be related to the fact that they were not very sensitive for trips and persons with a very high VTT (Kouwenhoven and van Cranenburgh, 2019).

The state of the art for modeling the choice data in national VTT studies are models that account for both observed and unobserved heterogeneity and can catch the long tails (very high VTTs; see Börjesson et al., 2012) of a VTT distribution (mixed logit, latent class). The more recent models also try to correct for sign (time gains vs losses) and size (small vs large time gains) effects, which are likely to be artifacts of the SP method (see Section 3.2).

In terms of statistical SP design, the first series of national studies used variants of an orthogonal or random design. The more recent studies select the combination of attribute levels that is presented to the respondents on the basis of the distinction in four quadrants (see Fig. 1) or use an efficient design, as the UK study of 2014–15 did. An efficient design means that the combination of attribute levels presented to the respondents in the SP is done in such a way that the coefficients of the discrete choice models can be estimated with optimal precision given the sample size (or with the smallest sample size given a level of precision; see Rose and Bliemer, 2009).

2.5 Three methods for the business VTT

In this chapter, business trips refer to trips made by employees on employer's business, excluding professional drivers (e.g., buses, taxis, lorries) and including blue-collar and white-collar workers, with some focus on briefcase travelers. A special case of business travelers are self-employed persons, where employer and employee refer to the same person.

The VTT for business travel is a more challenging research topic than for other trip purposes because it is determined by two decision-makers, the employer and the employee. For commuting trips, there may be a financial reimbursement for travel cost by the employer, but these trips usually take place in private time, as is the case for other (non-business, non-commuting) trips.

Several methods for determining the business VTT have been used in various studies in Europe, see Table 2. All three national VTT surveys in passenger transport in The Netherlands so far (Hague Consulting Group, 1990, 1998; Significance et al., 2013) have used the so-called Hensher equation HE (Hensher, 1977) for determining the business VTT.

The HE decomposes the business VTT into employee and employer components. It tries to take account of several phenomena, that the cost savings approach ignores (de Jong and Kouwenhoven, 2019):

- The VTT for business travel consists of an employer and an employee component;
- The employer component depends on the marginal productivity of work time;
- The employee component also depends of the value of leisure time;
- Some share of the travel time is spent working, though the productivity of this time is not quite as high as that of working at the workplace. When travel time is spent working, this reduces the overall VTT, which is perfectly in line with the underlying theory.

Table 2 Overview of methods to determine the business VTT as used in various national studies in Europe.

Study (country/year)		Method: Hensher equation (HE)	Cost savings approach (CSA)	Willingness-to-Pay (WTP)
Netherlands	1988	√		
	1997	√		
	2009–11	√		
Sweden	1994	√		
	2007–8		√	
Norway	1997	√		
	2009		√	
	2019	√		
UK	1994		√	
	2015			√

The formulation of the HE that is most widely accepted was first formulated in Fowkes et al. (1986):

$$VBTT = \underbrace{(1 - r - p \cdot q) \cdot MPL + MPF}_{\textit{Employer part}} + \underbrace{(1 - r) \cdot VW + r \cdot VL}_{\textit{Employee part}} \quad (7)$$

where

$VBTT$: the business VTT for use in appraisal;

MPL: the productive value of a unit of work time to the employer (the marginal product of labor);

r: the proportion of time savings returned to leisure; the remainder $(1 - r)$ is spent as work in the workplace;

p: the proportion of travel time saved that is at the expense of time spent working during the trip;

q: relative productivity of work undertaken while traveling (relative to working at the workplace);

MPF: the value of extra production as a result of reduced travel fatigue;

VW: the value to the employee of work time at the workplace relative to travel time;

VL: the value to the employee of leisure time relative to travel time.

The first two components on the right-hand side are for the employer, the third and fourth component are for the employee.

The HE can be derived from micro-economic theory (Batley, 2015). This however does not guarantee that employers and employees will follow these rules in their decision-making in practice, or that this rule can adequately explain their choices. This is an empirical question.

The Hensher approach has also been used in Sweden (Algers et al., 1995) and Norway (Ramjerdi et al., 1997). However, in Norway the HE was abandoned in 2009 (but Norway is moving to HE again in the 2019 study) and Sweden now only uses the cost savings approach (CSA). In the UK, an extensive scoping study was carried out (see Wardman et al., 2015) for business travel comparing three different approaches:

- The cost savings approach CSA (see Section 1), that had been used until that time for the official recommendations;
- The HE (in different restricted forms);
- The Willingness-to-Pay WTP approach, that uses SP and/or RP surveys among employers and/or employees to obtain the values.

Wardman et al. (2015) expressed serious reservations about the further use of CSA. A key problem with this approach is that it does not properly account for the productive use of travel time. The paper did not make a clear-cut choice between HE and WTP, but listed several possible research streams featuring these two approaches and combinations of these, and listed pros and cons. Among the disadvantages of the HE were mentioned: the difficulty of estimating the many coefficients of the HE in practice and different views in the literature on the interpretation of the employee component of the HE. The Department for Transport in its request for proposal for the 2014–15 national VTT study specifically ruled out the use of the HE. The new UK study (Arup et al., 2015) used the WTP approach for business travels. This means that the VTT is not build up bottom-up distinguishing employer and an employee components, but that an attempt is made to estimate a single overall VTT, that takes account of all the relevant considerations, by using choice observations (RP or SP) from employers or employees. The UK study collected RP data and SP data for business travel from employees and SP data from employers. In the employees SP, the aim was to get employees to respond in accordance with the company's interest. Both SPs gave similar values and it was decided to determine the official values on the basis of the SP among employees, because this was a much larger dataset with more robust estimation results, that could also be expanded using the National Travel Survey NTS (Batley et al., 2019).

- Different approaches have different consequences for the questionnaire to be used in the VTT/VTTR survey and the SP experiments used. The CSA does not require a business SP experiment. The average productive value of an hour worked *MPL* can be obtained from the business travelers' questionnaire on the basis of the responses to questions about income and hours worked, and external data on the wedge between gross and net wages.
- For the HE approach as used in The Netherlands (Significance et al., 2013), two types of inputs are needed from the survey among business travelers:
  - Weighted average values for *MPL*, *r*, *p* and *q*. These can be obtained from a sample of business travelers.
  - The private VTT for business travelers (*VP*) from one or more SP experiments in which it is made clear that it is the travelers whose values are sought, not those of the employer.
- In case one uses the WTP approach for business trips, there is no need to gather evidence on the marginal product of labor or the coefficients of the HE. All that is required is choice observations between alternatives with time and cost differences. In the most recent UK study (Arup et al., 2015), the official values were derived from an SP experiment among business travelers. Unlike the Dutch surveys, this experiment does not search for the private values that will come on top of the employers' values, but tries to get the employees to include the employer perspective in their SP responses.

2.6 Determination of representative values for use in CBA

The VTT that comes directly from an estimated model is not necessarily suited for use in project appraisal in a national context. The samples used for estimation are often not nationally representative, because targets have been set for specific strata (e.g., public transport, or business travelers) that have relatively low shares in the population but for which the estimation sample needs a certain minimum of interviews for successful model estimation. This is the reason that after the project stages of survey design, data collection and model estimation, a fourth phase often follows that is the establishment of an expansion scheme or application system to obtain nationally representative values. In the case of expansion, factors are derived from a national travel survey or similar survey that is representative, and then the estimation sample is made representative by applying these expansion factors. Alternatively, the estimated parameters can be applied on a different but representative sample, such as a national travel survey. In the latest UK national VTT and VTTR study for instance, the preferred models from the estimation phase were applied to a sample from the National Travel Survey NTS (Batley et al., 2019). The statistical population of interest for the VTT is not so much all persons in a country, but all kilometers or minutes traveled in a country, since an investment project is more likely to affect a long trip than a short one. A related issue is whether in appraisal one should use the above-calculated VTT and VTTR (if possible distance-weighted), which are based on willingness-to-pay, favoring those with high incomes who can afford to pay more, or adjust the values to reflect the income distribution of the travelers. These issues are discussed in Batley et al. (2019) and Börjesson and Eliasson (2014), going back to earlier discussions on equity values, such as Gálvez and Jara-Díaz (1998) or Mackie et al. (2001).

2.7 Determination of VTT in freight transport

Transport time savings, certainly in the long run, lead to reductions in the costs of transport staff and transport vehicles, as well as savings that are related to the goods themselves (reduction of the interest on the capital that is invested in the goods during the time of the transport, but also being out of stock). We therefore see two options for defining the scope of freight transport time benefits in CBA:

A. Narrow definition of the freight value of transport time (VTT): this excludes transport cost savings from VTT (only include the benefits of cargo time saved).

B. Broad definition of VTT: this includes cargo time saved, staff (crew, but in the medium to long run also company overheads, such as administration and office costs) time saved and vehicle time saved in VTT (only include distance cost saved in cost savings).

When using the narrow definition of the VTT, impacts of projects on staff and vehicle time saved need to be included in the CBA through the transport cost savings (together with the distance-based cost, including energy and access cost). Different countries use different definitions in their CBA (Vierth, 2013).

A difficult issue in SP surveys on freight VTT and VTTR is who to interview on what. In the latest Dutch national Freight VTT study (de Jong et al., 2014; Significance et al., 2013), specific assumptions (a priori hypotheses) were made on the extent to which particular actors take into account different components of the freight VTT—and should do so, when responding to the SP questions:.

- Carriers are in the best position to give the component of the VTT (and VTTR) that is related to the costs of providing transport services;
- Shippers that contract out are most interested in other aspects, as expressed by the VTT (and VTTR) that is related to the goods themselves.

If both these components of the VTT (VTTR) are properly distinguished, the carrier VTT (VTTR) and shipper (contract out) VTT (VTTR) can be added to obtain the overall VTT (VTTR) for use in CBA.

Previous studies have not tried to disentangle these two VTT (VTTR) components. However, in Significance et al. (2013) VTT and VTTRs were sought that include both components (not just the goods-related but also the services-related component), since in CBAs for transport projects in the Netherlands the user benefits of savings in vehicle and staff cost are included in the time savings of the project.

Of course, there may be exceptions to the general pattern depicted above, but in the questionnaires the researchers steered the shippers that contract out only to answer on the components they generally know most about, and likewise for carriers. This was done by giving very explicit instructions and explanations to get clearly defined component values from each type of agent. In other words, the researchers:

- explained to all respondents that the changes in time, cost and reliability are generic: these apply to all carriers using the same infrastructure and are not competitive advantages for their specific firm.
- explained to carriers that a shorter transport time might be used for other transports: the staff and vehicles/vessels can be released for other productive activities. A higher reliability means that the carriers can be more certain about such re-planning/re-scheduling. They also explained that the carriers do not have to take into account what would happen to the goods if they were late.
- explained to the shippers that contract out that they only have to take into account what would happen (deterioration, disruption of production process, running out of stock, etc.) to the goods if the transport time or its reliability would change. They were instructed not to take the impact on the transportation staff and vehicles into account.
- explained to shippers with own account transport that they have to take all of this (=cargo and staff/vehicle) into account.

In this way, the researchers obtained estimates for both components separately.

3. Methods used to determine the VTTR (P-side)

In the literature on valuing reliability/variability of travel time in passenger transport, two model specifications are used in most cases (see Batley et al., 2008; Carrion and Levinson, 2012; de Jong et al., 2004; OECD, 2010): the mean-dispersion approach and the scheduling approach.

3.1 Mean-dispersion models

In these models the utility function also includes some measure of the dispersion (spread) of the travel time distribution, usually the standard deviation or the variance. In the literature, these models are usually called 'mean-variance models,' which might be confusing given that most applications include the standard deviation, not the variance. We therefore use a more general name. These models use a utility function with linear cost, time and dispersion terms:

$$U = \beta_C \cdot C + \beta_T \cdot T + \beta_R \cdot \sigma \tag{8a}$$

or

$$U = \beta_C \cdot C + \beta_T \cdot T + \beta_R \cdot \sigma^2 \tag{8b}$$

where

β_R = Reliability coefficient (to be estimated)

σ = Standard deviation of the travel or transport time distribution

σ^2 = Variance of the travel or transport time distribution

The value of time can still be calculated by dividing the time coefficient by the cost coefficient. The value of reliability is calculated in a similar way by dividing the reliability coefficient by the cost coefficient. The reliability ratio is defined as the value of reliability divided by the value of travel time. This ratio can also be calculated by dividing the reliability coefficient (for the standard deviation) by the time coefficient.

3.2 Scheduling models

This specification defines (un)reliability as the amount of time that one will arrive earlier or later than preferred (the schedule delay terms or scheduling terms 'Early' and 'Late' below). This can also be defined as the number of minutes that one will depart earlier or later than preferred. This specification can be based on the scheduling model (departure time choice model) developed by Vickrey (1969) and Small (1982). A related alternative scheduling model that starts from the utility at the origin and the destination location over time was presented by Vickrey (1973) and Tseng and Verhoef (2008). The utility function has the following form:

$$U = \beta_C \cdot C + \beta_T \cdot T + \beta_{Early} \cdot Early + \beta_{Late} \cdot Late \tag{9}$$

where

β_{Early} = Coefficient on early arrival (to be estimated)
Early = Schedule delay early (amount of time earlier than preferred)
β_{Late} = Coefficient on late arrival (to be estimated)
Late = Schedule delay late (amount of time later than preferred)

In principle, it is possible to estimate both a coefficient on the standard deviation (or variance) and on the schedule delay terms. Such a utility function looks like:

$$U = \beta_C \cdot C + \beta_T \cdot T + \beta_R \cdot \sigma + \beta_{Early} \cdot Early + \beta_{Late} \cdot Late \tag{10}$$

There is a theoretical equivalence relation (under certain assumptions) between the Vickrey/Small scheduling approach and an approach using the mean and the standard deviation of travel time (Bates et al., 2001; Fosgerau and Karlström, 2010). There is also an equivalence relation between the Vickrey/Tseng/Verhoef scheduling model to a model with the mean and the variance of travel time (Fosgerau and Engelson, 2011). Therefore, it is theoretically possible to calculate a dispersion measure (and hence a VTTR) from a departure time choice model. The best approach will depend on how one can obtain the best empirical data and which model would fit best in the transport forecasting model system that is used (Börjesson et al., 2012).

3.3 Presentation of reliability in SP

The approach used in most studies that include the VTTR in passenger transport is to use the standard deviation of travel time. It is generally accepted that in the SP experiment, this variable cannot be presented as such to the respondents. A number of different presentation formats is discussed and evaluated in Tseng et al. (2009). The latest national passenger VTT studies in The Netherlands, UK and Norway have all used a presentation format with five possible (and equally likely) travel times, as in Fig. 2.

In freight transport, the mean-dispersion approach has been used as well, and also the presentation format with five possible transport times has been

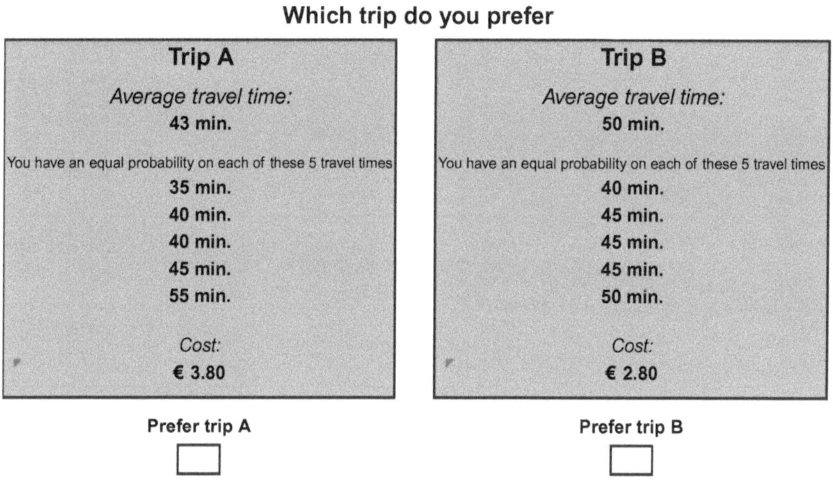

Fig. 2 Example of a choice screen including reliability.

applied in practice. However, most empirical VTT and VTTR studies in freight have presented unreliability as the percentage of goods not arriving on time, possibly combined with the size of the delay as another attribute.

4. Selected outcomes for VTT and VTTR

In order to give readers some flavor of the empirical outcomes for the VTT, we present in Table 3 below, some of the official values that were obtained in the national VTT studies in passenger transport. This table is taken from Wardman et al. (2016). The French values in this table, from CGSP (2013)—the report of the Quinet Commission, are not based on a specific new French national VTT survey, but on a review of 'the most recent studies in France and abroad.' For commuting trips, we see in these Western European countries many values around 10–12 euro. For trips with other purposes, we observe slightly lower values and for business trips we find values between 20 and 30 euro.

An overview of results on the VTTR in passenger transport, focussing on the reliability ratio, can be found in de Jong and Bliemer (2015). For a summary of empirical results for the freight VTT and VTTR we refer to de Jong (2014, 2020).

Table 3 Official values of travel time from national studies (€ per hour 2010 incomes and prices).

			Commute	Other	Business
Switzerland (2003)	Comm./Other: Swiss Ass. of Road and Transp. Exp. (2009); Busi.: Axhausen et al. (2006)	Car	26.7	6.19	37.87
		PT (Bus/Train)	16.19	8.72	35.31
Denmark (2004)	Fosgerau et al. (2007)	Car	11.87	11.87	
		PT (Bus/Train)	11.87	11.87	
Norway (2009)	Ramjerdi and Flügel (2010)	Car Short (<100 km)	11.7	10.01	49.4
		Car Long (>100 km)	26	18.98	49.4
		PT (Bus/Train) Short (<100 km)	7.8	5.98	49.4
		Train Long (>100 km)	20.28	11.96	49.4
		Bus Long (>100 km)	13.39	9.49	49.4
		Air	37.44	23.4	57.85
Sweden (2008)	Trafikverket (2012)	Car Long (>100 km)	10.96	10.96	29.54
		Bus Long (>100 km)	3.96	3.96	29.54
		Train Long (>100 km)	7.41	7.41	25.07
		Air		17.56	29.54
		Car Short (<100 km)	8.83	5.99	29.54
		Bus Short (<100 km)	5.38	3.35	29.54
		Train Short (<100 km)	7	5.38	25.07
Netherlands (2011)	Significance et al. (2013)	Car	9.25	7.5	26.25
		Train	11.5	7	19.75
		Bus/Tram	7.75	6	19
		Air		47	85.75

Table 3 Official values of travel time from national studies (€ per hour 2010 incomes and prices).—cont'd

			Commute	Other	Business
Germany (2012)	Axhausen et al. (2014)	Car Short (<50 km)	4.2	3.49/3.97	6.01
		PT (Bus/Train) Short (<50 km)	3.89	3.85/4.73	4.65
		Car Long (>50 km)	9.58	9.26/9.46	12.11
		Train Long (>50 km)	8.21	8.44/9.31	11.06
		Air Long		22.89	33.87
France (2013)	CGSP (2013)	All Urban (All of France)	10	6.8	17.5
		All Urban (Ile-de-France)	12.6	8.7	22.3
		Car		14.4	32.7
		Coach		12.1	27.6
		Train		22.7	43.3
		Air		53.4	72.9
United Kingdom (2014)	Department for Transport (2015)	All Modes	12.51	5.71	
		Car Urban 0–50 km			12.6
		Car Inter-Urban 50–100 km			20.38
		Car Inter-Urban 100 km+			31.4
		Train Urban 0–50 km			12.6
		Train Inter-Urban 50–100 km			20.38
		Train Inter-Urban 100 km+			45.24
		Bus/LRT Urban			12.6

Note: The German values for other distinguish leisure and shopping and we, respectively, give each of these.

Adapted from Wardman, M., Chintakayala, P.K., de Jong, G.C., 2016. Values of travel time in Europe: review and meta-analysis. Transport. Res. A 94, 93–111.

5. Methods used to forecast travel time gains and reliability gains (Q-side)

In this section we briefly discuss how time and reliability savings can be included in forecasting (Q-side) for a transport project. Forecasting the Q-side for VTT is relatively straightforward. There are many transport models around the world that can give the impact of a reduction in travel time on choice-making, e.g., on mode choice. These models then have to be run for a future situation with and without the transport project to yield the time savings as well as the modal shift brought about by the project. The modal shift predictions are needed to calculate the new users for the internal benefits in the CBA, but also for the external benefits of the project (e.g., change in emissions or safety).

Some countries now have official values of reliability available, also for reliability defined as the standard deviation of travel time. The Q-side of reliability has been studied to a lesser degree. Practically all of these studies on the Q-side have dealt with road transport, trying to explain the standard deviation of travel time on motorways from travel time, inverse speed, congestion or traffic flow. The data used for this were automatic induction loop speed and flow measurements or GPS data. For public transport, it is common practice in some countries to monitor the deviations from the timetable as a measure of reliability, but there are very few studies on modeling the Q-side of reliability in public transport.

The estimated models explaining the standard deviation of travel time can then be used, together with standard transport model outputs in terms of travel times to calculate the standard deviation of travel time for the case with and without the infrastructure project. This means that the unreliability model is used as a post-processing module, that is positioned after the transport model and that provides reliability benefits for use in the cost-benefit analysis (see de Jong and Bliemer, 2015 for a more extensive general discussion, and Kouwenhoven and Warffemius, 2016 for a comparison of models for forecasting the standard deviation of travel time and an application to road transport in the Netherlands).

6. Future research challenges

Below we list a number of research challenges for research on the VTT and VTTR in the coming years.

SP surveys on these topics suffer from a dependence of the results on the size of the time and cost changes offered (thus the SP design), relative to the reference values (Fosgerau, 2017). The research questions concern the size of the impact of SP design on the resulting VTT and VTTR, for various values of the estimated model coefficients, whether there are possibilities to reduce the dependence within SP and what the potential is for moving (partly) back to RP?

The available passenger VTT almost exclusively refer to car drivers or some forms of public transport. An extension to under-researched modes (car-passenger, bicycle, walking, or even MaaS) is highly recommended.

The VTT over time is impacted by changes in worthwhile use of travel time on the VTT (Kouwenhoven and de Jong, 2018; Wardman et al., 2019). Further research is needed on quantifying this impact on the VTT and on how to include other benefit components in the CBA for these user benefits. How precisely was travel time spent and why? Can the type of work of the respondent be done during a business or commute trip (or even during a trip for another purpose)? Further development of ICT technology could make travel more productive and worthwhile than it already is. However, it is difficult to predict technological developments, and especially the speed of their large-scale adoption. Probably the biggest game-changer in this respect would be the automated vehicle (Fosgerau, 2017). Private (or shared) cars where the driver doesn't need to pay any attention to driving, and where the car could be used as a sort of 'mobile office' would further reduce the VTT (de Almeida Correia et al., 2020; Pudāne and Correia, 2020; Steck et al., 2018). This will only result in a very low VTT if considerably more travelers than today would decide to spend the travel time performing an activity that has a similar utility as at the origin and destination (de Jong and Kouwenhoven, 2019).

Appraisal of investment projects in transport by its very nature takes a long-term perspective (e.g., looking 30 or 40 years ahead, which are not untypical lifespans for physical transport infrastructure). However, many of the VTTs and VTTRs are based on SP research. In SP choice situations, the respondents probably do not take such a long-term view, but provide answers that are more representative for the short-term. The potential impacts of this and possibilities to obtain more long-term values are discussed in Beck et al. (2017) and Peer and Börjesson (2018).

Studies that look at VTT and VTTR and other values used in appraisal from several perspectives need further investigation (consumer perspective, as used in the studies described above, or citizen perspective, or a social choice vs a private choice perspective, see Mouter and Chorus, 2016; Mouter et al., 2019), to find out what the differences will be and which perspective will be most appropriate for which valuation in which situation.

Studies on income effects, inter-modal differences (comfort and worthwhile use of travel time) and the application of equity values as a pragmatic approach to mitigate some of these issues are likely to become more prominent.

Even though some studies produced a VTTR, reliability benefits are seldomly included because forecasts of the impact of the project on reliability are still missing (for road transport, but even more so for public transport). The is a need for new forecasting models (the Q-side) for all modes that include reliability.

Finally, in CBA for transport projects in many countries, time benefits play a major role. It is likely that this role might become smaller in years to come because of worthwhile use of the travel time (see above). But there also is the possibility (for the moment still rather theoretical) that the calculation of time savings from a transport model, which are then multiplied by a standard VTT from some other source, will be replaced by a more encompassing and consistent measure, the logsum change (de Jong et al., 2007). The logsum change is a measure of consumer surplus change in the context of logit choice models. In spite of the very frequent use of logit models in transport, project assessment is only rarely done using logsums. Key reasons for this are that logsum changes are less intuitive and harder to explain to non-experts than time gains. When logit models are used for forecasting, the use of logsums in the appraisal of transport projects is already possible.

From this list, it can be concluded that though the value of travel time has already been studied for a long time, still many issues remain for future researchers in the years to come.

References

CGSP—Commissariat Général à la Stratégie et à la Prospective, 2013. Cost Benefit Analysis of Public Investment. Final Report—Summary and Recommendations. Commission Quinet, Paris.

Accent and Hague Consulting Group, 1999. The Value of Travel Time on UK Roads. Report to DETR, London/The Hague.

Algers, S., Dillen, J.L., Widlert, S., 1995. The national Swedish value of time study. In: Proceedings of Seminar F, PTRC Summer Annual Meeting.

Arup, ITS Leeds, Accent, 2015. Provision of Market Research for Value of Time Savings and Reliability, Phase 2 Report to the Department for Transport. Available at: https://www.gov.uk/government/uploads/system/uploads/attachment_data/file/470231/vtts-phase-2-report-issue-august-2015.pdf.

Axhausen, K., Ehreke, I., Glemser, A., Hess, S., Jödden, C., Nagel, K., Sauer, A., Weis, C., 2014. Ermittlung von Bewertungsansätzen für Reisezeiten und Zuverlässigkeit auf der Basis eines Modells für modale Verlagerungen im nicht-gewerblichen und gewerblichen

Personenverkehr für die Bundesverkehrswegeplanung. Entwurf Schlussbericht, TNS Infratest and ETH Zurich.

Axhausen, K.W., Hess, S., König, A., Abay, G., Bates, J., Bierlaire, M., 2006. State of the Art Estimates of the Swiss Value of Travel Time Savings. Institute of Transport Planning and Systems (IVT), ETH, Zurich.

Bates, J., Polak, J., Jones, P., Cook, A., 2001. The valuation of reliability for personal travel. Transport Res E-Log 37 (2–3), 191–229.

Batley, R.P., 2015. The Hensher equation: derivation, interpretation and implications for practical implementation. Transportation 42, 257–275.

Batley, R., Bates, J., Bliemer, M., Börjesson, M., Bourdon, J., Cabral, M.O., Chintakayala, P.K., Choudhury, C., Daly, A., Dekker, T., Drivyla, E., Fowkes, T., Hess, S., Heywood, C., Johnson, D., Laird, J., Mackie, P., Parkin, J., Sanders, S., Sheldon, R., Wardman, M., Worsley, T., 2019. New appraisal values of travel time saving and reliability in Great Britain. Transportation 46, 1–39. https://doi.org/10.1007/s11116-017-9798-7.

Batley, R.P., Grant-Muller, S., Nellthorp, J., de Jong, G.C., Watling, D., Bates, J.J., Hess, S., Polak, J., 2008. Multimodal Travel Time Variability, Final Report, Report for the UK Department of Transport. ITS Leeds, John Bates and Imperial College.

Beck, M.J., Hess, S., Cabral, M.O., Dubernet, I., 2017. Valuing travel time savings: a case of short-term or long term choices? Transport Res E-Log 100, 133–143.

Beesley, M.E., 1965. The value of time spent travelling: some new evidence. Economica 32, 174–185.

Binsuwadan, J., de Jong, G.C., Batley, R., Wheat, P., 2019. The value of travel time savings in freight transport: a meta-analysis. In: Paper Presented at UTSG 2019, University of Leeds.

Börjesson, M., Eliasson, J., 2014. Experiences from the Swedish value of time study. Transp. Res. A Policy Pract. 59, 144–158.

Börjesson, M., Eliasson, J., 2019. Should the value of travel time be differentiated? Transport. Rev. 39 (3), 357–375.

Börjesson, M., Eliasson, J., Franklin, J., 2012. Valuations of travel time variability in scheduling versus mean–variance models. Transp. Res. B Methodol. 46 (7), 855–873.

Börjesson, M., Fosgerau, M., Algers, S., 2012. Catching the tail: empirical identification of the distribution of the value of travel time. Transp. Res A 46 (2), 378–391.

Bruzelius, N., 1979. The Value of Travel Time. Croom Helm, London.

Carrion, C., Levinson, D., 2012. Value of travel time reliability: a review of current evidence. Transp. Res. A 46, 720–741.

de Almeida Correia, G.H., Looff, E., Van Cranenburgh, S., Snelder, M., Van Arem, B., 2020. On the impact of vehicle automation on the value of travel time while performing work and leisure activities in a car: theoretical insights and results from a stated preference survey. Transp. Res. A 119, 359–382.

Dalvi, M.Q., Lee, N., 1969. Variations in the Value of Travel Time. 37 Manchester School, pp. 213–236.

Daly, A.J., Tsang, F., Rohr, C., 2014. The value of small time savings for non-business travel. JTEP 48 (2), 205–218.

De Borger, B., Fosgerau, M., 2008. The trade-off between money and travel time: a test of the theory of reference-dependent preferences. J. Urban Econ. 64, 101–115.

de Jong, G.C., 2008. Value of freight travel-time savings, revised and extended chapter. In: Hensher, D.A., Button, K.J. (Eds.), Handbook of Transport Modelling, Handbooks in Transport. vol. 1. Elsevier, Oxford/Amsterdam.

de Jong, G.C., 2014. Values of service attributes and elasticities. In: Tavasszy, L., de Jong, G. (Eds.), Modelling Freight Transport. Elsevier Insights Series, Elsevier, London/Waltham, MA.

de Jong, G.C., 2020. Value of time in freight transport. In: Vickerman, R. (Ed.), Encyclopedia of Transportation. Elsevier, Oxford. Forthcoming.
de Jong, G.C., Bliemer, M.C.J., 2015. On including travel time reliability of road traffic in appraisal. Transp. Res. A 73, 80–96.
de Jong, G.C., Daly, A.J., Pieters, M., van der Hoorn, A.I.J.M., 2007. The logsum as an evaluation measure: review of the literature and new results. Special issue of Transp. Res. A Policy Pract. 41, 874–889.
de Jong, G.C., Kouwenhoven, M., 2019. Time use and values of time and reliability in the Netherlands. In: OECD/ITF (2018) Zero Value of Time of Travel Time Savings? ITF Round table 176.
de Jong, G.C., Kouwenhoven, M., Bates, J., Koster, P., Verhoef, E., Tavasszy, L., Warffemius, P., 2014. New SP-values of time and reliability for freight transport in the Netherlands. Transp. Res. E 64, 71–87.
de Jong, G.C., Kroes, E.P., Plasmeijer, R., Sanders, S., Warffemius, P., 2004. The value of reliability. In: Paper Presented at ETC 2004, Strasbourg.
Department for Transport, 2015. Understanding and Valuing Impacts of Transport Investment: Values of Travel Time Savings. https://www.gov.uk/government/uploads/system/uploads/attachment_data/file/470998/Understanding_and_Valuing_Impacts_of_Transport_Investment.pdf.
DeSerpa, A., 1971. A theory of the economics of time. Econ. J. 81, 828–846.
Dillén, J., Algers, S., 1998. Further research on the national Swedish value of time study. In: Selected Proceedings of the 8th World Conference on Transport Research. 3, pp. 135–148.
Evans, A., 1972. On the theory of the valuation and allocation of time. Scot. J. Polit. Econ. 19, 1–17.
Feo-Valero, M., Garcia-Menendez, L., Garrido-Hidalgo, R., 2011. Valuing freight transport time using transport demand modelling: a bibliographical review. Transp. Rev. 201, 1–27.
Flügel, S., Halse, A., Kouwenhoven, M., de Jong, G.C., Sundfør, H., Hulleberg, N., Jordbakke, G., 2019. A minute of your time: the impact of survey recruitment method and interview location on the value of travel time. In: Paper Presented at ITEA Conference 2019.
Fosgerau, M., 2006. Investigating the distribution of the value of travel time savings. Transp. Res. B 40 (8), 688–707.
Fosgerau, M., 2017. The Value of Travel Time, ETC 2017 Keynote Presentation. ETC, Barcelona.
Fosgerau, M., Engelson, L., 2011. The value of travel time variance. Transp. Res. B 45 (1), 1–8.
Fosgerau, M., Hjorth, K., Lyk-Jensen, S.V., 2007. The Danish Value of Time Study: Final Report. Danish Transport Research Institute, Knuth-Winterfeldt Allé, Bygning 116 Vest, 2800 Kgs, Lyngby, Denmark.
Fosgerau, M., Karlström, A., 2010. The value of reliability. Transp. Res. B 44 (1), 38–49.
Fowkes, A.S., Marks, P., Nash, C.A., 1986. The value of business travel time savings. In: Working Paper 214. Institute for Transport studies, University of Leeds.
Gálvez, T., Jara-Díaz, S., 1998. On the social valuation of travel time savings. Int. J. Transp. Econ. 25, 205–219.
Gunn, H.F., 2008. Valuation of travel time savings and losses. In: Hensher, D.A., Button, K.J. (Eds.), Handbook of Transport Modelling, Second ed. Pergamon, Oxford.
Hague Consulting Group, 1990. The Netherlands' Value of Time Study: Final Report. Report for DVK, HCG, Den Haag.
Hague Consulting Group, 1998. The Second Netherlands' Value of Time Study: Final Report, Report 6098–1 for AVV. HCG, Den Haag.
Hensher, D.A., 1977. Value of Business Travel Time. Pergamon Press.

Hensher, D.A., 2010. Hypothetical bias, choice experiments and willingness to pay. Transp. Res. B 44, 735–752.
Hess, S., Daly, A., Börjesson, M., 2020. A critical appraisal of the use of simple time-cost trade-offs for appraisal value of time measurement. Transportation 47, 1541–1570.
Hultkrantz, L., Savsin, S., 2018. Is 'referencing' a remedy to hypothetical bias in value of time elicitation? Evidence from economic experiments. Transportation 45 (6), 1827–1847.
Jara-Diaz, S.R., 2008. Allocation and valuation of travel time savings. In: Hensher, D.A., Button, K.J. (Eds.), Handbook of Transport Modelling, Handbooks in Transport. vol. 1. Elsevier, Oxford/Amsterdam.
Kahneman, D., Tversky, A., 1979. Prospect theory: an analysis of decision under risk. Econometrica 47, 263–291.
Kahneman, D., Tversky, A., 1992. Advances in prospect theory: cumulative representation of uncertainty. J. Risk Uncertain. 5 (4), 297–323.
Kouwenhoven, M., de Jong, G.C., 2018. Value of travel time as a function of comfort. J. Choice Model. 28, 97–108.
Kouwenhoven, M., de Jong, G.C., Koster, P., van den Berg, V.A.C., Verhoef, E., Bates, J., Warffemius, P., 2014. New values of time and reliability in passenger transport in the Netherlands. Res. Transp. Econ. 47, 37–49.
Kouwenhoven, M., van Cranenburgh, S., 2019. A systematic comparison of parametric and nonparametric methods for uncovering the value-of-travel-time distribution from binary stated-choice data. In: Paper Presented at International Choice Modelling Conference, Kobe 2019.
Kouwenhoven, M., Warffemius, P., 2016. Forecasting Travel Time Reliability in Road Transport: A New Model for the Netherlands. ITF-OECD Discussion Paper 2016-2, ITF-OECD, Paris.
Krčál, O., Peer, S., Staněk, R., Karlínová, B., 2019. Real consequences matter: why hypothetical biases in the valuation of time persist even in controlled lab experiments. Econ. Transp. 20, 100138.
Mackie, P., Jara-Díaz, S., Fowkes, T., 2001. The value of travel time savings in evaluation. Transp. Res. E 37, 91–106.
Mackie, P.J., Wardman, M., Fowkes, A.S., Whelan, G., Nellthorp, J., Bates, J., 2003. Values of Travel Time Savings in the UK. ITS Leeds and John Bates Services Report for the UK Department for Transport, Leeds.
Mackie, P., Worsley, T., Eliasson, J., 2014. Transport appraisal revisited. Res. Transp. Econ. 47, 3–18.
McFadden, D., 1981. Econometric models of probabilistic choice. In: Manski, C., McFadden, D. (Eds.), Structural Analysis of Discrete Data With Economics Applications. MIT Press, Cambridge, pp. 198–269.
Mouter, N., Chorus, C., 2016. Value of time: a citizen perspective. Transp. Res. A 91, 317–329.
Mouter, N., Cabral, M.O., Dekker, T., van Cranenburgh, S., 2019. The value of travel time, noise pollution, recreation and biodiversity: a social choice valuation perspective. Res. Transp. Econ. 76, 100733.
MVA, ITS Leeds, TSU Oxford, 1987. The value of travel time savings. Policy J. 1987
OECD, 2010. Improving Reliability on Surface Transport Networks. OECD, Paris.
Ojeda-Cabral, M., Batley, R., Hess, S., 2016. The value of travel time: random utility versus random valuation. Transportmetrica A Transp. Sci. 12 (3), 230–248.
Peer, S., Börjesson, M., 2018. Temporal framing of stated preference experiments: does it affect valuations? Transp. Res. A 117, 319–333.
Pudāne, B., Correia, G., 2020. On the impact of vehicle automation on the value of travel time while performing work and leisure activities in a car: theoretical insights and results from a stated preference survey—a comment. Transp. Res. A 132, 324–328.

Quarmby, D.A., 1967. Choice of travel mode for the journey to work. JTEP 1, 273–314.

Ramjerdi, F., Flügel, S., 2010. The 2009 Norwegian Value of Travel Time Study. Prepared for the Norwegian Public Roads Administration. The Norwegian National Rail Administration, The Norwegian Coastal Administration, Avinor AS and The Ministry of Transport and Communications.

Ramjerdi, F., Rand, L., Sætermo, I.A., Sælensminde, K., 1997. The Norwegian Value of Time Study Part 1. TØI Report 379, Report to Ministry of Transport and Communications, The Norwegian Railways, the Norwegian Public Road Administration and the Norwegian Civil Aviation Administration, TØI Oslo.

Rose, J.M., Bliemer, M.C.J., 2009. Constructing efficient stated choice experimental designs. Transp. Rev. 29, 587–617.

Significance, VU University, John Bates Services, TNO, NEA, TNS NIPO, PanelClix, 2013. Values of Time and Reliability in Passenger and Freight Transport in the Netherlands, Report for the Ministry of Infrastructure and the Environment, Significance. The Hague.

Small, K.A., 1982. The scheduling of consumer activities: work trips. Am. Econ. Rev. 72, 467–479.

Small, K., 2012. Valuation of travel time. Econ. Transp. 1 (1), 2–14.

Steck, F., Kolarova, V., Bahamonde-Birke, F., Trommer, S., Lenz, B., 2018. How autonomous driving may affect the value of travel time savings for commuting. Transp. Res. Rec. 2672 (46), 11–20.

Swiss Association of Road and Transportation Experts, 2009. Kosten-Nutzen-Analysen im Strassenverkehr; Zeitkosten im Personenverkehr. Swiss Association of Road and Transportation Experts, Zurich.

Trafikverket, 2012. Samhällsekonomiska principer och kalkylvärden för transportsektorn: ASEK 5. Available at http://www.trafikverket.se/Foretag/Planera-och-utreda/Planerings--och-analysmetoder/Samhallsekonomisk-analys-och-trafikanalys/ASEK---arbetsgruppen-for-samhallsekonomiska-kalkyl--och-analysmetoder-inom-transportomradet/.

Train, K.E., 2002. Discrete Choice Methods With Simulation. Cambridge University Press, New York.

Tseng, Y.Y., Verhoef, E.T., 2008. Value of time by time of day: a stated-preference study. Transp. Res. B 42 (7–8), 607–618.

Tseng, Y.Y., Verhoef, E.T., de Jong, G.C., Kouwenhoven, M., van der Hoorn, A.I.J.M., 2009. A pilot study into the perception of unreliability of travel times using in-depth interviews. J. Choice Model. 2 (1), 8–28.

Varela, J.M.L., Börjesson, M., Daly, A., 2018. Public transport: one mode or several? Transp. Res. A Policy Pract. 113, 137–156. https://doi.org/10.1016/j.tra.2018.03.018.

Vickrey, W.S., 1969. Congestion theory and transport investment. Am. Econ. Rev. 59, 251–261. Papers and Proceedings.

Vickrey, W.S., 1973. Pricing, metering, and efficiently using urban transport facilities. Highw. Res. Rec. 476, 36–48.

Vierth, I., 2013. Valuation of transport time savings and improved reliability. In: Ben-Akiva, M.E., Meersman, H., van de Voorde, E. (Eds.), Recent Developments in Transport Modelling: Lessons for the Freight Sector. Emerald, Bingley, UK.

Wardman, M., Chintakayala, P.K., de Jong, G.C., 2016. Values of travel time in Europe: review and meta-analysis. Transp. Res. A 94, 93–111.

Wardman, M., Batley, R., Laird, J., Mackie, P., Bates, J., 2015. How should business travel time savings be valued? Econ. Transp. 4 (4), 200–214.

Wardman, M., Chintakayala, P., Heywood, C., 2019. The valuation and demand impacts of the worthwhile use of travel time with specific reference to the digital revolution and endogeneity. Transportation 94, 1–26.

Welch, M., Williams, H., 1997. The sensitivity of transport investments benefits to the evaluation of small travel-time savings. JTEP 31 (3), 231–254.

CHAPTER THREE

The value of a statistical life

Henrik Andersson*
Toulouse School of Economics, University of Toulouse Capitole, Toulouse, France
*Corresponding author: e-mail address: henrik.andersson@tse-fr.eu

Contents

Abstract

The monetary value of preventing one statistical death is usually defined as the value of a statistical life (VSL), which is the focus of this chapter. It represents how much society would be willing to spend to prevent one unidentified death, but since no easily available prices exist for this value, non-market valuation approaches like stated- (SP) and revealed-preference (RP) methods need to be used to obtain it. We will in the chapter describe the theoretical economic model behind the VSL concept and the most common empirical SP and RP techniques used to obtain monetary estimates of the VSL.

Keywords: Fatality risk, Non-market valuation, Revealed preferences, Stated preferences, Value of a statistical life, Willingness to pay

1. Introduction

A well-functioning transport sector is essential to any society in its provision of bringing together goods and services from different markets and locations, and enabling individuals to travel for, e.g., business, education, and social reasons. But, it also creates many negative effects like pollution, noise, and congestion. One major negative effect from transportation is that

ISSN 2543-0009
https://doi.org/10.1016/bs.atpp.2020.07.004

individuals get injured or even die when traveling. For instance, statistics suggest that as many as 1.35 million individuals die annually in road traffic accidents alone (WHO, 2018). Since these injuries and deaths result in huge welfare losses to societies governments invest and design polices to reduce their numbers. But, why do governments not try to eliminate the injuries and the deaths? Reducing the risk of injury or fatality comes at a cost, and hence governments need to decide whether the social benefits from reducing the risks justify the costs.

One approach to evaluate safety measures is to compare them based on their outcomes in terms of reduced injuries and fatalities. The preferred measure would then be the one with the highest number of reduced injures and/or fatalities. However, since such an evaluation tool does not consider the costs, it risks systematically suggesting that large and costly policies should be implemented. An alternative decision tool would therefore be to evaluate the safety measures based on their cost per prevented injury and/or fatality. Normalizing the cost of the policy to one prevented injury or fatality allows for a comparison of the effectiveness of policies of different sizes and with different technologies and is often referred to as cost-effectiveness analysis (CEA). Whereas CEA allows for a more efficient resource allocation by identifying the most cost-effective safety policies, it fails to take into account how individual preferences may differ between policies. Hence, CEA is useful to evaluate the technical efficiency of policies with the same objective, e.g., reducing the risk of fatalities, but it usually cannot guide resource allocation between sectors, or even within sectors when polices cover several objectives. For instance, a more cost-effective policy regarding preventing traffic fatalities may have larger negative environmental effects compared to the other policies.

The evaluation tool favored by economists, i.e., cost-benefit analysis (CBA), allows for guidance of resource allocation between sectors and for polices with multiple objectives. Cost-benefit analysis is firmly grounded in welfare analysis and is based on the interventions' e.g., a policy effect on the welfare of the individuals affected.[a] Its decision rule is that if the benefits of a government policy exceed the costs then the policy is welfare improving and should be implemented.[b] Cost-benefit analysis as an

[a] Here we ignore the issue of standing, i.e., who's preferences count in the CBA. For a discussion on standing see, e.g., Whittington and MacRae Jr. (1986).

[b] This example is based on the simplistic interpretation of how CBA is implemented when decision makers do not face any budget constraints and can implement all policies/projects where benefits exceed the costs. In reality budgets are limited and hence the decision rule may need to be adjusted (Pearce et al., 2006).

evaluation tool has increased in use and importance (see, e.g., Andersson, 2018) which is reflected by the many manuals and guidelines on how to conduct and implement CBA published at national levels and also by the European Commission (DoT, 2016; EPA, 2010; European Commission, 2014; HM Treasury, 2003; Quinet et al., 2013). Daniels et al. (2019) provide a recent example of a systematic CBA of different road safety measures. Conducting a CBA requires, though, that all benefits and costs are measured in a common metric and manuals and guidelines usually provide recommendation on values to use. Money usually acts as this metric and whereas many effects' values are reflected by their market prices, not all effects have easily available prices. Traffic safety, i.e., reducing the risk of an accident with a negative health outcome, is an example of a good that does not have a market price per se. Instead, individuals' preferences for safety need to be elicited using non-market valuation techniques.

Non-market valuation techniques are usually (broadly) defined as either belonging to revealed-preference (RP) or stated-preference (SP) methods. The classification is based on whether preferences are elicited using market data where individuals' actual decisions are expected to reveal the individuals' preferences, or in hypothetical settings where non-binding decisions are used to inform about preferences (Freeman et al., 2014). In this chapter, we focus on preferences for traffic safety and examples of market behavior to elicit preferences for safety such as the use of seat-belts (Blomquist, 1979), bicycle helmets (Jenkins et al., 2001), and car purchases (Andersson, 2005). Since the other approach, i.e., SP methods, are not restricted to having access to market data the range of safety scenarios, from quite abstract to more market like, is wide (see, e.g., Andersson and Treich, 2011). Monetizing preferences for safety, i.e., assigning a monetary value to the prevention of deaths and injuries may seem strange and even unethical and the use of monetary risk values for safety-policy evaluations has been criticized (see, e.g., Ackerman and Heinzerling, 2004; Broome, 1978; Hauer, 1994). The aim with this chapter is to explain why monetizing preferences to reduce the risk of injury and death is neither strange, nor unethical, by first explaining what the monetary values actually represents, and then by explaining that they are meant to represent the public's own preferences.

We will in this chapter focus on the valuation of reducing the risk of dying in traffic, but the same theory and empirical methods are also applicable to valuing the reduction of injury risk. In the following section we will first briefly describe the history of the valuation of preventing death and provide its intuition, and then provide the theoretical models. We will then in

Section 3 describe the main empirical non-market valuation methods used to estimate monetary values. The chapter ends with a discussion.

2. Background and theory

In the following subsections we first provide a brief background and introduction to the concept of valuing fatality risk reductions, and then present the theoretical models, first the standard one-period model and then the multiperiod model. When describing the different models, we also provide a discussion of some of the main predictions from the models, which are of importance to the understanding and validity testing of results in empirical applications, and their policy relevance (Sunstein, 2004).

2.1 Monetizing preferences

Today it is well established that individuals' willingness to pay (WTP), or willingness to accept (WTA) (more below), is the appropriate measure of preferences for health risk reductions (Dreze, 1962; Schelling, 1968). Prior to the WTP approach becoming widely accepted as the appropriate valuation approach the human capital (HC) approach dominated, however. The HC approach assumes that an individual's social value is reflected by his/her market productivity (Mishan, 1982). Hence, in contrast to the WTP approach it is not a preference-based approach. This can be illustrated by Eq. (1). Let p_t, y_t, and r be the survival probability conditional on surviving until t, the income in t, and the discount rate, with t and T define the time periods and end of life. The value of preventing a death is then, according to the HC approach, given by the discounted expected future earnings, i.e.,

$$HC = \sum_{t=1}^{T} \frac{p_t y_t}{(1+r)^t}, \tag{1}$$

hence the individual's social value depends on his/her earnings, which reflect his/her market productivity. Despite its attractiveness of being intuitive and straightforward, and that data being relatively easily accessible, its two major drawbacks make it of limited use for policy purposes: (1) a zero value is assigned to non-market production, and (2) it does not reflect individuals' preferences to reduce their risk of death.[c] Since we expect that

[c] As shown in Wijnen et al. (2019), even if uncommon, the HC approach is still used in some places. An extension of the HC approach, i.e., the "reproduction-and resource-costs method," is discussed in Bahamonde-Birke et al. (2015).

society also cares for unemployed and retired individuals, who according to Eq. (1) would have a zero value, calculating a value based on Eq. (1) could be considered both unethical and illogical. Therefore, one suggestion has been to augment the value with monetary values reflecting non-market social contributions like goods and services produced in the household, and also monetary values for lost leisure time (Keeler, 2001). This addresses the issue regarding the first drawback, but it does not address the second drawback which is the main critique against the HC approach. It has also been shown that the HC approach may underestimate the social value of preventing a fatality since it, under reasonable and plausible assumptions of the utility function, can serve as a lower bound of a preference-based measure of preventing a fatality (Bergstrom, 1982; Rosen, 1988). For the reasons described, unless it is not feasible to obtain preference-based estimates, the HC approach is out of favor among economists to elicit monetary safety values.

Instead, monetary values should be derived based on preference-based approaches and the rest of this chapter will, therefore, focus on preference-based monetary safety measures. As described, individual WTP reflects preferences and we will focus on preferences for a reduced risk of death. Hence, the concept and the models will be based on fatality (mortality) risk scenarios, but they are also applicable to injury (morbidity) risks.[d] We will follow the standard and define the monetary value to prevent one fatality as the value of a statistical life (VSL). It is important to stress that the value does not reflect the value of saving an identified life, but since VSL contains the word "life" there is an ongoing discussion whether it is the best expression for the marginal WTP to reduce a fatality risk (Cameron, 2010; Simon et al., 2019). However, we opt to use it here as well since it is the established terminology, but to stress that it does not reflect an identified life, consider the following illustrative example:

> Assume a society (city/region/country/etc.) with a population of 100,000 in which 8 individuals die as a result of traffic accidents each year. A traffic safety program is proposed by the local government with the objective to reduce the number of traffic accident deaths to two per year. Thus, the safety program would lead to six fewer deaths per year and assume that each individual is willing to pay EUR 240 annually

[d] Whereas there is only is only one possible negative health outcome in the models describing fatality risk, i.e., death, models on injury risk also need to consider issues of severity and the duration of the injury (see, e.g., Andersson et al., 2015, for a discussion).

for it to be implemented. Knowing the WTP we can then estimate that per statistical death prevented the society is willing to pay EUR $240 \times 100{,}000/6 =$ EUR 4 million. That is, EUR 24 million would be collected to save 6 lives, which would mean that the VSL is equal to EUR 4 million.

2.2 One-period model

The VSL is the population mean of the marginal rate of substitution (MRS) between mortality risk and wealth when the individual MRS and the personal change in risk are uncorrelated (see e.g., Jones-Lee, 2003). The theoretical model is based on a state-dependent expected-utility framework where individuals are assumed to maximize their utility (Dreze, 1962; Jones-Lee, 1974; Rosen, 1988). Let p and $u_s(w)$ denote the survival probability and the state-dependent utilities of wealth (w), with the states either being staying alive ($s=a$) or dead ($s=d$), then the individuals are assumed to maximize,

$$EU(w,p) = pu_a(w) + (1-p)u_d(w). \tag{2}$$

Eq. (3) lists the standard assumptions in the literature; the utility functions are twice differentiable, utility of wealth is higher if alive than dead, marginal utility of wealth is non-negative and higher if alive than dead, and individuals are weakly risk averse to financial risks, i.e.,

$$u_a(w) > u_d(w), u_a'(w) > u_d'(w) \geq 0 \text{ and } u_s''(w) \leq 0 \tag{3}$$

That is, we assume that at any wealth level both the utility and the marginal utility are higher if alive than dead, and as illustrated in Fig. 1 with these assumptions the indifference curves over wealth and survival probability are decreasing and strictly convex.

The compensating and equivalent surplus, i.e., the WTP and WTA, for a change in the mortality risk Δp ε (Freeman et al., 2014) can be derived using Eq. (2). Focusing first on the WTP, which reflects the maximum amount a person is willing to give up to for the risk reduction, and let EU_0 be defined by Eq. (2) and $C(\varepsilon)$ denote the WTP for the risk reduction ε, then $C(\varepsilon)$ is given by,

$$(p+\varepsilon)u_a(w - C(\varepsilon)) + (1-p-\varepsilon)u_d(w - C(\varepsilon)) = EU_0, \tag{4}$$

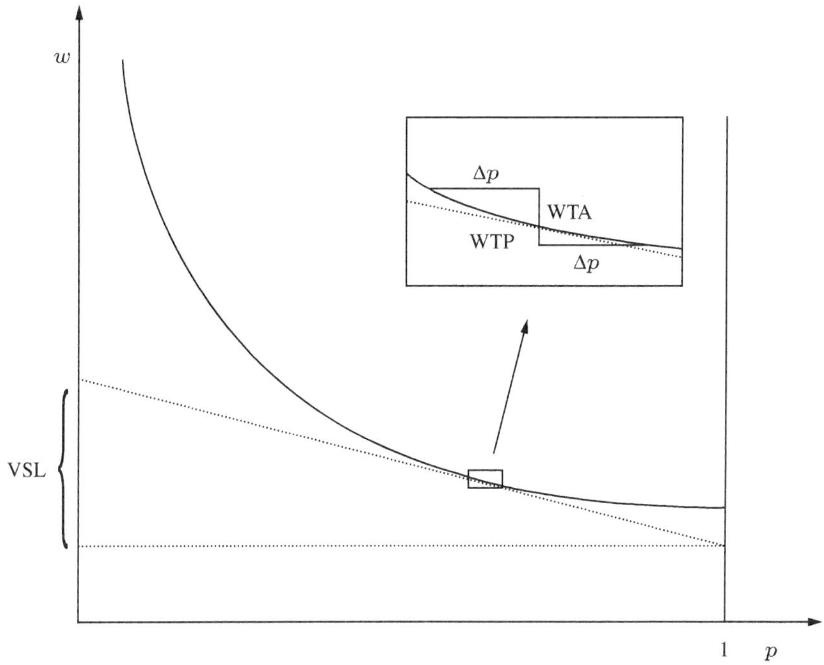

Fig. 1 The value of a statistical life. *Source: Lectures notes, Henrik Andersson, Toulouse School of Economics, inspired by lectures notes by James Hammitt, Harvard University.*

and similarly if we let *P(ε)* denote the WTA, which reflects the minimum amount a person is willing to accept as compensation for an increase in the risk level, and let the risk increase be defined by ε, then *P(ε)* is given by,

$$(p-\varepsilon)u_a(w+P(\varepsilon))+(1-p+\varepsilon)u_d(w+P(\varepsilon))=EU_0. \qquad (5)$$

It is evident from Eqs. (4) and (5) that WTP and WTA will depend on the size of ε, i.e., that the larger change in risk the larger is the WTP or the WTA, which is also illustrated in Fig. 1. However, the size of ε will be small and we expect WTP and WTA to be nearly equal and that they are near-proportional to the size of ε (Hammitt, 2000).

The WTP or WTA above is for an finite small change in risk and the marginal WTP, i.e., the MRS between wealth and mortality risk (VSL), can be obtained by taking the limit of WTP or WTA when $\varepsilon \cong 0$,

$$VSL=-\left.\frac{dw}{dp}\right|_{\text{EU constant}}=\frac{u_a(w)-u_d(w)}{pu'_a(w)+(1-p)u'_d(\mathrm{w})}. \qquad (6)$$

Eq. (6) is the ratio between the utility difference and the expected marginal utility and is derived by totally differentiating Eq. (2) and keeping utility constant. VSL is always strictly positive given the assumptions in Eq. (3).

In the empirical section we will describe that Eq. (6) can be empirically estimated, but in many empirical applications the risk reduction may be small but finite. For instance, in surveys where respondents are asked to consider hypothetical scenarios it does not make sense to ask about a truly marginal risk change. Instead the analyst asks the respondents about his/her WTP (or WTA) for a small change in the risk (Δp) and the VSL is then given by the ratio between the change in wealth, e.g., WTP, and the change in risk, i.e.,

$$VSL = \frac{WTP}{\Delta p} \tag{7}$$

In Eq. (7) the WTP is proportional to the change in risk. But, it should be interpreted as an approximation since the true relationship between WTP and Δp is only near-proportional, which is a necessary, but not sufficient, condition for WTP to be a valid measure of individuals' preferences (Hammitt, 2000).

2.2.1 The wealth and the dead-anyway effect

The theoretical framework described in the previous section is important to understand what VSL represents, but also to provide predictions for empirical applications where it is important to test the validity of the findings (Bishop and Boyle, 2019). The two core predictions from the model above are the wealth and dead-anyway effect. Regarding the former, i.e., the wealth effect, it is standard to all non-market valuation studies (i.e., not only for health risks) to examine how wealth influences WTP as a test of the validity of the estimates (see, e.g., Arrow et al., 1993). Given the assumptions in Eq. (3) it is straightforward to show with Eq. (6) that VSL increases with wealth (Weinstein et al., 1980), since the numerator and the expected marginal utility in the denominator increases and decreases in wealth, respectively. The intuition is also clear, i.e., that wealthier individuals (everything else equal) are willing to pay more for a good, since they have more to lose and that their utility cost of spending is smaller.

The dead-anyway effect suggests that WTP decreases with the survival probability (p) (or increases with the baseline risk, hence the expression) (Pratt and Zeckhauser, 1996). This effect only depends on the denominator in Eq. (6) and is a result of the denominator becoming larger when p

increases since $u'_a > u'_d$. Again, the prediction is intuitive with a high risk person having incentives to spend on increasing his/her survival probability.

2.2.2 Other selected predictions

The predictions that WTP and WTA depend on the size of the risk change, and that they are near-proportional to it, together with the ones on the wealth and the dead-anyway effect described in the previous section can be considered the core predictions of the standard one-period VSL model. But, several other useful predictions have also been derived from the one-period model. For instance, the survival probability above can be separated into different types of risks an individual faces. Let traffic risk define a specific risk of interest, and for simplicity all other risks an individual faces as a background risk. It can then be shown that the WTP for the specific risk can be influenced by the background risk. Assuming that the background risk is independent to the specific risk Eeckhoudt and Hammitt (2001) showed that the VSL will decrease with the size of the background risk, whereas with the risk being additive Andersson (2008) showed that the VSL would instead increase. Moreover, Eeckhoudt and Hammitt (2004, p. 13) showed that "Although aversion to financial risk increases VSL in definable cases, under many plausible assumptions the relationship between risk aversion and VSL is ambiguous," and Treich (2010) that VSL increases with ambiguity aversion.

One issue to consider when eliciting individual preferences for traffic safety is whether the safety measure will be a private or a public one. If individuals are purely selfish then their WTP for both type of safety measure will be the same. However, if their preferences express some form of altruism, pure or paternalistic, then it can be shown that the WTP for a private and a public measure, where the latter will also be available and paid for by others, may differ depending on the type of altruism (Andersson et al., 2019).[e]

2.3 Multiperiod model

The single-period model above can be extended to a multiperiod model. For many health effects this extension is of high relevance since it allows for an examination how latency, i.e., a delay from being exposed to the risk to experiencing the negative health effects, affect the WTP (Hammitt and Liu, 2004). However, whereas latency may be present for a risk like air

[e] Other predictions can also be made, e.g., the health effect on VSL being ambiguous (Hammitt, 2002; Strand, 2006), but in this chapter we limit the examples of predictions to a few that we consider of most relevance, and we also refer to provided references for more details.

pollution, the negative health outcome in traffic accidents are often immediate, like injury or death. Hence, the latency issue can be considered of less relevance when eliciting preferences for traffic safety. However, the multiperiod model is also used to examine how age may influence the WTP, which is of relevance also for evaluating traffic safety measures.

The multiperiod model is based on the life-cycle model in which individuals are assumed to maximize their expected value of the utility of consumption (see, e.g., Johansson, 2002; Yaari, 1965),

$$EU_\tau = \sum_{t=\tau}^{\infty} q_{\tau,t}(1+i)^{\tau-t}u(c_t), \tag{8}$$

where τ, $u(c_t)$, i, and $q_{\tau,t} = p_\tau \ldots p_{t-1}$, denote the point of reference, the utility of consumption at time t, the utility discount rate, and the probability at τ of surviving to t. We follow Hammitt and Liu (2004) and illustrate the derivation of the VSL with a two period model (to simplify, and for the same reason also assuming that the marginal utility of a bequest is equal to zero), i.e.,

$$EU = p_1 u_1(c_1) + p_1 p_2 u_2(c_2), \tag{9}$$

subject to the budget constraint,

$$c_1 + \frac{c_2}{1+i} = B, \tag{10}$$

where i is the discount rate, and the subscripts 1 and 2 referring to the first and second time period. The VSL will depend on the optimal consumption path which between the periods can be shown to be given by,

$$\frac{u_1'(c_1)}{u_2'(c_2)} = p_2(1+i) \tag{11}$$

We are now interested in the marginal WTP today for a risk reduction that appears today, i.e., both the payment and the risk reduction happen in 1, which we can obtain by totally differentiating Eq. (9),

$$VSL_{1,1} = -\left.\frac{dc_1}{dp_1}\right|_{\text{EU constant}} = \frac{u_1(c_1) + p_2 u_2(c_2)}{p_1 u_1'(c_1)}, \tag{12}$$

which corresponds to the expression in Eq. (6).

As discussed, the multiperiod model can be used to examine the effect of age on the WTP, something that has gained a lot of interest (see, e.g., Huang et al., 2018). Even if it intuitively could be expected that WTP would decline with age, younger individuals have more to lose, it has been shown that this may not necessarily be the case. The age effect on the WTP will depend, as shown by Eq. (11), on the individual's optimal consumption path over his/her life-cycle. Different studies have shown that this will depend on assumptions of the model. Shepard and Zeckhauser (1984), for instance, predicted the VSL to have an inverted U-shape with respect to age when assuming that individuals can only optimize their consumption path by saving but not borrowing, whereas the VSL will decline with age when borrowing against future earnings is feasible. Johansson (2002) took a broader perspective regarding assumptions of the model and showed that the WTP-age relationship is ambiguous, i.e., in addition to the predictions above it can also be positive or independent.

An additional use of the multiperiod model is to examine how the WTP may be affected if it does not represent the WTP for a one-period risk reduction, as described in both the one-period and multiperiod scenarios above, but as one that cover the risk reduction over several time periods. Since the WTP can be calculated as the summation of the WTP for a series of time periods with the risk reduction (Johannesson et al., 1997) it has frequently been used in the empirical literature as a mean to make the change in risk larger, and hence, more understandable to the respondents. Andersson et al. (2013) showed, though, based on the multiperiod model that when the time period is long and/or the discount rate is high such an approach can introduce a non-negligible bias of the WTP.

3. Empirical methods

As described, no easily available market prices exist for traffic safety per se. Instead analysts have to rely on non-market valuation techniques to estimate a WTP that is expected to reflect individuals' preferences for safety. Usually these techniques are classified based on whether they use market data, i.e., revealed-preference methods, or use hypothetical scenarios in questions, i.e., stated-preference methods, to elicit individual preferences. In the following sections we will describe the two approaches and provide examples of methods.[f]

[f] There exists several different techniques and there is now a rich empirical literature using these different techniques. In this section we have had to restrict ourselves to a broad overview and a few examples. We refer readers to textbooks and references in the reading lists for more details on the different methods (e.g., Freeman et al., 2014; Haab and McConnel, 2002; Hanley and Barbier, 2009).

3.1 Revealed-preference methods

The use of RP relies on the fact that individuals in markets make decisions that reveal how much they are willing to trade other goods, e.g., time saved or money, to reduce their risk of injury or fatality. Examples of such behavior is whether to use seat-belts, buy and use bicycle helmets, etc. (see, e.g., Svensson, 2009). For instance, an individual will buy and use a bicycle helmet if the benefit from using it, i.e., the reduced risk, exceeds its costs, which are both the financial cost of buying it and any disutility from using it. Not buying a bicycle helmet does not suggest, though, that the individual does not have preferences for safety, only that the costs are too high compared with the benefits. For instance, if the market price of the helmet, or the disutility of using it, would decrease the same individual could change its behavior and buy and use the helmet.

The examples above are typically defined as discrete choices. As described, an individual decides to use the equipment/device if the benefits exceed the costs. When using market data this means that the estimated WTP reflects the lower bound of the individual's preferences, which can be illustrated by rearranging Eq. (7),

$$WTP < VSL \bullet \Delta p. \quad (13)$$

It is important to stress that Eq. (13) is only the lower bound WTP for those using the safety device. Others who decide not to use the device have a lower WTP than the cost of using it, and when estimating the value to be used for policy purposes the preferences of both groups should be considered.

The fact that decisions are real, often made on more than one occasion (which would ensure familiarity with the good), and the simplicity of the choice situations means that discrete choice data are a valuable source of information for policy purposes. However, since the information most easily available, i.e., the expenditure, may be different from the total cost which also potentially includes disutility of using the equipment, and since buying a device not necessary means using it, caution needs to be taken. To illustrate, assume the purchase of a bicycle helmet. The analyst may observe the price of the helmet and have access to information on how much the fatality risk will be reduced for the user of this helmet. However, the analyst may not know to what extent and for how long the buyer intends? to use the helmet, and whether an individual experiences any disutility from using it, and if so, how much. Another issue, as always when examining individual decisions, is how well-informed consumers are when taking the decision. For instance, does the consumer use the same information about how much the helmet will reduce the risk as the analyst? These are all issues when analyzing discrete market choices, but they can all be mitigated by using good quality data, and by for instance combining market data with questionnaire data to have more information on consumers'/users' expectations from the safety product, actual usage, etc.

3.1.1 Hedonic prices

An empirical method that assumes a continuum of differentiated products, which means that choices are no longer discrete and consumers' marginal WTP can be estimated, is the hedonic regression method (Rosen, 1974). This method has been quite popular to monetize preferences for health risk reductions, especially using labor-market data where workers are assumed to require compensation to take on riskier jobs (Gentry and Viscusi, 2016; Viscusi, 2014), but also property data where the correlation between property prices and the level of health risks where the properties are located has been examined (Davis, 2004; Leggett and Bocksstael, 2000).

Rosen (1974), when formalizing the hedonic regression technique, based his model on the assumption that prices of composite goods depend on the utility bearing attributes of the goods (Becker, 1965; Lancaster, 1966). Hence, in a competitive market with utility maximizing individuals and profit maximizing firms, the price (P) of good $\mathbf{Q}=(q_1, q_2 \ldots, q_k)$, where the vector contains the attributes of the good, is given by,

$$P = P(q_1, q_2, \ldots, q_k). \tag{14}$$

In equilibrium the marginal WTP (MWTP) for a specific attribute (q_k) will equal its implicit price, which is given by the partial derivative of the hedonic price function with respect to that attribute, i.e.,

$$MWTP_{q_k} = \frac{\partial P(\mathbf{Q})}{\partial q_k} \tag{15}$$

Hence, the hedonic regression technique estimates the effect on the price from variations in the attribute of interest while controlling for other attributes influencing the price. When it comes to eliciting the MWTP for traffic safety the hedonic regression technique has been used to examine how much individuals are prepared to pay for safer cars (e.g., Andersson, 2005; Dreyfus and Viscusi, 1995).

If q_k in Eq. (15) is a safety feature of the car that reduces the risk of fatality in the event of an accident, then the MWTP can be interpreted as the VSL.

However, as discussed by Atkinson and Halvorsen (1990) access to an attribute that reflects the true fatality (and injury) risk of a car may not be feasible. Instead, analysts will rely on accident statistics? for different markets and models and examine how these are correlated with the prices of the markets and models. Accident statistics will be influenced by the drivers of the vehicles and external circumstances surrounding the accidents, like the age of the driver, one-vehicle accident, etc., and will therefore not reflect the true inherent risk of the vehicle. Let q_k, F, and $\mathbf{D}$, denote the true risk, the fatal accident rate, and a vector or accident characteristics. Assuming that F is a function of both q_k and $\mathbf{D}$, i.e., $F=g(q_k,\mathbf{D})$, and that the relationship between F and q_k is monotonic, then $q_k=g^{-1}(F,\mathbf{D})$ (p. 133). Therefore, instead of estimating the price function with the true risk,

$$P = P(q_k, \mathbf{Q}_{-k}), \tag{16}$$

which is not feasible if q_k is not available, Atkinson and Halvorsen (1990) suggest that a price equation substituting for q_k is estimated,

$$P = P(F, \mathbf{D}, \mathbf{Q}_{-k}). \tag{17}$$

The VSL can now be estimated by,

$$VSL = -\frac{\partial P(F, \mathbf{D}, \mathbf{Q}_{-k})}{\partial F}, \tag{18}$$

where the minus is included to ensure a positive VSL, since as defined P is a function of risk and not safety.

In addition to the issue of the risk variables described above, another issue to deal with is the functional form of the price equation. The theoretical model does not provide much guidance more than it should be non-linear (Rosen, 1974, p. 37). Instead, different functional forms need to be tested and decided upon empirically. Common functional forms in the literature are the semi-log and the log-linear, but other forms are also used. Here we have provided a brief overview of the hedonic pricing method with a focus on traffic safety. Freeman et al. (2014), e.g., provide a more comprehensive overview of the method.

3.2 Stated-preference methods

Compared to the RP methods described above, in the SP approach respondents face hypothetical choice scenarios without any real consequences. Data is collected through surveys, online, face-to-face, etc., and respondents are asked to behave as if decisions were real so that their answers can be interpreted as representing their true preferences. One way to address the hypothetical weakness and obtain more truthful preference revelation is to explain to respondents that there is a chance that their answers will influence actual policies, usually referred to "consequentiality" (Carson et al., 2014; Vossler et al., 2012). Even with this approach the decisions are not real, and this combined with that respondents often may be asked to make choices on subjects not familiar to them, like how much they would be willing to pay to improve the air quality to a certain level, are considered the main weaknesses of the SP approach. However, it also provides advantages to the RP approach. Since the hypothetical scenario is created by the analyst it allows for the elicitation of preferences for a wide range of scenarios, also for scenarios where market data is not available, and it also means that the analyst has control over the choice situations, including which information is assumed available to the respondents. A wide range of different SP methods exists (see, e.g., Bateman et al., 2002), but here we will only cover the two methods most commonly used to elicit individual WTP, i.e., the two methods usually labeled as the contingent valuation method (CVM) and discrete choice experiments (DCE). The description below will be relatively brief and focused on the WTP for traffic fatality risks, but for readers interested in a recent guidance on best-practice for SP studies we recommend Johnston et al. (2017).

3.2.1 The contingent valuation method

In a CVM survey with the purpose to estimate the VSL participants are presented with a hypothetical scenario that would reduce the risk of fatalities. The scenario could, e.g., be a government policy or a private safety measure, and the respondents are provided background information on the nature of the risk, how the policy/measure would reduce the risk, how much the risk would be reduced, etc. All to make sure that respondents understand the scenario, and that all of them have the same scenario in mind when answering the questions. In a survey on WTP to reduce health risks it would also be common to include some type of visual aid to help the respondents understand the change in risk they are presented (Corso et al., 2001). Moreover, demographic and socio-economic information about the respondents are usually also collected in the survey since this type of information can be used both to test the validity of the answer, e.g., whether WTP increases with wealth level, and for policy purposes, e.g., if the VSL should be age-adjusted.

The core of a CVM survey is the section where respondents' WTP is elicited. This can be done in different ways like with payment card or ladders, but most commonly used are the open-ended format, where respondents are asked to state their maximum WTP, and the referendum format where respondents are asked to answer yes or no to a proposed policy or an offer to purchase or rent a safety measure (e.g., some type of equipment for a car). The open-ended format would extract the maximum WTP as shown in Eq. (4) but due to it being cognitively demanding, not reflecting how most financial decisions are taken, and risk having a large share of strategic answers (respondents over- or understating their true WTP), it is not the preferred method among analysts. Instead most analysts prefer the referendum format where respondents face a yes or no question. For instance, respondents could be asked whether they would support a government policy that would reduce the risk by a specified amount at an also specified cost, or they could be asked whether they would buy a safety equipment for their car if the cost was X EUR. The cost shown to the respondents in the referendum format is usually referred to as bids and the format, in comparison to the open-ended format described above, often referred to as closed-ended. Since it better mimics voting scenarios and market transactions it is considered less cognitive demanding, and if well-designed less prone to strategic answering (Johnston et al., 2017). To illustrate, an example of a referendum format question:

> Assume that investments by the national transport authority will reduce the number of fatalities in the road network. Would you be willing to pay EUR 180 for a policy that would result in 6 fewer persons dying next year as a result of road accidents?
>
> Yes ☐ No ☐.

From the answer to the question above we will only know whether the respondents' WTP is at least, or below, EUR 180 for the fatality risk reduction. To obtain more precision of the individual WTP a follow-up question can be added where the bid is increased if the respondent accepts the first bid and lowered if he/she declines it. The one question format is usually defined as single-bounded, whereas the one with a follow-up bid is defined as double-bounded. Moreover, to obtain the distribution of the WTP for the population bids are varied among the respondents, i.e., all respondents do not get the same initial bid.

Since open-ended CVM data are straightforward to model using standard regression techniques, and since the closed-ended format is the preferred one we focus on the latter in our brief discussion of analyzing the respondents' answers. As described above, with closed-ended CVM data we only have information about the interval of the respondent's WTP, not the actual level, and such data are, therefore, modeled using a latent variable framework, in which the latent (unobserved) WTP is specified as:

$$WTP_i^* = \alpha + \mathbf{X}_i'\boldsymbol{\beta} + \varepsilon_i \tag{19}$$

where $\mathbf{X}_i$ is a vector of individual characteristics, α and $\boldsymbol{\beta}$ are a parameter and a vector of parameters to be estimated, and ε_i is an error term, typically assumed to be normally distributed with mean 0 and variance σ^2. In this framework we examine the probability that respondent i accepts a bid of the amount r_i which is given by:

$$\begin{aligned} P\left(WTP_i^* > r_i\right) &= P\left(\alpha + X_i'\beta + \varepsilon_i > r_i\right) = P\left(\varepsilon_i > r_i - \alpha - X_i'\beta\right) \\ &= 1 - \Phi\left(\frac{r_i - \alpha - X_i'\beta}{\sigma}\right) \end{aligned} \tag{20}$$

where Φ denotes the standard normal CDF, and the α and $\boldsymbol{\beta}$ parameters from Eq. (17) together with the σ parameter can be estimated by maximum likelihood. It has been shown that model specifications can have a substantial impact on the estimated WTP, and hence, thorough and extensive sensitivity analyses using different specifications should be conducted, including using distributional-free estimators such as the Turnbull estimator (see, e.g., Haab and McConnel 2002).

3.2.2 Discrete choice experiments

Many of the features of and considerations that need to be taken into account in the CVM are the same in DCEs; ensuring that respondents find the survey relevant and understand the importance of answering it, the importance of clear scenario descriptions, collection of information about demographics and socio-economics. The basic difference between the CVM and DCE is that the latter involves choices between different alternatives, and that they usually involve more than two attributes which is the case in the CVM, i.e., the attribute/good of interest and its cost. Fig. 2 provides an illustration of a choice situation were in addition to the fatality risk and cost attribute from the CVM scenario above the policy now also covers the reduced risk of injury.

A choice situation as illustrated in Fig. 2 is usually defined as a choice set. In this example respondents are asked to choose between two alternatives of the policy and also have the option to choose the current situation with no

Assume that investments by the national transport authority will reduce the number of fatalities in the road network.

	Policy A	Policy B
Number of fewer individuals who will die next year when the policy is implemented	3	6
Number of fewer individuals who will be severely injured next year when the policy is implemented	250	500
Your cost	EUR 100	EUR 180

Which option do you prefer

☐ Policy A

☐ Policy B

☐ None of the suggested policies (today's situation remains and no additional cost for you)

Fig. 2 Example DCE question.

policy being implemented, i.e., the status quo. Hence, the choice situation is more complex than the one in the CVM example above, but it is also straightforward to see that the choice set is an extended version of the CVM scenario. If injury risk would not be affected by the policy, and therefore could be removed as an attribute, and if Policy A would be assumed to no longer be a relevant alternative and also removed from the choice set, then the choice situation in Fig. 2 would be identical to the CVM scenario in the previous section. Hence, DCE can be interpreted as an extended version of the CVM.

Since usually more than two attributes are included it allows for the extraction of more information compared to the CVM. In the example in Fig. 2 the answers would, e.g., allow for an examination of fatality-injury risk tradeoffs, and not only fatality-dollar tradeoffs. The introduction of more attributes and alternatives means, though, that the scenarios become more complex for the respondents, and hence it is important for the analyst to mitigate the risk of the scenarios becoming too cognitively demanding. However, this complexity also seems to mitigate issues like anchoring and starting-point bias that is a concern in the more simplistic CVM. In DCE surveys respondents are, therefore, typically presented with several choice sets where the levels of the attributes vary, which enables the analyst, with the same number of respondents, to collect more information from a DCE compared with a CVM survey. The combination of the attribute levels in the different choice sets presented to the respondents is constructed according to an experimental design, for which there is a quite rich literature (see, e.g., Carlsson and Martinsson, 2003).

The setup for the analysis of DCE data is typically the random utility model framework. Let *die*, *injury* and *cost* denote the three attributes in the choice set above, then the utility that respondent n derives from choosing alternative j in choice set t can be given by,

$$U_{njt} = \beta_0 sq_{njt} + \beta_1 die_{njt} + \beta_2 injury_{njt} + \beta_3 \cos t_{njt} + \varepsilon_{njt} \tag{21}$$

where sq is a dummy variable for the status quo alternative, ε is a random error term which is assumed to be IID type I extreme value, and the βs are the coefficients to be estimated (subscripts dropped for ease of reading). From the specification in Eq. (21) the VSL, i.e., the marginal rate of substitution between cost and lives saved, is given by the ratio of the coefficients for *die* and *cost*, i.e.,

$$-\frac{\partial U_{njt}/\partial die_{njt}}{\partial U_{njt}/\partial \cos t_{njt}} = -\frac{\beta_1}{\beta_3}, \tag{22}$$

where the ratio is multiplied by minus one to convert the expression to a positive value ($\beta_1 > 0$ since die defined as number of fewer fatalities).

The conditional logit (also referred to as the multinomial logit) (Cameron and Trivedi, 2005) is the standard model to examine the probability that respondent n chooses alternative j in choice set t,

$$P_{njt} = \frac{exp\left(\beta_0 sq_{njt} + \beta_1 die_{njt} + \beta_2 injury_{njt} + \beta_3 \cos t_{njt}\right)}{\sum_{j=1}^{J} exp\left(\beta_0 sq_{njt} + \beta_1 die_{njt} + \beta_2 injury_{njt} + \beta_2 \cos t_{njt}\right)}, \tag{23}$$

where the parameters can be estimated using maximum likelihood.[g] The specification above assumes that preferences for changes in the attributes are the same among the respondents. This can be relaxed by introducing interactions between the attributes and respondent characteristics in the

[g] See, e.g., Lancsar et al. (2017) for a practical guide on the modeling of DCE data with examples using different software packages.

conditional logit model. However, this relies on knowledge of the analyst of which interactions are of interest, and that those respondent characteristics are observable (available to the analyst). Typically, the analyst does not have perfect information of all characteristics related to preference heterogeneity, and even if he/she would, not all of them would be observable. More advanced discrete choice models can take into account such unobserved preference heterogeneity and are commonly used in DCE studies. For instance, the mixed logit model relaxes the assumption of a fixed parameter and allows the parameters to vary randomly, assuming a particular continuous distribution (see, e.g., Train 2009). An alternative to the mixed logit is the latent class logit model which assumes a discrete coefficient distribution, i.e., preferences vary among the respondents but not within the discrete classes (see, e.g., Greene and Hensher 2003; Hole 2008).

3.3 VSL and transportation—Empirical findings

As explained, monetary values that reflect the social benefit of reducing fatality risk are commonly used to evaluate transport policies (DoT, 2016; Wijnen et al., 2019). Decision makers can today rely on a rich literature on the social value of preventing a fatality based on preference estimates, from both revealed- and stated-preference studies. There is robust evidence that individuals value risk reduction, i.e., are willing to pay (demand compensation) to reduce (increase) their risk exposure. Whereas there is also evidence that suggests that monetary values are both valid and reliable estimates of individual preferences, evidence also suggests that methods used, where the study was conducted, type of safety measure, etc., may influence the values (see, e.g., Andersson et al., 2019; Andersson and Treich, 2011; Blomquist, 2004; de Blaeij et al., 2003; Hultkrantz and Svensson, 2012; Lindhjelm et al., 2011). Hence, the evidence suggests that individuals' preferences may be context dependent, which means that there is not one unique value for VSL, but instead it is expected to vary depending on, e.g., the risk context and the wealth of a population.

4. Discussion

We have in this chapter provided a brief introduction to the theory and empirics on the valuation of preventing a fatality. There is strong consensus among economists that WTP is the appropriate approach to assign monetary values to individual health risks. However, even if there is consensus in economics about the appropriateness of the WTP approach to value health risk reductions, among non-economists it is controversial. It is therefore important to stress that the VSL is not the value of an identified life but the value of preventing a statistical death, and when used for policy purposes it is not known who will benefit from the policies, only that a certain number of deaths (or injuries) will be prevented (i.e., there is a veil of ignorance). Moreover, as described in the section on RP methods, individuals do make daily decisions in their lives that suggest that they have a finite WTP to reduce their risk of fatality, injury, illness, etc. Hence, it is important to stress that the objective of the valuation of health risk changes is to obtain estimates that reflect such decisions.

Even among advocates of the use of WTP studies there is awareness of the challenges analysts face when implementing health valuation studies. Traditionally, economists have preferred RP methods, since they rely on actual behavior. But market data do not always exist for the good of interest, and even if they do, they need to be of good quality to enable the estimation of high-quality values. Moreover, RP methods also rely on individuals making well-informed decisions. Therefore, SP methods have an important role to play. But, as explained, their main weakness is that they are hypothetical and, hence, respondents do not have incentives to be well informed when making their decision, or even make the decision that reflect their true preferences. Issues with SP methods have resulted in a larger literature focusing on the limitations and drawbacks of SP methods (see, e.g., Hausman, 2012), but there is also vast evidence that well-designed studies can address many of these limitations and drawbacks (see, e.g., Carson, 2012).

There is agreement that the VSL is the appropriate measure of preventing a statistical death. Much of the research, therefore, focuses on better understanding of individual behavior, by both theoretical extensions of the models and empirical research, and to elicit values that are valid and reliable estimates of individual preferences. As discussed above, RP and SP methods both have their weaknesses, but since no easily available prices are available for health risk reductions both have a key role to play in eliciting risk preferences. It is also important to stress the significant progress that has been taken place over the last couple of decades in estimating WTP for health risk reductions, not only methodological improvements but also data access, resulting in improved validity and reliability of the estimated values (Robinson and Hammitt, 2015; Viscusi, 2014).

References

Ackerman, F., Heinzerling, L., 2004. Priceless: On Knowing the Price of Everything and the Value of No\thing. The New Press, New York, NY, USA.

Andersson, H., 2005. The value of safety as revealed in the Swedish car market: an application of the hedonic pricing approach. J. Risk Uncertain. 30 (3), 211–239.

Andersson, H., 2008. Willingness to pay for car safety: evidence from Sweden. Environ. Resource Econ. 41, 579–594.

Andersson, H., 2018. Application of BCA in Europe—experiences and challenges. J. Benefit-Cost Anal. 9, 84–96.

Andersson, H., Treich, N., 2011. The value of a statistical life. In: de Palma, A., Lindsey, R., Quinet, E., Vickerman, R. (Eds.), The Handbook in Transport Economics. Edward Elgar Publishing Ltd, Cheltenham, UK, pp. 396–424.

Andersson, H., Hammitt, J.K., Lindberg, G., Sundström, K., 2013. Willingness to pay and sensitivity to time framing: a theoretical analysis and an application on car safety. Environ. Resource Econ. 56 (3), 437–456.

Andersson, H., Hammitt, J.K., Sundström, K., 2015. Willingness to pay and QALYs: what can we learn about valuing foodborne risk? J. Agric. Econ. 66 (3), 727–752.

Andersson, H., Levivier, E., Lindberg, G., 2019. Private and public willingness to pay for safety: a validity test. Accid. Anal. Prev. 123, 170–175.

Arrow, K.J., Solow, R., Portney, P., Leamer, E., Radner, R., Schuman, H., 1993. Report of the NOAA Panel on Contingent Valuation. National Oceanic and Atmospheric Administration. 58 Federal Register 46.

Atkinson, S.E., Halvorsen, R., 1990. The valuation of risks to life: evidence from the market for automobiles. Rev. Econ. Stat. 72 (1), 133–136.

Bahamonde-Birke, F.J., Kunert, U., Link, H., 2015. The value of a statistical life in a road safety context—a review of the current literature. Transplant. Rev. 35 (4), 488–511.

Bateman, I.J., Carson, R.T., Day, B., Hanemann, N., Hett, T., Hanley, N., Jones-Lee, M.W., Loomes, G., Mourato, S., Ozdemiroglu, E., 2002. Economic Valuation With Stated Preference Techniques: A Manual Cheltenham. Edward Elgar Publishing.

Becker, G.S., 1965. A theory of the allocation of time. Econ. J. 75 (299), 493–517.

Bergstrom, T.C., 1982. When is a man's life worth more than his human capital? In: Jones-Lee, M.W. (Ed.), The Value of Life and Safety. North-Holland Publishing Company, Amsterdam, The Netherlands, pp. 3–26.

Bishop, R.C., Boyle, K.J., 2019. Reliability and validity in nonmarket valuation. Environ. Resource Econ. 72 (2), 559–582.

Blomquist, G.C., 1979. Value of life saving: implications from consumption activity. J. Polit. Econ. 87, 540–558.

Blomquist, G.C., 2004. Self-protection and averting behavior, values of statistical lives, and benefit cost analysis of environmental policy. Rev. Econ. Househ. 2, 89–110.

Broome, J., 1978. Trying to save a life. J. Public Econ. 9, 91–100.

Cameron, T.A., 2010. Euthanizing the value of a statistical life. Rev. Environ. Econ. Policy 4 (2), 161–178.

Cameron, A.C., Trivedi, P.K., 2005. Microeconometrics: Methods and Applications. Cambridge University Press, New York, NY, USA.

Carlsson, F., Martinsson, P., 2003. Design techniques for stated preference methods in health economics. Health Econ. 12, 281–294.

Carson, R.T., 2012. Contingent valuation: a practical alternative when prices aren't available. J. Econ. Perspect. 26 (4), 27–42.

Carson, R.T., Groves, T., List, J.A., 2014. Consequentiality: a theoretical and experimental exploration of a single binary choice. J. Assoc. Environ. Resour. Econ. 1 (1/2), 171–207.

Corso, P.S., Hammitt, J.K., Graham, J.D., 2001. Valuing mortality-risk reduction: using visual aids to improve the validity of contingent valuation. J. Risk Uncertain. 23 (2), 165–184.
Daniels, S., Martensen, H., Schoeters, A., Van den Berghe, W., Papadimitriou, E., Ziakopoulos, A., Kaiser, S., Aigner-Breuss, E., Soteropoulos, A., Wijnen, W., Weijermars, W., Carnis, L., Elvik, R., Perez, O.M., 2019. A systematic cost-benefit analysis of 29 road safety measures. Accid. Anal. Prev. 133, 105292.
Davis, L.W., 2004. The effect of health risk on housing values: evidence from a cancer cluster. Am. Econ. Rev. 94 (5), 1693–1704.
de Blaeij, A., Florax, R.J.G.M., Rietvald, P., Verhoef, E., 2003. The value of statistical life in road safety: a meta-analysis. Accid. Anal. Prev. 35 (6), 973–986.
DoT, 2016. Benefit-Cost Analysis (BCA) Resource Guide. US Department of Transport. https://www.transportation.gov/office-policy/transportation-policy/benefit-cost-analysis-guidance-2017.
Dreyfus, M.K., Viscusi, W.K., 1995. Rates of time preference and consumer valuations of automobile safety and fuel efficiency. J. Law Econ. 38 (1), 79–105.
Dreze, J.H., 1962. L'utilité sociale d'une vie humaine. Rev. Fr. Rech. Operat. 22, 93–118.
Eeckhoudt, L.R., Hammitt, J.K., 2001. Background risks and the value of a statistical life. J. Risk Uncertain. 23 (3), 261–279.
Eeckhoudt, L.R., Hammitt, J.K., 2004. Does risk aversion increase the value of mortality risk? J. Environ. Econ. Manag. 47 (1), 13–29.
EPA, 2010. Guidelines for Preparing Economic Analyses (Appendix B). Available at: https://www.transportation.gov/office-policy/transportation-policy/revised-departmental-guidance-on-valuation-of-a-statistical-life-in-economic-analysis.
European Commission, 2014. Guide to Cost-Benefit Analysis of Investment Projects: Economic Appraisal Tool for Cohesion Policy 2014–2020. European Commission, Directorate-General for Regional and Urban policy, Brussels, Belgium.
Freeman, A.M., Herriges, J.A., Kling, C.L., 2014. The Measurement of Environmental and Resource Values. RFF Press, New York, NY, USA.
Gentry, E.P., Viscusi, W.K., 2016. The fatality and morbidity components of the value of statistical life. J. Health Econ. 46, 90–99.
Greene, W., Hensher, D.A., 2003. A latent class model for discrete choice analysis: contrasts with mixed logit. Transp. Res. B 37, 681–698.
Haab, T.C., McConnel, K.E., 2002. Valuing Environmental and Natural Resources: The Econometrics of Non-Market Valuation. Edward Elger.
Hammitt, J.K., 2000. Evaluating contingent valuation on environmental health risks: the proportionality test. J. Assoc. Environ. Resour. Econ. 20 (1), 14–19.
Hammitt, J.K., 2002. QALYs versus WTP. Risk Anal. 22 (5), 985–1001.
Hammitt, J.K., Liu, J.-T., 2004. Effects of disease type and latency on the value of mortality risk. J. Risk Uncertain. 28 (1), 73–95.
Hanley, N., Barbier, E.B., 2009. Pricing Nature: Cost-Benefit Analysis and Environmental Policy. Edward Elgar Publishing, Cheltenham, UK.
Hauer, E., 1994. Can one estimate the value of life or is it better to be dead than stuck in traffic? Transp. Res. A Policy Pract. 28 (2), 109–118.
Hausman, J.A., 2012. Contingent valuation: from dubious to hopeless. J. Econ. Perspect. 26, 43–56.
HM Treasury, 2003. "The Green Book—Appraisal and Evaluation in Central Government." Treasury Guidance. London TSO.
Hole, A.R., 2008. Modelling heterogeneity in patients' preferences for the attributes of a general practitioner appointment. J. Health Econ. 27 (4), 1078–1094.
Huang, D., Andersson, H., Zhang, S., 2018. Willingness to pay to reduce health risks related to air quality: evidence from a choice experiment survey in Beijing. J. Environ. Plan. Manag. 61, 2207–2229.

Hultkrantz, L., Svensson, M., 2012. The economic value of preventing fatalites: recent evidence on the value of a statistical life in Sweden. Health Policy 108, 302–310.
Jenkins, R., Owens, N., Wiggins, L.B., 2001. Valuing reduced risks to children: the case of bicycle safety helmets. Contemp. Econ. Policy. 19 (4), 397–408.
Johannesson, M., Johansson, P.-O., Löfgren, K.-G., 1997. On the value of changes in life expectancy: blips versus parametric changes. J. Risk Uncertain. 15 (3), 221–239.
Johansson, P.-O., 2002. On the definition and age-dependency of the value of a statistical life. J. Risk Uncertain. 25 (3), 251–263.
Johnston, R.J., Boyle, K.J., Adamowicz, W., Bennett, J., Brouwer, R., Cameron, T.A., Hanemann, W.M., Hanley, N., Ryan, M., Scarpa, R., Tourangeau, R., Vossler, C.A., 2017. Contemporary guidance for stated preference studies. J. Assoc. Environ. Resour. Econ. 4 (2), 319–405.
Jones-Lee, M.W., 1974. The value of changes in the probability of death or injury. J. Polit. Econ. 82 (4), 835–849.
Jones-Lee, M.W., 2003. Safety and the saving of life: the economics of safety and physical risk. In: Layard, R., Glaister, S. (Eds.), Cost-Benefit Analysis. Cambridge University Press, Cambridge, UK, pp. 290–318.
Keeler, E.B., 2001. The value of remaining lifetime is close to estimated values of life. J. Health Econ. 20 (1), 141–143.
Lancaster, K.J., 1966. A new approach to consumer theory. J. Polit. Econ. 74 (2), 132–157.
Lancsar, E., Fiebig, D.G., Hole, A.R., 2017. Discrete choice experiments: a guide to model specification, estimation and software. Pharmacoeconomics 35 (7), 697–716.
Leggett, C.G., Bocksstael, N.E., 2000. Evidence of the effects of water quality on residential land prices. J. Environ. Econ. Manag. 39, 121–144.
Lindhjelm, H., Navrud, S., Braathen, N.A., Biausque, V., 2011. Valuing mortality risk reductions from environmental, transport, and health policies: a global meta-analysis of stated preference studies. Risk Anal. 31 (9), 1381–1407.
Mishan, E.J., 1982. Cost-Benefit Analysis, third ed. George Allen & Unwin, London, UK.
Pearce, D., Atkinson, G., Mourato, S., 2006. Cost-Benefit Analysis and the Environment—Recent Developments. OECD Publishing, Paris, France.
Pratt, J.W., Zeckhauser, R.J., 1996. Willingness to pay and the distribution of risk and wealth. J. Polit. Econ. 104 (4), 747–763.
Quinet, E., Baumstark, L., et al., 2013. Cost Benefit Assessment of Public Investments: Summary and Recommendations. Commissariat Général à la Stratégie et à la Prospective. Policy Planning Commission, Paris, France.
Robinson, L.A., Hammitt, J.K., 2015. Research synthesis and the value per statistical life. Risk Anal. 35 (6), 1086–1100.
Rosen, S., 1974. Hedonic prices and implicit markets: product differnetiation in pure competition. J. Polit. Econ. 82 (1), 34–55.
Rosen, S., 1988. The value of changes in life expectancy. J. Risk Uncertain. 1 (3), 285–304.
Schelling, T.C., 1968. The life you save may be your own. In: Chase, S.B. (Ed.), Problems in Public Expenditure Analysis. The Brookings Institution, Washington D.C, pp. 127–162.
Shepard, D.S., Zeckhauser, R.J., 1984. Survival versus consumption. Manag. Sci. 30 (4), 423–439.
Simon, N.B., Dockins, C., Maguire, K.B., Newbold, S.C., Krupnick, A.J., Taylor, L.O., 2019. Policy brief—what's in a name? A search for alternatives to "VSL". Rev. Environ. Econ. Policy 13 (1), 155–161.
Strand, J., 2006. Valuation of environmental improvements in continuous time with mortality and morbidity effects. Resour. Energy Econ. 28 (3), 229–241.
Sunstein, C.R., 2004. Valuing life: a plea for disaggregation. Duke Law J. 54, 385–445.
Svensson, M., 2009. Precautionary behavior and willingness to pay for a mortality risk reduction: searching for the expected relationship. J. Risk Uncertain. 39, 65–85.

Train, K., 2009. Discrete Choice Methods With Simulation. Cambridge University Press, Cambridge.
Treich, N., 2010. The value of a statistical life under ambiguity aversion. J. Environ. Econ. Manag. 59 (1), 15–26.
Viscusi, K., 2014. Chapter 7—the value of individual and societal risks to life and health. In: Machina, M., Viscusi, K. (Eds.), Handbook of the Economics of Risk and Uncertainty. 1, pp. 385–452. North-Holland.
Vossler, C.A., Doyon, M., Rondeau, D., 2012. Truth in consequentiality: theory and field evidence on discrete choice experiments. Am. Econ. J. Microecon. 4 (4), 145–171.
Weinstein, M.C., Shepard, D.S., Pliskin, J.S., 1980. The economic value of changing mortality probabilities: a decision-theoretic approach. Q. J. Econ. 94 (2), 373–396.
Whittington, D., MacRae Jr., D., 1986. The issue of standing in cost-benefit analysis. J. Policy Anal. Manage. 5 (4), 665–682.
WHO, 2018. Global Status Report on Road Safety 2018. World Health Organization.
Wijnen, W., Weijermars, W., Schoeters, A., van den Berghe, W., Bauer, R., Carnis, L., Elvik, R., Martensen, H., 2019. An analysis of official road crash cost estimates in European countries. Saf. Sci. 113, 318–327.
Yaari, M.E., 1965. Uncertain lifetime, life insurance, and the theory of the consumer. Rev. Econ. Stud. 32 (2), 137–150.

CHAPTER FOUR

Transport models

Rob van Nes[a,*] and Gerard de Jong[b,c]
[a]Transport & Planning, Faculty of Civil Engineering and Geosciences, Delft University of Technology, Delft, The Netherlands
[b]Significance, The Hague, The Netherlands
[c]ITS, University of Leeds, Leeds, United Kingdom
*Corresponding author: e-mail address: R.vanNes@tudelft.nl

Contents

Abstract

This chapter aims to provide an overview of the overall set-up of transport models and their applications, plus a reflection on transport modeling itself. Main characteristics of transport models are discussed with special attention for the four main components: trip generation, trip distribution, modal split, and network assignment. Both aggregate and disaggregate model approaches are considered. Furthermore, a description is given of practical issues when building and using these models in practice, with special attention for quality control. The main focus is on passenger transport but related models for freight transport models and land use and transport interaction are briefly discussed. The chapter concludes with a reflection on the value and limitations of transport modeling and an overview of new modeling developments.

Keywords: Transport modeling, Trip generation, Trip distribution, Modal split, Assignment, Aggregate, Disaggregate, Application, Quality control

Advances in Transport Policy and Planning, Volume 6
ISSN 2543-0009
https://doi.org/10.1016/bs.atpp.2020.08.001

1. Introduction

Transport models may seem an unusual topic in a book on appraisal methods, as they are not appraisal methods themselves. Transport models have been developed and are used for other purposes. On the other hand, transport models provide important input for appraisal methods for transport policy and planning, such as time gains and cost savings and changes in the use of the different travel modes, which have an impact on emissions and safety, among other things. In practice there might even be more debate on the transport model results than on the actual appraisal methods used. Given the specific nature of transport models in this context, the goal of this chapter is different from that of most other chapters. The aim is to provide an overview of the overall set-up of transport models, the main issues when using these models in practice, and to give a reflection on transport modeling itself.

Transport models have been developed since the 1950s, originating from a car traffic engineering perspective. The goal of the models was and is to have a systematic quantitative method to analyze the consequences of changes in the transport system. Such changes could be changes in the external environment of the transport system, e.g., land use, demography and economy, and changes in the transport system itself, such as fares and travel costs, new infrastructure or new public transport services. Over time, transport models evolved from small simple models focusing on car traffic in the peak hour to large complex models covering the main transport modes for a full working day plus both peak periods. These changes also demonstrate that the model results are used for a larger variety of studies: from purely traffic engineering (what is the flow on this road and is there any congestion?) to input for environmental models such as air quality and noise, while travel times are used for cost-benefit analyses. At the same time the modeling paradigms changed from analogy-based aggregate models to empirical choice-based disaggregate models. Yet despite these developments, transport models still have a number of typical elements in common:

- *Zones*: The area that is studied is represented using a zoning system, usually split up in a detailed study area (with relatively small zones), an influence area and a coarser external area (with larger zones). It is assumed that all trips originate in a zone and end in a zone. For these zones data on the number of inhabitants, households, jobs, facilities, etc., is used.
- *Networks*: The networks are used to travel from one zone to another zone. The infrastructure networks for road traffic are modeled using

graphs having nodes and links, while the service networks for public transport are modeled using nodes and lines having frequencies.

- *Model components*: In nearly all transport models four components can be distinguished:
  1. Trip generation: which calculates the number of trips leaving each zone and the number of trips arriving in a zone, and thus the total number of trips in the model;
  2. Trip destination: which calculates for each zone (origin) the distribution of all trips leaving the zone over all other zones (destinations); this gives the origin-destination (OD) matrix of the transport flows;
  3. Modal split: which calculates for every set of trips going from one zone to another zone, how these trips are split up over the modes, usually car and public transport (possibly distinguishing various modes within public transport, such as train and bus), and more and more also cycling;
  4. Assignment: calculates for each mode how all flows of that mode use the corresponding network, leading to flows of cars on links and of passengers on public transport lines.
- *Trip purposes*: For these models, especially for the first three models, it has been found that a distinction by trip purpose leads to a much better description of what is observed in reality, which is due to differences between trip purposes in locations to travel to and from, and in sensitivities for travel costs, travel distance and travel time. Commonly used trip purposes are for instance commuting, business, education, and shopping.

The transport system is a complex large-scale integrated open system (Sussman, 2004): millions of people, firms and organizations make choices to perform activities, to travel, to choose residential locations, and all are affected by weather, economy, etc. The scoping of transport models to using zones, simplified network descriptions, considering four modeling components and a limited set of modes and trip purposes only, makes it clear that transport models only capture a part of this complexity. Model results are therefore never an exact forecast of what will happen if the context changes or a policy measure is implemented. However, transport model results do give an interesting indication—in order of magnitude—of what the main effects of such changes could be in terms of differences compared to a reference, e.g., an increase or decrease of traffic flows. Note that this statement on the usefulness of transport model results may conflict with expectations and in some cases even requirements for appraisal methods and legal regulations.

Since travel models by definition deal with travel times and travel costs, a related issue is the conversion of times into costs or vice versa. For this conversion the so-called Value of Time is used, which is also an important input for cost-benefit analyses. This topic is further discussed in the chapter on Value of travel time and travel time reliability (De Jong and Kouwenhoven, 2020).

In the following section the main modeling principles and the overall set-up of transport models will be discussed. The next section then relates to transport modeling in practice: the processes of building transport models, applying them in projects, and the issue of quality control. This is followed by a reflection on transport modeling itself and a discussion on new developments. The chapter ends with some concluding remarks.

2. Overall set-up of transport models

As stated, transport models assume that the spatial distribution of inhabitants, jobs, facilities etc., is known, as are the networks for the modes distinguished in the analysis. Based on this input, transport models determine the demand in trips per time period within an average working day for each mode and secondly assign this demand to the corresponding networks.

The basic unit in many models is a trip, i.e., the movement of a person from one location to another, or in other words from an origin to a destination. Many models focus on trips made within a specific period such as the morning or evening peak as in such periods the demand patterns are somewhat more homogeneous, but also because peak flows are important for decision-making on the capacity of a link, node or line. Modeling individual trips separately (e.g., separately for the morning and the afternoon peak), however, can lead to inconsistencies in mode choice for the trip going to work and the trip going back home (e.g., a car left behind at the work location). Therefore, there are also models that have tours as a basic unit. A tour is a series of consecutive trips starting and ending at the same location, usually the home. At the minimum, a tour consists of an outbound and a return trip, but there may also be stops at secondary destinations (e.g., for shopping or picking up the children from school) that may be modeled explicitly. Using tours leads to similar modeling steps, yet prior to the assignment component the tours are split into trips for the corresponding periods.

A second characteristic of transport models is the way they describe travel behavior. The classic models are usually based on statistical descriptions at an aggregate level and use analogies like the gravity model. In order to capture more detail often a segmentation is made by trip purpose and by travelers having a car available or not. However, this does not capture the real heterogeneity in travel behavior.

The alternative method is to describe travel behavior at the disaggregate level (that is the level of individual households and persons), the level of the actual decision-makers. Since most decisions at this level address a discrete choice (a choice among a limited set of, often qualitative, alternatives) the disaggregate models are usually discrete choice models, such as the logit model. Discrete choice models at the disaggregate level are commonly based on the theoretical foundation of the random utility maximization model (McFadden, 1974, 1978, 1981).

The main concept is that travelers choose between discrete alternatives in a choice set based on their utility, and that they prefer the alternative having the highest utility. The utility U_i of an alternative i is based on observed attributes V_i, usually a weighted sum of attributes X_{ik}, and a random term ε_i representing the non-observed characteristics of the alternative:

$$U_i = V_i + \varepsilon_i = \sum_{k=1,m} c_k \cdot X_{ik} + \varepsilon_i$$

The attributes X_{ik} could relate to characteristics of the alternative as well as of the decision maker, i.e., the traveler. This allows for modeling the interaction between travel and traveler characteristics, and for capturing the variety in travel behavior at a higher level of detail than is possible with aggregate models. The coefficients c_k denote the behavioral coefficients of the model, that need to be estimated on disaggregate data.

Given specific assumptions on the distribution of the random term, i.e., being independent and identically distributed for all alternatives and having an extreme value distribution, the logit-formula can be derived. This formula specifies the probability $P(i)$ that alternative i is chosen from a choice set C:

$$P(i|C) = {}^{\exp(\beta \cdot V_i)} \Big/ \sum_{j \in C} \exp\left(\beta \cdot V_j\right)$$

The parameter β is the scale parameter, as it represents the sensitivity of travelers for differences between the utilities of the alternatives: a value of 0 states that the utilities are not relevant and a high value for β indicates that travelers are very sensitive for such differences and tend to prefer the alternative having the highest utility only. For more information on disaggregate models see Ben-Akiva and Lerman (1985) and Train (2002).

Disaggregate models are especially useful if a large range of policy measures need to be analyzed. Note that it is also possible to use a logit model at the aggregate level to explain for instance market shares of modes for zone pairs. However, such an aggregate logit modal split model does not have the foundation on a theory of behavior that the logit model at the disaggregate level has.

Fig. 1 shows the main structure of the transport model and its four components for both the aggregate and disaggregate approach. In the following description of the four model components, both modeling approaches will be discussed. For a more in-depth description the reader is referred to Cascetta (2001) and Ortuzar and Willumsen (2011).

2.1 Trip generation

In this component the model determines the production and attraction per trip purpose for the specific time period, or more precisely, the model calculates the number of trips leaving each zone (departures) and the number of trips arriving at a zone (arrivals). Usually this is calculated per trip purpose, as this allows for more (spatial) detail by using trip purpose specific attributes.

2.1.1 Aggregate approach

A typical method used in classic models is linear regression on a dataset of zones. The departures and arrivals per trip purpose are calculated as a

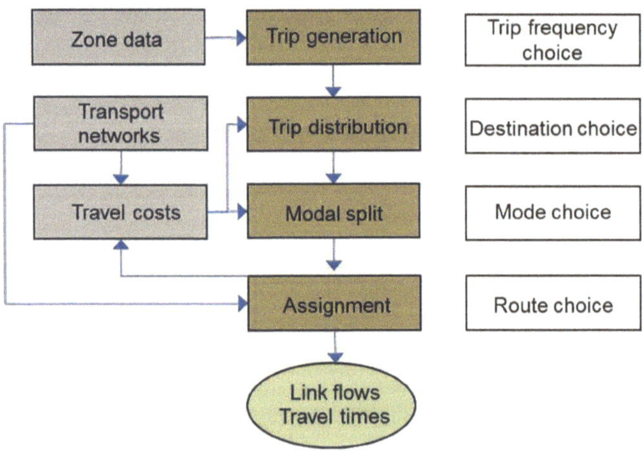

Fig. 1 Overview model components for the aggregate model (in the middle) and disaggregate model (right hand side).

function of, for example, the number of inhabitants, households, jobs, etc. For a morning peak the departures might be a function of the number of inhabitants or the labor force (i.e., for commuting) in a zone, and the arrivals a function of the number of people or jobs (again for commuting). For the evening peak it will be the opposite. In general trip numbers based on person or household data are considered to be more reliable than trip numbers based on for instance number of jobs.

2.1.2 Disaggregate approach

In case of discrete choice models, logit models can be used to determine the number of trips or tours per travel purpose per person or per household, or better put, per person type or per household type. In these models, tours are more suitable as they are clearly related to activities: one makes a trip to perform an activity and return to one's original location, and the individual could decide to make second tour for the same type of activity, and even a third tour could be an option. In the discrete choice framework this can be modeled using a binary logit for the choice between zero and one or more tours and a binary logit for the conditional choice (given one or more) whether to make one or more additional tours on a given day or not (the latter models are also referred to as stop—repeat-models). Note that these models focus on the production of tours and not on the arrivals for activity locations.

2.2 Trip distribution

This component describes how the trips or tours leaving each zone are distributed over the possible destinations. The result is a so-called origin-destination (OD-) matrix where a cell T_{ij} represents the number of trips traveling from zone i to zone j. The sum over each row thus represents the total number of departures per zone, and the sum over each column represents the arrivals per zone. Again, a distinction between trip purposes is applied.

When analyzing trip distribution patterns two basic "principles" can be distinguished. Obviously, there's a correlation between the number of trips between two zones and both the production and the attraction of these zones. By definition, zones having a high production produce more trips while attractive zones attract more trips. Secondly, locations that are further away or that are more difficult to reach, attract fewer trips than locations nearby or that are easier to reach.

2.2.1 Aggregate approach

These two "principles" lead to the following formulation of the trip distribution model (see also Casey, 1955):

$$T_{ij} = Q_i \cdot X_j \cdot f(c_{ij})$$

in which the trips between zones i and j are calculated as the product of a production factor of zone i, an attraction factor of zone j, and a deterrence function f, which is a decreasing function that describes the influence of the travel costs (usually including travel time) between both zones. This influence can differ per trip purpose. This formulation is usually referred to as the gravity model. The analogy with Newton's formulation of the gravity model is obvious, yet this multiplicative formulation can also be derived from an analogy based on the entropy maximization (Wilson, 1970), or from a choice modeling approach.

If this multiplicative formulation is combined with the production and attraction determined in the trip generation component, we get the doubly constrained gravity model. The two constraints are then that the sum over each row should equal the given production or number of departures for that zone and that the sum over each column should result in the given attraction or number of arrivals. Given the calculated production and attraction, the travel costs between each pair of zones (the so-called skim matrix), and the deterrence function f, the origin-destination matrix can be calculated using a simple iterative algorithm (Furness, 1965) in which the values for each cell T_{ij} and implicitly the production and attraction factors are determined. The result is an OD-matrix that is based on the two main principles and that matches the production and attraction derived from the trip generation.

In specific cases the doubly constrained gravity model can be simplified to a singly constrained gravity model. If the modeler believes that for instance the production is more reliable than the attraction, a singly constrained model might be considered. In that case the attractions are not used as a constraint, and the trips leaving a zone are distributed over the possible destinations based on the values of the deterrence function. And if the attractions are considered to be more reliable, the trips arriving at a zone are similarly distributed over the origins.

2.2.2 Disaggregate approach

In case of discrete choice models, the destination choice is mostly modeled using a logit model. If for instance the production is determined in tours, the utility for each destination is specified as a function of activity-related attraction attributes such as the number of jobs, the travel cost (and time) and socio-economic attributes, where each attribute has its own parameter. In this case the example of the number of jobs represents an attraction factor that captures the first main principle while the travel costs will have a negative sign to account for the second main principle. It should also be noted that in this case there's only a single constraint, i.e., the number of tours generated by each zone.

2.3 Modal split

This third component models the distribution of trips over the modes. Since preferences and sensitivities for modes might differ per trip purpose, this component is also applied per trip purpose.

2.3.1 Aggregate approach

For classical models this can be modeled using empirical curves that for instance describe the share of public transport as a function of the ratio of the travel costs for public transport to the travel costs for car use. However, this approach assumes that the trip distribution is calculated for all modes together. For trip generation this poses no problems, in fact it is even more realistic to model the total number of trips by purpose. An important question then is what needs to be used for the travel costs c_{ij} when calculating the trip distribution: the travel costs for the car, for public transport or a kind of aggregate costs?

A solution to this problem is to calculate trip distribution and modal split simultaneously using mode-specific deterrence functions. The model then changes into:

$$T_{ij} = Q_i \cdot X_j \cdot \sum_m f_{\mathrm{m}}\left(c_{ijm}\right)$$

The modal split is computed as:

$$T_{ijm} = f_m\left(c_{ijm}\right) \Big/ \sum_k f_k\left(c_{ijk}\right) \cdot T_{ij}$$

that is, the modal split is based on the ratio of the deterrence function values for the modes for each OD-pair. This simultaneous trip distribution modal split model is solved with a similar iterative algorithm as described for the trip distribution model.

2.3.2 Disaggregate approach

For the discrete choice model approach, the mode choice can be modeled with logit models in which the utilities consist of the relevant mode-specific attributes for a trip or tour. Here too, the comment can be made: what are the travel costs used in the trip distribution model? This can be solved in two ways, the first of which is estimating a simultaneous model of destination and mode choice using a nested logit model. The second solution is estimating the mode choice model first based on travel costs per mode (c_{ijm}), calculating the expected travel cost (c_{ij}) from it (in a logit model, this is the so-called "logsum"), which is then used as explanatory variable in the destination choice model:

$$c_{ij} = \frac{1}{\beta} \cdot \ln\left(\sum_{m} \exp\left(\beta \cdot c_{ijm}\right)\right)$$

In the case of simultaneous estimation it has been found that for certain trip purposes the destination choice is modeled at the upper level and the mode choice within the nests of the model, and for other trip purposes the order is reversed: mode choice at the upper level and destination choice within the nests. The order of the choices in the nesting structure affect the sensitivities, for instance for changes in travel costs of a mode, as the lower level choices are most sensitive for such changes.

The result of the modal split component is a set of OD-matrices per mode, and per trip purpose if requested, which are the input to the last component: network assignment. However, there's one issue that requires special attention in this stage. All three model components discussed so far relate to trips or tours made by persons while considering typical modes as car, public transport and bicycles. However, the mode car can be split up into car driver and car passenger. For the assignment to the road network only car drivers are relevant. In the classical models this usually dealt with by applying an average car occupancy factor per trip purpose. A more elegant method is to distinguish car drivers and car passengers as different modes, as is often done in disaggregate mode (and destination) choice models.

2.4 Assignment

In this final component the OD-matrices per mode are assigned to the corresponding networks to calculate the flows on the links, and for public transport the flows on the lines. For practical reasons, usually no distinction is made between trip purposes.

2.4.1 Aggregate approach

In its simplest form this can be done by determining the shortest path for each OD-pair (e.g., using the well-known Dijkstra algorithm (Dijkstra, 1959)) and by assigning the flow for that OD-pair to the links of that path. Summing these flows for all OD-pairs yields the total flow for each link. Although this simple method has certain benefits, it doesn't do justice to actual phenomena. It assumes that all travelers from an origin to a destination use the same route in the network, while travelers will have different route preferences and moreover the method doesn't consider the fact that travel times on roads or links depend on the actual flow: higher flows lead to higher travel times (congestion).

Given these two phenomena four assignment methods can be distinguished:

- All-or-nothing, all travelers opt for the shortest path and link travel times are fixed;
- Stochastic assignment, travelers have different preferences and multiple routes are used, yet link travel times are fixed;
- Deterministic equilibrium assignment (DUE): travelers all opt for the shortest path, but now link travel times are dependent on the link flows;
- Stochastic equilibrium assignment (SUE): travelers have different preferences, and link travel times depend on the link flows.

Stochastic assignment can be modeled using logit route choice models, however, standard logit models assume independent alternatives, while in transport networks there can be large sets of overlapping routes, giving rise to correlated alternatives. Therefore, often the probit-model is used, which can be solved using the Monte-Carlo method. For each iteration step the link travel times are sampled from a distribution, the shortest paths are determined, and a proportion of the flow is assigned to the routes found. This can be done for a limited number of iterations or until the final links flows converge. This method is for instance used for modeling bicycle networks.

The latter two methods consider the congestion effect, that is link travel times depend on the link flows. The relation between link travel time and link flow is often described using the formula from the Bureau of Public Roads:

$$t_a(q_a) = t_{a0} \cdot \left(1 + \alpha \cdot \left({q_a}/{c_a}\right)^{\beta}\right)$$

which states that the travel time is equal to a free flow travel time of that link and increases with the ratio of the link flow and link capacity (Bureau of

Public Roads, 1964). The parameters α and β describe the sensitivity of the travel time for the flow. Note that other formulations can be used as well.

The equilibrium assignment models aim to achieve consistency between the travel times used to assign the flows and the travel times resulting from those flows. This equilibrium condition has been formulated by Wardrop (1952) and states that at equilibrium no traveler can reduce her or his travel time by changing routes unilaterally, and thus that in equilibrium conditions the travel times of all used routes are equal and shorter than the travel times of unused routes.

The equilibrium can be found using an iterative algorithm that starts with an all-or-nothing (for a DUE) or a stochastic assignment (for a SUE). In each following step the travel times are adapted based on the latest flows, after which another assignment is performed. These latest flows are a weighted average of the flows resulting from the previous iterations. Depending on the weighting method, the algorithm is called the Method of Successive Averages (MSA or Flow averaging) or the more advanced Frank-Wolfe algorithm. The method stops when the link and route flows converge and thus the travel times of the used routes are equal. Note, that in this case the assignment also provides the travel times considering the delay due to congestion on the network.

Public transport requires special attention because of the specific network structure consisting of links for access and egress, public transport lines that have frequencies, and the need for transfers. Travelers can thus choose at which stop to board, experience a waiting time due to the frequencies, might have multiple lines available between a pair of stops, and might avoid or choose transfer nodes. The shortest path might then be too simple as within a period different shortest paths might be relevant. Therefore, most public transport assignment methods consider a set of routes and distribute travelers over these routes based on the frequencies (e.g., Spiess and Florian, 1989) or using route choice models. Just like car traffic the actual usage of public transport affects the travel costs, however, these effects are more complex. Crowding can affect boarding times and thus affect waiting times, but also affects the comfort in the vehicle. Furthermore, the possibility that travelers cannot board a full vehicle complicates the modeling. Therefore, many models in practice do not include these effects yet.

2.4.2 Disaggregate approach

While for demand models it is relatively common and intuitive to consider the individual or household as decision maker and thus to exploit the benefits of disaggregate models, assignment models tend to focus on flows only, not on types of travelers or even individual travelers/vehicles. The main reason for this is the computational requirements of finding equilibrium conditions in networks, as a systematic distinction between traveler types would lead to more complex multi-user class assignment models.

As stated above logit models can be used for stochastic assignment, stochastic user equilibrium, and public transport assignment. These models tend to limit the analysis to route attributes only and do not consider personal or household characteristics. A consequence is that when logit models are used in assignment models they are usually applied at an aggregate level. Furthermore, the issue of overlapping, and thus correlated, route alternatives in a network requires more advanced logit models to cope with these correlations.

2.5 Concluding comments on the overall model set-up

If in the assignment component congestion is considered, the resulting car travel times and thus travel costs might differ from the car travel costs that were considered in the trip distribution and modal split components. In order to achieve a consistent model an iterative procedure is applied by re-computing the trip distribution and modal split using the latest car travel costs, assigning the new matrix and to deriving new car travel costs, etc. This iterative process stops after a fixed number of iterations or when the car travel times have converged.

In the description of the model components a fixed period, e.g., a morning peak hour, was considered. The time dimension itself was not explicitly discussed. There are two different notions that are relevant to distinguish here: modeling the time of day when modeling a 24-h period, and dynamics within a modeled period.

Originally transport models focused on peak periods. Later 24-h models became important for instance in order to provide input for environmental models. Within a 24-h model a fifth component is added that addresses the time of day choice, that is whether a trip is made in the morning peak, the evening peak, or in an off-peak period. This can be represented by fixed time-of-day fractions (for each travel purpose) or by explicit logit-choice models, which might be integrated with destination and mode choice models (De Jong et al., 2003).

The network assignment methods described are classified as static assignments. A typical characteristic is for instance that the demand is present on the full route, i.e., the flow is assigned to all links of the route, independent of the travel time needed or bottlenecks on the route. In reality, traffic propagates through the network and bottlenecks might lead to queues that can block upstream links and intersections, and because of the limited outflow might prevent other bottlenecks from becoming a bottleneck in practice. These phenomena can be modeled with dynamic assignment models leading to a more realistic assignment. The consequences of this are higher input requirements and longer computation times.

For public transport the time dimension plays a different role. Using frequencies is a simple method, yet it might lead to optimistic assumptions for frequencies in case of parallel lines and pessimistic assumptions for transfer waiting times. If the schedule would be considered (time-table-based assignment), the assignment to the lines would be more realistic, especially in case of low frequency public transport. Again, the consequences are higher input requirements and longer computation times.

Finally, the scoping of the transport models to the four components discussed in this section, excludes other phenomena that are relevant in transport studies, e.g., development of the population, car ownership, economy and so on. For a base year such data is likely to be available, but for a forecast such data needs to be forecasted as well. This can be done by specifying different scenarios and by using other types of models such as car ownership models and population synthesis models. Similarly, the results of the transport model are used as input for other models, e.g., for noise hindrance and air quality. However, these models are not within the scope of this chapter.

3. Use of transport models in practice

Transport models are more than the mathematical description of transport systems and the actual software. The models have many parameters that need to be estimated and require large datasets as input. So, the first step is building a model and calibrating it for the study area. If a calibrated model is available, it can be applied for exploration studies and for the assessment of transport effects of policy measures. In both cases quality assurance is relevant. These three topics will be discussed in Sections 3.1, 3.2, and 3.3.

3.1 Building a transport model

The first step in building a transport model is defining the specifications for the model. Starting point is the type of questions the model needs to be used for and the criteria that are used in analysis and assessment. On the other hand, there are constraints regarding the state of practice, the available modeling tools, and the available budget. For a small municipality, available software based on a classical four-step model might often be a suitable and feasible solution, while for a regional or national authority a wider range of measures is studied, thus setting higher requirements and making an advanced choice-model-based transport model a realistic option, possibly even with dedicated model development for one or more of the components.

It is important to note that in both cases the expected questions and the trade-off with the state-of-practice and the available budget set the scope of the model to be built. Furthermore, building a model is expensive and takes time. A simple model might take a few months and a more elaborate model 1½–2 years. Since these models are used for exploration and assessment studies, authorities are reluctant to switch to new types of transport models while these types of projects are still in progress: new models might yield different results and complicate the analysis and more importantly the decision process. Together this implies that there is a serious risk of a lock-in, i.e., choices setting the scope may limit future developments for analysis and assessment.

The second step in building a transport model is specifying the level of detail and collecting the input data, travel behavior data to estimate or calibrate the model parameters, and validation data to assess the realism of the model. The level of detail refers to the specification of the model area: the study area that is modeled in full detail, the influence area around it, and the external area to guarantee a proper modeling of ingoing, outgoing and through traffic. Furthermore, it refers to the specification of the related networks: the study network for which the flows need to be modeled and the network needed to assure that traffic coming from and going to zones have realistic access to the study network. For the resulting zones, the zonal data needs to be collected, just as for the networks. In both cases digital databases are often available making data collection easier, yet often the data is not always directly applicable, for instance having other geographic areas than the proposed zones, and the data needs to be thoroughly checked.

Data on travel behavior is needed for parameter estimation for trip generation, trip distribution and modal split, a process that is also called parameter calibration. Note that network assignment is often not based on an estimated model. Important sources on travel behavior are travel surveys (trip diary surveys for one or more days), especially household and person surveys as they capture actual travel patterns. If a regular travel survey is available often the number of respondents is still too low, however, combining 2 or 3 years of such a survey might be a suitable solution. In other cases, additional surveys or even a full new survey might be required. As these data sources relate to actual travel behavior, the models are based on revealed preference. However, for a number of model parameters travel surveys might not be sufficient, for instance if there's insufficient variation in the attributes (e.g., all busses having a similar frequency) or if an attribute is not relevant yet (e.g., no road pricing). In that case a stated preference survey can be used. In such a stated preference survey, respondents are provided with a number of choice options having different attribute values. The choices made by the respondents allow for estimating the required parameters. Note that classical aggregate models have lower data requirements than disaggregate discrete choice models, especially if for the latter a substantial variety of household or person types is distinguished.

Once the parameters for trip generation, deterrence and modal split functions have been estimated and all input for the base year is available, the model can be applied yielding the network flows for the base year. The next step is to check the model results with other data sources, a process also referred to as validation. Do the flows match traffic counts? Are the predicted bottlenecks on the right locations? Do the trip length distributions per mode match the observed trip length distributions? Experience shows that this analysis often reveals significant differences between model results and observations.

The first step then is to check the input data, especially the networks, the estimations and the modeling process, and the other data sources as well. Usually this leads to a considerable improvement of the match with other data sources, yet it is likely that there will still be differences with for instance traffic counts. Key point to bear in mind here, is that transport models always describe only a subset of all possible behavioral mechanisms. Second, the consistency concepts discussed before are very valuable: they lead to unique solutions given the input of the model. Yet they assume that everyone has the same level of information and all choices are optimal, while in reality there will always be travelers having limited knowledge of the transport system and there will always be people whose situation recently changed and who haven't updated all relevant choices yet. A typical example of the latter is for instance the historic relation that inhabitants in new neighborhoods or new towns have with the city they originated from.

If the differences with other data sources are considered to be too great while the calibrated model parameters are considered to be correct and reliable, the OD-matrices themselves can be calibrated to achieve a better match with for instance counts. Such a matrix calibration aims to find an

OD-matrix that is comparable with the matrix that resulted from the model while having a better match with other constraint such as counts. For OD-matrix calibration there are powerful mathematical tools available, yet this process requires extra attention as small errors in the data used, can lead to unwanted effects (see e.g., Joksimovic and Van Grol, 2016). Ideally, it should be possible to have an explanation for the systematic changes in the OD-matrices. A consequence of this step is that we have a model describing the main mechanisms in the transport system, OD-matrices per mode directly following from the model, and OD-matrices that have been calibrated using external data sources. This will have consequences for the application of the model.

3.2 Model application

There are two main types of model applications that can be distinguished:

- Exploration of the impacts of for instance future scenarios for autonomous factors;
- Analysis of the impact of specific policy measures.

In both cases a further distinction can be made with respect to whether the scenarios and measures are within the original scope of the model or not. In the first case, the applications are in line what the model was developed for. In the second case, however, it isn't. Options then range between using the available model and accepting the limitations, and developing a new model tailored to the new requirements. In many cases there will be substantial arguments for exploiting the available model as much as possible, such as financial constraints, time constraints, and a preference for consistency with previous analyses. A consequence of this choice is that the interpretation of the results requires extra attention.

For the exploration of a future scenario the model application is relatively straightforward. The model input for the zones and the network for the future year needs to be adapted according to the scenario. Key assumption is that the travel behavior itself remains the same. This implies that the model and the original parameters can be used to calculate the new OD-matrices and the corresponding flows on the networks. If the OD-matrix has been calibrated to achieve a better match with counts, a choice has to be made whether to apply the corrections for the future scenario as well or not. The common way to maintain the results of the matrix calibration is the pivot point method in which the future year matrix (FY_m) from the model and the base year matrix from the model (BY_m) are used to determine the relative growth for each OD-pair, and where these growth factors are multiplied with the calibrated OD-matrix (*BYM*) to obtain the future year matrix (*FYM*):

$$FYM = {}^{FY_m}/_{BY_m} \cdot BYM$$

In this way the strength of the model, a systematic description of the main mechanisms and thus sensitivities of the transport system, is combined with the benefit of a good match with observed flows.

Having a model for a future situation allows for a systematic analysis of changes in the number of trips, trip distribution, modal split, and network usage. Since the mechanisms that are included in the model are known, there is a logical explanation for the observed changes in the model results. Such an analysis is useful for presenting the results to decision-makers as well as for developing possible solution measures. Since there is always uncertainty about what the future will bring, it is recommended to analyze a number of scenarios in order to develop an idea of possible bandwidths for future developments.

Application of the model for evaluating specific policy measures is even simpler, provided that the measure can be easily translated to model inputs (e.g., introducing new links in the networks, improving links, changing travel costs). A (future) scenario is used as a reference, and the only change in the model input is the proposed policy measure. The model can then be applied, and the results can be systematically compared with those of the reference.

3.3 Quality control

Given the size and complexity of the models and the consequences of possible errors for decision processes, quality assurance has become more and more important. There are various ways to do so, for instance audits, guidelines, standardization, and protocols.

Audits are used to assess the quality and appropriateness of models. A team of experts analyzes the model set-up, compare it with the state-of-the-art, and judge to which extent the model is suitable for answering the questions it is used for. An import aspect in such an audit is an analysis of the sensitivities of the model, or more precisely a comparison of the time and cost elasticities of the model and values in relevant literature.

A good example of guidelines can be found in the Transport Analysis Guidance (Department for Transport, 2019). These guidelines provide a description of the model set-up, modeling methods per model components, and data sources, together with quality standards for applying these models and methods in practice. Examples of such quality standards are bandwidths for time and costs elasticities, guidelines for setting up future scenarios, and guidelines for convergence of iterative processes in for instance assignment models. Interesting characteristic of such guidelines is that they allow freedom in building transport models while guaranteeing a quality standard. The documentation on London's strategic transport models explicitly states that the demand model, the assignment models, and other model components are all build following the TAG to ensure robust and reliable models. (TfL Planning, 2017).

If consistency between model results is important, for instance for a consistent comparison of assessment and appraisal studies performed in different regions, standardization of the modeling tools is an option. Authorities can then prescribe a specific modeling suite including specific future scenarios that need to be used for all studies requiring a formal appraisal. An example is that in The Netherlands the National Model System and the related regional models (Netherlands Regional Model) are prescribed for all national and regional transport projects (see e.g., Joksimovic and Van Grol (2012) for a description of these models). The fact that in this case both a national model and the corresponding regional models are prescribed, also implies that consistency between all these models is an important issue when building and calibrating these models (see Joksimovic and Van Grol, 2016).

An issue that regularly appears in practice is that multiple models are available for the same study, e.g., a regional and an urban model. From a scientific perspective having multiple models could enrich the analysis, however, in practice this could also lead to actors opting for the model that suits their perspective best. Therefore, authorities usually provide clear guidelines on which models should be used for which purposes, e.g., the regional model is the standard for the freeways in urban regions and the local model is the standard for all urban roads. Furthermore, they can develop protocols on how and to which extent the preferred models can be adapted using the insights from the other models. Such protocols are also useful in cases where it is found that for a specific part of the study area the results of the preferred model are less reliable than expected.

4. Reflections on transport models

Sections 2 and 3 focused mostly on passenger transport models. However, for transport appraisal studies freight transport is also relevant and for large projects the interaction between transport and land use could be considered as well. Since these two topics are closely related to passenger transport models, they are briefly discussed. Furthermore, a reflection is given on the value and limitations of transport models in practice. This section concludes with a brief overview of new developments in transport modeling.

4.1 Freight modeling and land use and transport interaction modeling

Freight transport is clearly different from passenger transport, e.g., freight doesn't make decisions, there are many other actors involved, there is a large variety in commodity types, the time scale is much longer, and intermediate storage is an option. Yet freight transport models tend to have a similar model structure as passenger transport models, albeit with some clear differences. The demand models for freight transport, i.e., trip generation and trip distribution, are based on trade relations per commodity type and are usually expressed in monetary values, however, the gravity model concept might still be recognized. Once the OD-pattern is determined it is translated in volumes (tons) to be transported. New in some freight transport models is a separate component related to logistics. In this component the freight going from a sender to a receiver is translated in actual transport trips. Logistics deals with decisions on shipment size, inventory policy, warehousing etc. Note that the logistic perspective also includes empty rides, as freight transport is not balanced in both directions. For mode choice and network assignment again similar concepts as in passenger transport are used. Two main differences can be noted. In freight transport multimodality is more common than in passenger transport and for network assignment round trips, for instance trucks serving multiple clients, are relevant as well. Of course, the travel patterns by truck are valuable input for car assignment models as well (e.g., as pre-loads on the links). For more information on freight modeling the reader is referred to the book by Tavasszy and De Jong (2014).

In transport models the spatial pattern is assumed to be given. In reality land use is influenced by the transport system as well. Key notion here is that locations that are accessible by car or public transport are more attractive locations and thus are more likely to be developed further. Wegener and Fürst (2004) present a conceptual model for the interaction between land use and transport and provide empirical evidence for the relations in this model. The extension from transport modeling to land use and transport interaction (LUTI) models leads to the introduction of four new markets or new modeling components: the land use market, real estate market, housing market and labor market. Typical for most of these models is that they use a stepwise method to forecast the future land use and transport system: based on the accessibility of the base year, the spatial development for the next period is modeled which is again used as input for the transport model for that period. This process is repeated until the forecast year is modeled. A consequence of this approach is that the results depend on the scenario specifying when new infrastructure or new transport services become available.

4.2 Value and limitations of transport models in practice

In appraisal studies transport models are used to predict quantitative effects of future developments and policy measures. These predictions, however, are by definition limited by the simplifications made when modeling the complex transport system and by the quality of the input of other complex systems as demography, spatial developments, economy and so on. On the other hand, transport models allow a systematic analysis of changes between two applications of the transport models given the differences in input, with respect to both the final modeling results and all the intermediate results from the individual modeling components. As a result, there is a kind of dilemma between the benefits of using transport models and the limitations that are inherent to modeling. In this section a number of issues related to this dilemma are discussed.

A systematic comparison facilitates a clear discussion on the expected impacts, which is according to Epstein (2008) one of the 16 reasons other than prediction why modeling is important. Key in modeling is trying to understand systems by representing them in a mathematical form. Analysis of differences between model and reality leads to new questions and new theories. Based on these theories specific data collections can be set-up and more elaborate models can be developed, leading to a better understanding and a more comprehensive explanation of the system at hand.

This process of model improvement is clearly visible for transport models in which the simple unimodal gravity model evolved into large-scale multimodal choice-based models that consider a large variety in traveler characteristics and trip types, and this process is still going on. Examples are the introduction of activity schedules to achieve a more realistic description of the relation between people's activities and travel behavior (see e.g.,

Scherr et al., 2019; Timmermans and Arentze, 2011), or models that aim to link the separate modes in a truly multimodal transport model in which travelers can use combinations of modes for making a trip, e.g., using car to drive to the train station, and using the train to travel to their destination, possibly including bicycle or metro for the last part of their trip (see e.g., Rasmussen et al., 2016; Van Eck et al., 2014).

Parallel to this process of model improvement, there is, however, also a trend that the complexity of the transport system itself increases due to the introduction of new technologies, new transport concepts, and a changing society. Therefore, the net effect is that transport models will remain tools that describe the key mechanisms of a complex system and that are very useful if not essential when analyzing transport systems for short term of long-term changes.

It should be noted that this development of models, both in complexity and scale, brings in a new choice for model applications: Which model should be used for which question? It is not about using the best possible model available. The question is which model is useful for answering the questions at the table: for simple policy measure a basic transport model might be appropriate, while a national transport policy does require an elaborate transport model, yet quite likely with a lower level of spatial detail.

In the early years of model development, the expectations of integrating transport models and planning where high, and practice didn't meet these expectations. This led to a critical paper by Lee (1973) on the seven sins for large-scale urban models. These seven sins are hyper-comprehensiveness, grossness, hungriness, wrong-headedness, complicatedness, mechanicalness, and expensiveness. A recent analysis by Te Brömmelstroet et al. (2014) suggests that many of these issues are still unsolved. There is wider range of models available for the description of the urban system and the urban transport system, yet the level of detail in the models is high and the data requirements are still enormous. In applications, limitations of the models are not always acknowledged, the logic of the models sometimes remains unclear, and the model itself as well as the model results can still influence the planning process more than is justified. The costs of transport model applications decreased, yet tailored large-scale models are still expensive. Some valuable recommendations by Te Brömmelstroet et al. (2014) are that uncertainty of models and the systems themselves should be acknowledged, that transparency on assumptions and relations included in the models is key, and that always a broader view is required than using model results only.

4.3 New developments in transport modeling

As stated above models are being improved for all kinds of reasons coming from different perspectives. A rough distinction could be that these improvements result from developments in the transport system itself, new requirements from practice, and scientific interests. Since the scope of research on transport models is so wide, only a selection of developments is discussed in this section.

New developments in the transport system are for instance automated driving, new transport service concepts such as Mobility as a Service (MaaS) and a growing interest in environmentally friendly modes such as cycling.

Automated driving (see e.g., Snelder et al., 2019) requires that no longer a simple car availability is relevant, but that the type of vehicle that is available needs to be included in the model as well. This concept is also relevant for developments as car sharing or electric driving. Depending on the available vehicle type(s) all following choices in the modeling framework could be affected. Furthermore, automated driving will also affect the way the network is used: differences in routing and an impact on capacities of roads. Also, it could affect the worthwhile use of travel time, and in this way the value of transport time.

The concept of Mobility as a Service (see e.g., Jittrapirom et al., 2017; Kamargianni et al., 2018) includes on-demand transport services, shared transport services, and shared transport means. The latter is already briefly discussed above, the other two transport service types lead to logistic or empty rides and will affect the chosen routes as well since the vehicle will facilitate the demand of multiple travelers in an efficient way. This will require new model components that model the transport service providers' processes as well (comparable with the logistics component for freight transport models). At the same time these service concepts introduce an uncertainty for the traveler of the actual service that will be provided, which need to be included in the demand models and which suggests another iterative process in the modeling framework.

Cycling (see e.g., Liua et al., 2020, Prato et al., 2018) is an environmentally friendly mode that requires limited space compared to private cars. Innovations as *E*-bikes make cycling an even more attractive alternative. Therefore, there is an increasing demand for a better representation of cycling in transport models. A consequence of this development is that there is a need for a better understanding of why travelers opt for a bike or an E-bike and of the route choice of cyclists. Typical questions here are the usage of bicycles by young people and kids as well, groups that are sometimes ignored in standard transport models, the usage of the bike as access or egress mode to public transport, and the traffic dynamics of cyclists. The latter becomes more complicated as well due to the increasing variety in bicycle types in size and speed.

From a *transport policy perspective*, new assessment criteria become important, such as reliability of travel times, demand management, and traffic management.

Modeling reliability (see e.g., Mattsson and Jenelius, 2015; Snelder et al., 2012), and the related concept of robustness, requires new modeling techniques to account for the stochasticity that affects the network performance. This stochasticity relates to wide range of phenomena, such as variation in demand, effect of weather on demand and traffic conditions, accidents, road works and events. Modeling techniques can focus on accounting for stochastic travel times or focus on the probabilistic nature of all kinds of events requiring a large set of model runs. Also, one could try to model how travelers or carriers respond to uncertainty.

Demand management (see e.g., Lessan and Fu, 2019) on the other hand focuses on changing the mode choice, but possibly also the number of trips and the time of day choice, of travelers to main activity locations, e.g., large firms. Usually such demand management strategies are tailored to specific conditions of the activity locations, and in case of commuting also to the specific conditions of the employees. Therefore, it requires a high level of detail for modeling the demand to and from such locations.

Traffic management aims to use the network as efficiently as possible, while regular assignment models assume that all travelers try to find the routes that best suit their own purposes. Traffic management can affect the departure time, the route choice, the speed and the availability of infrastructure (e.g., peak lanes). All of these measures are based on the actual traffic conditions. Again, a higher level of detail is required, in this case especially for the network assignment. Note that there might be a relation with modeling techniques related to reliability as well.

From a *research perspective*, there are many directions for improving transport models, for instance by changing the theoretical foundations underlying the transport models such as replacing the random utility maximization model by the random regret minimization model (Chorus, 2010). For this chapter, two directions are discussed in more detail: the availability of new data sources and simulation-based modeling.

Given the abundant availability and usage of mobile phones, route planners, and apps, huge datasets on travel patterns become available showing (partial) origin-destination patterns and possibly route usage as well, evolving within a day and over days, weeks, and months (see e.g., Anda et al., 2017; Milne and Watling, 2019). Compared to the traditional surveys this type of data has a high level of spatial and temporal detail. Such data can be linked with other sources, such as weather conditions or incidents, to study travelers' behavior in specific conditions. There's however, one major drawback of this data: there's no information of the traveler itself, nor of the type of trip that is made (e.g., trip purpose). This is partly due to privacy regulations or simply because that type of data is not collected. This implies that empirical data from these data sources is very valuable for describing current situations in a much richer way than before, e.g., for determining base year matrices, yet household survey type data collection and detailed demand models are still needed for longer term forecasts for appraisal studies.

All modeling approaches discussed in Section 2 still group travelers in a few categories for aggregate models or in a larger number of person or household types, while the actual transport system is used by thousands or millions of users. Simulation-based modeling (see e.g., Kaghoa et al., 2020; Vovsha, 2017) aims to capture the variety and dynamics resulting from that level of detail. Each traveler is considered to be an individual entity and the model simulates the travel related choices, for instance modeling activity schedules for persons in households (activity-based models) or traveling in a multimodal network. In a simulation-based model framework as MATSim (Horni et al., 2016) the assignment is performed using simulation as well. At first sight such an approach might seem computationally demanding, however, the fact that only travelers are modeled instead of fractions of OD-flows as in the regular transport models, might actually reduce computation times for large-scale models.

5. Concluding remarks

The transport system is a complex system having a large societal impact. Many changes in the transport system require large investments and will have a long-term impact. Therefore, a proper analysis and appraisal of proposed measures is essential both from a transport engineering and from a decision-making perspective. Transport models are able to provide quantitative estimates on the effect of measures on the transport system, and more importantly, they allow a systematic comparison between alternatives. Furthermore, they also provide insight in the way the measures affect travel choices and travel patterns leading to those estimates.

Since the transport system is a complex system, however, transport models cannot be anything else than a simplification of reality. Therefore, both transport modelers and users of the results from transport models, should be aware of the strengths and weaknesses of the models that are applied. Transport modelers should be transparent on what the model is capable of and what not. Users of model results should be critical on the model results and ask questions if results do not seem logical. A good understanding of the main components of the four-stage model, and of the practical issues that arise when using transport models in a study, is crucial for having a dialog between transport modelers and users of the results.

Since transport models are a simplification, they can be improved and expanded. In this context, there are two dilemmas to be aware of. When modeling new developments (e.g., mobility as a Service, autonomous vehicles), it is often necessary to make exogenous assumptions of the future market share of such developments. On the one hand there is a gain by having a wider ranging and more detailed description of the transport system, but on the other hand the dependency on assumptions of such future developments introduces new uncertainties. The second dilemma is somewhat similar. There might be a tendency to use the most recent and most detailed transport model. In some cases, this could be the best thing to do, especially if the new model captures phenomena that are essential for the measures that are studied. In many cases, however, an "older and simpler" model might be just as suitable, with practical benefits as lower data requirements, lower computational requirements and more experience in analyzing and interpreting the results. From this perspective the main question is not about selecting the best model, but about selecting the most useful model in a given situation.

References

Anda, C., Erath, A., Fourie, P.J., 2017. Transport modelling in the age of big data. Int. J. Urban Sci. 21 (Suppl. 1), 19–42. https://doi.org/10.1080/12265934.2017.1281150.

Ben-Akiva, M., Lerman, S.R., 1985. Discrete Choice Analysis: Theory and Application to Travel Demand. The MIT Press, Cambridge.

Bureau of Public Roads, 1964. Traffic Assignment Manual. Urban Planning Division, US Department of Commerce, Washington D.C.

Cascetta, E., 2001. Transportation Systems Engineering: Theory and Methods. Springer Science + Business Media, Dordrecht.

Casey, H.J., 1955. Applications to traffic engineering of the law of retail gravitation. Traffic Q. IX (1), 23–35.

Chorus, C.G., 2010. A new model of random regret minimization. Eur. J. Transp. Infrastruct. Res. 10 (2), 181–196.

De Jong, G., Kouwenhoven, M., 2020. Value of travel time and travel time reliability. In: Mouter, N. (Ed.), Standard Transport Appraisal Methods. Advances in Transport Policy and Planning, vol. 6. Elsevier, Amsterdam, pp. 43–74 (Chapter 2).

De Jong, G.C., Daly, A.J., Vellay, C., Pieters, M., Hofman, F., 2003. A model for time of day and mode choice using error components logit. Transp. Res. E 39, 245–268.
Department for Transport, 2019. Transport Analysis Guidance. https://www.gov.uk/guidance/transport-analysis-guidance-webtag. London.
Dijkstra, E.W., 1959. A note on two problems in connection with graphs. Numer. Math. 1, 269–271.
Epstein, J.M., 2008. Why model? J. Artif. Soc. Soc. Simul. 11 (4), 12.
Furness, K.P., 1965. Time function iteration. Traffic Eng. Control 7, 458–460.
Horni, A., Nagel, K., Axhausen, K.W. (Eds.), 2016. The Multi-Agent Transport Simulation MATSim. Ubiquity Press, London. https://doi.org/10.5334/baw.
Jittrapirom, P., Caiati, V., Feneri, A.M., Ebrahimigharehbaghi, S., Alonso-Gonzalez, M.J., Narayan, J., 2017. Mobility as a service: a critical review of definitions, assessments of schemes, and key challenges. Urban Plan. 2 (2), 13–25. https://doi.org/10.17645/up.v2i2.931.
Joksimovic, D., Van Grol, R., 2012. New generation Dutch national and regional models—an overview of theory and practice. In: ETC Conference Papers. Association for European Transport.
Joksimovic, D., Van Grol, R., 2016. Consolidated calibration of Dutch national and four regional models—recent developments. In: ETC Conference Papers. Association for European Transport.
Kaghoa, G.O., Balaca, M., Axhausen, K.W., 2020. Agent-based models in transport planning: current state, issues, and expectations, The 9th international workshop on agent-based mobility, traffic and transportation models, methodologies and applications (ABMTRANS). Procedia Comput. Sci. 170, 726–732.
Kamargianni, M., Yfantis, L., Muscat, J., Azevedo, C.L., Ben-Akiva, M., 2018. Incorporating the Mobility as a Service Concept Into Transport Modelling and Simulation Framework. Extended abstract, Transportation Research Board 2019. https://discovery.ucl.ac.uk/id/eprint/10061860/7/Kamargianni_TRB2019_MaaSsim_Extended%20Abstract_full.pdf.
Lee, D.B., 1973. Requiem for large-scale models. J. Am. Inst. Plann. 39, 163–178.
Lessan, J., Fu, L., 2019. Credit- and permit-based travel demand management state-of-the-art methodological advances. Transp. A: Transp. Sci. 1–24. https://doi.org/10.1080/23249935.2019.1692963.
Liua, C., Tapania, A., Kristoffersson, I., Rydergren, C., Jonsson, D., 2020. Development of a large-scale transport model with focus on cycling. Transp. Res. A 134, 164–183.
Mattsson, L.G., Jenelius, E., 2015. Vulnerability and resilience of transport systems—a discussion of recent research. Transp. Res. A 81, 16–34.
McFadden, D., 1974. Conditional logit analysis of qualitative choice-behavior. In: Zarembka, P. (Ed.), Frontiers in Econometrics. Academic Press, New York, pp. 105–142.
McFadden, D., 1978. Modeling the choice of residential location. In: Karlqvist, A., Lundqvist, L., Snickars, F., Weibull, J. (Eds.), Spatial Interaction Theory and Residential Location. North-Holland, Amsterdam.
McFadden, D., 1981. Econometric models of probabilistic choice. In: Manski, C., McFadden, D. (Eds.), Structural Analysis of Discrete Data: With Econometric Applications. The MIT Press, Cambridge, Massachusetts, pp. 198–272.
Milne, D., Watling, D., 2019. Big data and understanding change in the context of planning transport systems. J. Transp. Geogr. 76, 235–244.
Ortuzar, J.D., Willumsen, L.G., 2011. Modeling Transport, fourth ed. John Wiley & Sons, Chichester.
Prato, C.G., Halldórsdóttir, K., Nielsen, O.A., 2018. Evaluation of land-use and transport network effects on cyclists' route choices in the Copenhagen Region in value-of-distance space. Int. J. Sustain. Transp. 12 (10), 770–781. https://doi.org/10.1080/15568318.2018.1437236.

Rasmussen, T.K., Anderson, M.K., Nielsen, O.A., Prato, C.G., 2016. Timetable-based simulation method for choice set generation in large-scale public transport networks. Eur. J. Transp. Infrastruct. Res. 16, 3. https://doi.org/10.18757/ejtir.2016.16.3.3153.

Scherr, W., Joshi, C., Manser, P., Frischknecht, N., Métrailler, D., 2019. An Activity-based Travel Demand Model of Switzerland Based on Choices and Constraints. hEART 2019. https://transp-or.epfl.ch/heart/2019/abstracts/hEART_2019_paper_128.pdf.

Snelder, M., van Zuylen, H.J., Immers, L.H., 2012. A framework for robustness analysis of road networks for short term variations in supply. Transp. Res. A 46, 828–842.

Snelder, M., Wilmink, I., van der Gun, J., Bergveld, H.J., Hoseini, P., van Arem, B., 2019. Mobility impacts of automated driving and shared mobility—explorative model and case study of the province of North-Holland. Eur. J. Transp. Infrastruct. Res. 19 (4), 291–309.

Spiess, H., Florian, M., 1989. Optimal strategies: a new assignment model for transit networks. Transp. Res. B Methodol. 23 (2), 83–102.

Sussman, J., 2004. 1.221J transportation systems. In: Fall 2004. Massachusetts Institute of Technology: MIT OpenCourseWare. https://ocw.mit.edu. License: Creative Commons BY-NC-SA.

Tavasszy, L., De Jong, G.C. (Eds.), 2014. Modeling Freight Transport. Elsevier.

Te Brömmelstroet, M., Peltzer, P., Geertman, S., 2014. Commentaries: Forty years after Lee's Requiem: are we beyond the seven sins? Environ. Plann. B. Plann. Des. 41, 381–391.

TfL Planning, 2017. London's Strategic Transport Models. Transport for London, London.

Timmermans, H., Arentze, T.A., 2011. Transport models and urban planning practice: experiences with Albatross. Transp. Rev. 31 (2), 199–207. https://doi.org/10.1080/01441647.2010.518292.

Train, K.E., 2002. Discrete Choice Methods With Simulation. Cambridge University Press, Cambridge.

Van Eck, G., Brands, T., Wismans, L.J.J., Pel, A.J., van Nes, R., 2014. Model complexities and requirements for multimodal transport network design: assessment of classical, state-of-the-practice, and state-of-the-research models. Transp. Res. Rec. 2429, 178–187. https://doi.org/10.3141/2429-19.

Vovsha, P., 2017. Microsimulation travel models in practice in the US and prospects for agent-based approach. In: Bajo, J., et al. (Eds.), Highlights of Practical Applications of Cyber-Physical Multi-Agent Systems. PAAMS 2017. Communications in Computer and Information Science. vol. 722. Springer, Cham, pp. 52–67.

Wardrop, J.G., 1952. Some theoretical aspects of road traffic research. Proc. Inst. Civ. Eng. 1, 325–362. Part II.

Wegener, M., Fürst, F., 2004. Land-Use Transport Interaction: State of the Art. Available at SSRN https://ssrn.com/abstract=1434678. or https://doi.org/10.2139/ssrn.1434678.

Wilson, A.G., 1970. Entropy in Urban and Regional Modeling. Pion, London.

CHAPTER FIVE

The wider economic benefits of transportation

Csaba G. Pogonyi*

Imperial College London, London, United Kingdom
*Corresponding author: e-mail address: csabagaborpogonyi@gmail.com

Contents

Abstract

The wider economic benefits of transportation are additional to direct user benefits typically measured in standard cost-benefit analysis. As various guidelines define wider economic benefits differently, this chapter concentrates on their underlying mechanism—agglomeration benefits. The chapter reviews recent literature on the theoretical and empirical foundations of agglomeration impacts and connects it to transportation induced benefits. Furthermore, finally, it explains in detail how one of the most advanced methodology, the United Kingdom's guideline measures agglomeration benefits. The end of the chapter provides a brief overview of the possible future directions of understanding the wider economic benefits of transportation.

Keywords: Transportation, Mass transit, Urban economics, Project appraisal, Additionality

1. Introduction

Societies spend a large share of their income on transportation infrastructure; however, the economic justification for their benefits is often lacking or incomplete. This chapter concentrates on the wider economic

Advances in Transport Policy and Planning, Volume 6
ISSN 2543-0009
https://doi.org/10.1016/bs.atpp.2020.09.001

benefits of transportation which are essential for the economic appraisal of large-scale public transportation projects. Research on the wider economic benefits (and disbenefits) of transportation is essential as the results are used in evaluating multibillion dollar transport investments. Disregarding these benefits leads to inaccurate cost-benefit calculations and can ultimately lead to decision makers choosing an option which does not maximize the welfare of the society. More and more countries use sophisticated project appraisal methodologies with a wide range of wider economic benefits, and more and more funding is spent in urban areas, which make research with a special focus on wider economic benefits essential.

It is important to note that the precise calculation of wider economic benefits is even more challenging than it is for direct user benefits. This additional challenge means higher cost of analysis which has led many countries and international bodies to instead use a simple rule-of-thumb approach (like the Netherlands) to capture the potential wider economic benefits of transportation projects. This higher cost of analysis may be disproportionally high for small-scale projects; however, they are still essential in deciding on investing in multibillion dollar transport projects.

The United Kingdom's transport analysis guidance (Department for Transport, 2019) is probably the most advanced and well-founded methodology, and it has several chapters on the quantification of wider economic impacts (Department for Transport, 2017). It identifies three main wider economic impacts: induced investment, employment effects and productivity impacts. Increasing transport accessibility changes the attractiveness of an area, which leads to more intensive usage of space, leading to a change in land use. Employment effects arise as households increase their labor supply: lower generalized cost of transportation increases their connection to employment centers which leads to labor supply impacts. Moreover, increased accessibility leads to the relocation of jobs to high productivity locations, which mostly lead to a move to more productive jobs. The guidelines explicitly connect agglomeration economies to productivity impacts: as the density of economic activity increases, workers and firms become more productive. They identify two different types of mechanisms of densification: static clustering and dynamic clustering. Static clustering is when the density of economic activity increases due to changes in generalized costs, which brings firms and workers closer—without them changing their locations. Dynamic clustering is when workers and jobs change their location after a change in the transport network, leading to—most of the time—increased densification, which leads to an increase in productivity.

The UK guidance is a great starting point to understand how to quantify wider economic benefits and this is also due to its drive to ensure that benefits are not double counted. Double counting—or additionality—is in the center of any debate on innovation in project appraisal. A decision maker is usually interested in a range of impacts before making a decision on a large infrastructure project: how many jobs will be created, what will happen with housing prices, what will happen with productivity and wages, and many more. An economic appraisal is able to produce—with varying precision—some cost/benefit numbers for all of these. However, adding up all the monetized benefits of extra jobs, extra productivity and land value uplift would lead to double counting. The simplest example is the link between land values and labor productivity/wages: a new transport investment increases the value of land as the workers/firms who wish to move there are now ready to pay more for the location—as they can be more productive and can get higher wages.

Additionality is a key concept in economic project appraisal, and this is why some European countries (like Norway) decided not to include wider economic benefits in their project appraisal guidelines—from fear of overestimating impacts. The United Kingdom's Homes and Communities Agency provides a comprehensive overview of additionality for all public sector projects (UK Homes and Communities Agency, 2019). Another good source is the EBRD's additionality guidance, which focuses on the role of structured financial support offered by the bank (EBRD, 2018).

This chapter concentrates on the most established part of wider economic benefits: agglomeration benefits. The author of this chapter—together with many empirical economists—is on the view that most of the benefits (and disbenefits) which occur in addition to direct user benefits are due to agglomeration economies.

The literature on the economics of agglomeration is well-established and has been developing for more than a hundred years. The calculation of wider economic benefits rests on the theory of agglomeration externalities developed by Marshall (1890). Increasing the density of the economy leads to productivity improvements through increased opportunities for labor market pooling, knowledge interactions, specialization and sharing of inputs and outputs. The literature on the economic impacts of transportation benefits from the current data revolution as new disaggregate microdata provides opportunities to apply advanced quasi-experimental methodologies. State-of-the-art transportation project appraisal connects theory and empirical study as quantifying the wider economic benefits of transportation requires both understanding the underlying agglomeration externalities and providing precise causal estimates for the impact of large-scale projects.

The easiest way of understanding how agglomeration benefits connect to direct user benefits is through the three levels of benefits UK TAG guidelines also support this approach. Level 1 benefits are direct user benefits—existing and future users of the transport network benefit from reduced generalized costs. Level 2 benefits are static benefits: reduced generalized costs increase accessibility in the economy which leads to increased economic density. Increased economic density is associated with higher productivity for both workers and firms, leading to wider economic benefits. It is important to add that these benefits occur for all the economic agents in the market—not just for the beneficiaries of the new transport link and therefore they are not double-counting level 1 benefits. Level 3 benefits are dynamic agglomeration benefits: due to the change in generalized costs in the economy, firms and workers decide to relocate, often leading to an increase of clustering which leads to productivity increase not captured in level 1 or level 2. It is important to note that improving the transport network can lead to negative impacts as well through the displacement of economic activity and sprawl, which may be captured at level 3.

After reviewing the fields of economics of agglomeration and the impacts of transportation, this chapter shows how the findings are used in transportation project appraisal. The wider economic benefits section connects urban and transport economics with project appraisal and the last section highlights some of the possible future directions of this dynamic field of economics.

2. The economics of agglomeration

Cities are locations where both people and firms move despite high land prices and other costs. This spatial concentration of economic activity is often called agglomeration in spatial and urban economics. The rationale behind moving to cities is that spatial concentration leads to agglomeration benefits, which outweigh their costs. This section first reviews the theoretical background behind the economics of agglomeration then provides an overview of the empirical evidence supporting it.

There have been many theories and branches of economics which have investigated the existence of cities and their rise throughout the centuries. The tendency for spatial concentration has been apparent for centuries in science, the first theory explaining it is attributed to Von Thunen's theory (Von Thunen, 1966). His model explains how agricultural activities distribute in space around a central city. The theory poses a simple trade-off between land rents and transport costs, and this sorts different activities to different distances from the central city. Fujita and Thisse (2002) represent this relationship with a downward sloping land rent curve: land prices decrease as distance to the city increases in order to compensate for increased transportation costs.

While Von Thunen's theory provides a good representation of the economy of space in the first half of the 19th century, the industrial revolution dramatically changed the structure of the economy. Still, the decreasing importance of agriculture did not diminish the importance of transport costs. Transportation costs are the main drivers for the optimal location of industrial activity in the model of Weber (1929). A firm chooses its location by minimizing transportation costs for its inputs and also for the delivery of its outputs; so, its optimal location is determined by the input- and output-weighted costs of transportation. An important limitation of Weber's model is that it assumes that input factors are homogeneous across regions. This limitation was solved by the Weber-Moses model as it allows for factor substitution; however, it assumes equal access to all output markets. This results in a model where location choice depends only on heterogeneous input factors and their relative price ratios (McCann, 2001).

Alonso (1964) extends Von Thunen's model and develops a general theory for land values and land uses in cities and regions. He argues that the relationship between land rents and transportation costs is more complex than Von Thunen's model and his theory explains how economic agents choose their locations around a central business district (CBD). These agents maximize their utility by trading transport costs for larger housing units, and this behavior self-sorts consumers to different distances from the CBD. Fujita and Thisse (2002) represent this relationship with a downward sloping bid rent curve: residential land prices decrease as distance to the CBD increases.

Another important addition to the literature stems from the analysis of market potential (Harris, 1954). The Harris market potential index is used in many empirical studies even today to incorporate in the analysis the phenomenon of spatial spillovers and distance decay in agglomeration forces. This index is, for a location, the distance-weighted sum of opportunities (e.g., population, employment, or production) provided by other locations nearby.

The general criticism toward these theories is that they assume a certain structure of the economy without connecting it to the behavior of economic agents—even though the theory was around at least since the end of the 19th century. In his 1890 and 1920 volumes, Marshall (1890, 1920) defined the three principal sources of urban agglomeration. The first is labor market pooling, as people move to the same place to find jobs, allowing firms to have a greater variety to choose from. The second is input and output sharing between intermediate good producers and final good producers, which make firms more productive. The third source is knowledge spillovers, which is based on the observation that ideas tend to spread easier in close proximity. Marshallian benefits are used even today in explaining urban agglomeration. Duranton and Puga (2004) a hundred years later similarly defined the mechanisms of agglomeration, mentioning the most important mechanisms: increased opportunities for labor market pooling, knowledge interactions, specialization and sharing of inputs and outputs.

Krugman's 1990 article "Geography and Trade" (Krugman, 1996) is generally accepted as the founding article of the "New Economic Geography" (NEG) discipline. This article united the two previously separate disciplines of international trade and economic geography. On the one hand, trade models assuming constant returns to scale and perfect competition did not permit economists to explain why similar rich economies trade with each other more intensively than with different poor ones. Their mathematical models were not able to handle the economies of scale assumptions, which seemed to provide the solution. On the other hand, economic geography has long been using models, which assume economies of scale to explain the location of economic activity. Since Krugman's article, international trade and economic geography have been learning from each other. The article emphasizes the same fundamental forces which simultaneously determine specialization across countries for some factors of production (trade theory) and the location choice of these factors across countries (economic geography). After Krugman, many general equilibrium models with economies of scale and imperfect competition were developed. According to Combes et al. (2008), these models have been able to model the utility and profit maximization location choice of firms and people well.

NEG models assume that the economy is in equilibrium among centripetal and centrifugal forces. Centripetal forces are driven by the circular causation of backward (suppliers aim to locate close to large markets) and forward linkages (consumers and workers aim to locate close to suppliers of goods and varieties). Centrifugal forces arise from the immobility of input factors such as land. The theory incorporates transport infrastructure by arguing that it changes the balance between the opposing forces, with a new link leading to a modified equilibrium.

Duranton and Puga (2004) enumerate a number of potential mechanisms on how agglomeration impacts economic agents. They argue that urban agglomeration makes the sharing of nondivisible goods more efficient.

Large and nonshareable goods (like roads or a conference hall) are too big or complex for producing lots of small ones, and they require close access. The trade-off between the costs and benefits of accessing these goods defines the equilibrium size of a city.

Another mechanism is the love of variety (home market effect) which states that increasing the number of inhabitants or the number of firms increases growth in utility more than proportionally. In this sense, the central market functions as a nondivisible good, and it induces positive agglomeration externalities.

A larger market also leads to more specialization. This argument is related to Marshall's labor pooling argument, namely that a bigger pool of workers makes it possible for people to specialize and increase their productivity.

Another sharing mechanism is the sharing of risk. Firms and workers are facing various types of shocks (like an economic depression). In such a situation, it is in the interest of both firms and workers to move to higher density areas, as there the chances are better for recruiting new employees or finding a job.

Not just sharing, but matching is also more efficient in agglomerated areas. The labor matching model of Mortensen and Pissarides (1999) shows that increased agglomeration reduces the cost of matching between employees and employers. The success of matching depends on the number of searchers and suppliers, and in a city, firms can select from a wider range of workers; moreover, workers also get more offers. This way, a more effective matching increases quality and lowers costs.

The final mechanism is learning, which is more efficient in cities. Cities are more suitable to generate knowledge: Duranton and Puga (2000) show, cities work like "nurseries" for ideas: they allow firms to try out new ideas, create new ventures and later these firms may move away to cheaper locations.

Graham and van Dender (2011) find that it is challenging to distinguish the role of density from other explanations on productivity increase. Connecting to Marshall (1920) and Duranton and Puga (2004) they mention five potential externalities arising from wider access to economic mass: increased opportunities for labor market pooling, scope for industry specialization, greater efficiency in knowledge or technology sharing, and a better input-output association. These effects are either increasing productivity or lowering average costs. They claim that for understanding the economic benefits of transportation, quantifying the magnitude of these externalities is crucial; however, at the current stage of development, not even their existence and the channels through which they impact the economy are thoroughly understood.

Proximity also improves the spread of knowledge or information. There are two broad types of knowledge spillovers. The Marshall–Arrow–Romer (MAR) externalities are called "localization" externalities (Combes, 2000): this theory is connected to the endogenous growth theory and models how in a certain sector, knowledge spreads. Specialization has increasing returns to scale and thus—mostly in high-tech sectors—proximity leads to specialization, which leads to higher productivity. The Jacobs externalities are called "urbanization" externalities. Here the emphasis is on diversity and complementarity, and the theory states that all sectors benefit from being close to other sectors.

2.1 Empirical evidence on agglomeration

Empirical evidence has been growing to support the mechanisms of agglomeration benefits. Most of the studies use a measure for the size of agglomeration similar to Harris (1954):

$$\rho_i = \sum_{j=1}^{n} m_j f(g_{ij}), \tag{1}$$

where ρ is the measure of agglomeration (effective density (ED) in most studies), m_j is economic mass (employment or population in most of the cases) at area j, g_{ij} is a measure for the cost of travel between areas i and j (often geographical distance, travel time or generalized cost of travel), and $f()$ is the impedance function which is a decreasing function of g_{ij}. This measure captures the effects of both scale and spatial proximity, and through the decreasing function of distance it incorporates an implicit transport dimension.

There have been many studies which evaluated the correlation between ED and various economic outcomes. A recent metastudy (Ahlfeldt and Pietrostefani, 2019) use density elasticities from 180 studies and present a set of recommended elasticities which may be used in many applications. Table 1 presents their results. Due to the availability of research, these elasticities mostly refer to large cities in high-income countries. It is also important to mention that these elasticities represent only correlations: providing causal estimates needs a thorough identification strategy which is especially challenging for long-run density benefits.

The results of Ahlfeldt and Pietrostefani (2019) show that density creates both benefits and costs for the society. Wage and productivity are positively correlated; however, rents seem to increase even more with density.

Table 1 Economic density elasticities by category (Ahlfeldt and Pietrostefani, 2019).

Elasticity	Value
Wage	0.04
Patent intensity	0.21
Rent	0.15
Inter-quintile wage gap reduction	−0.035
Self-reported wellbeing	−0.0037
Variety value (price index reduction)	0.12
Local public spending	0.17
Crime rate reduction	0.085
Mortality rate reduction	−0.09
Pollution reduction	−0.13
Green density	−0.28
Energy use reduction	0.07
Car use reduction	0.05
Vehicle miles traveled (VMT) reduction	−0.06

The negative inter-quintile wage gap reduction suggests that wage differences increase with density, pointing toward an economically more unequal society. The negative self-reported wellbeing value understates this. Local public spending and crime rate reduction are both positive, suggesting that public services and safety are better in higher density areas. Mortality reduction decreases with density; however, the negative pollution reduction value and green density show that living in high density areas can be less healthy for locals. Living in high density is beneficial for environmental concerns as their findings show a reduction in energy use, in car usage and in vehicle miles traveled.

Ahlfeldt and Pietrostefani (2019) use monetary equivalents to understand the impact of increasing density on the quality of life. They find that increasing the density of a city by 1% implies an increase in yearly wages by \$280 (\$190 after taxes) and \$347 in rent. This leads to a \$156 decrease in real wages net of taxes; moreover, increased amenities, and other positive welfare effects do not make up for this loss. They explain this rather striking result by arguing that the rent increase may be attributable to the higher cost of providing space and is not exclusive to amenities and that policy-induced densification may still lead to aggregate welfare gains. This result shows that even after half a century of increasing interest, there is still much to learn on the impact of density on the quality of life.

2.2 Economic performance and agglomeration

Most empirical investigations use production functions to estimate the impact of agglomeration on economic performance. This approach connects urban economics to standard microeconomics and to a well-established literature on productivity. These studies typically define a wage or firm production function with a measure of access to economic mass embedded and then estimate the function on large country-level datasets.

The density of economic activity is the source of increasing aggregate returns. Ciccone and Hall (1993) developed an approach often used in the literature: they investigate if agglomeration raises the productivity of firms through externalities. They find that doubling employment density increases average labor productivity by around 6%. Moreover, more than half of the variance of output per worker across states in the United States can be explained by differences in the density of economic activity.

There has been much attention on the relationship between economic density and wages or firm productivity. Graham and Gibbons (2017) review 47 international empirical studies and find that most of them find a significant positive relationship between the size of agglomeration and productivity, with a mean agglomeration elasticity of 0.046: a 10% increase in city size leads to a 0.46% increase in productivity. The density plot of their results shows that most of the elasticities are between 0 and 0.1 (see Fig. 1).

Spatial proximity to economic mass impacts the sectors of the economy differently. The retail sector benefits more from locating close to a large pool of final consumers, whereas the manufacturing sector prefers to locate close to its intermediate suppliers of inputs. Graham (2007a) analyses the link between agglomeration and productivity for a set of detailed sectors of the UK economy. He finds that there are positive externalities from increasing urban densities and that these can be substantial, particularly for service industries. Pogonyi et al. (2018) find that new metro stations clustered the retail sector the most. New stations clustered financial services as well, and manufacturing was affected negatively.

As many studies have shown, there is much heterogeneity for the returns to density depending not just on the level of agglomeration or the sector, but also on the methodology employed. Melo et al. (2013) review empirical

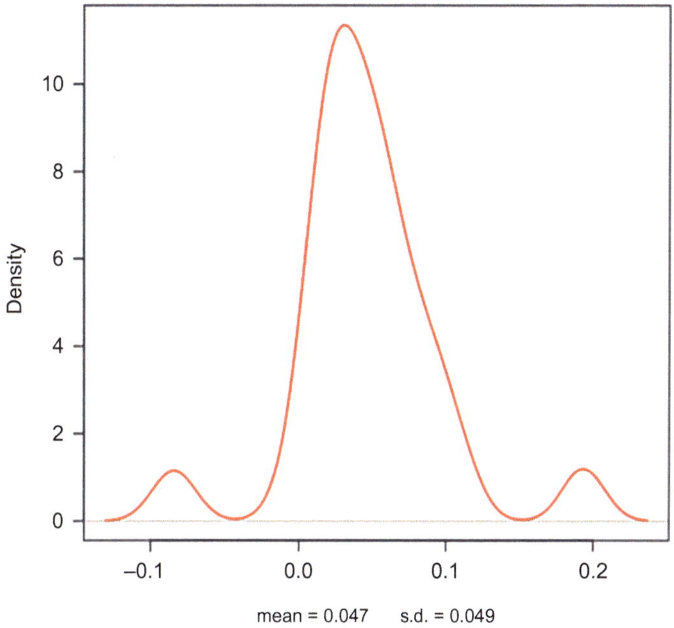

Fig. 1 Histogram of urban agglomeration elasticities (Graham and Gibbons, 2019).

evidence on the impact of transportation infrastructure on economic density and how this impacts productivity. They find that agglomeration elasticities tend to be the highest in the developing world (the median elasticity is 0.082 as opposed to 0.013 in Europe and 0.014 in the US). Elasticities for the economy as a whole are small (median is 0.016), and they are the highest in manufacturing and primary industries (median is 0.057 and 0.051, respectively), whereas they can be even negative in the energy industry (median elasticity is −0.002). There are also significant differences between transport modes: for all transport modes and for airport they are close to zero (0.005 and 0.006 is the median, respectively), for port/ferry and railway they are small but positive (0.0016 and 0.011, respectively), whereas for roads they are large and positive (0.045).

Graham and van Dender (2011) use a set of sophisticated panel and semiparametric methods to estimate transportation induced agglomeration benefits. They find nonlinear relationships between the size of agglomeration and productivity, with no positive effects for a wide range of increases in accessibility. They fit their firm productivity estimates on accessibility using four different specifications (see Fig. 2): (A) shows the relationship for all

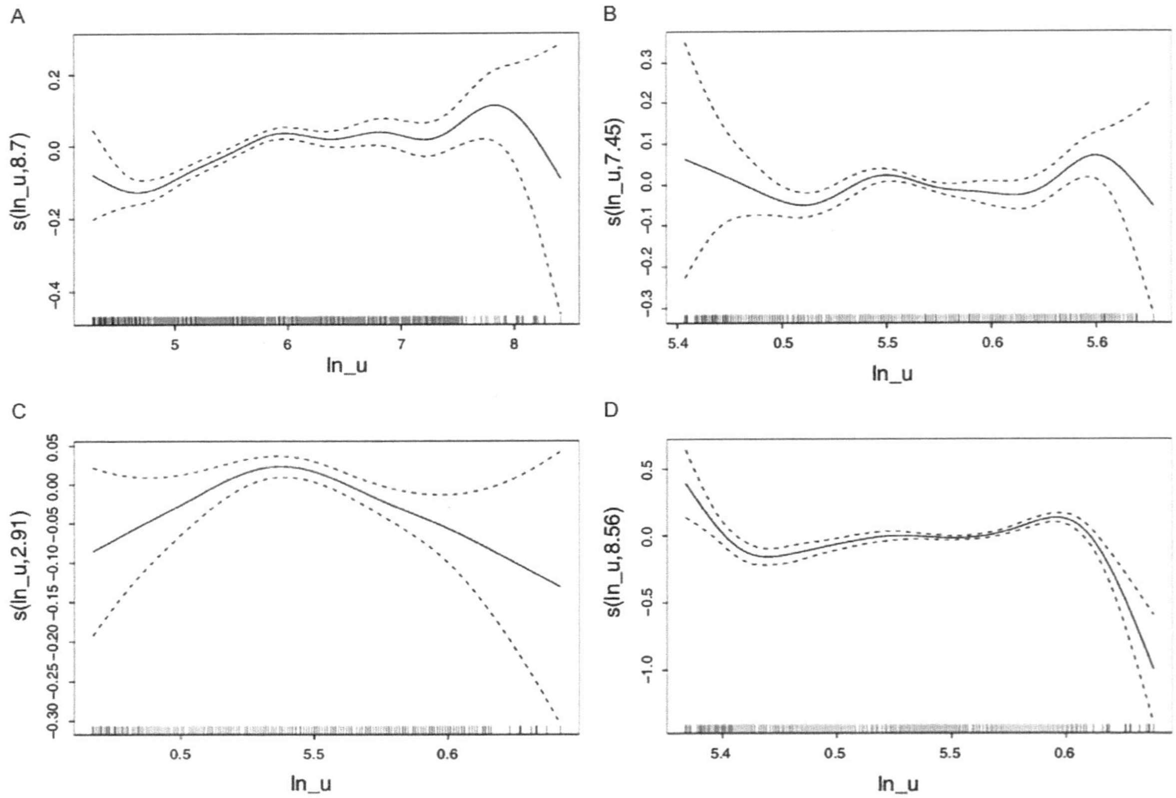

Fig. 2 Semiparametric estimates of effects of log accessibility on total factor productivity (Graham and van Dender, 2011).

areas, (B) shows only for conurbations, (C) for urban big areas (>250,000 pop) and (D) for large urban areas (>1,000,000 pop). Interestingly, moving to higher accessibility areas does not necessarily lead to higher productivity; moreover, very high accessibility even decreases productivity.

Graham and van Dender (2011) also estimate elasticities separately for major industries of the economy. They find positive and significant elasticities for the economy as a whole and all industries as well. The largest effects are observed for business services (0.127) and transport & communications (0.116), with manufacturing (0.077), construction (0.095) and wholesale & retail (0.064) showing lower elasticities. The elasticity for all industries is 0.105. These estimates are in line with the usual literature averages (for a review, see for example Melo et al. (2009)).

2.3 Distance decay

Another important question is how fast agglomeration effects decay with distance. The body of evidence has been growing in the last 20 years; however, there is not much evidence on distance decay in a within-city setting. This literature typically uses a market potential measure similar to Eq. (1). Eq. (2) shows a less general representation of the market potential measure with a separate distance decay parameter, α:

$$\rho_i = \sum_{j=1}^{n} \frac{m_j}{d_{ij}^{\alpha}}, \tag{2}$$

where all the letters denote the same variables like in Eq. (1), and α is a parameter which denotes how sensitive are agglomeration externalities to increasing distance (d_{ij} in this setting). Some variations of this measure also incorporate the size of the own-area (like in Graham, 2007b).

This setting allows the gravitational definition of access to economic mass where agglomeration externalities diminish with distance. If α is greater than 1, the further away the economic mass, the less it affects market potential. A smoother spatial distance decay is achieved if α is less than 1. Much of the literature, assume that α equals 1 as it is difficult to estimate it directly in a regression setting together with other variables of interests.

There have been many studies estimation the distance decay parameter, and the most widely used setting is using distance bands. This approach divides the plain to a number of distance bands with their respective economic mass as weight, and this way a separate coefficient can be estimated for every band. Empirical studies usually find that agglomeration effects are stronger within short distances, and further out the effect sharply declines (see Pogonyi et al. (2018) for an overview of these findings)

Rosenthal and Strange (2008) estimate the spatial decay parameter using wage data from the US census using distance bands. They employ a set of estimation strategies and instrumental variables, and they find that the spatial concentration of employment within five miles is positively related to wage and that this effect attenuates sharply with distance. Di Addario and Patacchini (2008) follow their approach and estimate a similar model for Italy. They find that every additional 100,000 inhabitants in the local labor market raise earnings by 0.1% and that this effect decays very rapidly with distance, losing significance beyond approximately 12 km.

Rice et al. (2006) use subregional data from Great Britain to analyze the determinants of spatial variations in income and productivity. They measure proximity by travel time and show that effects decline sharply with time and that they disappear beyond approximately 80 min. They use an exponential distance decay function for working-age population and find that α is 1.37 and 1.51 when they use a nonlinear least squares estimator. They estimate the same model for wages and find an α of 1.2 and 1.41 for the nonlinear least squares estimator.

Graham et al. (2009) estimate firm-level production functions using a large panel dataset for firms in Great Britain, using a control function approach which addresses potential sources of endogeneity. Using a nonlinear least squares approach, they find that the overall distance decay is 1.66. They estimate the distance decay for separate industries as well and find that it is approximately 1 for manufacturing, 1.8 for consumer and business services and 1.6 for construction.

A particularly relevant study is by Arzaghi and Henderson (2008), where they analyze the extent of spatial decay among advertising companies in Manhattan. They find that scale externalities are large; however, externalities decay rapidly by geographical distance and disappear after 750 m. They argue that this is due to the importance of networking and information spillovers in high-end service industries.

3. The economic impacts of transportation

As the previous section showed, there are several theories which emphasize the importance of transport infrastructure for economic activity. Classical location theory (Alonso, 1964; Moses, 1958; Predöhl, 1928) states that the most important determinant for the location of economic activity is transport cost. The New Economic Geography (Krugman, 1996) literature understates that and inserts transport costs into the setting of imperfect competition and interregional labor mobility. Standard macroeconomic theory (Aschauer, 1990; Garcia-Mila and McGuire, 1992; Munnell, 1992) takes transport as one of the main ingredients of public infrastructure, which is one of the sources of economic growth as it contributes to technical change.

New Economic Geography emphasizes the role of transport costs as one of the most important factors in the location choice of firms and people. Any intervention which makes people and firms locate closer to each other can induce agglomeration externalities. Transport infrastructure impacts the economy through cost, accessibility and quality mechanisms, providing new opportunities for both consumers and producers. In addition to simple direct effects (revenue of the operator, travel time savings of the users, and others), transportation improvements induce agglomeration externalities as well. Areas with better access to markets with economic activity will be—ceteris paribus—more competitive and more productive. So better connected regions are more successful than remote areas.

Redding and Turner (2015) develop a multiregion model of economic geography, which makes it possible to understand the general equilibrium implications of an improvement in the transport infrastructure. Their model provides results on wages, population, trade and industry composition as well. They differentiate between interregional and intraregional transport investments and argue that interregional investments increase market access and wages as they decrease the cost of transporting goods to demand markets. Intraregional investments (like a metro) decrease commuting costs within the region and increase the supply of labor. Their model assumes that the density-increasing impact overweights the urban sprawl impact, and thus this increased supply of labor raises total income and wages.

Improving transportation connectivity can induce agglomeration effects without increasing the physical size of the city. Venables (2007)'s model suggests that there are significant gains from urban transport improvements. His computable equilibrium model argues that agglomeration externalities can be induced without increasing the physical size of cities by improving connectivity. He divides the economy of a city to 20,000 spatial cells and defines a transport network, which is defined by four lines which intersect at the central business district (CBD), where workers commute to. The CBD consists of an endogenously determined number of cells and areas further out are residential until the edge of the city. Productivity is highest at the center of the CBD and declines toward the edge. The edge of the city

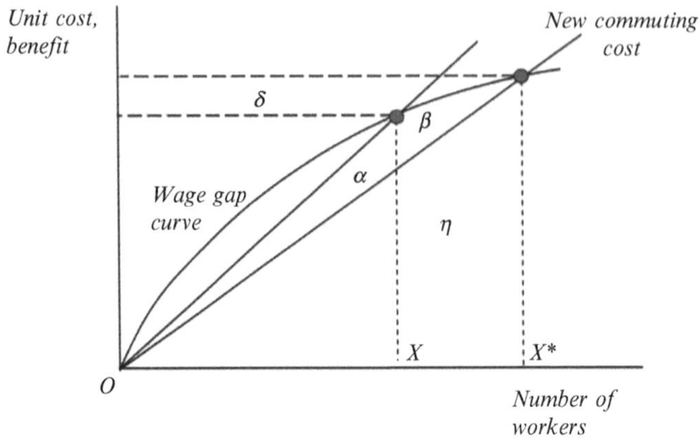

Fig. 3 Net gains from transport improvement with endogenous productivity (Venables, 2007).

is where the city versus outsider wage gap equals the travel costs to the CBD. Fig. 3 illustrates the impact of a transport improvement with endogenous productivity assumed. The commuting cost line is flatter as the generalized cost of commuting decreases after the transport investment. This increases the size of the city (*X* moves to *X**), which leads to increased productivity and wages as positive endogenous productivity due to agglomeration effects means that increasing city size increases its productivity. An important finding is that all the workers of the city benefit: not just those who are now able to live and work in the city, but also former residents as agglomeration benefits increased their productivity. New residents benefit as now they are able to commute to the CBD and earn higher salary, and former residents as well as due to the increase in the size of the city, their wages are also higher due to productivity improvements.

Empirical evidence shows that transportation projects tend to have a positive impact on the economy. Table 2 provides an overview of some of the important empirical studies on the impact of transportation on economic activity which employ a credible causal estimation strategy. Most of the evidence estimates the impact of transportation on long-run population movements. Redding and Turner (2015) compare the study of Baum-Snow (2007) interested in the redistribution of population and the study of Duranton and Turner (2012) estimating the growth of population. These two use a similar sample of cities and years; therefore, it is possible to make a strained comparison. Baum-Snow (2007) finds that central city

Table 2 Review of some of the studies on the causal economic impacts of transportation.

Study	Country	Impact	Measure	Result
Chandra and Thompson (2000)	United States	Interstate highway	Total earnings	6%–8%
Chandra and Thompson (2000)	United States	Interstate highway	Total earnings for adjacent areas	−1% to 3%
Baum-Snow (2007)	United States	Radial highway	Central city population	−14%
Duranton and Turner (2012)	United States	Within-city highway	Central city population	15%
Baum-Snow (2017)	United States	Radial highway	Central city population	−16%
Baum-Snow (2017)	United States	Radial highway	Number of jobs	−6%
Baum-Snow et al. (2017)	China	Radial highway	Central city population	−4%
Holl (2004)	Spain	Highway	Firm birth	14%
Garcia-López et al. (2015)	Spain	Radial highway	Central city population	−8% to 9%
Garcia-López et al. (2015)	Spain	Radial highway	Population in the suburbs	+20%
Gibbons et al. (2019)	Great Britain	+1% Accessibility (highway)	Number of business units	0.4%
Gibbons et al. (2019)	Great Britain	+1% Accessibility (highway)	Employment	0.3%
Donaldson and Hornbeck (2013)	United States	19th century railroads	Agricultural land values	1.1%
Ahlfeldt and Feddersen (2018)	Germany	High-speed rail	GDP	8.5%
Holl (2011)	Spain	High-speed rail	Number of firms	3.3%
Holl (2011)	Spain	High-speed rail	Labor productivity	1.08%

Continued

Table 2 Review of some of the studies on the causal economic impacts of transportation.—cont'd

Study	Country	Impact	Measure	Result
Carbo et al. (2018)	Spain	High-speed rail	Economic output	2.4%
Carbo et al. (2018)	Spain	High-speed rail	Number of firms	3.3%
Carbo et al. (2018)	Spain	High-speed rail	Labor productivity	1.1%
Mayer and Trevien (2017)	France	Suburban rail	Employment	8.8%
Mayer and Trevien (2017)	France	Suburban rail	Population	No impact
Ahlfeldt (2011)	Germany	Inter-city rail in city	Real estate prices	No impact
Billings (2011)	United States	Light rail	Real estate prices (single-family)	4%
Billings (2011)	United States	Light rail	Real estate prices (condominiums)	11.3%
Billings (2011)	United States	Light rail	Real estate prices (commercial)	No impact
Gonzalez-Navarro and Turner (2018)	Global	Metro	Population	No impact
Gibbons and Machin (2005)	Great Britain	Metro	Real estate prices	9.3%

population decreases by 14% due to a one standard deviation increase in the number of radial highways, keeping the overall population constant. Duranton and Turner (2012) find that a one standard deviation increase in within-city lane kilometers of interstate highways increases population by 15%. The comparison of these two studies suggests that the growth and redistribution components are of similar magnitude. Baum-Snow et al. (2017) use a similar approach to Baum-Snow (2007) for Chinese highway and railway investments and find that radial highways decrease central city population by about 4%. They show that radial highways decentralize service sector activity, radial railways decentralize industrial activity, and ring roads decentralize both. Garcia-López et al. (2015) estimate the effects of highways in Spain using historical evidence. They find that radial highways decreased central city population by 8%–9% between 1960 and 2011, and that population in the suburbs increased by 20%.

Evidence interested in the impact of transportation on economic output has also been growing. Chandra and Thompson (2000) find that new interstate highways in the US raised total earnings for counties close to the investment by 6%–8% between 1969 and 1993. However, total earnings fell by 1%–3% for counties adjacent to highway counties. Their model finds that the net effect of new highways is essentially zero for regional growth. Baum-Snow (2017) use planned proportions of the US highway system to show that each radial part displaced 16% of central city workers, but only 6% of jobs to the suburbs. Besides, they find that a large part of the overall agglomeration economies affect the economy at spatial scales below the metropolitan area as they find an implied elasticity of central city firm productivity to central city employment relative to suburban employment is 2%–5%. Banerjee et al. (2012) are interested in whether access to transportation leads to a permanent increase in growth rates or only affects the level of activity. Their research studies long-term GDP per capita and GDP per capita growth on a fine regional level in China between 1986 and 2006. They find a moderate positive effect on GDP per capita closer to historical transport schemes. They estimate zero impact on GDP per capita growth, which suggests that transport infrastructure impacted only the level of activity in the area, not its growth prospects. Faber (2014) constructs a hypothetical least-cost transport networks which connect major Chinese cities to estimate the impact of highways on economic activity. He finds that new highways led to a reduction in GDP growth for nontargeted peripheral areas, and this is mostly due to reduced industrial output. Holl (2004) analyses the location of new manufacturing establishments in Spain between

1980 and 1984. She finds that areas within 10 km of new highways benefited the most. Further off locations experienced a decline in the number of firms, indicating that the effect of redistribution is strong. The strength of the impact differs across sectors; moreover, she finds evidence for geographical specialization among firms. Gibbons et al. (2019) find increases in output per worker and wages for existing firms in areas where transportation accessibility increased due to new road infrastructure in the United Kingdom between 1997 and 2008.

Evidence is growing on the impact of rail on productivity. Ahlfeldt and Feddersen (2018) find that GDP increased on average by 8.5% after the introduction of the German high-speed rail for areas which were treated incidentally as they are located in-between two important cities. Holl (2011) also uses the incidental treatment approach to study the impact of the Spanish high-speed rail the regional economy and find that the number of firms increased by 3.3% and labor productivity by 1.08%. Carbo et al. (2018) evaluate economic impacts arising from the introduction of high-speed rail between Madrid and Barcelona. They find similar results to Holl (2011) as the average treatment effect for provinces with stops on the line was 2.4% for economic output, 3.3% for numbers of firms, and 1.1% for labor productivity. Donaldson and Hornbeck (2013) estimate the impact of railroads on land values in the 19th century United States (which one might assume that are closely correlated with productivity). They find that changes in market access associated with railroads increased agricultural land values with an estimated elasticity of 1.1.

Evidence for intracity transportation changes is rare. Gibbons and Machin (2005) study the impact of the Jubilee line extension (JLE) and find that residential real estate prices increased by 9.3% on average for those areas where the minimum distance to the nearest metro station decreased, and the nearest JLE station is within 2 km. Billings (2011) estimates the impact of a light rail system on property prices in Charlotte, United States in 2000. Using an identification strategy which uses planned, but abandoned rail corridors and a difference-in-differences setting, he finds that light rail access increased single-family property prices by 4%, and condominiums by 11.3% within one mile of stations. It is interesting that he finds no impact on commercial prices, which may indicate that new stations provided more opportunities for commuting to the central business district, but did not induce local economic benefits. Mayer and Trevien (2017) study the impact of the Regional Express Rail in the Paris metropolitan region between 1970 and 2000, and find that employment increased by 8.8% but find no effect on the overall population. Unfortunately, they do not study the impact on productivity.

Ahlfeldt et al. (2015) use a fine spatial scale to study the impact of the Berlin Wall on the spatial distribution of economic activity in Berlin. They find that the wall resulted in the clustering of business activity around the center of West Berlin and that the center of whole Berlin moved; however, after the fall of the wall the center of activity moved back to its original location.

A recent development is an analysis by Heblich et al. (2018), where they estimate how the mid-19th century transport revolution (the invention of the steam engine) shaped the urban agglomeration of London. Their quantitative urban model can model commuting flows in the city, and this enables them to understand how improved transportation helped the development of the city. They find that much of the aggregate growth of Greater London can be explained by the new transport technology of the railway and this is due to dramatically reduced travel times which permitted the first large-scale separation of workplace and residence.

The cross-city study by Gonzalez-Navarro and Turner (2018) is interested in how metros affected population across the world's cities for 60 years. They find that metros have an economically insignificant effect on urban population growth; however, the introduction of subways cause cities to decentralize.

There is a growing interest in the spatial distribution of the impact as well. Ahlfeldt and Feddersen (2018) finds for the German high-speed rail that the spillover effect declines by 50% with every 30 min of travel time and diminishes to 1% after 200 minutes. Hodgson (2018) estimates the impact of railroad construction on the spatial distribution of towns in the American West in the late 19th century. His results imply that railroads generated an agglomeration shadow, as towns close to the railroads but not directly treated were more likely to decline than those which remained isolated.

4. Transportation project appraisal

Theory and evidence for the benefits of transportation are used to develop and expand methodologies, which aim to quantify these benefits and thus to provide precise calculations for transportation project appraisal. These methods help the efficient allocation of public funds as they aim to calculate all the long-run costs and benefits of the project in a unified framework. This section first briefly reviews the history of project appraisal with a focus on the United Kingdom, and then it shows how user benefits and overall benefit-to-cost ratios are calculated.

The benefit-to-cost ratio of a transportation project has been for long one of the most important determinants for the viability of a project. According to Worsley (2011), benefits were restricted to passenger time savings, including savings in walking and waiting time in the United Kingdom until the late 1980s. The early 1990s brought improvements in appraisal methodology, which made it possible to estimate crowding levels and consider this disutility in calculations. Benefits for those transport users who switched mode and thus reduced road congestion were also included. In 1996, the British government asked for advice on the relationship between transport and the economy from the Standing Advisory Committee (Department of the Environment Transport and the Regions, 1999). That time policymakers were debating whether the Jubilee Line Extension in East London should be continued after multiple delays and escalating costs. Conventional methods—valued travel times savings, changes in transportation operating costs and operator revenues—were amended with a reduction in the variability of travel times and environmental costs. The resulting method works well in a setting where prices for transport are close to the marginal cost of travel based on the assumption of perfect competition. However, as the previous section showed, transportation improvements provide extensive externalities which are not borne by the direct user of the improvement.

In 2006, the Eddington report (HMSO, 2006) refined transport appraisal methods further, with emphasis on the role of transportation in sustaining productivity and competitiveness. The Department of Transportation's 2005 paper "Transport, Wider Economic Benefits and Impacts on GDP" (Department for Transport, 2005) identified four sources of market imperfection that had the potential to influence the level of welfare benefits. These four were the potential for providing agglomeration externalities by changing the effective density of an area; increasing competition in the market due to the transport project; imperfect competition in transportation markets changes the values of estimated transport cost savings, and; by changing the cost of joining the labor market increasing the labor supply through two channels: increase in the number of people employed and existing workers shifting to more productive jobs. Appraisal methodology has developed further since; however, it still uses the principles formulated in the Eddington report (HMSO, 2006).

Venables (2016) argues that appraisals should not be context-specific. He argues that building a structural model for some large projects may make sense. However, this is not a general solution as it is expensive to build a specific model for every transport project and it holds the risk that the same model would be mechanically applied in a different setting with insufficient attention to detail. He argues that the transport appraisal methodology has to be independent of context, and high-quality empirical evidence has to quantify the mechanisms. Forecasting the true social costs and benefits of the project is challenging, as double-counting should be avoided while adding up different components; moreover, the model should be exhaustive (a positive impact may cause a negative impact elsewhere, and both have to be accounted for).

4.1 User benefits of transportation

Venables et al. (2015) provides an excellent overview of the effects of a transport improvement (see Fig. 4). A new investment saves time and other costs

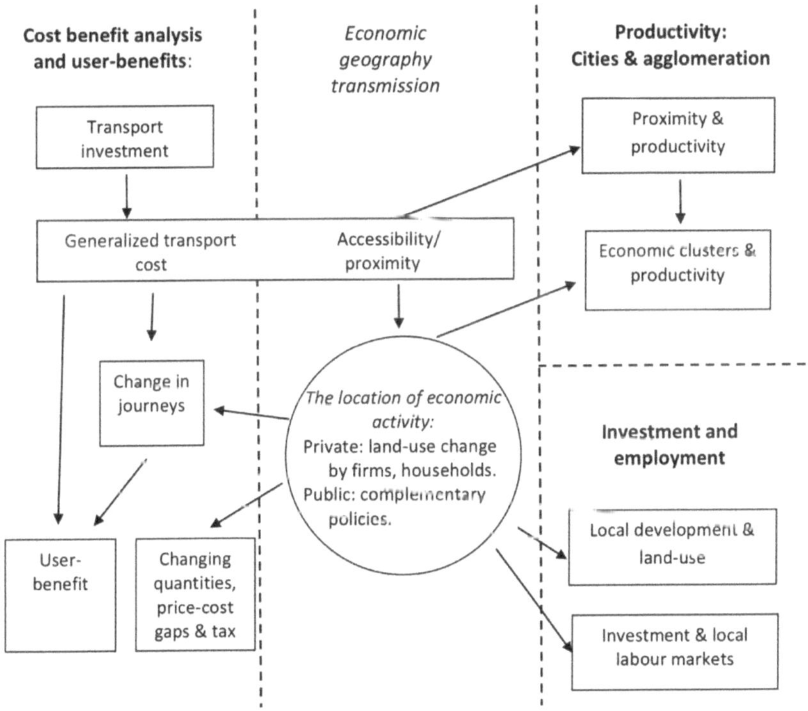

Fig. 4 The effects of a transport improvement (Venables et al., 2015).

to users of the transport network, whether they are individuals, households or firms. These changes in the generalized cost of transportation change traffic flows, increasing flows at one part of the network but ideally decreasing elsewhere. These changes in journeys lead to user benefits, which usually constitute the largest part of benefits. Transport investments also change accessibility in the economy, which lead to changes in land use patterns: some sectors of the economy benefit, some may lose, and the reorganization leads to many changes: changing locations of activity (firms and households) lead to changes in traffic flows and taxation of activity. At the same time, reorganization creates winner areas where growing investment levels and developing local labor markets induce more intensive local development. Some areas may even lose due to displacement. The third impact of reorganization is that the economy clusters, which leads to increased productivity through agglomeration economies (see the next section on the wider economic benefits of transportation). Besides, increased accessibility has a direct, nonreorganizational impact on proximity as well, leading to increased productivity of labor and firms.

As Graham and Gibbons (2017) put it, direct user benefits capture the benefits of the scheme for new and existing users of the transport system as well. As the generalized cost of travel falls or the quality of service increases due to the project, there is a change in journeys and users benefit. It is important to note that much of the effects are transmitted to the nonusers of the network: for instance, part of the benefit from cutting travel times is transferred to landlords through increased rent, or firms transfer their benefits to their consumers through increased quality or decreased cost.

Evaluations use sophisticated land use and transportation (LUTI) models to forecast changes in traffic flows in the network. These models are mostly based on travel surveys and transport modeling, and they predict changes in the number of journeys and the mode choice caused by the transportation scheme. Atkins (2013) found that around 25% of the appraisals forecasted traffic flow changes inaccurately, and 40% of the errors were due to an incorrect prediction of land use changes caused by the scheme. This shows the importance of understanding how changes in transportation change the location choice of firms and people even for direct user benefits.

Graham (2017) explains that an ex-ante CBA process first defines alternative projects which can be compared based on their aims and cost-to-benefit ratios. The next step models the impact of the projects on the transport network: how demand for certain modes would change, whether travel times are affected, how costs of using the network change, whether there is decreased risk of accidents, how the environment is affected, and many more impacts depending on the project. The results of the modeling exercise are then monetized, and their costs and benefits are calculated for stakeholders. Transport users are impacted through fares, travel times, safety and quality. Transport operators are impacted via investment, operating costs and revenues. Nonusers of the intervention are impacted through accidents, environmental impacts and other externalities. The wider economy is affected through changes in the size of agglomeration, competition and labor markets. Also, the government is affected through taxes, subsidies, and other policy tools. After all the costs and benefits are calculated for all the stakeholders, these have to be extrapolated for a fitting time frame and then discounted to present values. In the end, these discounted present values can be used to decide which alternative should be chosen to maximize social welfare.

User benefits are calculated using a simple microeconomic framework (see chapter XX for more details). The aim is to calculate either the net present value (*NPV*) or the benefit-to-cost ratio (*BCR*) of the scheme:

$$NPV = PVB - PVC \tag{3}$$

$$BCR = PVB/PVC \tag{4}$$

The net present value shows in monetary terms all the benefits which will be created by the scheme, whereas the benefit-to-cost ratio shows how the costs and benefits compare to each other. There are minimum acceptable BCRs defined for different project types (which are typically higher than 1).

Under conditions of perfect condition, constant returns to scale and no market failures, all welfare impacts of the transport scheme are captured by direct user benefits. This means that even if the project changes prices in the economy, this will be a net effect: a transfer between users and nonusers. Housing prices and land values generally increase after the opening of a new transport project, increasing the welfare of the nonuser landowner. This should not be included in the CBA calculation if the user tenant already accrued the benefit: the housing market transfers the welfare benefit to the landlord; however, this increase equals the benefit that the user received due to decreased generalized costs of travel. Including the landowner's benefit would lead to double-counting of benefits and thus, to overestimating overall welfare benefits.

5. The wider economic benefits of transportation

Wider economic benefits arise due to market failures in the economy and thus are additional to direct user benefits. Transport investments enhance proximity which induce agglomeration externalities, generally leading to benefits for firms and workers. Moreover, households and firms may relocate to change job markets or suppliers after the intervention.

As it was discussed in the introduction, the additionality of WEBs to DUBs is often debated, even though the theory defines clearly that introducing WEBs do not lead to the double-counting of benefits. As I have discussed in the previous section, wider economic benefits are not synonymous to impacts on nontransport markets (like the landowners' benefits) but are rather additional benefits arising from the market failures of imperfect competition, nonconstant returns to scale and externalities. The calculation of changes in consumer surplus due to DUB assumes the absence of these market failures, and the calculation for WEBs shown in this chapter stem exclusively from the presence of these failures.

According to Graham and Gibbons (2017), the three most important WEBs are imperfect competition, tax revenues, and agglomeration economies. Imperfect competition benefits are welfare gains arising from increasing competition in monopolistic markets. A fall in the generalized cost of transportation decreases the cost of interaction between economic actors, which may lead to expanding output. A welfare gain is achieved if the marginal willingness to pay for increased output is higher than the cost of producing it in a monopolistic market. Tax revenues for the government are increased if economic agents become more productive and thus pay more tax. The location choices of firms and workers change due to the transport scheme, and this reorganization leads to labor market gains: workers move to more productive areas or increase their participation rate, which results in productivity benefits. Most of these benefits are captured by DUBs (in rents for example); however, increased tax revenues to the state are WEBs (mostly through income tax, national insurance contributions or corporate tax).

Graham and Gibbons (2017) explain how increased provision of transportation determines agglomeration via increased access to economic mass. Transport constraints reduce the extent of agglomeration, and increased access changes the effective scale of access to economic activity for agents, which makes them more productive (Venables, 2007).

As a first step, an investigation calculates how access to economic mass is affected. The methodology uses the effective density (ED) function Eq. (1), where often employment is chosen as economic mass, and as a function of distance either simple geographical distance, mode-specific travel times or generalized costs. This measure incorporates an implicit transport network dimension and captures the effects of both scale and spatial proximity. Ideally, such ED is calculated for small spatial zones and they are free of arbitrary administrative boundaries.

The next step is to estimate agglomeration elasticities, ideally for small spatial blocks and different sectors of the economy. The theory builds on standard microeconomics and starts with a production function:

$$y_i = f(\rho_i, Z_i), \tag{5}$$

where y_i is the output of a firm, ρ_i is its access to economic mass (often proxied with effective density, Eq. (1)) and Z_i is a vector of variables representing all other variables which have an impact on output. The current methodology does not use firm-level predictions. Instead, it calculates for regions as unit of analysis. As Venables et al. (2015) noted, this makes sense since there is a trade-off between the specificity of the model and its cost. This means that the model is interested in how average productivity in an area is affected by the transport investment. Estimating productivity for firms or workers is a separate economic discipline and sophisticated control function semiparametric techniques are advised to be used (for more on this, see Van Beveren, 2012); therefore, most empirical investigations are interested in how the previously estimated productivity metric is impacted by a change in the access to economic mass:

$$\omega_i = f(\rho_i, Z_i), \tag{6}$$

where overall productivity is ω_i and ρ_i is taken as a productivity shifter. WEB calculations are interested in how a certain area is affected; therefore, usually, the unit of observation is not an individual economic actor (a firm or a worker), but an area. The shift in productivity caused by increasing the level of access to economic mass for area i can be calculated as

$$\partial \log \omega_i = \sum_{i=1}^{n} \epsilon_{\omega,\rho} * \partial \log \rho_i \tag{7}$$

where $\epsilon_{\omega,\rho}$ is the elasticity of production with respect to a change in access to economic mass (the agglomeration elasticity), the wider economic benefit of a transport project can thus be calculated by using an appropriate measure as agglomeration elasticity ($\epsilon_{\omega,\rho}$) and predicting the change in effective density ($\partial \log \rho_i$) and summing their products for all affected spatial areas. It is important to stress that these benefits are additional to direct user benefits as through the agglomeration benefits channel all workers in the area are affected, not just the users of the transport project.

Investigating Eq. (7) further shows the difference between static and dynamic agglomeration effects (or level 2 and level 3 in the UK webTAG framework). Substituting ρ_i to Eq. (7) yields:

$$\partial \log \omega_i = \sum_{i=1}^{n} \epsilon_{\omega,\rho} \left[\sum_{i=1}^{n} \epsilon_{\rho_i,g_{ij}} \partial \log g_{ij} + \sum_{i=1}^{n} \epsilon_{\rho_i,m_j} \partial \log m_j \right] \tag{8}$$

where the first part ($\epsilon_{\rho_i,g_{ij}} \partial \log g_{ij}$) shows the static agglomeration effect: a transport investment decreases the generalized cost of travel between two areas, which leads to increased access to economic mass. This change in generalized cost can be forecasted with a transport model. The second part ($\epsilon_{\rho_i,m_j} \partial \log m_j$) is the dynamic agglomeration effect: the transport investment induces the spatial reorganization of economic activity and population. If this reorganization leads to increased economic mass access to economic mass, the area benefits from agglomeration externalities. Some areas may also experience a decrease in economic mass, which leads to decreased access, and this decreases productivity benefits. Dynamic agglomeration effects can be forecasted by spatial econometric models like Pogonyi et al. (2019).

Some studies investigate the wider economic benefits of transportation to provide better evidence for project appraisal. Graham et al. (2009) estimate various econometric methods to provide agglomeration parameter values for the UK appraisal methodology. Graham (2007a) applies agglomeration elasticity calculations on the London CrossRail scheme. He uses a methodology similar to Venables (2007) and studies how externalities would affect the projected benefits of investment. His calculations show that agglomeration benefits due to CrossRail increase the welfare to the society by 25% (3.1 billion pounds, from 12.8 billion to 15.9).

Gibbons et al. (2010) investigate the relationship between improved accessibility and increased productivity. Their firm-level research analyses all road schemes which were completed between 1998 and 2003 in England. They find no significant effect of increased accessibility on productivity; however, they claim that this is due to the very small average impact of transport projects on agglomeration—road schemes increased effective density by 1.8% on average within 10 km of the project.

Gibbons et al. (2016) use a measure of accessibility based on generalized costs, and their approach makes a distinction between road and rail accessibility. Their wage equation is estimated using microdata on individuals, which is a more precise measure than usual estimates based on regional aggregates. They use wage data for the UK (the Annual Survey of Hours and Earnings database) and control for a wide variety of worker characteristics and fixed effects in order to obtain precise productivity estimates. Their rail measure captures accessibility at an aggregate regional level, whereas road accessibility is defined on a more local level. They find that the agglomeration elasticity using car accessibility is slightly higher (0.069) than rail (0.049); however, they are not significantly different from each other.

The estimated agglomeration elasticities can be used to calculate the wider economic benefits of a transport scheme. There are many different ways to estimate WEBs; here I show only how the UK WebTAG methodology suggests this (for a review, see Graham, 2017). They use the same underlying TFP model as 6 and calculate economic density as:

$$\rho_i^g = \frac{1}{n}\sum_{j=1}^{n}\frac{m_j}{g_{ij}^{\alpha}} = \frac{1}{n}\sum_{j=1}^{n}\rho_{ij}^g, \tag{9}$$

where ρ_i is economic density for area i, n is the number of areas, m_j is economic mass (often employment) in area j and g_ij is the generalized cost between areas i and j. This equation can be used to estimate elasticities between agglomeration and generalized costs, and agglomeration and economic mass:

$$\eta_{\rho_i^g, \log g_{ij}} = -\frac{\alpha \rho_{ij}^g}{n \rho_i^g} \tag{10}$$

$$\eta_{\rho_i^g, \log m_j} = \frac{1}{n}\frac{\rho_{ij}^g}{\rho_i^g}. \tag{11}$$

The WebTAG calculation uses both a geographical distance-based ED and an average generalized cost-based ED. Changes in the transport system are proxied by the elasticity which uses generalized costs (ρ^g), but this elasticity was actually empirically estimated with a geographical distance-based ED(ρ^D). Holding all other variables constant, the total proportional change in productivity can thus be calculated as

$$\mathrm{d}\log\omega = \sum_{i=1}^{n} \frac{\partial \log \omega}{\partial \log \rho_i^D} \mathrm{d}\log\rho_i^g = \sum_{i=1}^{n} \eta_{\omega,\rho^D} \mathrm{d}\log\rho_i^g, \tag{12}$$

and the total proportional change in ED thus can be decomposed to "static" and "dynamic" components:

$$\mathrm{d}\log\rho_i^g = \sum_{j=i}^{n} \frac{\partial \log \rho_i^g}{\partial \log m_j} \mathrm{d}\log m_j + \sum_{j=1}^{n} \frac{\partial \log \rho_i^g}{\partial \log g_{ij}} \mathrm{d}\log g_{ij}. \tag{13}$$

"Static" agglomeration calculations assume that the spatial distribution of economic mass does not change due to the new infrastructure, and thus they assume that the first part of Eq. (13) equals zero (as $d\log m_j = 0$). However, changes in the transport infrastructure lead to a significant redistribution of activity; therefore, for precise calculations, the whole equation has to be calculated.

The calculation of WEBs thus equals

$$\mathrm{d}\log\omega = \sum_{i=1}^{n} \eta_{\omega,\rho^D} \left[\sum_{j=1}^{n} \eta_{\rho_i^g,\log m_j} \mathrm{d}\log m_j + \sum_{j=1}^{n} \eta_{\rho_i^{g_{ij}}} \mathrm{d}\log g_{ij} \right]. \tag{14}$$

The WebTAG methodology balances between being too specific and being too general as even though it uses the literature average for agglomeration elasticity (η_{ω,ρ^D}), all other components are calculated from the project-specific dataset. Graham (2017) recommend accounting for probable heterogeneity in agglomeration effects: Graham and van Dender (2011) show that agglomeration effects can be sharply different for different levels of conurbations. The results of these WEB calculations should be added to DUBs, extrapolated for the length of the project and then all the costs and benefits should be discounted to present value (see the previous section for details).

6. Literature gaps and future directions

This chapter briefly reviewed the literature on the wider economic benefits of transportation. There are several literature gaps in this field. A gap is that the current WEB methodology provides results for fairly large spatial areas, and this leads to imprecise estimation; moreover, the urban displacement impact predicted by Redding and Turner (2015) cannot be detected at such a scale. A second gap is that the current WEB methodology does not account for the displacement effect explicitly and uses regional averages instead of smaller spatial scales. New data available for small spatial areas should enable studies building robust, empirical evidence-driven spatial models. The third gap is that there has not been much attention to other, non-Marshallian agglomeration economies, for example, crime or air pollution may significantly reduce people's access to economic mass.

The data revolution provides more and more precise data for spatial models, and this may be one of the reasons why there is an increased interest in urban economics (Gabriel Ahlfeldt's spatial model which studies the spatial reorganization of Berlin (Ahlfeldt et al., 2015) was the first ever urban economics paper which received the prestigious Frisch Medal by the Econometric Society in 2018 (The Econometric Society, 2018)). In addition to increased computational abilities and the growing public interest in cities; high-quality micro-geographic data make such research possible and relevant. New data provides an opportunity to study the usual topics of transport and urban economics with more precision.

The general interest in social inequality inspired the work of Tsivanidis (2018). His paper takes a step beyond estimating the treatment effect for the average citizen of a transport intervention, as it estimates how the gains are shared between low- and high-skilled workers. These results are important in assessing the overall welfare impact of transportation; moreover, they provide essential, evidence-based insights about benefits and costs, which can be used in policy debates.

More weight is put in policy debates on the developing world; moreover, this interest has been growing even more rapidly for large metropolitan areas. Urban and transport economics have already provided several innovative approaches for generating data and answering policy-relevant questions. Pinkovskiy et al. (2014) combined satellite-recorded night-time lights with household survey-based income per capita data to calculate precise income per capita measures for the developing world and its regions. Akbar et al. (2018) use the Google Directions API to estimate city level vehicular mobility indices and apply it to 154 Indian cities. Moreover, Gonzalez-Navarro and Turner (2018) construct panel data that describe all of the world's subway networks (632 cities) for sixty years, which enables them to understand the long-run effects of metros on city growth.

References

Ahlfeldt, G.M., 2011. The train has left the station: do markets value intracity access to intercity rail connections? German Econ. Rev. 12 (3), 312–335. https://doi.org/10.1111/j.1468-0475.2010.00521.x.

Ahlfeldt, G.M., Feddersen, A., 2018. From periphery to core: measuring agglomeration effects using high-speed rail. J. Econ. Geogr. 18 (2), 355–390. https://doi.org/10.1093/jeg/lbx005.

Ahlfeldt, G.M., Pietrostefani, E., 2019. The economic effects of density: a synthesis. In: International Trade and Regional Economics (DP13440). Centre for Economic Policy Research, London School of Economics and Political Science.

Ahlfeldt, G.M., Redding, S.J., Sturm, D.M., Wolf, N., 2015. The economics of density: evidence from the Berlin wall. Econometrica 83 (6), 2127–2189. https://doi.org/10.3982/ECTA10876.

Akbar, P., Couture, V., Duranton, G., Storeygard, A., 2018. Mobility and Congestion in Urban India. National Bureau of Economic Research, Cambridge, MA.

Alonso, W., 1964. Location and Land Use. Toward a General Theory of Land Rent. Harvard University Press, Cambridge, MA, p. 204.

Arzaghi, M., Henderson, J.V., 2008. Networking off Madison avenue. Rev. Econ. Stud. 75 (4), 1011–1038. https://doi.org/10.1111/j.1467-937X.2008.00499.x.

Aschauer, D.A., 1990. Why is infrastructure important? In: Conference Series [Proceedings]. vol. 34. Federal Reserve Bank, Boston, pp. 21–68.

Atkins, 2013. Post opening project evaluation of major schemes meta-analysis. In: Main Report. Report to the Highways Agency, https://www.gov.uk/government/collections/post-opening-project-evaluation-pope-of-major-schemes.

Banerjee, A., Duflo, E., Qian, N., 2012. On the Road: Access to Transportation Infrastructure and Economic Growth in China. National Bureau of Economic Research, Cambridge, MA. http://www.nber.org/papers/w17897.pdf.

Baum-Snow, N., 2007. Did highways cause suburbanization? Q. J. Econ. 122 (2), 775–805. https://doi.org/10.1162/qjec.122.2.775.

Baum-Snow, N., 2017. Urban Transport Expansions, Employment Decentralization, and the Spatial Scope of Agglomeration Economies. Technical report. https://www.brown.edu/Departments/Economics/Faculty/Matthew_Turner/ec2410/readings/BaumSnow_unp_2017.pdf.

Baum-Snow, N., Brandt, L., Henderson, J.V., Turner, M.A., Zhang, Q., 2017. Roads, railroads, and decentralization of Chinese cities. Rev. Econ. Stat. 99 (3), 435–448. https://doi.org/10.1162/REST_a_00660.

Billings, S.B., 2011. Estimating the value of a new transit option. Reg. Sci. Urban Econ. 41 (6), 525–536. https://doi.org/10.1016/J.REGSCIURBECO.2011.03.013.

Carbo, J.M., Graham, D.J., Anupriya, C.D., Melo, P.C., Anupriya, 2018. Evaluating the causal economic impacts of transport investments: evidence from the Madrid–Barcelona high speed rail corridor. J. Appl. Stat. 46 (9), 1714–1723.

Chandra, A., Thompson, E., 2000. Does public infrastructure affect economic activity?: evidence from the rural interstate highway system. Reg. Sci. Urban Econ. 30 (4), 457–490. http://www.sciencedirect.com/science/article/pii/S0166046200000405.

Ciccone, A., Hall, R., 1993. Productivity and the Density of Economic Activity. National Bureau of Economic Research, Cambridge, MA. http://www.nber.org/papers/w4313.pdf.

Combes, P.-P., 2000. Marshall-Arrow-Romer Externalities and City Growth. CERAS working paper no. 99-06, http://www.enpc.fr/ceras/combes/.

Combes, P.-P., Mayer, T., Thisse, J.-F., 2008. Economic Geography: The Integration of Regions and Nations. Princeton University Press, ISBN: 0691139423, p. 399.

Department for Transport, 2005. Transport, Wider Economic Benefits and Impacts on GDP. http://webarchive.nationalarchives.gov.uk/+/http:/www.dft.gov.uk/pgr/economics/rdg/webia/webmethodology/sportwidereconomicbenefi3137.pdf.
Department for Transport, 2017. Transport Analysis Guidance: WebTAG. https://www.gov.uk/guidance/transport-analysis-guidance-webtag.
Department for Transport, 2019. Transport analysis guidance—GOV.UK. https://www.gov.uk/guidance/transport-analysis-guidance-webtag.
Department of the Environment Transport and the Regions, 1999. Transport and the economy (SACTRA). http://webarchive.nationalarchives.gov.uk/20050301192906/http:/dft.gov.uk/stellent/groups/dft_econappr/documents/pdf/dft_econappr_pdf_022512.pdf.
Di Addario, S., Patacchini, E., 2008. Wages and the city. Evidence from Italy. Labour Econ. 15 (5), 1040–1061. https://doi.org/10.1016/J.LABECO.2007.09.003.
Donaldson, D., Hornbeck, R., 2013. Railroads and American Economic Growth: A "Market Access" Approach. National Bureau of Economic Research, Cambridge, MA. http://www.nber.org/papers/w19213.pdf.
Duranton, G., Puga, D., 2000. Nursery cities: urban diversity, process innovation, and the life cycle of products. Am. Econ. Rev. 91 (5), 1454–1477.
Duranton, G., Puga, D., 2004. Micro-foundations of urban agglomeration economies. In: Henderson, J.V., Thisse, J.F. (Eds.), first ed. Handbook of Regional and Urban Economics, vol. 4. Elsevier, pp. 2063–2117. (Chapter 48).
Duranton, G., Turner, M.A., 2012. Urban Growth and Transportation. Rev. Econ. Stud. 79 (4), 1407–1440. https://doi.org/10.1093/restud/rds010.
EBRD, 2018. Additionality in the EBRD—review of concept and application. Evaluation Cooperation Group. https://www.ecgnet.org/document/additionality-ebrd-%E2%80%93-review-concept-and-application.
Faber, B., 2014. Trade integration, market size, and industrialization: evidence from China's national trunk highway system. Rev. Econ. Stud. 81 (3), 1046–1070. https://doi.org/10.1093/restud/rdu010.
Fujita, M., Thisse, J. F., 2002. Agglomeration and Market Interaction. https://papers.ssrn.com/sol3/papers.cfm?abstract_id=315966.
Garcia-López, M.-A., Holl, A., Viladecans-Marsal, E., 2015. Suburbanization and highways in Spain when the Romans and the Bourbons still shape its cities. J. Urban Econom. 85 (C), 52–67. https://doi.org/10.1016/j.jue.2014.11.002.
Garcia-Mila, T., McGuire, T.J., 1992. The contribution of publicly provided inputs to states' economies. Reg. Sci. Urban Econ. 22 (2), 229–241. http://www.sciencedirect.com/science/article/pii/016604629290013Q.
Gibbons, S., Machin, S., 2005. Valuing rail access using transport innovations. J. Urban Econom. 57 (1), 148–169. https://doi.org/10.1016/J.JUE.2004.10.002.
Gibbons, S., Overman, H.G., Lyytikäinen, T., Laird, J., 2010. Evaluating the productivity impacts of road transport schemes: report on pilot study findings. https://www.researchgate.net/publication/48910180_Evaluating_the_productivity_impacts_of_road_transport_schemes_report_on_pilot_study_findings. LSE SERC.
Gibbons, S., Lyytikainen, T., Overman, H.G., Sanchis-Guarner, R., 2016. New road infrastructure: the effects on firms. CEPR Discussion Papers. https://ideas.repec.org/p/cpr/ceprdp/11239.html.
Gibbons, S., Lyytikäinen, T., Overman, H.G., Sanchis-Guarner, R., 2019. New road infrastructure: The effects on firms. J. Urban Econ. 110, 35–50. https://doi.org/10.1016/J.JUE.2019.01.002.
Gonzalez-Navarro, M., Turner, M.A., 2018. Subways and urban growth: evidence from earth. J. Urban Econom. 108, 85–106. https://doi.org/10.1016/J.JUE.2018.09.002.

Graham, D.J., 2007a. Agglomeration, productivity and transport investment on JSTOR. J. Transport Econ. Policy 41 (3), 317–343. http://www.jstor.org/stable/20054024?seq=1#page_scan_tab_contents.

Graham, D.J., 2007b. Variable returns to agglomeration and the effect of road traffic congestion. J. Urban Econ. 62 (1), 103–120. https://doi.org/10.1016/j.jue.2006.10.001.

Graham, D.J., 2017. Inverse demand, consumers surplus and transport appraisal. In: Lecture note, Transport Demand and Economics, Imperial College London.

Graham, D.J., Gibbons, S., 2017. Updating Agglomeration Elasticities: Phase 1a. Technical Report. Department for Transport.

Graham, D.J., Gibbons, S., 2019. Quantifying wider economic impacts of agglomeration for transport appraisal: Existing evidence and future directions. Econ. Transp. 19, 100121. https://doi.org/10.1016/j.ecotra.2019.100121.

Graham, D.J., van Dender, K., 2011. Estimating the agglomeration benefits of transport investments: some tests for stability. Transportation 38 (3), 409–426. https://doi.org/10.1007/s11116-010-9310-0.

Graham, D.J., Gibbons, S., Martin, R., 2009. Transport investment and the distance decay of agglomeration benefits. Report to the Department of Transport. http://personal.lse.ac.uk/GIBBONS/Papers/Agglomeration%20and%20Distance%20Decay%20Jan%202009.pdf.

Harris, C.D., 1954. The market as a factor in the localization of industry in the United States. Ann. Assoc. Am. Geogr. 44 (4), 315–348. https://doi.org/10.1080/00045605409352140.

Heblich, S., Redding, S.J., Sturm, D.M., Couture, V., Dingel, J., Glaeser, E., Henderson, V., Moser, P., Platt-Boustan, L., Strange, W., Steinwender, C., White, J., Wolmar, C., 2018. The making of the modern metropolis: evidence from London. https://personal.lse.ac.uk/sturmd/papers/wp/MMM_7Sept2018_paper.pdf.

HMSO, 2006. The Eddington Transport Study. http://webarchive.nationalarchives.gov.uk/+/http:/www.dft.gov.uk/about/strategy/transportstrategy/eddingtonstudy/.

Hodgson, C., 2018. The effect of transport infrastructure on the location of economic activity: railroads and post offices in the American West. J. Urban Econ. 104, 59–76. https://doi.org/10.1016/J.JUE.2018.01.005.

Holl, A., 2004. Start-ups and relocations: manufacturing plant location in Portugal. Papers Reg. Sci. 83 (4), 649–668. https://doi.org/10.1111/j.1435-5597.2004.tb01932.x.

Holl, A., 2011. Market potential and firm-level productivity in Spain. J. Econ. Geogr. 12, 1191–1215. https://doi.org/10.1093/jeg/lbr030.

Krugman, P.R., 1996. Geography and Trade. Leuven University Press. ISBN: 0262610868, p. 142. https://books.google.co.uk/books?hl=en&lr=&id=AQDodCHOgJYC&oi=fnd&pg=PP7&dq=geography+and+trade+krugman&ots=Pzm-2kGMdr&sig=8G8tCO9pQPlbu8QzdK4rGP3YPrM#v=onepage&q=geography and trade krugman&f=false.

Marshall, A., 1890. Principles of Economics: An Introductory Volume. Palgrave Macmillan UK. http://classnet.yizhong.xm.fj.cn/zyw/up/4030002.PDF.

Marshall, A., 1920. Industry and Trade. http://socserv2.mcmaster.ca/ econ/ugcm/3ll3/marshall/Industry%26Trade.pdf.

Mayer, T., Trevien, C., 2017. The impact of urban public transportation evidence from the Paris region. J. Urban Econ. 102, 1–21. https://doi.org/10.1016/J.JUE.2017.07.003.

Melo, P.C., Graham, D.J., Noland, R.B., 2009. A meta-analysis of estimates of urban agglomeration economies. Regional Sci. Urban Econ. 39 (3), 332–342. https://doi.org/10.1016/j.regsciurbeco.2008.12.002.

McCann, P., 2001. Urban and regional economics. Oxford University Press. https://EconPapers.repec.org/RePEc:oxp:obooks:9780198776451.

Melo, P.C., Graham, D.J., Brage-Ardao, R., 2013. The productivity of transport infrastructure investment: a meta-analysis of empirical evidence. Reg. Sci. Urban Econ. 43 (5), 695–706. https://doi.org/10.1016/j.regsciurbeco.2013.05.002.

Mortensen, D.T., Pissarides, C.A., 1999. New developments in models of search in the labor market. In: Ashenfelter, O.C., Card, D. (Eds.), Handbook of Labor Economics, vol. 3. PartB. http://www.sciencedirect.com/science/article/pii/S1573446399300250.

Moses, L.N., 1958. Location and the theory of production. Q. J. Econ. 72 (2), 259. https://doi.org/10.2307/1880599.

Munnell, A.H., 1992. Policy watch: infrastructure investment and economic growth. J. Econ. Perspect. 6 (4), 189–198. https://doi.org/10.1257/jep.6.4.189.

Pinkovskiy, M., Sala-I-Martin, X., Barro, R., Chakrabarti, R., Crump, R., Deaton, A., Herman, H., Negro, M.D., Van Der Klaauw, W., Lee, D., Meng, K., Notowidigdo, M., Papaioannou, E., Pelech, D., Piketty, T., Rokkanen, M., Sacarny, A., Sheiner, L., Shleifer, A., Steinsson, J., Topa, G., Verhoogen, E., Wolfers, J., Zafar, B., Zhang, C., 2014. Lights, Camera,…Income! Estimating Poverty Using National Accounts, Survey Means, and Lights. NBER Working Papers 19831. National Bureau of Economic Research, Inc.

Pogonyi, C.G., Graham, D.J.M., Carbo, J., 2018. Growth or displacement? A metro Line's causal impact on the spatial distribution of business units and employment: evidence from London. SSRN Electron. J. https://doi.org/10.2139/ssrn.3272152.

Pogonyi, C.G., Graham, D.J., Carbo, J.M., 2019. Metros, agglomeration and firm productivity. Evidence from London. SSRN Electron. J. https://doi.org/10.2139/ssrn.3350505.

Predöhl, A., 1928. The theory of location in its relation to general economics. J. Polit. Econ. 36 (3), 371–390. https://doi.org/10.1086/253950.

Redding, S.J., Turner, M.A., 2015. Transportation costs and the spatial organization of economic activity. Duranton, G., Vernon Henderson, J. (Eds.), Handbook of Regional and Urban Economics. In: vol. 5. Elsevier, pp. 1339–1398. https://doi.org/10.1016/B978-0-444-59531-7.00020-X.

Rice, P., Venables, A.J., Patacchini, E., 2006. Spatial determinants of productivity: analysis for the regions of Great Britain. Reg. Sci. Urban Econ. 36 (6), 727–752. https://doi.org/10.1016/j.regsciurbeco.2006.03.006.

Rosenthal, S.S., Strange, W.C., 2008. The attenuation of human capital spillovers. J. Urban Econom. 64, 373–389. https://doi.org/10.1016/j.jue.2008.02.006.

The Econometric Society, 2018. 2018 Frisch Medal Awarded. https://www.econometricsociety.org/content/2018-frisch-medal-awarded.

Tsivanidis, N., 2018. The aggregate and distributional effects of urban transit infrastructure: evidence from Bogotá's TransMilenio. https://economics.stanford.edu/sites/g/files/sbiybj9386/f/tsivanidis_jmp.pdf.

UK Homes and Communities Agency, 2019. Public Sector Economic Appraisal Guide. https://specificationonline.co.uk/sections/housing/articles/2016-03-23/hca/hca-publish-public-sector-economic-appraisal-guide. Specification Online.

Van Beveren, I., 2012. Total factor productivity estimation: a practical review. J. Econ. Surv. 26 (1), 98–128. https://doi.org/10.1111/j.1467-6419.2010.00631.x.

Venables, A., 2007. Evaluating urban transport improvements: cost-benefit analysis in the presence of agglomeration and income taxation. J. Transp. Econ. Policy 41 (2), 173–188.

Venables, A.J., 2016. Incorporating Wider Economic Impacts Within Cost-Benefit Appraisal. International Transport Forum, Discussion Paper 2016-05. www.itf-oecd.org.

Venables, A.J., Laird, J., Overman, H., 2015. Transport Investment and Economic Performance: Implications for Project Appraisal. Department for Transport. https://assets.publishing.service.gov.uk/government/uploads/system/uploads/attachment_data/file/386126/TIEP_Report.pdf.

Von Thunen, J.H., Hall, P. (Eds.), 1966. The Isolated State. Pergamon Press, Oxford. Translated by C.M. Wartenberg. Edited with an introduction.

Weber, A., 1929. Über den Standort der Industrien, Tübingen, JCB Mohr–English Translation: The Theory of the Location of Industries. Chicago University Press, Chicago.

Worsley, T., 2011. The Evolution of London's Crossrail Scheme and the Development of the Department for Transport's Economic Appraisal Methods. http://www.oecd-ilibrary.org/transport/the-evolution-of-london-s-crossrail-scheme-and-the-development-of-the-department-for-transport-s-economic-appraisal-methods_5kg0prk600jk-en.

CHAPTER SIX

Multi-criteria analysis

Marco Dean*
Bartlett School of Planning, University College London, London, United Kingdom
*Corresponding author: e-mail address: marco.dean@ucl.ac.uk

Contents

Abstract

Multi-criteria analysis (MCA), in the literature also known under the names of multiple-criteria decision-making (MCDM), multiple-criteria decision analysis (MCDA), multi-objective decision analysis (MODA), multiple-attribute decision-making (MADM) or multi-dimensional decision-making (MDDM), comprises various classes of methods, techniques and tools (with different degrees of complexity) which explicitly consider multiple objectives and criteria (or attributes) in decision-making problems. Since the late 20th century, MCA methods have ignited an increasing interest among researchers and practitioners working in a number of fields, including transport policy and planning. The threefold purpose of this chapter, based on a comprehensive examination of the academic and gray literature, is to: (1) provide a brief, yet comprehensive overview of the different MCA methods available; (2) illustrate the current state of the art in the use of MCA in the transport sector; and (3) discuss the potential advantages and limitations of MCA by adopting, as far as possible, a balanced and neutral stance on the subject. This chapter, in particular, contends that while extremely useful for framing and structuring complex problems, MCA is not always a synonym for better and more comprehensive decisions. It also highlights that a fundamental disconnection exists between theory and transport assessment practice, with several methods proposed in the academic literature (*e.g.*, sophisticated MCA methods based on elaborated procedures and advanced mathematical principles, or participatory approaches to MCA grounded

Advances in Transport Policy and Planning, Volume 6
ISSN 2543-0009
https://doi.org/10.1016/bs.atpp.2020.07.001

on rather idealistic assumptions) which are rarely employed in real-world applications. Hence, more dialogue and collaborative research between scholars, practitioners and decision-makers is encouraged to close this gap and develop theoretically robust but also more realistic and pragmatic MCA techniques.

Keywords: Transport projects, Appraisal, Evaluation, Decision-making, Multi-criteria analysis, Participatory multi-criteria analysis

1. Introduction

Ex ante appraisal and *ex post* evaluation have always been part of the planning and decision-making process. However, while until the beginning of the 20th century these steps presented a rather informal character, since the 1930s, the progressive adoption of more rigorous planning procedures has increased the need for formal methods capable of ensuring more systematic (*ex ante* and *ex post*) assessments of both "soft" policies and "hard" plans and projects (Alexander, 2006). Hence, in the course of time, a number of different appraisal and evaluation methods, techniques and tools have been proposed in the attempt to ensure more informed decisions, and, at the same time, embrace new planning paradigms and respond appropriately to sustainable development concerns and other emerging global challenges (Dean, 2018; Dimitriou et al., 2016; Goodman and Hastak, 2006; McAllister, 1982). The existing appraisal and evaluation methods can be classified in several ways (*e.g.*, Faludi and Voogd, 1985; Oliveira and Pinho, 2010; Rogers and Duffy, 2012; Söderbaum, 1998). One of the simplest classification schemes is based on the number of objectives and decision criteria considered in the analysis. From this point of view, it is possible to distinguish between two families of methods, although, as highlighted further below, their boundaries are frequently blurred:

- *Mono-criterion methods*, which assess a given plan against a single and specific objective. This family includes, for instance, cost-benefit analysis (CBA), which assesses a plan primarily against the objective of economic efficiency (as shown by the benefit-cost ratio or the net present value of the plan), by translating all impacts into discounted monetary terms.
- *Multi-criteria methods*, which appraise or evaluate a plan by taking into account (more explicitly than mono-criterion methods) the various dimensions of interest, and the interplay between multiple, often contrasting, objectives, and different decision criteria and metrics.

Hence, contrary to what is commonly believed, multi-criteria analysis (MCA) does not constitute a single specific method. Rather, it should be intended as an umbrella term for a number of different techniques and tools by which multiple objectives and decision criteria (or attributes) can be formally incorporated into the analysis of a problem. MCA is generally assumed to have originated in the fields of mathematics and operational research during the second half of the previous century, with the works of Kuhn and Tucker (1951) and Charnes and Cooper (*e.g.*, Charnes et al., 1955; Charnes and Cooper, 1961) on goal programming which are commonly regarded as one of the major stimuli for the development of MCA methods. However, as pointed out by Köksalan et al. (2011), the real roots of this discipline are much more ancient and are deeply entwined with studies of classical economists and mathematicians, which are also at the origin of CBA. Over the decades, the evolution of MCA has been directly or indirectly influenced by research in different areas of study (*e.g.*, utility and value theories, social choice theory, revealed preference theory, game theory, and fuzzy and rough set theories) so that, presently, the realm of MCA comprises many subfields and different schools of thought (Bana e Costa et al., 1997; Figueira et al., 2005a; Köksalan et al., 2011). Since the late 20th century, MCA methods have ignited a growing interest among both researchers and practitioners working across a range of disciplines. This can be primarily attributed to an ever-greater awareness of the fact that many contemporary planning and policy problems facing society have a multi-dimensional nature and therefore require the careful examination of a variety of different, often conflicting, perspectives and aspects (Giampietro, 2003; Munda, 1995, 2008). MCA has thus progressively gained importance as an appraisal and evaluation approach in a number of fields, including ecology, sustainability and environmental science (Herath and Prato, 2006; Huang et al., 2011; Wang et al., 2009), health care decision-making (Thokala et al., 2016), banking and finance (Aruldoss et al., 2013), urban and regional planning (Nijkamp and Rietveld, 1990; Voogd, 1983) and transport project appraisal and evaluation (Macharis and Bernardini, 2015). A significant contribution to the introduction and diffusion of MCA in the field of land use and transport planning was given, in particular, by Nathaniel Lichfield and Morris Hill, whose studies on appraisal and evaluation methods, conducted between the 1950s and 1970s, culminated in the introduction of the Planning Balance Sheet (Lichfield, 1956, 1960, 1966, 1969), later expanded and renamed as

Community Impact Evaluation (Lichfield, 1996), and the Goal-Achievement Matrix (Hill, 1966, 1968, 1973). These methods, which at that time became soon regarded as the foremost challengers to the long-established CBA, can be considered to have represented a sort of benchmark for many other MCA techniques and approaches proposed in this field over the course of time (Dean, 2018; Dimitriou et al., 2016). Against this backdrop, this chapter, drawing on a comprehensive analysis of the academic and gray literature, has a threefold objective. Firstly, it seeks to bring order to this "methodological chaos" by providing a brief, yet comprehensive overview of the different MCA methods available. Secondly, it aims at illustrating the current state of the art in the use and application of MCA in the transport sector, highlighting differences between theory and practice. Thirdly, it also attempts to discuss the potential advantages and limitations of MCA by adopting, as far as possible, a balanced and neutral perspective so as to break down clichés and false beliefs on the subject.

The chapter consists of six further sections. Section 2 describes the main elements and features of MCA. Section 3 offers an examination of the key principles and theoretical foundations of the most widely known MCA methods, while Section 4 illustrates the MCA tools and techniques which are used by practitioners in transport project appraisal and evaluation. Section 5 analyses the strengths and weaknesses of MCA. Section 6 focuses on participatory MCA methods, which, especially over the past two decades, have been devised and promoted by many scholars with the view to producing more thorough, transparent and democratic assessments of transport policies and projects. Finally, Section 7 concludes the chapter by highlighting its key insights and outlining future research needs in this area.

2. Key elements of multi-criteria analysis

Decisions on transport projects, especially the major ones, always involve difficult trade-offs between multiple and divergent criteria due to the complexity of the problem at hand (Dean, 2018). Indeed, first of all, large-scale transport projects rarely constitute single, stand-alone pieces of infrastructure. Rather, in many cases, they assume the features of complex programs of different projects, framed as a single unitary package, and planned and constructed under a unique policy umbrella (Dimitriou et al., 2012). As a case in point, a high-speed railway line generally consists of different sections connecting different cities along the route. Usually, it also provides interconnections to other existing railway lines, thus complementing and integrating other transport networks, at different scales. The construction of the line involves a series of sub-projects such as bridges or tunnels and is also associated with the redevelopment or construction of new stations. The latter, in turn, can spawn important urban regeneration schemes. Ultimately, the new transport corridor may even function as a backbone for the whole territory, fostering wider social, economic, and political development strategies. Secondly, it must be noted that every infrastructure investment produces numerous and diverse consequences. Some of these consequences are planned, desirable and beneficial, whereas others are not. Hence, while promising great benefits, major transport projects require high capital investment costs (and thus are extremely likely to result in a lack of resources for other societal needs) and unavoidably imply substantial adverse impacts in the form, for example, of severe disruptions for people, and degradation, loss and isolation of wildlife habitats. Typically, then, such benefits and costs are distributed unevenly over space and time and this contributes to create or exacerbate social imbalances between population groups. Finally, it should not be forgotten that decisions on transport projects as well as on other major planning and policy problems are embedded in a world of various and competing interests, where, most of the time, the objectives and priorities of the various stakeholder groups can hardly be reconciled or aligned with each other. For such problems MCA can thus constitute a useful decision-support model, which can help analysts and policy-makers master large amount of complex and contrasting data and advance toward a solution.

As illustrated in the previous section, the MCA literature covers a high number of methods (and several variants of the standard methods) accounting for multiple objectives and decision criteria. Already in the 1980s, a review undertaken by Despotin et al. (1983) identified more than a hundred different MCA approaches Although these methods can differ even substantially from one another, many of them have certain aspects in common and exhibit a framework which includes the following key elements:

- *Option*: alternative course of actions proposed in order to address a perceived problem and achieve an overarching end result.
- *Objective*: specific goal against which any proposed option is being assessed. Objectives are usually clustered around different overarching appraisal and evaluation dimensions (*e.g.*, sustainability policy problems generally include the economic, environmental and social dimensions).

Given the arbitrariness of these dimensions, often, however, the same objectives can be easily allocated to different dimensions.

- *Criterion*: specific measurable indicators of the performance of an option in relation to an objective, which allows measuring the extent to which an option meets that objective. For instance, the objective of "promoting economic growth" can be measured through a criterion such as the "GDP growth rate" (see Table 1). In principle, however, any objective may imply a number of different criteria (another possible criterion for assessing growth maximization is, for example, the actual individual consumption per capita). It is possible to distinguish between quantitative indicators, measuring the performances of an option in a numerical fashion (*e.g.*, monetary units or bio-physical units), and qualitative indicators, containing a (qualitative) description of the performance of the option.
- *Performance score*: constructed measure pertaining to a given scale (*e.g.*, a 0 to 1 scale, a 1 to 100 scale or a −5 to 5 scale) which identifies the performance of an option against a specific objective/criterion.

Table 1 Examples of objectives and associated criteria.

Appraisal/ evaluation dimensions	Objectives	Possible appraisal/evaluation criteria
Economic	To promote economic growth	GDP growth rate
	To improve the accessibility of an area	Access cost indicator
Environmental	To minimize the adverse effects on local air quality	Change of CO_2 emissions across the local area/region/country in a given period
	To promote modal shift from private vehicles to trains	Number or portion of automobile trips shifted to train mode
Social	To protect the archeological and cultural heritage of an area	[Qualitative descriptions of the impacts produced by a project/plan on the archeological/cultural resources of the area]
	To provide adequate public transport service in an area	Public transport accessibility level of the area

Author's own elaboration.

High-performing options are ascribed high scores, while low-performing options score lower on the scale. Critical objectives and criteria may also be assigned some constraints in the form of specific threshold values, which place some restrictions concerning the worst acceptable performance of an option against those criteria (Nijkamp and Ouwersloot, 1997). Threshold values can be set in compliance with policy targets and legal instruments, scientific criteria, which identify limits to natural processes and systems, or ethical standards (Rosenberger, 2001).

- *Criterion weight*: coefficient which is commonly intended to represent the level of importance of an objective and corresponding criterion relatively to the other objectives and criteria under consideration (*i.e.*, high-importance objectives and criteria are identified with high weights). The actual meaning of weights can, however, change substantially according to the different MCA methods adopted (Belton and Stewart, 2002; Bouyssou et al., 2000; Munda, 2008).

Typically, in a multi-criteria decision-making problem one or more project options are assessed against a number of different objectives, for which a set of criteria have been identified. The performances of an option against the various objectives and criteria, which can be assigned different weights, are identified by scores. Overall, what formally defines a multi-criteria method is the set of rules establishing the nature of options, objectives, criteria, scores and weights as well as the way in which objectives/criteria, scores and weights are used to assess, compare, screen in/out or rank options.

3. Classification of multi-criteria analysis methods

Given the deep variety of MCA methods developed over the years, the identification of a comprehensive scheme of classification, mapping all the existing techniques and systematically capturing their similarities and differences remains problematic. In the course of time, a number of different (partial) taxonomies have been suggested (*e.g.*, Belton and Stewart, 2002; Ishizaka and Nemery, 2013; Janssen and Munda, 1999; Kodikara, 2008; Munda, 1995; Rogers et al., 2000; Rogers and Duffy, 2012; Roy, 1996; Zardari et al., 2015). The belonging (or not) of a method to a specific category within a given classification system is not always obvious and can easily become the object of a fierce dispute among experts. The classification proposed by Dean (2018) and illustrated in Fig. 1 is particularly convenient for the purpose of this paper. According to this classification

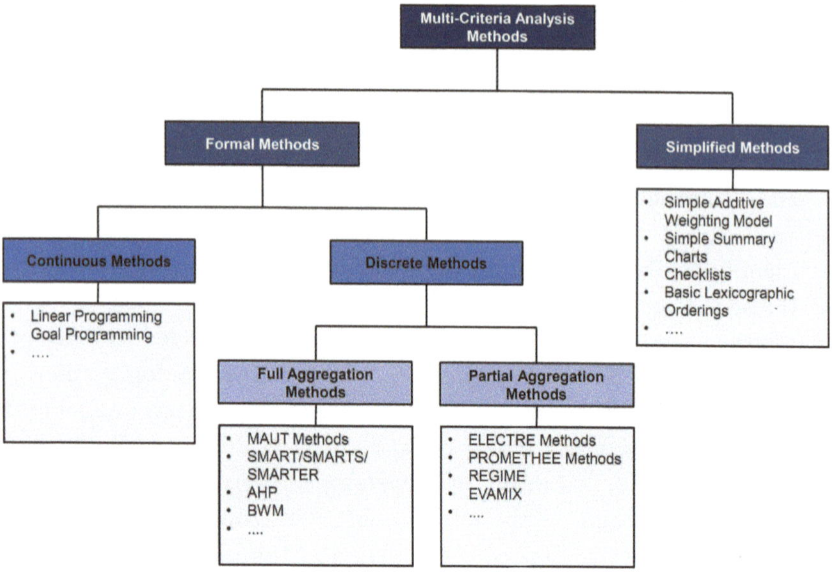

Fig. 1 Classification of MCA methods. *Adapted from Dean, M., 2018. Assessing the Applicability of Participatory Multi-Criteria Analysis Methodologies to the Appraisal of Mega Transport Infrastructure. Ph.D. Dissertation. The Bartlett School of Planning, University College London, UK. (https://www.academia.edu/43180035/Assessing_the_Applicability_of_Participatory_Multi-Criteria_Analysis_Methodologies_to_the_Appraisal_of_Mega_Transport_Infrastructure).*

scheme, a first important distinction has to be made between *formal* and *simplified* methods. Formal MCA methods (illustrated briefly in Section 3.1) are based on elaborated procedures, a number of rather rigorous (although often arbitrary) rules and, sometimes, also on advanced mathematical principles. Computer support is also often needed to implement such methods, which, however, are still susceptible to inaccuracies and errors. A comprehensive examination of formal MCA methods can be found in many books and textbooks (*e.g.*, Belton and Stewart, 2002; Bouyssou et al., 2006; Chankong and Haimes, 1983; Figueira et al., 2005b; Ishizaka and Nemery, 2013; Roy, 1996; Triantaphyllou, 2000; Vincke, 1992), which, however, are not easily readable and understandable by the general readers. By contrast, simplified methods (presented in Section 3.2) entails simple and frequently rough MCA applications.

Despite the great variety of approaches may be seen as a strong point of MCA, this "methodological chaos" often creates several critical dilemmas. Practical applications have demonstrated that, when applied to the same decision-making situation, different methods typically lead to different results (*e.g.*, Banihabib et al., 2017; Bouyssou et al., 2000; Jeffreys, 2004; Roy and Bouyssou, 1986; Triantaphyllou, 2000; Tsamboulas et al., 1999; Zanakis et al., 1998). Indeed, each method has its own properties as well as its own advantages and disadvantages when it comes to analyzing and presenting data and information. Therefore, selecting an appropriate MCA method can turn out to be, almost paradoxically, a multi-criteria problem itself (Triantphyllou and Mann, 1989). Whereas the choice of which technique to employ in a decision-making problem should be well justified, in practice, this is rarely done. The selection of a MCA method is usually taken in a largely arbitrary manner and motivated only by the analysts and decision-makers' knowledge of a given method, the availability of software and tools for carrying out the analysis, or the existence of examples and similar studies that can be emulated without too much difficulty. Over the years, some tentative guidelines to assist analysts and decision-makers in their selection process have been produced (*e.g.*, Guitouni and Martel, 1998; Li and Thomas, 2014; Ozernoy, 1992). However, many of these guidelines consider and compare only a relatively limited number of methods and do not actually provide clear and unambiguous advice (Watróbski et al., 2018). Being based on different selection criteria and procedures, these guidelines also tend to produce contrasting recommendations.

3.1 Formal methods

3.1.1 Continuous methods

Formal MCA methods can be categorized in *continuous* and *discrete* methods. Continuous MCA methods typically deal with problems where an infinite (or, however, extremely large) number of possible alternatives exist, although they are not explicitly known at the outset. This category encompasses multi-objective programming methods such as linear programming and goal programming, where alternatives are generated during the resolution of complex equation systems, including an infinite or semi-infinite number of variables, constraints and objectives (Charnes and Cooper, 1977; Ehrgott, 2005; Korhonen, 2005). Such methods are generally suitable for technical design and optimization problems (*e.g.*, identification of the preferable highway alignment; configuration of the most convenient layout for a port or an airport; traffic signal optimization studies), which typically follow higher-level strategic decisions, and can be properly mastered only by mathematicians and experts.

3.1.2 Discrete, full aggregation methods

Discrete methods, by comparison, reflect real-world planning and policy problems, where the alternatives to assess are limited in number and relatively well-defined at the beginning of the analysis. The large majority of formal, discrete MCA methods can be encompassed in two broad categories, namely *full aggregation* and *partial aggregation* methods, representing two different schools of thought. The former category, corresponding to the American MCA school, aims at synthetizing the performances of an option against all the different criteria into a single, global score. Discrete, full aggregation MCA methods comprise, among others, the Multi-Attribute Utility Theory (MAUT) methods, whose aim is to determine the overall utility of an option under study with reference to a given number of decision criteria, which here are termed "attributes" (Keeney and Raiffa, 1976). Similarly to CBA, with MAUT methods, the concept of "utility" conveys a decision-maker's level of satisfaction with a particular outcome (Fishburn, 1970). Each criterion (attribute) has its own utility function which expresses varying levels of satisfaction according to the different possible performances of an option against that specific criterion. With MAUT methods all the marginal (or partial) utility functions for the individual criteria are ultimately combined within one mathematical expression, called multi-attribute utility function, representing the overall utility (*i.e.*, the global attractiveness) of that option. In assessing two or more alternative courses of action with MAUT methods, the preferred option is the one with the highest value for the overall utility. The multi-attribute utility function can assume different forms according to the nature of the problem at hand and the types of criteria considered in the analysis. In the simplest case, it presents a linear form so that the overall utility of an option can be calculated as a weighted sum of the utility functions for each individual criterion. In other words, given an option a and a set of N appraisal criteria, the overall utility U of a, measured against the N criteria, is determined in accordance with the following mathematical rule:

$$\begin{aligned} U(a) &= \sum_{j=1}^{N} w_j \times u_j(a) \\ &= w_1 \times u_1(a) + w_2 \times u_2(a) + \ldots + w_N \times u_N(a) \qquad (1) \\ &\sum_{j=1}^{N} w_j = 1 \text{ and } 0 \leq w_j \leq 1 \end{aligned}$$

where $u_j(a)$ represents the partial utility function for the j-th criterion, expressing the performance (utility) of option *a* on the j-th criterion; and w_j is the weight of the j-th criterion, through which $u_j(a)$ is scaled to a 0–1 interval.

The single-criterion value functions $u_j(a)$ are typically expressed in a 0–1 interval scale, with 0 that indicates the worst performance and 1 that indicates the best available performance. Therefore, given the fact that the value of criterion weights varies between 0 and 1, also the multi-attribute utility function $U(a)$ assumes values comprised between 0 (worst utility) and 1 (best utility).

This weighted additive model is perfectly valid only if the utility of each criterion is independent of that of the others (Keeney and Raiffa, 1976). This property, known as "mutual preferential independence," implies, loosely speaking, the absence of phenomena of synergy or conflict between different criteria so that the marginal contribution of each criterion to the overall utility can be assessed separately. Criteria, therefore, must be selected carefully and a huge number of conditional clauses have to be checked in order to minimize the possibility of such interactions to occur (Keeney, 1977). When, however, mutual preferential independence between criteria is not verified, the multi-attribute utility function combining the single utility functions assumes more complex forms (Keeney and Raiffa, 1976; Zeleny, 1982). Some of these forms (*e.g.*, multiplicative, quasi-pyramid, semi-cubic, multi-linear utility functions), which entail weaker independence conditions between criteria are presented in Table 2. According to Zeleny (1982), additive or multiplicative utility functions are the only practical, manageable models for cases with more than four criteria.

In the course of time, difficulties in employing MAUT methods have led to the introduction of the Simple Multi-Attribute Rating Technique (SMART), which represents a less complex (but also a less theoretically sound) multi-attribute approach (von Winterfeldt and Edwards, 1986). The SMART analysis relies on a weighted additive function, although it considers the condition of mutual preferential independence to be rather superfluous and easily by-passable through an opportune definition of the criteria (Edwards, 1977). A few variants of this method, namely the SMARTS (Simple Multi-attribute Rating Technique using Swings) and SMARTER (Simple Multi-attribute Rating Technique Exploiting Ranks) approaches, have also been developed in the attempt to address concerns over the logical consistency of SMART (Bouyssou et al., 2000; Edwards and Barron, 1994).

Table 2 Common forms for multi-attribute utility function.

Types of multi-attribute utility function	**Three-criterion representations**
Weighted additive model	$U(a) = w_1u_1(a) + w_2u_2(a) + w_3u_3(a)$
Multiplicative model	$U(a) = w_1u_1(a) + w_2u_2(a) + w_3u_3(a) + kw_1w_2u_1(a)u_2(a) + kw_1w_3u_1(a)u_3(a) + kw_2w_3u_2(a)u_3(a) + k^2w_1w_2w_3u_1(a)u_2(a)u_3(a)$ With *k* scaling factor
Quasi-pyramid model	$U(a) = w_1u_1(a) + w_2u_2(a) + w_3u_3(a) + w_{12}u_{12}(a) + w_{13}u_{13}(a) + w_{23}u_{23}(a) + w_{123}u_1(a)u_2(a)u_3(a)$
Semi-cubic model	$U(a) = w_1u_1(a) + w_2u_2(a) + w_3u_3(a) + w_{12}u_{12}(a) + w_{13}u_{13}(a) + w_{23}u_{23}(a) + w_{123}f_1(a)f_2(a)f_3(a)$ With $f_i(a)$ normalised utility difference functions
Multi-linear model	$U(a) = w_1u_1(a) + w_2u_2(a) + w_3u_3(a) + w_{12}w_1w_2u_1(a)u_2(a) + w_{13}w_1w_3u_1(a)u_3(a) + w_{23}w_2w_3u_2(a)u_3(a) + w_{123}w_1w_2w_3u_1(a)u_2(a)u_3(a)$

Adapted from Zeleny, M., 1982. Multiple Criteria Decision Making. McGraw-Hill.

Another well-known method aimed at assessing options through the calculation of a global score is the Analytic Hierarchical Process (AHP) (Saaty, 1980), whose preference structure, although presented by its proponents as completely distinct from MAUT methods (Saaty, 1990), can be reconciled to a weighted additive model (Belton, 1986; Rogers and Duffy, 2012). The AHP, in particular, seeks to reduce a multi-criteria decision-making problem to a series of smaller, self-contained analyses based on the assumption that the human mind is incapable of considering simultaneously too many factors when taking a decision (Arrow and Raynaud, 1986; Miller, 1956; Saaty, 1980). It begins by arranging the elements of the analysis in three main hierarchical levels as shown in Fig. 2: the overall goal of the decision-making problem at the top; a set of (ideally, mutually preferential independent) decision criteria in the middle layers; and a group of competing options at the bottom. A further middle layer can be added if criteria need to be broken down in sub-criteria.

Once this three-level hierarchy has been created, the AHP requires determining the relative priority of each criterion (second level) with respect to the goal of the analysis (first level). This is established by firstly carrying out a series of pairwise comparisons of criteria. Overall, with N criteria, $N(N-1)/2$ comparisons are necessary. The subjective judgments regarding

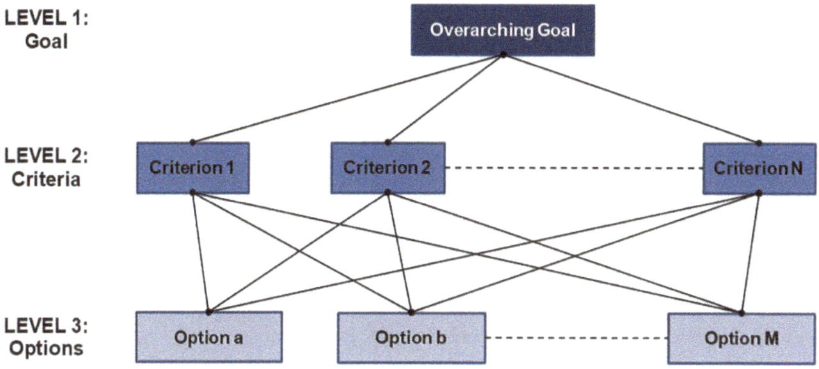

Fig. 2 Typical AHP structure for a decision problem. *Author's own elaboration.*

'Greenhouse Gas Reduction' is more important than 'Economic Growth'

'Greenhouse Gas Reduction' is slightly more important than 'Equity'

'Greenhouse Gas Reduction' is strongly more important than 'Strategic Fit'

Criteria	Greenhouse Gas Reduction	Economic Benefits	Equity	Strategic Fit	Geometric mean*	Normalised Weights
Greenhouse Gas Reduction	1	4	3	7	3.03	3.03/5.54 = 0.55
Economic Growth	1/4	1	1/3	3	0.71	0.71/5.54 = 0.13
Equity	1/3	3	1	5	1.50	1.50/5.54 = 0.27
Strategic Fit	1/7	1/3	1/5	1	0.31	0.31/5.54 = 0.06
				Total	5.54	1

*Geometric mean = $\sqrt[n]{x_1 x_2 \cdots x_n}$

Fig. 3 Example of pairwise comparison between four criteria with the AHP method. *Author's own elaboration*

the relevance of the different criteria are translated into quantitative scores by using a discrete, nine-point semantic scale, ranging from 1 (when the two criteria under examination are "equally preferred") to 9 (when one criterion is "preferred very strongly" over the other one). The results of the pairwise comparison of different criteria are arranged in a matrix as illustrated in Fig. 3. After the construction of the pairwise comparison matrix, the next step is to retrieve the actual priority (or weight) of each criterion. The most rigorous, but also the most computationally demanding approach consists in calculating the normalized principal eigenvector (Saaty, 2003). A much easier approach consists instead in the calculation of the geometric mean of each row and the successive normalization of the resulting new column (Saaty, 2001), as shown in Fig. 3. This approximation approach produces sufficiently close results to the eigenvector method in many situations (Barfod and Leleur, 2014; Rogers and Duffy, 2012).

Successively, also the local priority of each option (third level) with respect to the decision criteria (second level) needs to be determined. The relative merit of each option is also established through a pairwise comparison (based on the same nine-point semantic scale) of the relative performance ratings for all combinations of project options, separately for each decision criterion considered in the analysis. Overall, with M options there are $M(M-1)/2$ comparisons for each criterion. The same procedure, involving the computation of the normalized principal eigenvector (or the normalized geometric means) of the pairwise comparison matrices of the options (one matrix for each decision criterion considered in the analysis), is then implemented to determine the local priority (or score) of each option with reference to each criterion.

Finally, once weights and scores have been determined (both of them are assigned on a 0–1 scale and sum to 1), the overall valuation V of an option a with respect to the overall goal of the analysis and a set of N decision criteria is calculated by summing together the products of each criterion weight and the performance of a with respect to that criterion. Mathematically this is expressed as:

$$\begin{aligned} V(a) &= \sum_{j=1}^{N} w_j \times x_j(a) \\ &= w_1 \times x_1(a) + w_2 \times x_2(a) + \ldots + w_N \times x_N(a) \end{aligned} \tag{2}$$

where $x_j(a)$ is the local priority (performance score) of option a with respect to the j-th criterion; and w_j is the priority (weight) of the j-th criterion.

The reliability of the ranking results produced with the AHP has, however, been the subject of substantial debate among MCA specialists, with several authors questioning, among other things, the validity of the eigenvector method, the coherence of the pairwise comparisons and the justification for the interpretation of the associated semantic scale as a ratio scale (*e.g.*, Asadabadi et al., 2019; Bana e Costa and Vansnick, 2008; Harker and Vargas, 1987; Ishizaka and Labib, 2011). Over the years, there have been several attempts to modify this method with the view to correcting some logical errors and making the process less time-consuming (*e.g.*, Belton and Stewart, 2002; Dyer, 1990; Ferrari, 2003). Rezaei (2015), for instance, has proposed the Best-Worst Method (BWM), which uses only the best criterion and the worst criterion for the pairwise comparisons. In this BWM, after the identification of criteria, two criteria, namely the best and the worst ones are (arbitrarily) selected. Two rounds of pairwise comparisons are undertaken respectively between the best criterion and the remaining criteria, and between the worst criterion and the remaining criteria. Hence, with N criteria the BWM requires only $2N-3$ comparisons. The results of these comparisons, which are coded into a predefined numerical scale (*e.g.*, the nine-point scale of the AHP), are ultimately used to derive the weights of the criteria.

As it is evident from Eqs. (1) and (2), full aggregation methods provide full compensation between criteria. Indeed, with such methods high performances on some criteria can compensate for a low score against one or more criteria. Hence, an option that has fairly good performances with respect to all criteria may turn out to have the same overall performance as an option that scores exceptionally high against many criteria but present very poor performances for some other criteria (Dean, 2020a). Compensation can, however, be decreased by using nonlinear aggregation functions or by fixing some thresholds regarding the acceptable performance levels against some criteria. Weights, in such methods, assume primarily the meaning of trade-off coefficients, that is, the amount of achievement of one criterion that must be sacrificed in order to gain a unitary increase on another criterion (Belton and Stewart, 2002; Bouyssou et al., 2000; Munda, 2008). Weights modulate the marginal contribution of each criterion to the overall-performance score (or overall utility) of each option and are highly linked to and dependent on the measurement scales employed to assess performance scores against the criteria (Dean, 2020a).

3.1.3 Discrete, partial aggregation methods

A typical multi-criteria problem is represented by a situation where there is no optimal solution: an option a_1 may be better than an option a_2 according to one criterion but, at the same time, it may be worse than a_2 according to another criterion, so that eventually it is impossible to identify the "best" course of action. This situation, as depicted in Fig. 4, is generally referred to as the "multi-criteria imbroglio" (Schärlig, 1985). As highlighted in the previous section, however, with full aggregation MCA methods such a multi-dimensional problem is translated into a mono-criterion

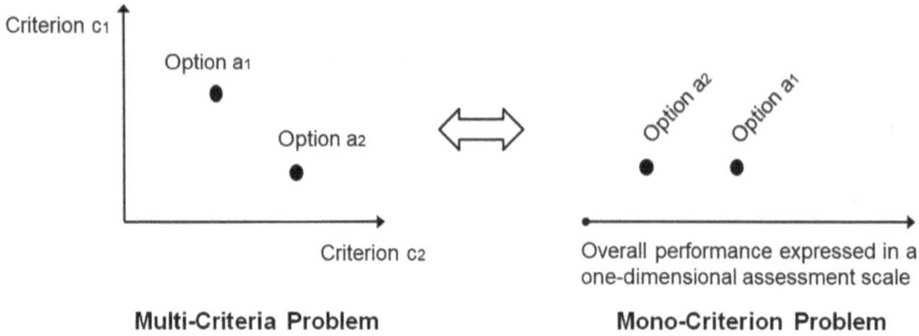

Fig. 4 Multi-criteria and mono-criterion problems. *Author's own elaboration.*

one, where different options are assessed and ranked on the basis of their overall-performance index expressed in a unidimensional scale. The American MCA School thus implicitly assumes that the decision-makers involved in the analysis have a complete preference system which enables them to produce a complete rank order of the options at hand.

Partial aggregation MCA methods, by comparison, representing the European (French) MCA School, question the existence of a complete preference system for any decision-making problem and reject the full aggregation of the single performance scores into a unique common scale on account of the strong heterogeneity which often characterizes objectives and criteria. With such methods, based on the notion of outranking, the comparison of options takes place on a pairwise basis with respect to each individual criterion. The objective is to establish the degree of dominance that one option has over another. An option is said to outrank (or dominate) another one if there is strong enough argument to support a conclusion that the former outperforms the latter on enough criteria (of sufficient importance), while there is no essential evidence to show that this statement is false with respect to the remaining criteria (Roy, 1996). Hence, with discrete, partial aggregation methods the output of an analysis is not an overall value for each option, but an outranking relation on the set of options (see Fig. 5).

The various discrete, partial aggregation (or outranking) MCA methods differ for the types of data and information which they can handle (*e.g.*, quantitative or qualitative, complete or fuzzy) and for the rules and procedures employed for determining the level of dominance of an option over the others (compare *e.g.*, Brans and Mareschal, 2005; Figueira et al., 2005c; Martel and Matarazzo, 2005). For example, the Preference Ranking Organization Method for Enrichment Evaluation (PROMETHEE), in its

Criteria	Weights	Performance Scores of Options			
		a_1	a_2	a_3	a_4
C_1	1/5	1	4	3	5
C_2	1/5	4	3	4	1
C_3	1/5	3	3	4	1
C_4	1/5	3	5	4	2
C_5	1/5	4	2	3	1

⇨

$X_1(a_3)=3 < X_1(a_4)=5$

$X_2(a_3)=4 > X_2(a_4)=1$

$X_3(a_3)=4 > X_3(a_4)=1$

$X_4(a_3)=4 > X_4(a_4)=2$

$X_5(a_3)=3 > X_5(a_4)=1$

⇨ Enough evidence to conclude that $a_3 > a_4$

Fig. 5 Illustrative example of decision model implied by partial aggregation (outranking) MCA methods. *Author's own elaboration.*

simplest form (*i.e.*, PROMETHEE I), tries to calculate a Preference Index which measures the strength of the statement "option a_1 outranks option a_2" (Brans and Vicke, 1985). The first version of the ELECTRE family methods, whose French acronym stands for *ELimination Et Choix Traduisant la REalité*, namely Elimination and Choice Translating Reality, brings this approach a stage further through the calculation of a Concordance Index and a Discordance Index as a complementary indicator to the former (Roy, 1968). The Concordance Index, similarly to the Preference Index of PROMETHEE I, quantifies the preference for option a_1 over option a_2. The Discordance Index, by comparison, highlights information that may contradict the statement "option a_1 dominates option a_2" and measures the degree to which on any of the criteria a_1 is worse than a_2. To account for imprecision and uncertainty in preference elicitation, specific thresholds levels, which the concordance and discordance measures are required to comply with for the evidence to be convincing, are defined (Rogers et al., 2000; Roy, 1996). Concordance and discordance thresholds, however, assume different values depending on the specific outranking method and application. This subjectivity regarding indices, preference thresholds as well as all the other key parameters and steps of the analysis creates unquestionably some concerns from a reliability standpoint (Cook et al., 1988; Roy and Bouyssou, 1986).

Outranking MCA methods are partially or totally non-compensatory since a low score against one criterion cannot (or can only partially) be compensated for by a better score against another criterion. Therefore, which such methods an option that has good performances with respect to all criteria is likely to outperform another option with present high scores against many criteria but performs quite poorly in some other criteria. Weights here assume the (more intuitive) meaning of importance coefficients which measure the influence that each criterion should have in building up the case for the assertion that one alternative is better than another (Belton and Stewart, 2002; Bouyssou et al., 2000; Munda, 2008). Such methods not always lead to a complete ranking of the options as the notion of "incomparability" is allowed (*i.e.*, when there is no essential evidence to demonstrate that one option is superior or inferior to another one). Whereas often problematic for decision-making, the conclusion of incomparability between some options may also be helpful in highlighting some aspects of the problem that would perhaps require a more thorough analysis (Rogers and Duffy, 2012).

3.2 Simplified methods

Notwithstanding the large number of sophisticated MCA methods developed over time, simplified MCA techniques are very popular, mainly due to practicality reasons. Indeed, many people involved in MCA applications simply do not have enough time, resources or even the knowledge for solving complex equation systems, assessing utility functions or performing long pairwise comparisons. Elementary MCA methods include, among others, simple summary charts, simple additive weighting methods, checklists and other screening tools. Whereas such techniques can be ran and understood virtually by anyone, including non-MCA experts, if used improperly (with no consideration of even the most basic rules and principles), they are extremely likely to lead to many inconsistencies and flaws (*e.g.*, inaccurate selection of criteria leading to the violation of the preferential independence condition and double-counting problems; incorrect weighting and scoring procedures; discrepancies between the weighting elicitation methods and the actual meaning of weights; methodologically unsound rules to combine scores and weights) (Dean, 2020a).

3.2.1 Simple multi-criteria summary charts

With such methods the performances of the option(s) at hand against the different criteria employed for the analysis are simply displayed using tables, graphs or diagrams without the inclusion of scores and weights. While, in some cases, (quantitative or qualitative) performance scores may be assigned, there is no attempt to either determine mathematically a global score or rank the project options under examination in a mechanistic manner (see Table 3 and Fig. 6). The focus of this approach, which is presentational in nature, is clearly on "opening up" the analysis (Stirling, 2006, 2008), with different types of charts which provide analysts and decision-makers with a comprehensive overview of the key features and impacts of the option(s) under study and assist them in better understanding the problem situation.

Table 3 Example of simple summary table displaying the performances of a hypothetical road project against different criteria without scoring and weighting the impacts of the option.

Objectives/criteria	Quantitative impacts	Qualitative impacts
Greenhouse gases	Increase in greenhouse gas emissions as a result of the project: • change in carbon emissions over 60 year appraisal period = 120 tons; • change in carbon emissions in opening year = 2 tons	Not applicable
Heritage of historic resources	No demolition of any historic building would be required	The proposal could be implemented with full respect of the historical character of the area. No major alterations to historic landmarks or sites
Accident reduction	Several car accidents potentially prevented from the construction of the project: • fatal = 20; • serious = 125; • slight = 400	Not applicable
Transport economic efficiency	The project would generate large benefits for business users from travel time and vehicle operating cost savings: • Present Value of Benefits = £125.8 m	Not applicable
Integration/strategic fit	Not applicable	The project aligns with local and regional transport objectives which support the scheme Conflicts with environmental and sustainability objectives at all levels

Author's own elaboration.

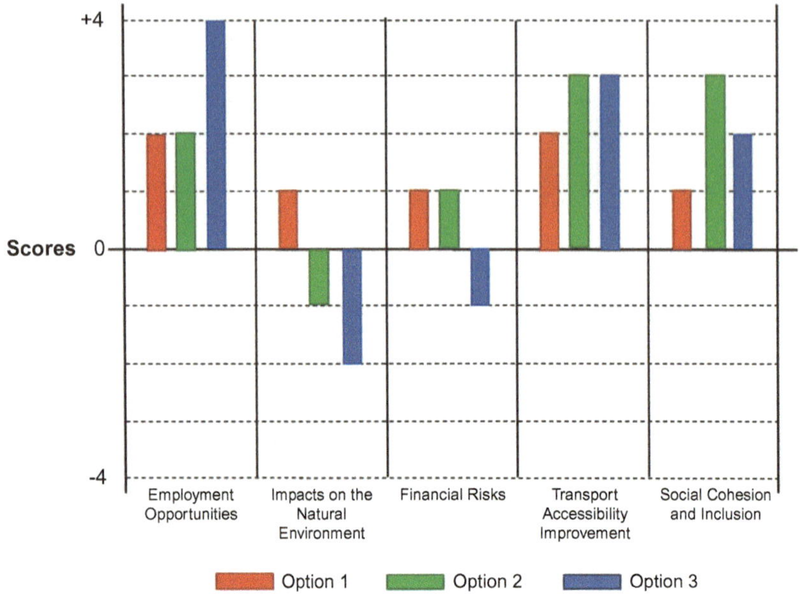

Fig. 6 Example of simple MCA summary diagram showing the performances of three different options without any attempt to rank them in a mechanistic way. *Author's own elaboration.*

3.2.2 Simple additive weighting methods

Simple additive weighting methods represent one of the most well-known and widely used decision-support methods based on different criteria. These methods adopt the rather straightforward and captivating weighted additive model (typical of some MAUT applications, AHP, SMART and several other full aggregation MCA methods) in the attempt to calculate the overall performance of the different options under investigation. Here the focus is thus on "closing down" the analysis (Stirling, 2006), with global scores, obtained as the weighted sum of the single performance scores, which clearly point out to analysts and decision-makers what the "best" option to address the problem at hand is. The results of the process are generally presented by means of performance tables, similar to the one illustrated in Table 4. In such tables, each row identifies a specific criterion and the columns show the respective weights and performance scores of the option(s) under study against that criterion. While easy to understand and clear-cut, these methods usually lack the theoretical rigor of formal methods and, very often, turn out to resemble rudimental weighted average calculations which have very few or even no links with MCA theory.

Table 4 Example of performance table presenting the result of a MCA based on a simple additive weighting model.

		Option 1		Option 2		Option 3	
Objectives/ criteria	**Weights (0 ÷ 100%)**	**Scores (0 ÷ 10)**	**Weighted scores**	**Scores (0 ÷ 10)**	**Weighted scores**	**Scores (0 ÷ 10)**	**Weighted scores**
Strategic fit	25%	4	1	8	2	10	2.5
Wider Ec. benefits	10%	4	0.4	6	0.6	5	0.5
Env. impacts	15%	2	0.3	7	1.05	4	0.6
Equity	30%	5	1.5	7	2.1	8	2.4
Implement risks	20%	9	1.8	2	0.4	8	1.6
Total	**100%**		**5**		**6.15**		**7.6**
Preference rank		**3**		**2**		**1**	

Author's own elaboration.

Objective/ Criteria	Options			
	a1	a2	a3	a4
Strategic Fit	V	X	V	V
Social Acceptability	V	V	V	X
Affordability	V	V	V	V
Implementation Risks	X	V	V	X

Fig. 7 Example of multi-criteria checklist. *Author's own elaboration.*

3.2.3 Multi-criteria checklists and other screening tools

This category comprises various elementary and intuitive forms of MCA, which do not involve numerical procedures and are also often employed (instinctively) by many people in their everyday decisions. The most typical examples of such methods include basic checklists (see Fig. 7) and lexicographic orderings (see Fig. 8) which can be conveniently used at the beginning of the planning and decision-making process to screen some options out and find the most feasible options, which will then be developed and examined further. With basic lexicographic orderings, in particular, the different objectives and criteria are ordered into different priority levels and the various options are ranked or screened in/out against one criterion at a time, commencing with the most important one, and ending with the less important one. If an option appears clearly the best with reference to the first criterion the process ends and that option is selected as the preferred one. Conversely, if more than one option performs reasonably well against the most important criterion, this subset of options is then compared against the second most important criterion. The process continues in this way in a sequential manner until a single option is chosen or all the criteria have been gone through and complete separation between options proves impossible.

4. Current use of MCA in the transport sector

As highlighted by several studies carried out over the past two decades (*e.g.*, Bristow and Nellthorp, 2000; Grant-Muller et al., 2001; Hayashi and Morisugi, 2000; Mackie and Worsley, 2013; OECD, 2005), nowadays, MCA is widely used in many countries to assess transport projects, although, in most of the cases, it is seen only as complementary to CBA and employed to capture impacts not properly accounted by the latter method. Several reviews of the literature (Deluka-Tibljaš et al., 2013; Macharis and Bernardini, 2015; Mardani et al., 2015) also underline the increased interest

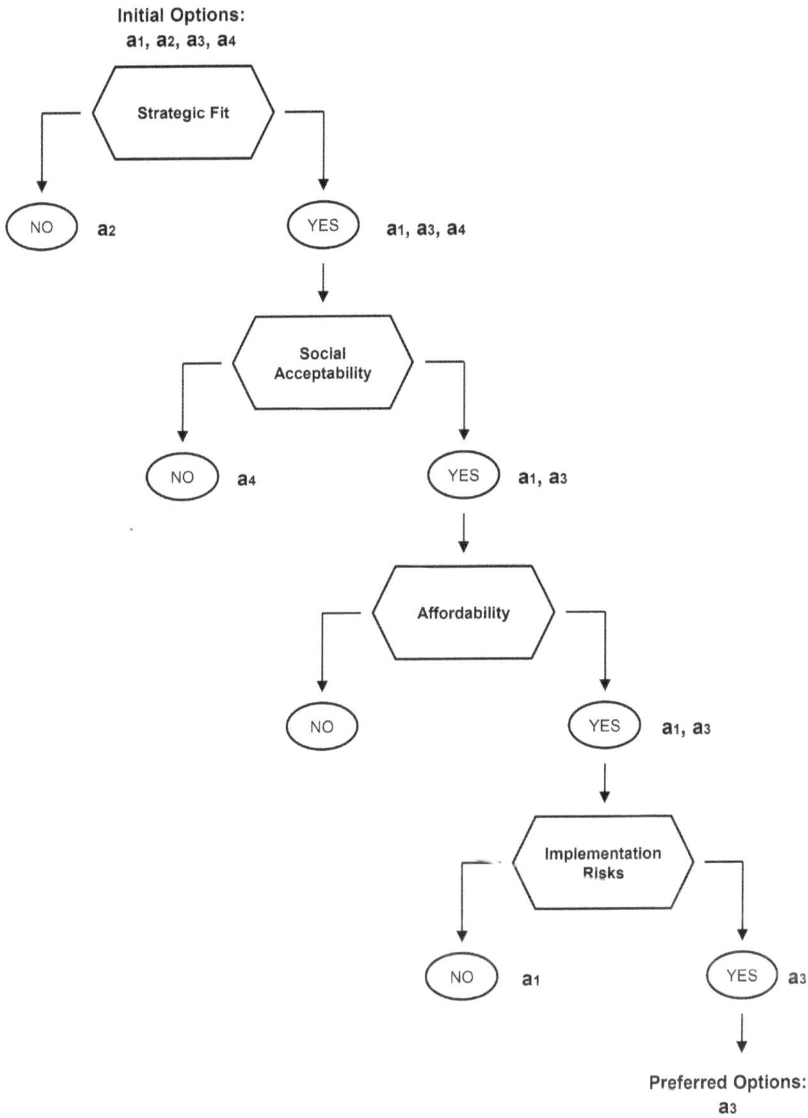

Fig. 8 Example of lexicographic ordering. *Author's own elaboration.*

in the use of MCA in the transport sector, with hundreds of journal articles published on this topic since the 1980s. However, one aspect which has not been sufficiently emphasized by these works and which, instead, deserves particular attention is that, while the academic literature on transport planning abounds with theoretical applications of Goal Programming,

MAUT, AHP, ELECTRE and other formal MCA methods, practitioners, most of the times, mainly employ simplified MCA techniques. This, for example, is particularly evident in the UK, which is currently considered to be at the forefront in the employment of MCA in transport project appraisal and evaluation (Macharis and Bernardini, 2015; Worsley and Mackie, 2015). In England, the New Approach to Appraisal (NATA) was introduced, in the late 1990s, in the attempt to ensure a more holistic transport assessment process (DETR, 1998a,b), which, until that moment, had mainly relied on CBA (Vickerman, 2000). The core of this appraisal framework was represented by a simple multi-criteria summary chart in the form of a single sheet Appraisal Summary Table accounting for both the readily monetisable impacts of development proposals (*e.g.*, travel time and vehicle operating cost savings), and their wider environmental and social implications, which had been frequently omitted in the past. Initially adopted only for informing the prioritization of trunk road investment proposals (DETR, 1998a,b), NATA has progressively evolved and has been included into WebTAG (Web-based Transport Analysis Guidance), namely the transport appraisal guidance and toolkit adopted in England (DfT, 2014, 2018a). The Appraisal Summary Table, which includes several quantitative and qualitative criteria grouped into economic, environmental, social and public accounts dimensions (see Table 5), thus now provides the overall framework for the appraisal of all the major (public and private) transport projects. Similar multi-criteria assessment procedures based on multi-criteria summary charts have been also introduced in Wales (WAG, 2008; WG, 2017) and Scotland (TS, 2008). These multi-criteria frameworks seeks to assist promoters, objectors, local authorities and any other relevant stakeholders in understanding the potential multifold impacts and consequences of a given project proposal, without, however, intending to provide a mechanistic way of reaching decisions. Indeed, they do not contain either any pre-determined weighting scheme for the criteria or an algorithm capable of generating a global project score (DfT, 2005, 2014, 2018a). The omission of weights as well as the selection of criteria to be included in these frameworks has, however, raised concerns among experts. Concerning criteria, in particular, it is evident, as illustrated in Table 5, that while the WebTAG Appraisal Summary Table may appear very comprehensive, it involves the risk of double-counting of impacts. Indeed, the inclusion of redundant and overlapping criteria (although not summed-up together) is likely to lead to misleading interpretations of the pros and cons of the options under examination.

Table 5 The Appraisal Summary Table included in the WebTAG.

Dimensions	Objectives	Qualitative impacts	Quantitative impacts	Monetary impacts
Economy	Business users & transport providers Reliability impact on business users Regeneration Wider Impacts			
Environmental	Noise Air quality Greenhouse gases Landscape Townscape Historic environment Biodiversity Water environment			
Social	Commuting and other users Reliability impact on commuting and other users Physical activity Journey quality Accidents Security Access to services Affordability Severance Option and non-use values			
Public accounts	Cost to broad transport budget Indirect tax revenues			

Adapted from https://www.gov.uk/government/publications/webtag-appraisal-tables.

The transport appraisal process described in the WebTAG also involves some preliminary assessments of the project proposals, with the view to discarding unpromising options and identifying the alternatives which can undergo further rounds of examination. The initial sifting of the options is undertaken by means a multi-criteria checklist which includes a wide range of aspects and factors (see Table 6). This preliminary analysis is

Table 6 The Sifting Tool recommended by the WebTAG.

Dimensions	Objectives
Strategic case	What are the key transport problems to be solved and the main objectives of the option?
	To what extent does the option alleviate the identified problems?
	How does the option fit within the wider transport and government objectives?
	How does the option fit with the other planning and policy objectives?
	What are the most uncertain assumptions that have been made?
	What consultation has taken place with relevant stakeholders?
Economic case	Will the option reduce the travel time and costs?
	Will the option impact on the day to day variability in journey times or the average minutes of lateness?
	Will there be any impact on the number of incidents?
	Will the option produce any significant wider economic impacts which would require detailed consideration at a later stage?
	Does the option have an impact on the vulnerability of the network to terrorism, severe weather events or the effects of climate change?
	Will the option support housing provision?
	What impacts will the option have on carbon emissions?
	What impacts will the option have on the local environment (*e.g.*, air quality, noise, natural environment, heritage and landscape, streetscape and urban environment)?
	What impacts will the option have in terms of well being (*e.g.*, physical activity, crime reduction, social mobility)?
	Are the potential impacts of the option (regarding noise, air quality, severance, accessibility, security, accidents, user benefits and personal affordability) significantly concentrated in terms of the people groups or spatial areas affected? Might the option have negative impacts on specific groups of people, can these expected negative impacts be eliminated through some form of amendment to or redesign of the initial option?
	Does the option have an impact on a targeted regeneration area?
	Will the option address (or cause or exacerbate) regional imbalances?

Table 6 The Sifting Tool recommended by the WebTAG.—cont'd

Dimensions	**Objectives**
Managerial case	Implementation timetable from inception to delivery
	Will there be any issues around the public acceptability of the option?
	Has the option been tested and proven to be practical and effective?
	How well-developed is the supporting evidence around the practical feasibility of the option at this stage?
	What risks have been identified with regard to implementing such an option/project?
Financial case	How affordable is the option?
	What are the capital costs of the option? Has an optimism bias analysis been undertaken?
	What are the expected revenue costs of the option?
	Are there any additional implementation, operation, maintenance and enforcement costs?
	Overall cost risk rating: from 1 (low risk) to 5 (high risk)
Commercial case	To what extent can the option be scaled up or down depending on the level of funding available?
	How easily could the option be amended to fit with changing circumstances?
	How easy would it be to stop the option once it has been put into operation? Or before it starts operating?
	Where is funding coming from?
	Will any income be generated?

Adapted from DfT (Department for Transport), 2018b. Early Assessment and Sifting Tool (EAST) Guidance, Department for Transport.

aimed at investigating the project proposals from five different perspectives, namely strategic, economic, commercial, financial and management, in line with the "Five Business Case" model recommended by the UK Government (DfT, 2018b).

To promote the use of MCA in the transport sector, but also in other policy fields, the UK Department of the Environment, Transport and the Regions has commissioned a specific *Manual for Multi-Criteria Analysis*

(Dodgson et al., 2009), providing practical guidance for government officials and other practitioners on how to undertake and make the best use of MCA in decision-making processes. Whereas presenting an overview of the various MCA techniques currently available, including the more formal and complex ones, the manual strongly recommends the use of elementary methods in the forms of basic summary charts or simple additive weighting models.

Similar approaches to the use of MCA can be found in the transport assessment guidelines of several other nations including, for example, Australia (COA, 2006; TFNSW, 2016) and New Zealand (Alberquerque, 2013; Douglas et al., 2013). Moreover, as highlighted by Beinat (2001) and Janssen (2001) simplistic MCA tools are also frequently adopted in many countries as decision-support systems for Environmental Impact Assessment (EIA) procedures. Indeed the need for summarizing and highlighting the key results of long EIA reports, containing complex data and information regarding the multifold impacts of a project proposal on the environment, make simple multi-criteria summary charts particularly convenient. Sometimes, a simple weighted summation model is also used to calculate a global score, expressing (roughly) the overall sustainability of the proposal.

Appraisal and evaluation procedures adopted by multilateral development banks and other international institutions also mirror this trend toward the employment of rather simple MCA tools and techniques. The World Bank, for example, has recently developed the Infrastructure Prioritization Framework to help governments prioritize infrastructure investments under conditions of limited resources, multiple policy goals, and uncertainty (Darwin et al., 2016, 2018). The framework consists in a MCA decision-support tool based on a simple additive weighting model which assesses and compares different investment options with respect to two overarching dimensions: a financial-economic dimension, including mainly quantitative criteria such as the financial internal rate of return, the multiplier effects and the net present value of the proposals; and a social-environmental dimension, which may encompass the carbon footprint of the proposals, the number of job created, the number of people affected by the repurposing of land use and several other qualitative criteria. Whereas the selection of criteria differs depending on the application context (*i.e.*, specific government's policy goals and project stakeholders' interests and priorities), the risk of double-counting seems rather high. For each

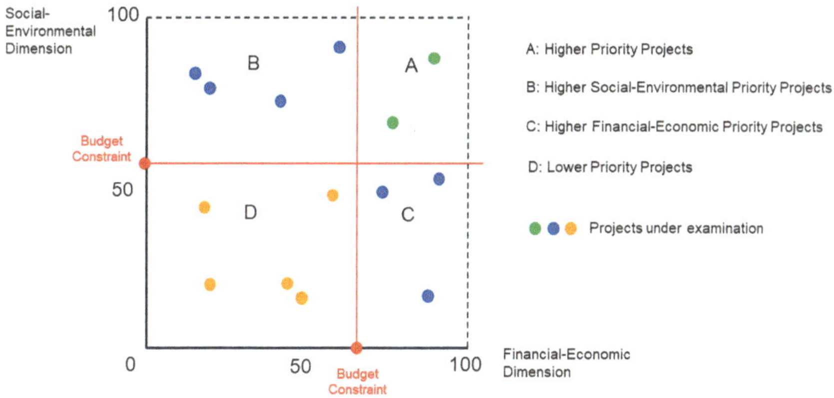

Fig. 9 Infrastructure prioritization framework devised by the World Bank. *Adapted from Darwin, M., Cledan, M.-P., Schuyler, H and Schwartz, J.Z., 2016. Prioritizing Infrastructure Investment a Framework for Government Decision Making. Policy Research Working Paper No. 7674, The World Bank Group.*

investment proposal, two overall global indexes (one for each dimension) are calculated as the weighted sum of the single performances of the proposals against each criterion included in each dimension. While it is specified that weights may be determined either with statistical methods or through a deliberation process with key stakeholders, it is evident that these two approaches are likely to lead to completely different weighting schemes. There also seems to be some ambiguity with regard to whether criteria are considered as trade-off or importance coefficients. As illustrated in Fig. 9, the financial-economic and the social-environmental global indexes are then used as coordinates to plot the investment proposals onto a Cartesian plane whose axes represent each dimension. Thereafter, the specific budget constraint for the sector is imposed along each axis. The result is a matrix with four quadrants which can be used to inform project selection. In Fig. 9, Quadrant A contains "high-priority" infrastructure investment projects, which simultaneously score high on both the dimensions and which, consequently, are likely the best candidates for implementation. In contrast, projects falling into quadrant D are of lower priority status, since they score low on both dimensions. Infrastructure projects in quadrants B and C are considered medium-priority for implementation as they score relatively high only on one dimension (either the financial-economic or the social-environmental dimension).

The European Investment Bank (EIB), the European Commission (EC) and the Asian Development Bank (ADB), in their guidelines for the economic appraisal of investment projects, all recommend the use of MCA based on a simple additive weighting model to inform and supplement CBA, especially in those situations when it is not possible to express all costs and benefits of projects in monetary terms (ADB, 2017; EC, 2008, 2015; EIB, 2013).

The EIB and the ADB are also currently working on the development of novel multi-criteria appraisal and evaluation tools. In recent years, in particular, a working group within the ADB's Transport Community of Practice, has conceived a new framework with the view to promoting the design of more sustainable transport projects. The new framework, termed Sustainable Transport Appraisal Rating, assesses projects against 18 criteria grouped in four main dimensions, namely economic, environmental and social dimensions, representing the key pillars of sustainable development, and a risk dimension, which refers to the risk that expected outcomes may not be realized or sustained (Véron-Okamoto and Sakamoto, 2014). As showed in Table 7, an equal 30% weight is given to the economic, environmental and social dimensions, while the risk dimension accounts for the remaining 10%. This predefined and fixed weighting scheme is then combined with the performance scores based on the judgments of the evaluators (*e.g.*, a group of transport, social development and environmental specialists, and economists from the ADB). The scoring system adopted to assess the performance of the projects against the various criteria belonging to the economic, environmental and social dimensions is based on a seven-point ordinal scale, ranging from "very strongly positive" performances (+3) to "very strongly negative" performances (−3). A three-point ordinal scale, running between +1 and −1, is instead used for the risk rating. The overall rating is derived according to a simple additive weighting model. It is apparent, however, that this procedure, which implicitly assimilates these Likert-type scales (*i.e.*, ordinal scales in which the distance between the different levels on each scale is not clearly defined) to interval scales (where there is, instead, a specific standard unit that ensures equal distance between each value on the same scale) is not particularly sound.

Finally, as the last example of this brief overview it can be worth to mention the Japan International Cooperation Agency (JICA), which employs a purely qualitative multi-criteria framework for conducting its *ex ante*

Table 7 Sustainable transport appraisal rating framework proposed by the Asian Development Bank.

Dimensions	Objectives	Weights	Scores
Economic	Efficiency: People	30%	−3 ÷ +3
	Efficiency: Businesses		
	Quality and reliability		
	Fiscal burden		
	Wider economic benefits		
	Security		
Environmental	Greenhouse gas emissions	30%	−3 ÷ +3
	Transport-related emissions and pollution		
	Resource efficiency		
	Climate resilience		
	Natural and built environment		
Social	Basic accessibility	30%	−3 ÷ +3
	Employment		
	Affordability		
	Safety		
	Inclusion and social Cohesion		
Risk	Design and evaluation risk	10%	−1 ÷ +1
	Implementation risk		
	Operational risk		
TOTAL		100%	

Adapted from Véron-Okamoto, A. and Sakamoto, K., 2014. Toward a Sustainability Appraisal Framework for Transport. Asian Development Bank Sustainable Development Working Paper Series, No. 31.

appraisals and *ex post* evaluations (JICA, 2004). The JICA's framework, which does not include weighted scores, comprises five main decision criteria (*i.e.*, relevance, effectiveness, efficiency, impact, sustainability) which allow making a value judgment on the projects under examination (see Table 8).

Table 8 Qualitative multi-criteria framework adopted by the Japan International Cooperation Agency.

Criteria	Meaning	Key investigated aspects
Relevance	A criterion for considering whether the implementation of project has benefited (or will benefit) the intended beneficiaries or the target society	• Is the project consistent with the Japan's foreign assistance policy and JICA's country programs? • Is the project consistent with a partner country's development plans? • Does the project match the needs of a target area or society? • ...
Effectiveness	A criterion for considering the validity and necessity of a project	• Is the project purpose specific enough? • Has the project purpose been achieved (or is it going to be achieved)? • ...
Efficiency	A criterion for considering how economic resource/inputs are converted to results. The main focus is on the relationship between project cost and effects	• Was (or is) the cost of inputs justified by the degree of achievement of outputs? • Were (or are) there any alternatives that would have achieved (or will achieve) same level at lower costs? • Could (can) higher level of achievement be expected at the same costs? • Was (or is) the cost of inputs justified by the degree of achievement of the project's purpose? • ...
Impact	A criterion for considering the effects of the project with an eye on the longer term effects, including direct or indirect, positive or negative, intended or unintended outcomes	• Has the overall goal been achieved (or is it going to be achieved)? • Did (or does) the achievement of the overall goal result from the project purpose? • Is there any unexpected positive or negative influence (*i.e.*, policies, economics and finance, organization and institution, technologies, society and culture, and environment) including ripple effects? • ...
Sustainability	A criterion for considering whether produced effects continue after the termination of the assistance	• Are the expected effects described in both the project purpose and the overall goal going to be sustained after the termination of assistance? • ...

Adapted from JICA (Japan International Cooperation Agency), 2004. JICA Guideline for Project Evaluation—Practical Methods for Project Evaluation. Office of Evaluation, Planning and Coordination Department Japan International Cooperation Agency (JICA).

5. Strengths and weaknesses of MCA

In the literature many discussions can be found on the pros and cons of MCA. Quite often these claimed strengths and weakness are compared to those of CBA (*e.g.*, Dean and Hickman, 2018; Dimitriou et al., 2016; Dobes and Bennett, 2009, 2010; Ergas, 2009; Hickman and Dean, 2018). However, due to the fact that CBA is a single specific assessment method and MCA encompasses, instead, a number of (very different) appraisal and evaluation techniques, such a comparison is difficult to make and can easily result in very generic and vague discussions. Whereas chapter "Comparing cost-benefit analysis and multi-criteria analysis" by Mouter et al. includes an examination of the difference, similarities and complementary aspects of CBA and MCA, this section focuses mainly on potential advantages and limitations of simplified MCA tools and techniques. There seem to be three main properties which are frequently mentioned when it comes to explaining the merits of MCA:

- Comprehensiveness: by taking explicit account of multiple objective and criteria, MCA techniques can provide better insights into the nature of the problem at hand relative to mono-criterion methods such as CBA (Dimitriou et al., 2010, 2016; Leleur, 2012; Macharis and Bernardini, 2015).
- Flexibility: MCA methods make it possible to study different types of problems and deal with a wide array of data and information, whether quantitative or qualitative in nature (Barfod and Leleur, 2014; Brown et al., 2001; Browne and Ryan, 2011; Guhnemann et al., 2012).
- Transparency: the displaying, through tables, graphs or diagrams, of all the objectives, appraisal criteria, weights and scores adopted during the assessment as well as all the data and information employed during the analysis provides a clearer and more transparent approach to appraisal and evaluation (Cornet et al., 2018a; Hickman, 2019; Macharis et al., 2018; Ward et al., 2016a).

These properties, however, should not always be taken for granted. For instance, it is, in principle, true that analyzing a problem in a multidimensional fashion may lead to more thorough decisions. However, as illustrated in Sections 3 and 4, both formal and simplified MCA methods are not immune from logical flaws and inconsistencies. The possibility of making more informed judgments also clearly depends, among other things, on the breadth of the value tree of objectives and criteria considered in the analysis. This, in turn, implies the difficult issue of what perspective to take and what interests to consider in the appraisal or evaluation exercise. While, for example, the purpose of CBA is to estimate (from the economic efficiency point of view) the pros and cons of a given project or policy measure by trying to take into account the effects experienced by all members of society, the scope of MCA is less clear-cut. On the one hand, the MCA literature emphasizes the importance of adequately representing the concerns and priorities of all the parties involved in or affected by the problem situation under examination (*e.g.*, Dimitriou et al., 2010; Dodgson et al., 2009; Macharis and Bernardini, 2015; Macharis and Nijkamp, 2011). On the other hand, for major policy decisions having far-reaching consequences with regard to both space and time, the identification of all the potential stakeholders and their agendas is rather problematic and, in many cases, is made even more difficult by time and budget constraints to undertake the analysis (Dean, 2018). Hence, in selecting a set of relevant objectives to account for the possible impacts of the options under study, analysts would probably tend to adopt (implicitly or explicitly) the client perspective (*e.g.*, the Minister, Government Department, project promoter, agency or group that has commissioned the analysis) and/or take mainly into account (intentionally or unintentionally) the positions of only some key stakeholders (*i.e.*, typically the most organized, and often most powerful groups, that have consolidated themselves as a public presence), while neglecting other interested or affected parties. Moreover, compared to other appraisal and evaluation methods, in many MCA applications, objectives and criteria are selected with only scant attention paid to the geographical and temporal dimensions of the analysis. Hence, especially in simplistic MCA approaches, the performances of options against the different criteria risk to become simply a collection of snapshots, often with no common (spatial or temporal) basis for comparison. In such situations, the aggregation of the performance scores is likely to lead to misleading results.

As discussed in Section 3.1, whereas the adoption of a linear aggregation rule to combine scores and weights into an overall-performance index responds to the needs of arriving at a final judgment over the desirability of the various alternative options, it may result in excessive oversimplifications of the decision situation (as this tends to deny the multi-dimensional nature of the problem at hand) with the consequent omission of critical information (Lichfield, 1990; Voogd, 1983), including also distribution of effects and equity aspects. Hill, whose work, as previously explained, has pioneered the development of MCA methods in land use and transport planning, also explicitly acknowledged this issue (Hill, 1985:174):

"Although in some of my early writing I have suggested a weighted overall-performance score as a possible option when assessing alternative plans in terms of multiple objectives (Hill, 1968, 1973), I have come to have serious reservations about this. A weighted overall-performance score may result in the loss of important information which might be relevant for arriving at a decision. In addition, it provides a numerical value which is extremely difficult to interpret."

Concerning the last point made by Hill, it must be stressed that the global score obtained by combining scores and weights does not offer any indications about the possible net social benefits generated by the options under study (Dobes and Bennet, 2009, 2010; Lichfield, 1993). Hence, theoretically, even the "best" option (*i.e.*, the one with the highest overall-performance score) might constitute an economically inefficient allocation of resources and lead to a reduction in overall welfare within society.

On the other hand, it should also be emphasized that, although useful to stimulate thinking and discussions over a decision problem, simple summary charts such as the NATA/WebTAG framework, which do not rely on a global performance index, may result equally problematic for moving toward a solution. Indeed, whereas the need for deciding and acting, once the relevant information has been collected, remains firm, with this approach to MCA there is nothing self-evident about how to process systematically and comprehensively the data and information included in tables, graphs or diagrams and derive clear outcomes and actions (Dean, 2018).

Concerning the second property, then, whereas, in principle, MCA allows the assessment of options against a large variety of both quantitative and qualitative objectives, in practice, the performance of the options against many of these objectives may result very difficult to measure either in a quantitative or qualitative manner. In many cases, "intangible" and "soft" aspects such as equity, cohesion, happiness, quality of life, sense of place may be even difficult to define objectively and translate into specific indicators (Miller, 1985; Vanclay, 1999). Given the high level of uncertainty surrounding appraisal and evaluation studies, for several criteria, often, it might be possible to gather only rough and vague data and information concerning the performance of the options under study. For other criteria the information search process might be considered too long, difficult, or costly. Finally, for some other criteria the needed data and information might simply not exist (Dom, 1999; Gustavson et al., 1999). Therefore, eventually, the actual MCA exercise might turn out to be based only on a very few objectives and criteria.

Finally, it is undeniable that simplified MCA methods are more transparent than CBA and other sophisticated MCA methods, whose mechanics is often seen by people without much formal training as a kind of "scientific witchcraft." However, it must also be emphasized that the highly arbitrary nature of MCA makes the results of the analysis hardly capable of proper technical reviews and third-party audits. In MCA, in particular, there are no many specific rules and universally accepted guidelines concerning the selection of appropriate MCA techniques applicable to a particular decision-making situation, the identification of objectives and criteria, scoring and weighting procedures, aggregation rules as well as all the other parameters which can strongly affect the results of the analysis. The already mentioned UK *Manual for Multi-Criteria Analysis* (Dodgson et al., 2009) exemplifies this matter. First of all, while recommending the use of simplified MCA methods (Dodgson et al., 2009: 29), the Manual does not offer any strong justification for this choice. The Manuel also states that, in a MCA process, the time spent determining objective and criteria "is the most important time of all" (Dodgson et al., 2009: 144) and that it is fundamental to ensure that "the objectives included in any MCA analysis are sufficiently wide to encompass the main concerns of people as a whole" (Dodgson et al., 2009: 12). On the other hand, it does not offer any concrete advice about how to derive these parameters. According to the Manual, the number of criteria should "range from 6 to 20" (Dodgson et al., 2009: 33). However, this obviously is a too broad range to be of any help to government officials. Hence, in absence of any rules of thumb, two analysts running the same MCA are extremely likely to adopt different lists of objectives and criteria. The Manual also does not include any indications regarding the most appropriate scale of measurement for scores and weight, but it only states that "scales extending from 0 to 100 are often used" (Dodgson et al., 2009: 22). However, it is clear that the ranking of the options obtained by adopting a 100-point scale may turn out to be different from the one produced, for example, with a 7-point scale (*e.g.*, a −3 to +3 scale). Finally, the Manual acknowledges that the identification of appropriate weighting scheme is "fundamental to the effectiveness of a MCA" (Dodgson et al., 2009: 64), although weighting procedures unavoidably entail "the question of whose preferences count most" (Dodgson et al., 2009: 64). However, quite surprisingly, instead of attempting to address this issue, the Manual points out that it "can go no further than identify this as an issue which should be recognized explicitly rather than implicitly" (Dodgson et al., 2009: 64).

Weights, in particular, seem to constitute the most controversial aspects of any MCA exercise. In the course of time, difficulties in determining suitable weighting schemes have hampered the use of MCA in several countries (Annema et al., 2015; Quinet, 2000). Hill, in this regard, has also cautioned that MCA "is not very useful if weights cannot be objectively determined or assumed" (Hill, 1968:27). An examination of the relevant literature reveals the existence of different currents of thought over the best way to derive weights:

- According to Nijkamp and Rietveld (1990), weights could be derived (directly or indirectly) from past decisions regarding problems similar to the decision-making situation in question.
- Van Pelt (1993) explains that, in principle, weights could be used in the attempt to differentiate and strike a balance between short-terms and long-term objectives.
- Munda (2004, 2008), suggests that weights should reflect some ethical principles (*e.g.*, "ecological stability" position, leading to higher weights for criteria related to environmental dimension; "economic prosperity" position, implying a strong consideration for economic criteria; "social equity" position, entailing the assignment of higher weights to social objectives) and different weighting schemes should thus be used to examine their consequences on the final option ranking.
- In its guidelines on MCA, the Australian Resource Assessment Commission also recommends changing and testing different set of weights as part of an interactive process between the analysts and decision-makers (RAC, 1992).
- Dimitriou et al. (2010) and Brown et al. (2001) claim that weights should be derived from policy documents and government guidelines.
- Finally, several authors including Macharis and Bernardini (2015), Barfod (2018) and Hickman (2019) argue that weights should be elicited directly from project stakeholders as part of a wide participatory and deliberative process (see Section 6).

However, none of the approaches to weighting suggested so far seems to be capable of solving this impasse. For example, although seeking to guarantee consistency with past decisions, the first of the above approaches may be problematic as detailed information on previous choices might not be available. Past decisions also might not have been the brightest resolutions.

Whereas the need for appraisal and evaluation studies to differentiate the effects occurring in the short-term from those produced in the long-term appear evident to almost anyone, there is little consensus on the priority level to assign to these two categories of impacts, as clearly demonstrated by the long-standing debate over discounting procedures in CBA and, more generally, by the multiple divergent viewpoints on the topic of sustainable development and intergenerational equity.

If weights are chosen by the analysts or the decision-makers, they unavoidably turn out to be largely arbitrary. They will thus tend to vary according to the will of the person (people) in charge of the process. This may produce inconsistent decisions, with some projects being accepted on the basis of one particular weighting scheme, and other rather similar projects being instead rejected due to the use of different weights. Even the employment of different sets of weights, although useful for examining the robustness of the analysis, cannot solve this issue as, ultimately, a definitive weighting scheme, leading to a particular option ranking, must be chosen.

Notwithstanding the idea of having an appraisal and evaluation process directed by policies may be appealing to someone, it must be noted that, in policy documents, objectives and strategies are defined at a too-high level of generality, so that specific information concerning decision criteria and weights cannot be immediately derived. Assuming, however, the possibility of locating weights in policy documents and government guidelines, several questions yet remain. Indeed, such policy weights are likely to vary from year to year, according to the composition of legislatures, political fashions, and the exigencies of bureaucrats. Hence, one may anticipate continued struggles over the weights to be adopted and the danger that special-interest groups will be offered the opportunity to have an undue degree of influence in the decision-making process.

Lastly, eliciting weights from stakeholder groups having different agendas will unavoidably lead to clashing weighting schemes and any attempt to reconcile these differences (through negotiation or, more simply, by calculating the average of a wide spectrum of values) may easily result in deadlocks of the process (Dean, 2018, 2020b). Chadwick (1971:276) summarizes the situation as follows: group weighting is a process that is not only difficult but also "theoretically impossible [...]. How might groups agree to a weighting which placed their own weight lower than that of others?" Echoing Chadwick's opinions, Manheim et al., 1975) argue that "Only a very naive group would agree to a compromise on a set of weights beforehand and then find that the resulting "highest score" alternative has disastrous results for them."

Hence, in an effort to avoid (or at least reduce) subjectivity and conflicts, some MCA tools and techniques, such as the NATA/WebTAG multi-criteria framework, have started not incorporating weights. However, also this approach has come under heavy criticism. Sayers et al. (2003), for instance, claim that the absence of any guidance relatively on which dimension and objective matter most may result in a reduction of the transparency of the process and lack of coherence in decision-making. A similar point is made by Dimitriou et al. (2010) who claim that owing to the omission of weights the analysis risks addressing social and environmental concerns as secondary to economic ones.

Overall, what clearly emerges from this discussion is that MCA cannot be clearly singled out as superior to other appraisal and evaluation methods, and its use should not be necessarily regarded as a panacea for better decisions.

6. Non-participatory and participatory approaches to multi-criteria analysis

Appraisal and evaluation can be undertaken either in *non-participatory* (*i.e.*, analyst-led) or *participatory* manner. In non-participatory assessments, the analysis is carried out autonomously by one of more analysts, according to a typical technocratic approach. The analysts gather, process and interpret data and information (by employing different decision-support methods and tools) and provide recommendations for the decision-maker(s) (*e.g.*, a Minister or a Government Department; a person, a few individuals or a committee with responsibility for the decision). A key argument in favor of this approach is that a group of trained specialists is best suited to support complicated and critical decisions. By contrast, participatory techniques adopt a more collaborative and (in principle more democratic) decision-making style, with the direct involvement of different interested and affected parties (*i.e.*, problem stakeholders) in the analysis. This thus may help analysts and decision-makers account, to the largest extent possible, for neglected perspectives, excluded possibilities and ignored issues. The choice over which approach is more appropriate depends on the nature of the problem at hand as well as on the resources available to carry out the analysis. Ideally, an analyst-led approach with no inputs from stakeholders may be more suitable for solving purely technical problems, characterized by a relatively low levels of uncertainty and ambiguity. On the contrary, more intricate and uncertain policy issues, affecting society at large, may be better addressed through (longer and more expensive) participatory processes in the attempt to ensure that all the different viewpoints regarding the decision situation are adequately represented (Funtowicz and Ravetz, 1991; Renn, 2015; Stirling, 1998, 2006).

While MCA has been originally conceived to be employed in a non-participatory manner, in the course of time, due to the ever growing demand for public participation in planning and decision-making processes, many arguments have been put forward to go beyond this technocratic model (Banville et al., 1998; Petts and Leach, 2000; Stagl, 2007; Stirling, 2006; Vari, 1995). Hence, especially over the past three decades, methodologies combining participatory and deliberative procedures with (in many cases, simplistic forms of) MCA have appeared in a rather diffuse way, in many planning and policy fields (*e.g.*, Burgess et al., 2007; Gregory and Keeney, 1994; Mcdowall and Eames, 2007; Munda, 2008; Proctor and Drechsler, 2006; Renn et al., 1993; Stagl, 2006; Stirling and Mayer, 2001). A number of multi-actor multi-criteria methods and approaches have also been expressly conceived for the transport sector. The most well-known methods are briefly summarized in Table 9. As it is noticeable from this table, however, it is not totally clear whether these techniques have enjoyed real-world applications or constitute mere academic proposals and how they fit (or would fit) with the current, conventional planning procedures, (analyst-led) appraisal and evaluation methods and public inquiry processes (Dean, 2018, 2020b).

In participatory MCA methods it is generally possible to distinguish two main categories of actors:

- A research team of analysts and specialist advisors, who run the process, taking (to the greatest extent possible) a general and independent view of the problem at hand, and ultimately present the results of the analysis to the decision-maker(s).
- Group decision-making participants, typically comprising problem stakeholders and, in some cases, in the attempt to incorporate a more scientific perspective in the analysis, also academics and experts. In principle, participants may take part in the multi-actor multi-criteria exercise individually or as representatives of organized groups (*e.g.*, local community groups, landowners, business groups, environmental experts).

In operational terms, the steps of participatory MCA methodologies resemble those of analyst-led MCA and typically encompass the following stages (which can take place in different orders and in different ways): development of options; identification of objectives and criteria against which to test options; weighting of criteria; and scoring of impacts of options against

Table 9 Key features of some participatory MCA methods proposed for the transport sector.

Methods	References	Application to real planning and decision-making processes	MCA Techniques employed	Actors involved	Level of participant involvement	Engagement techniques	Treatment of individual preferences
Goal-achievement matrix	Hill (1966, 1968, 1973)	Several application in the UK but generally applied in a non-participatory manner	Simple additive weighting model combined with some elements of the CBA framework	A few stakeholder groups. Types of stakeholder groups not always clear. Number of stakeholders per group not specified	Stakeholders can partially affect weights	Not specified	Mathematical aggregation of the weights provided by the various stakeholder groups
COSIMA, SUSTAIN, EcoMobility, Customized decision-support systems and other similar appraisal frameworks	Salling (2008), Leleur (2012), Barfod (2012), Jensen (2012), Jensen et al. (2013), Barfod and Salling (2015) and Salling et al. (2005, 2018)	Unclear—Apparently only theoretical application to real case studies	Combination of MCA based on the weighted additive model, CBA and different types of sensitivity analyses	Types and number of participants/groups not specified	Participants can affect objectives/criteria and weights	Workshops, Decision Conferences	The parties involved are required to reach an agreement over objectives and weights

Continued

Table 9 Key features of some participatory MCA methods proposed for the transport sector.—cont'd

Methods	References	Application to real planning and decision-making processes	MCA Techniques employed	Actors involved	Level of participant involvement	Engagement techniques	Treatment of individual preferences
Multi-actor multi-criteria analysis	Macharis et al. (2009, 2010, 2012), Macharis and Nijkamp (2011, 2013) and Macharis and Baudry (2018)	Several applications especially in Belgium, but real implications not clear	Typically, AHP and PROMETHEE but it is envisaged that any MCA method can be used	The few most important stakeholder groups (typically 3–6 groups). Number of stakeholders per group not specified	Stakeholders can affect objectives/criteria and weights	Interviews, workshops, surveys	The viewpoints of the different groups are both kept separated and aggregated together mathematically
Policy-led multi-criteria analysis	Dimitriou et al. (2010, 2016) and Ward et al. (2016a, 2016b)	None—Only used as part of theoretical role-play exercises	Simple additive weighting model	Different stakeholder and expert groups. A single representative for each group	Participants can partially affect options and objectives/criteria. They can also directly determine scores	Workshops	The viewpoints of the different groups are kept separated and used to explore possibilities of convergence of interests among the various actors

ANP/InViTO approach (participatory MCA combined with data visualization tools)	Lami et al (2011, 2014) and Pensa et al. (2013)	Unclear—Method developed as part of the Interreg IVB NWE Project Code24	Analytic Network Process (variation of AHP)	A few tens of people including citizen representatives, decision-makers and experts	Participants can affect options the priority of different criteria (weights) and the local priority of each option with reference to each criterion (scores)	Workshops and questionnaires supported by data visualization tools (InViTO)	The viewpoints of the different participants are aggregated together mathematically
Two-Stage MCA	De Brucker et al. (2015)	Limited/ Unclear	AHP	The few most important stakeholder groups. Number of stakeholders per group not specified	Stakeholders can affect objectives/ criteria and weights	Workshops	The viewpoints of the different groups are kept separated and used to explore possibilities of convergence of interests among the various actors

Adapted from Dean, M., 2018 Assessing the Applicability of Participatory Multi-Criteria Analysis Methodologies to the Appraisal of Mega Transport Infrastructure. Ph.D. Dissertation. The Bartlett School of Planning, University College London, UK. (https://www.academia.edu/43180035/Assessing_the_Applicability_of_Participatory_Multi-Criteria_Analysis_Methodologies_to_the_Appraisal_of_Mega_Transport_Infrastructure).

the different criteria. However, differently from analyst-led methods, in participatory MCA techniques group decision-making participants can contribute to the identification of the key elements of the multi-criteria framework (*i.e.*, options, objectives and criteria, weights and scores). Methodological adaptations of MCA to group decision-making seem thus to have taken place primarily in three main domains (Dean, 2018):

- Identification, classification and selection of group decision-making participants.
- Involvement of stakeholders (and experts) in the analysis and management of group processes.
- Collection, processing and inclusion of the group decision-making participants' preferences in the multi-criteria framework.

Each domain, however, entails some critical dilemmas and methodological challenges. Regarding the first domain, for example, it is possible to notice that with a few exceptions (*e.g.*, Banville et al., 1998; Ward et al., 2016a, 2016b), the literature on participatory MCA is rather vague on how group decision-making participants are identified and selected. On the one hand, echoing the literature on discursive democracy (*e.g.*, Forester, 1999; Healey, 1998, 2003; Innes, 1996), proponents of multi-actor multi-criteria methods (*e.g.*, Macharis and Nijkamp, 2011) emphasize that, ideally, in a MCA exercise all the parties that are affected by the issue under discussion should be involved or represented, with no viewpoint excluded a priori. On the other hand, the practical need for creating a workable and efficient process, limits drastically the number of group decision-making participants. In this regard a comprehensive review of participatory MCA techniques (Dean, 2018) have revealed that such processes rarely involve more than 30 people overall. Obviously, an appraisal or evaluation exercise regarding a major planning and policy problem which involves only a few actors and groups does not satisfy the requirements of statistical representativeness and, paradoxically, risks even representing a step backwards with reference to democracy and equity (Dean, 2018, 2020b).

In order to engage with stakeholders, a large variety of participatory techniques, ranging from simple interviews and structured questionnaires to in-depth group discussions, can be employed. Each technique has its own potential benefits and drawbacks. For example, individual interviews prevent interactions and discussions between the different participants and groups. However, they enable a more thorough investigation of each participant's interests and priorities, while avoiding groupthink (Dean, 2020b). In the attempt to facilitate the processes and generate some fruitful discussions, some methods (*e.g.*, Lami et al., 2011, 2014; Pensa et al., 2013) also make large use of specialized software and visualization tools. The involvement of actors and groups can also be realized with different degrees of intensity and in a wide variety of forms. Methods range from limited-participatory techniques, where participants take part only in some stages of the process and thus have the possibility of affecting only partially the multi-criteria framework, to fully-participatory techniques, in which instead the various parties are involved in the definition of options, objectives/criteria, weights, scores (Dean, 2018). As shown in Fig. 10, at one extreme of the spectrum it is possible to find methods such as the aforementioned Goal-Achievement Matrix (Hill, 1966, 1968, 1973), where participants' preferences are considered by the research team only during the determination of the weighting scheme. At the other extreme of the spectrum, there is, for instance, the Policy-Led Multi-Criteria Analysis (Dimitriou et al., 2010, 2016; Ward et al., 2016a,b), in which, instead, participants are directly or indirectly involved in the determination of options, objectives/criteria, and scores. However, it must be stressed that while it is reasonable to assume that different problems would require different engagement techniques and a different level of involvement of group decision-making participants, in the papers and articles presenting such methods, clear explanations and justifications for the approaches adopted are rarely provided (Dean, 2018).

Moreover, it is also clear that, although potentially important to ensure a comprehensive examination of the problem, the inclusion of stakeholder groups and other interested parties in the analysis, increases exponentially the complexity of the MCA exercise as clearly illustrated by Figs. 11 and 12. Indeed, under an analyst-led approach, a typical discrete multi-criteria decision-making problem, involving a finite set A of M options, $A=\{a_1, a_2, a_3, \ldots a_M\}$, and a set C of N criteria, $C=\{c_1, c_2, c_3, \ldots c_N\}$, characterized by and a set of weights $W=\{w_1, w_2, w_3, \ldots, w_N\}$, can be synthetically represented by a $N \times M$ matrix, whose typical element $x_j(a_i)$ ($i=1, 2, \ldots, M$; $j=1, 2, \ldots, N$) represents the evaluation of the i-th alternative by means of the j-th criterion (see Fig. 11).

By comparison, with a multi-actor multi-criteria exercise involving G group decision-making participants, the problem is described by a three-dimensional matrix $N \times M \times G$, which captures also the preferences of the different parties involved in the exercise. When participants are provided with the possibility of scoring the impacts of the options under study, the generic element of the matrix $x_j(a_i)^K$ ($i=1, 2, \ldots, M$; $j=1, 2, \ldots, N$; $k=1, 2, 3, \ldots, G$) represents the evaluation of the i-th alternative by

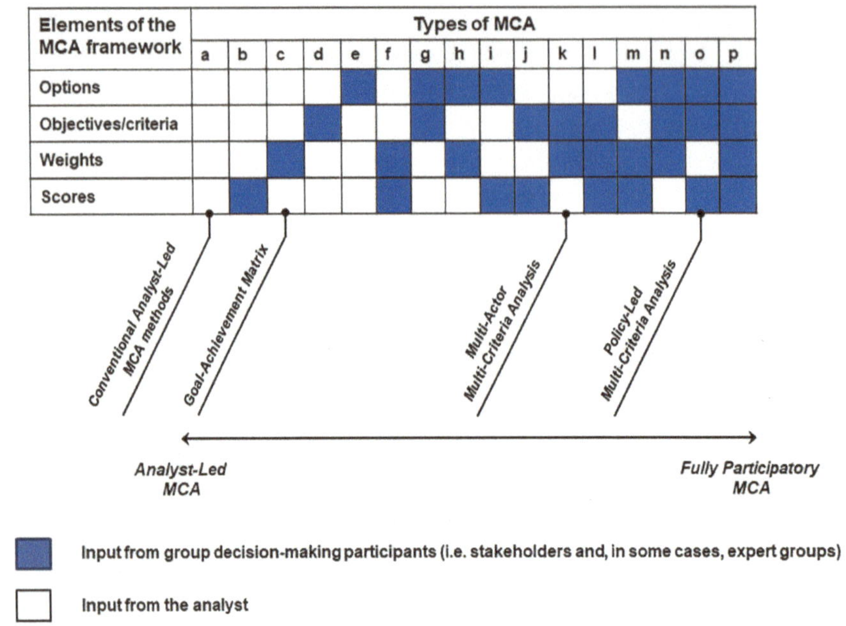

Fig. 10 Types of participatory MCA methods. *Adapted from Dean, M., 2018. Assessing the Applicability of Participatory Multi-Criteria Analysis Methodologies to the Appraisal of Mega Transport Infrastructure. Ph.D. Dissertation. The Bartlett School of Planning, University College London, UK. (https://www.academia.edu/43180035/Assessing_the_Applicability_of_Participatory_Multi-Criteria_Analysis_Methodologies_to_the_Appraisal_of_Mega_Transport_Infrastructure).*

Criteria	Weights	Options				
		a_1	a_2	a_3		a_M
c_1	w_1	$x_1(a_1)$	$x_1(a_2)$	$x_1(a_3)$		$x_1(a_M)$
c_2	w_2	$x_2(a_1)$	$x_2(a_2)$	$x_2(a_3)$		$x_2(a_M)$
c_3	w_3	$x_3(a_1)$	$x_3(a_2)$	$x_3(a_3)$		$x_3(a_M)$
c_N	w_N	$x_N(a_1)$	$x_N(a_2)$	$x_N(a_3)$		$x_N(a_M)$

Fig. 11 Tabular representation of a multi-criteria decision-making problem under an analyst-led approach to MCA. *Author's own elaboration.*

means of the j-th criterion according to the viewpoint of the k-th group decision-making participant. Moreover, if participants are also offered the opportunity to identify their own list of objectives and criteria and the weights of these criteria (Approach 'L' in Fig. 10), the set C or criteria

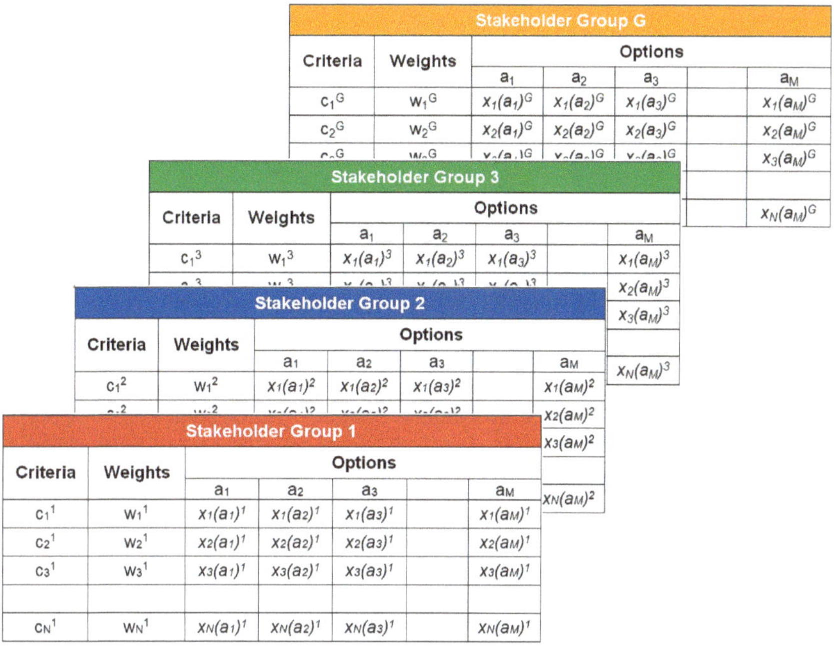

Fig. 12 Tabular representation of a multi-criteria decision-making problem under a participatory approach to MCA. *Author's own elaboration.*

and the set W of weights can also vary according to the viewpoint of the person (or group) undertaking the assessment (see Fig. 12). In general, since stakeholder groups typically present different interests and priorities, a participatory MCA process may lead to as many lists of criteria, weighting schemes and sets of scores as the number of groups involved. When the multi-actor multi-criteria exercise involves a high number of participants (as a participatory process on a large-scale transport project or another major policy problem would theoretically require) the multi-criteria framework can thus easily become very difficult (if not impossible) to manage and analyze.

Finally, one of the most critical aspects of participatory MCA is represented by the ways in which the interests and priorities of the different stakeholder groups are collected and processed to determine the options, the list of objectives and criteria, the set of scores and/or the weighting scheme. Different approaches, each having its own advantages and drawbacks, are possible (Dean, 2018; Dean et al., 2019). The points of view of the actors and groups taking part in the process can be kept separate from each other with the view to highlighting better differences and similarities in the

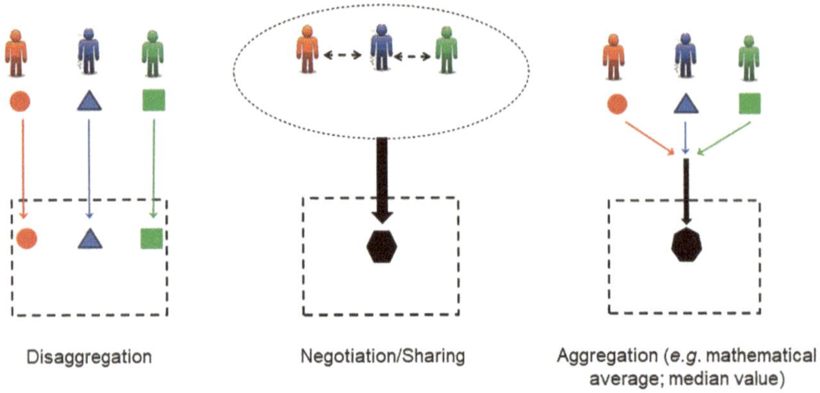

Fig. 13 Possible strategies for integrating multiple stakeholders' perspectives in participatory MCA. *Adapted from Dean, M., 2018. Assessing the Applicability of Participatory Multi-Criteria Analysis Methodologies to the Appraisal of Mega Transport Infrastructure. Ph.D. Dissertation. The Bartlett School of Planning, University College London, UK. (https://www.academia.edu/43180035/Assessing_the_Applicability_of_Participatory_Multi-Criteria_Analysis_Methodologies_to_the_Appraisal_of_Mega_Transport_Infrastructure).*

positions of the various group decision-making participants. In alternative, participants' viewpoints can be aggregated together (either through discussions and negotiations between participants or in a more mechanical way by determining the "average" between the various participants' preferences) in order to obtain a more practical synthesis between the positions of the various groups and actors (Fig. 13). Also regarding this aspect, the various participatory MCA methods proposed in the literature adopt different strategies, in many cases, however, without explaining the rationale behind this choice (Dean, 2018).

According to many proponents of such methods, participation and deliberation can strengthen the key attributes of MCA. In particular it is often mentioned that:

- The inclusion of stakeholders (and experts) in the analysis can further enrich the multi-criteria framework, by leading to the identification of the full spectrum of interests and values in dispute, thus improving the overall quality of any appraisal and evaluation exercise (Cornet et al., 2018b; Leleur, 2012; Macharis and Baudry, 2018; Salling, 2008).
- When combined with MCA methods, deliberative procedures can enhance even more the transparency of the appraisal exercise (Cornet et al., 2018a; Lami et al., 2011; Macharis et al., 2012).

- Finally, the involvement of different stakeholders in the appraisal exercise is expected to promote mutual learning and build trust among the interested parties (Barfod, 2018; Cornet et al., 2018b; Lami et al., 2014). It also supposed to increase the likelihood of acceptance of the results of the analysis by stakeholders themselves, as group decision-making participants are much more likely to take ownership of the decisions that emerge from the process (Macharis et al., 2009, 2010; Macharis and Nijkamp, 2013).

To date, however, impartial empirical testing of multi-actor multi-criteria methods does not seem to have been very common. So far, only a couple of studies aimed at investigating (objectively) the strength and weaknesses of such methods (rather than promoting them) have been published. These studies, undertaken by Dean et al. (2019) and Dean (2020b), have aroused doubts regarding many of the presumed benefits of participatory MCA techniques (see also Dean, 2018). These studies have shown, in particular, that participants may experience difficulties in formulating meaningful objectives and criteria, so that the direct involvement of stakeholders and experts in the appraisal or evaluation exercise may not necessarily increase the breadth of the assessment compared to a purely analyst-led approach to MCA. Furthermore, It has been stressed that several people may also experience difficulties in understanding the basic principle of MCA, with consequent concerns over the reliability of the outcome of the process. Questions have also been raised over the real willingness of stakeholders to share entirely their agendas during the process and engage in a cooperative dialog with the other parties. In decision-making situations where stakes are high, multi-actor multi-criteria methods seem also dangerously exposed to the risks of bias and dishonesty, implying people setting (unintentionally or intentionally) scores and weights to increase the probability that a particular goal will occur or to put deliberately other parties at a disadvantage. As already highlighted, then, when many different actors and groups are involved, the process can easily become very difficult to manage and deriving clear conclusions from different constellations of opinions can be quite problematic. Finally, it is also evident that there is also a huge potential for arbitrariness in such processes with many parameters (*e.g.*, number and types of group decision-making participants taking part in the exercise; level of participants involvement; and approach adopted to handle the participants' point of view), whose selections can alter dramatically the results of the process and thus further increase the intrinsic subjectivity of MCA.

7. Conclusions

The last 50 years have seen the rise in the popularity of MCA and the consequent establishment of a number of different assessment methods, tools and techniques accounting for multiple objectives and decision criteria. On the one hand, this diversity makes MCA a dynamic and highly versatile appraisal and evaluation approach, which can be tailored to suit the needs of the problem at hand. Surely one of the greatest values of MCA is in offering a rather natural and attractive framework for structuring complex problems, handling large amounts of data and information in a consistent way, and stimulating thinking and reflections over the different possible alternative solutions and their implications. On the other hand, it is also undeniable that this huge assortment of approaches, the great diversity between these methods and the lack of axiomatic foundations of many of them, render MCA a rather chaotic field and confer to this discipline a high degree of subjectivity, often making the results of the analysis open to debate and incapable of proper third-party audits.

This chapter, in particular, has highlighted a fundamental disconnection between the academic literature on MCA and transport assessment practice. Indeed, whereas many researchers seem to focus on the use, refinement, and development of sophisticated MCA techniques, most practitioners rely on simplified and frequently rough MCA implementations. The reasons for this primarily lie in the unfamiliarity of many planners, officials, decision-makers and other interested parties with formal MCA methods, but also in the lack of attention paid by scholars to the political character of transport planning and policy-making. Indeed, it must not be forgotten that decisions over major transport investments and other complex policy issues involving intense power struggles between stakeholders are rarely based (only) on technical reports and elaborated mathematical calculations concerning the benefits and costs of the possible alternative solutions (Dean, 2018). Hence, more dialogue and collaborative research between academics and practitioners would be fundamental for the formulation of MCA methods capable of ensuring a good compromise between standardization and rigor of the analysis, on the one hand, and ease of implementation and understandability of the assessment process, on the other hand. Surveys investigating the opinions of politicians, government officials, civil servants and other real transport decision-makers regarding the perceived pros and cons of multi-criteria tools and techniques, which are actually supposed to help them, would also be critical for the development of methods based on pragmatic and realistic implementations of robust theories. So far, such studies have been conducted only with reference to CBA (*e.g.*, Annema et al., 2015; Beukers et al., 2012; Mouter, 2017; Nyborg, 1998; Sager and Ravlum, 2005).

Participatory MCA methods also constitute another area where there seem to be a strong discrepancy between theory and practice. Notwithstanding the growing number of publications on this subject, so far several critical aspects have been largely neglected by the proponents of such methods. Also in this case, a closer collaboration between scholars and professionals and further empirical research to test the potential advantages and limitations of the different multi-actor multi-criteria approaches would be important. However, given the simplistic and idealistic assumptions which many of participatory MCA techniques seems to rely on (*e.g.*, the willingness of the various stakeholder groups to cooperate, learn about each other's social identities, and refrain from using power to influence decision-making), faith in the ability of such methods to open new perspectives and opportunities for transport project and policy assessment may turn out to be deeply misplaced.

References

ADB (Asian Development Bank), 2017. Guidelines for the Economic Analysis of Projects. Asian Development Bank.

Alberquerque, E., 2013. The NZ transport agency's transport appraisal framework. Policy Q. 9 (4), 66–70.

Alexander, E.R., 2006. Evolution and status: where is planning evaluation today and how did it get here? In: Alexander, E.R. (Ed.), Evaluation in Planning—Evolution and Prospects. Ashgate, pp. 3–16.

Annema, J.A., Mouter, N., Razaei, J., 2015. Cost-benefit analysis (CBA), or multi-criteria decision-making (MCDM) or both: politicians' perspective in transport policy appraisal. Transp. Res. Proc. 10, 788–797.

Arrow, K.J., Raynaud, H., 1986. Social Choice and Multicriterion Decision-Making. The MIT Press.

Aruldoss, M., Lakshmi, T.M., Venkatesan, V.P., 2013. A survey on multi criteria decision making methods and its applications. Am. J. Inf. Syst. 1 (1), 31–43.

Asadabadi, M.R., Chang, E., Saberi, M., 2019. Are MCDM methods useful? A critical review of analytic hierarchy process (AHP) and analytic network process (ANP) Cogent Eng. 6 (1). https://www.tandfonline.com/doi/full/10.1080/23311916.2019.1623153.

Bana e Costa, C.A., Vansnick, J.-C., 2008. A critical analysis of the eigenvalue method used to derive priorities in AHP. Eur. J. Oper. Res. 187 (3), 1422–1428.

Bana e Costa, C.A., Stewart, T.J., Vansnick, J.-C., 1997. Multicriteria decision analysis: some thoughts based on the tutorial and discussion sessions of the ESIGMA meetings. Eur. J. Oper. Res. 99 (1), 28–37.

Banihabib, M.B., Hashemi-Madani, F.-S., Forghani, A., 2017. Comparison of compensatory and non-compensatory multi criteria decision making models in water resources strategic management. J. Water Resour. Manag. 31, 3745–3759.
Banville, C., Landry, M., Martel, J.M., Boulaire, C., 1998. A stakeholder approach to MCDA. Syst. Res. Behav. Sci. 15 (1), 15–32.
Barfod, M.B., 2012. Optimising Transport Decision Making Using Customised Decision Models and Decision Conferences. Ph.D. Dissertation, Department of Transport, Technical University of Denmark.
Barfod, M., 2018. Sustainable transport planning: involving stakeholders in the decision support process using planning workshops and MCDA. Transport 33 (4), 1052–1066.
Barfod, M.B., Leleur, S. (Eds.), 2014. Multi-Criteria Decision Analysis for Use in Transport Decision Making, second ed. DTU Transport.
Barfod, M.B., Salling, K.B., 2015. A new composite decision support framework for strategic and sustainable transport appraisals. Transp. Res. A 72 (1), 1–15.
Beinat, E., 2001. Multi-criteria analysis for environmental management. J. Multi-Criteria Decis. Anal. 10 (2), 51.
Belton, V., 1986. A comparison of the analytic hierarchy process and a simple multi-attribute value function. Eur. J. Oper. Res. 26, 7–21.
Belton, V., Stewart, T., 2002. Multiple Criteria Decision Analysis: An Integrated Approach. Kluwer Academic Publisher.
Beukers, E., Bertolini, L., Te Brömmelstroet, M., 2012. Why cost benefit analysis is perceived as a problematic tool for assessment of transport plans: a process perspective. Transp. Res. A 46, 68–78.
Bouyssou, D., Marchant, T., Pirlot, M., Perny, P., Tsoukias, A., Vincke, P., 2000. Evaluation and Decision Models: A Critical Perspective. Kluwer Academic Publishers.
Bouyssou, D., Marchant, T., Pirlot, M., Tsoukias, A., Vincke, P., 2006. Evaluation and Decision Models With Multiple Criteria: Stepping Stones for the Analyst. Springer.
Brans, J.-P., Mareschal, B., 2005. Promethee methods. In: Figueira, J., Greco, S., Ehrgott, M. (Eds.), Multiple Criteria Decision Analysis: State of the Art Surveys. Springer, pp. 163–195.
Brans, J.P., Vicke, P., 1985. A preference ranking organization method. Manag. Sci. 31, 647–655.
Bristow, A.L., Nellthorp, J., 2000. Transport project appraisal in the European Union. Transp. Policy 7 (1), 51–60.
Brown, M., Milner, S., Bulman, E., 2001. Assessing transport investment projects: a policy assessment model. In: Giorgi, L., Pohoryles, R.J. (Eds.), Transport Policy and Research: What Future? Ashgate, pp. 44–89.
Browne, D., Ryan, L., 2011. Comparative analysis of evaluation techniques for transport policies. Environ. Impact Assess. Rev. 31, 226–233.
Burgess, J., Stirling, A., Clark, J., Davies, G., Eames, M., Staley, K., Williamson, S., 2007. Deliberative mapping: a novel analytic deliberative methodology to support contested science-policy decisions. Public Underst. Sci. 16 (3), 299–322.
Chadwick, G.F., 1971. A Systems View of Planning: Towards a Theory of the Urban and Regional Planning. Pergamon Press.
Chankong, V., Haimes, Y.Y., 1983. Multiobjective decision making: theory and methodology. In: Sage, A.P. (Ed.), vol. 8. North-Holland Series in System Science and Engineering. Elsevier Science Publishing.
Charnes, A., Cooper, W.W., 1961. Management Models and Industrial Applications of Linear Programming. John Wiley & Sons.
Charnes, A., Cooper, W.W., 1977. Goal programming and multiple objectives optimisations. Eur. J. Oper. Res. 1, 39–54.

Charnes, A., Cooper, W.W., Ferguson, R., 1955. Optimal estimation of executive compensation by linear programming. Manag. Sci. 1, 138–151.
COA (Commonwealth of Australia), 2006. National Guidance for Transport System Management in Australia. Commonwealth of Australia.
Cook, W.D., Golan, I., Kazakov, A., Kress, M., 1988. A case study of a non-compensatory approach to ranking transportation projects. J. Oper. Res. Soc. 39 (10), 901–910.
Cornet, Y., Barradale, M., Gudmundsson, H., Barfod, M., 2018a. Engaging multiple actors in large-scale transport infrastructure project appraisal: an application of MAMCA to the case of HS2 high-speed rail. J. Adv. Transp. 18, 1–22.
Cornet, Y., Barradale, M., Barfod, M., Hickman, R., 2018b. Giving future generations a voice: constructing a sustainability viewpoint in transport appraisal. Eur. J. Transp. Infrastruct. Res. 18 (3), 316–339.
Darwin, M., Cledan, M.-P., Schuyler, H., Schwartz, J.Z., 2016. Prioritizing Infrastructure Investment a Framework for Government Decision Making. Policy Research Working Paper No. 7674. The World Bank Group.
Darwin, M., Schuyler, H., Aditi, R., 2018. Prioritizing Infrastructure Investments: A Comparative Review of Applications in Chile. Policy Research Working Paper No. 8602. The World Bank Group.
De Brucker, K., Macharis, C., Verbeke, A., 2015. Two-stage multi-criteria analysis and the future of ITS-based safety innovation projects. IET Intell. Transp. Syst. 9 (9), 842–850.
Dean, M., 2018. Assessing the Applicability of Participatory Multi-Criteria Analysis Methodologies to the Appraisal of Mega Transport Infrastructure. Ph.D. Dissertation, The Bartlett School of Planning, University College, London, UK. https://www.academia.edu/43180035/Assessing_the_Applicability_of_Participatory_Multi-Criteria_Analysis_Methodologies_to_the_Appraisal_of_Mega_Transport_Infrastructure.
Dean, M., 2020a. A Practical Guide to Multi-Criteria Analysis. Forthcoming, ResearchGate.
Dean, M., 2020b. Participatory multi-criteria analysis methodologies: comprehensive, inclusive, transparent and user-friendly? An application to the case of the London gateway port. Res. Transp. Econ. https://authors.elsevier.com/tracking/article/details.do?aid=100887&jid=RETREC&surname=Dean.
Dean, M., Hickman, R., 2018. Comparing cost-benefit analysis and participatory multi-criteria analysis methodologies. In: Baudry, G., Macharis, C. (Eds.), Decision-Making for Sustainable Transport and Mobility: Multi Actor Multi Criteria Analysis. Edward Elgar, pp. 100–119.
Dean, M., Hickman, R., Chen, C.-L., 2019. Testing the application of participatory MCA: the case of the South Fylde Line. Transp. Policy 73, 62–70.
Deluka-Tibljaš, A., Karleuša, B., Dragičević, N., 2013. PReview of multicriteria-analysis methods application in decision making about transport infrastructure. Gradjevinar 65, 619–631.
Despotin, M., Moscarola, J., Spronk, C., 1983. A user oriented listing of multiple criteria decision methods. Revue Belge de Statistique, d'Informatique et de Recherche Operationnelle 23 (4), 4–110.
DETR (Department of the Environment, Transport and the Regions), 1998a. A New Deal for Trunk Roads in England: Understanding the New Approach to Appraisal. DETR, London.
DETR (Department of the Environment, Transport and the Regions), 1998b. A New Deal for Trunk Roads in England: Guidance on the New Approach to Appraisal. DETR, London.
DfT (Department for Transport), 2005. Introduction to Transport Analysis—Tag Unit 1.1. Department for Transport, Transport Analysis Guidance.
DfT (Department for Transport), 2014. Transport Analysis Guidance (TAG). URL, www.webtag.org.uk.

DfT (Department for Transport), 2018a. Transport Analysis Guidance: The Transport Appraisal Process. Department for Transport.

DfT (Department for Transport), 2018b. Early Assessment and Sifting Tool (EAST) Guidance. Department for Transport.

Dimitriou, H.T., Ward, E.J., Wright, P., 2010. Incorporating Principles of Sustainable Development within the Design and Delivery of Major Projects: An International Study with Particular Reference to Major Infrastructure Projects for the Institution of Civil Engineering and the Actuarial Profession. OMEGA Centre, The Bartlett School of Planning, University College London.

Dimitriou, H.T., Wright, P., Ward, E.J., 2012. Lessons for Decision-Makers: A Comparative Analysis of Selected Large-Scale Transport Infrastructure Projects in Europe, USA and Asia-Pacific. Executive Summary, OMEGA Centre, The Bartlett School of Planning, University College London.

Dimitriou, H.T., Ward, E.J., Dean, M., 2016. Presenting the case for the application of multi-criteria analysis to mega transport infrastructure appraisal. Res. Transp. Econ. 58, 7–20, Special Edition.

Dobes, L., Bennett, J., 2009. Multi-criteria analysis: good enough|| for government work? Agenda 16 (3), 7–29.

Dobes, L., Bennett, J., 2010. Multi-criteria analysis: ignorance or negligence? In: Paper presented at the 'Australasian Transport Research Forum 2010', Canberra, Australia, 29 September–1 October.

Dodgson, J.S., Spackman, M., Pearman, A., Phillips, L.D., 2009. Multi-Criteria Analysis: A Manual. Department for Communities and Local Government, London.

Dom, A., 1999. Environmental impact assessment of road and rail infrastructure. In: Petts, J. (Ed.), Handbook of Environmental Impact Assessment Volume 2—Environmental Impact Assessment in Practice: Impact and Limitation. Blackwell Science Ltd, pp. 331–350.

Douglas, N.J., Wallis, I., Lawrence, A., Wignall, D., 2013. International Comparison of Transport Appraisal Practice—Annex 7 New Zealand Country Report. Institute for Transport Studies, University of Leeds.

Dyer, J.S., 1990. Remarks on the analytic hierarchy process. Manag. Sci. 36 (3), 249–258.

EC (European Commission), 2008. Guide to Cost–Benefit Analysis of Investment Projects. European Commission, Brussels.

EC (European Commission), 2015. Guide to Cost–Benefit Analysis of Investment Projects: Economic Appraisal Tool for Cohesion Policy 2014–2020. European Commission, Brussels.

Edwards, W., 1977. How to use multiattribute utility measurement for social decision making. IEEE Trans. Syst. Man Cybern. 7 (5), 326–340.

Edwards, W., Barron, F.H., 1994. SMART and SMARTER: improved simple methods for multiattribute utility measurement. Organ. Behav. Hum. Decis. Process. 60, 306–325.

Ehrgott, M., 2005. Multiobjective programming. In: Figueira, J., Greco, S., Ehrgott, M. (Eds.), Multiple Criteria Decision Analysis: State of the Art Surveys. Springer, pp. 667–722.

EIB (European Investment Bank), 2013. The Economic Appraisal of Investment Projects at the EIB. European Investment Bank.

Ergas, H., 2009. In defence of cost-benefit analysis. Agenda 16 (3), 31–40.

Faludi, A., Voogd, H., 1985. Evaluation of complex policy problems: some introductory remarks. In: Faludi, A., Voogd, H. (Eds.), Evaluation of Complex Policy Problems. Delftsche Uitgevers Maatschappij B.V., pp. 1–6

Ferrari, P., 2003. A method for choosing from among alternative transportation projects. Eur. J. Oper. Res. 150 (1), 194–203.

Figueira, J., Greco, S., Ehrgott, M., 2005a. Introduction. In: Figueira, J., Greco, S., Ehrgott, M. (Eds.), Multiple Criteria Decision Analysis: State of the Art Surveys. Springer, pp. xxi–xxxvi.
Figueira, J., Greco, S., Ehrgott, M. (Eds.), 2005b. Multiple Criteria Decision Analysis: State of the Art Surveys. Springer.
Figueira, J., Mousseau, V., Roy, B., 2005c. ELECTRE methods. In: Figueira, J., Greco, S., Ehrgott, M. (Eds.), Multiple Criteria Decision Analysis: State of the Art Surveys. Springer, pp. 135–162.
Fishburn, P.C., 1970. Utility Theory for Decision Making. Research Analysis Corporation.
Forester, J., 1999. The Deliberative Practitioner: Encouraging Participatory Planning Processes. The MIT Press.
Funtowicz, S.O., Ravetz, J.R., 1991. A new scientific methodology for global environmental issues. In: Costanza, R. (Ed.), Ecological Economics: The Science and Management of Sustainability. Columbia University Press, pp. 137–152.
Giampietro, M., 2003. Multi-Scale Integrated Analysis of Agroecosystem. CRC Press.
Goodman, A.S., Hastak, M., 2006. Infrastructure Planning Handbook—Planning, Engineering, and Economics. ASCE Press.
Grant-Muller, S.M., MacKie, P., Nellthorp, J., Pearman, A., 2001. Economic appraisal of European transport projects: the state-of-the-art revisited. Transplant. Rev. 21 (2), 237–261.
Gregory, R., Keeney, R.L., 1994. Creating policy alternative using stakeholder values. Manage. Sci. 40 (8), 1035–1048.
Guhnemann, A., Laird, J.J., Pearman, A.D., 2012. Combining cost-benefit and multi-criteria analysis to prioritise a national road infrastructure programme. Transp. Policy 23, 15–24.
Guitouni, A., Martel, J.-M., 1998. Tentative guidelines to help choosing an appropriate MCDA method. Eur. J. Oper. Res. 109 (2), 501–521.
Gustavson, K., Lonergan, S., Ruitenbeek, H., 1999. Selection and modelling of sustainable development indicators: a case study of the Fraser River Basin, British Columbia. Ecol. Econ. 28 (1), 117–132.
Harker, P.T., Vargas, L.G., 1987. The theory of ratio scale estimation: Saaty's analytic hierarchy process. Manag. Sci. 33 (1), 1383–1403.
Hayashi, Y., Morisugi, H., 2000. International comparison of background concept and methodology of transportation project appraisal. Transp. Policy 7 (1), 73–88.
Healey, P., 1998. Collaborative planning in a stakeholder society. Town Plan. Rev. 69 (1), 1–21.
Healey, P., 2003. Collaborative planning in perspective. Plan. Theory 2 (2), 101–123.
Herath, G., Prato, T. (Eds.), 2006. Using Multi-Criteria Decision Analysis in Natural Resource Management. Ashgate.
Hickman, R., 2019. The gentle tyranny of cost–benefit analysis in transport appraisal. In: Docherty, I., Shaw, J. (Eds.), Transport Matters. Policy Press, pp. 131–152.
Hickman, R., Dean, M., 2018. Incomplete cost—incomplete benefit analysis in transport appraisal. Transplant. Rev. 38 (6), 689–709.
Hill, M., 1966. A Method for Evaluating Alternative Plans: The Goals-Achievement Matrix Applied to Transportation Plans. Ph.D. Dissertation, Graduate School of Arts & Science, University of Pennsylvania.
Hill, M., 1968. A goals-achievement matrix for evaluating alternative plans. J. Am. Inst. Plann. 34 (1), 19–29.
Hill, M., 1973. Planning for Multiple Objectives—An Approach to the Evaluation of Transport Plans. Technion.
Hill, M., 1985. Can multiple-objective evaluation methods enhance rationality in planning? In: Breheny, M., Hooper, A. (Eds.), Rationality in Planning—Critical Essay on the Role of the Rationality in Urban and Regional Planning. Pion Limited, pp. 166–182.

Huang, I.B., Keisler, J., Linkov, I., 2011. Multi-criteria decision analysis in environmental sciences: ten years of applications and trends. Sci. Total Environ. 409 (19), 3578–3594.
Innes, J.E., 1996. Planning through consensus building: a new view of the comprehensive planning ideal. J. Am. Plann. Assoc. 62 (4), 460–472.
Ishizaka, A., Labib, A., 2011. Review of the main developments in the analytic hierarchy process. Expert Syst. Appl. 38 (11), 14336–14345.
Ishizaka, A., Nemery, P., 2013. Multi-Criteria Decision Analysis: Methods and Software. John Wiley & Sons, Ltd.
Janssen, R., 2001. On the use of multi-criteria analysis in environmental impact assessment in the Netherlands. J. Multi-Criteria Decis. Anal. 10 (2), 101–109.
Janssen, R., Munda, G., 1999. Multi-criteria methods for quantitative, qualitative and fuzzy evaluation problems. In: van den Bergh, J. (Ed.), Handbook of Environmental and Resource Economics. Edward Elgar, pp. 837–852.
Jeffreys, I., 2004. The use of compensatory and non-compensatory multi-criteria analysis for small-scale forestry. Small Scale For. Econ. Manag. Policy 3 (1), 99–117.
Jensen, A.V., 2012. Appraisal of Transport Projects: Assessing Robustness in Decision Making. Ph.D. Dissertation, Department of Transport, Technical University of Denmark.
Jensen, A.V., Salling, K.B., Leleur, S., 2013. The sustain appraisal framework: flexible decision support for national sustainable transport planning. In: Paper Presented at the '13th World Conference of Transport Research' Rio de Janeiro, Brazil, July–1518.
JICA (Japan International Cooperation Agency), 2004. JICA Guideline for Project Evaluation—Practical Methods for Project Evaluation. Office of Evaluation, Planning and Coordination Department Japan International Cooperation Agency (JICA).
Keeney, R.L., 1977. The art of assessing multiattribute utility functions. Organ. Behav. Hum. Perform. 19, 267–310.
Keeney, R., Raiffa, H., 1976. Decisions With Multiple Objectives: Preferences and Value Tradeoffs. Wiley.
Kodikara, P.N., 2008. Multi-Objective Optimal Operation of Urban Water Supply Systems. Ph.D. Dissertation, Victoria University, Australia.
Köksalan, M.M., Wallenius, J., Zionts, S., 2011. Multiple Criteria Decision Making: From Early History to the 21st Century. World Scientific Publishing.
Korhonen, P., 2005. Interactive methods. In: Figueira, J., Greco, S., Ehrgott, M. (Eds.), Multiple Criteria Decision Analysis: State of the Art Surveys. Springer, pp. 641–665.
Kuhn, H.W., Tucker, A.W., 1951. Nonlinear Programming. Proceedings of the 2nd Berkeley Symposium on Mathematics, Statistics and Probability. University of California Press, Berkeley, pp. 481–492.
Lami, I.M., Masala, E., Pensa, S., 2011. Analytic network process (ANP) and visualization of spatial data: the use of dynamic maps in territorial transformation processes. Int. J. Anal. Hierarchy Process 3 (2), 92–106.
Lami, I.M., Abastante, F., Masala, E., Pensa, S., 2014. Integrating multicriteria evaluation and data visualization as a problem structuring approach to support territorial transformation projects. EURO J. Decis. Process. 2, 281–312.
Leleur, S., 2012. Complex Strategic Choices: Applying Systemic Planning for Strategic Decision Making. Springer.
Li, Y., Thomas, M.A., 2014. A multiple criteria decision analysis (MCDA) software selection framework. In: Paper Prepared for the 47th Hawaii International Conference on System Science.
Lichfield, N., 1956. Economics of Planned Development. The Estates Gazette Ltd.
Lichfield, N., 1960. Cost benefit analysis in city planning. J. Am. Inst. Plann. 26 (4), 89–91.
Lichfield, N., 1966. Cost benefit analysis in town planning: a case study: Swanley. Urban Stud. 3, 215–249.

Lichfield, N., 1969. Cost benefit analysis in urban expansion. Reg. Stud. 3 (2), 123–155.
Lichfield, N., 1990. Plan evaluation methodology: comprehending the conclusion. In: Shefer, D., Voogd, H. (Eds.), Evaluation Methods for Urban and Regional Plans. Pion, pp. 79–97.
Lichfield, N., 1993. Problems of valuation discussed. In: Banister, D., Button, K. (Eds.), Transport, the Environment and Sustainable Development. Routledge, pp. 205–211.
Lichfield, N., 1996. Community Impact Evaluation. UCL Press.
Macharis, C., Baudry, G., 2018. The multi actor multi criteria analysis framework. In: Baudry, G., Macharis, C. (Eds.), Decision-Making for Sustainable Transport and Mobility. Edward Elgar, pp. 2–27.
Macharis, C., Bernardini, A., 2015. Reviewing the use of multi-criteria decision analysis for the evaluation of transport projects: time for a multi-actor approach. Transp. Policy 37, 177–186.
Macharis, C., Nijkamp, P., 2011. Possible Bias in Multi-Actor Multi-Criteria Transportation Evaluation: Issues and Solutions. Research Memorandum 2011–31. Faculty of Economics and Business Administration, VU University Amsterdam.
Macharis, C., Nijkamp, P., 2013. Multi-actor and multi-criteria analysis in evaluating mega-projects. In: Priemus, H., van Wee, B. (Eds.), International Handbook on Mega-Projects. Edward Elgar. ch. 11.
Macharis, C., De Witte, A., Ampe, J., 2009. The multi-actor multi-criteria analysis methodology (MAMCA) for the evaluation of transport projects: theory and practice. J. Adv. Transp. 43 (2), 183–202.
Macharis, C., De Witte, A., Turcksin, L., 2010. The Multi-Actor Multi Criteria Analysis (MAMCA) application in the Flemish long-term decision making process on mobility and logistics. Transp. Policy 17, 303–311.
Macharis, C., Turcksin, L., Lebeau, K., 2012. Multi actor multi criteria analysis (MAMCA) as a tool to support sustainable decisions: state of use. Decis. Support. Syst. 54, 610–620.
Macharis, C., De Brucker, K., Van Raemdonck, K., 2018. When to use multi actor multi criteria analysis or other evaluation methods? In: Baudry, G., Macharis, C. (Eds.), Decision-Making for Sustainable Transport and Mobility. Edward Elgar, pp. 28–47.
Mackie, P., Worsley, T., 2013. International Comparisons of Transport Appraisal Practice—Overview Report. Institute for Transports Studies, Faculty of Environment, University of Leeds.
Manheim, M., Suhrbier, J., Bennett, E., Neumann, L., Colcord, F., Reno, A., 1975. Transportation Decision-Making: A Guide to Social and Environmental Consideration. National Cooperative Highway Research Program Report 156, Transportation Research Board, National Research Council, Washington, DC.
Mardani, A., Zavadskas, E.K., Khalifah, Z., Jusoh, A., Nor, K.M.D., 2015. Multiple criteria decision-making techniques in transportation systems: a systematic review of the state of the art literature. Transport 31 (3), 359–385.
Martel, J.-M., Matarazzo, B., 2005. Other OUTRANKING approaches. In: Figueira, J., Greco, S., Ehrgott, M. (Eds.), Multiple Criteria Decision Analysis: State of the Art Surveys. Springer, pp. 197–262.
McAllister, D.M., 1982. Evaluation in Environmental Planning: Assessing Environmental, Social, Economic and Political Trade-Offs. The MIT Press.
Mcdowall, W., Eames, M., 2007. Towards a sustainable hydrogen economy: a multi-criteria sustainability appraisal of competing hydrogen futures. Int. J. Hydrogen Energy 32 (18), 4611–4626.
Miller, G.A., 1956. The magical number seven, plus or minus two. Psychol. Rev. 63 (1), 81–97.

Miller, D.H., 1985. Equity and efficiency effects of investment decisions: multicriteria methods for assessing distributional implications. In: Faludi, A., Voogd, H. (Eds.), Evaluation of Complex Policy Problems. Delftsche Uitgevers Maatschappij B.V, pp. 35–50.
Mouter, N., 2017. Dutch politicians' use of cost–benefit analysis. Transportation 44, 1127–1145.
Munda, G., 1995. Multicriteria Evaluation in a Fuzzy Environment—Theory and Applications in Ecological Economics. Springer.
Munda, G., 2004. Social multi-criteria evaluation: methodological foundations and operational consequences. Eur. J. Oper. Res. 158 (3), 662–677.
Munda, G., 2008. Social Multi-Criteria Evaluation for a Sustainable Economy. Springer.
Nijkamp, P., Ouwersloot, H., 1997. A decision support system for regional sustainable development: the flag model. In: van der Bergh, J.C.J.M., Hofkes, M. (Eds.), Theory and Implementation of Sustainable Development Modeling. Kluwer, Dordrecht.
Nijkamp, P., Rietveld, P., 1990. In: Voogd, H. (Ed.), Multicriteria Evaluation in Physical Planning. Elsevier, North-Holland.
Nyborg, K., 1998. Some Norwegian politicians' use of cost–benefit analysis. Public Choice 95, 381–401.
OECD (Organisation for Economic Cooperation and Development), 2005. National systems of transport infrastructure planning. In: Report of the 128th Round Table on Transport Economics, Paris on 26th–27th February 2004. OECD Publishing.
Oliveira, V., Pinho, P., 2010. Evaluation in urban planning: advances and prospects. J. Plan. Lit. 24 (4), 343–361.
Ozernoy, V.W., 1992. Choosing the "best" multiple criteria decision-making method. Inf. Syst. Oper. Res. 30 (2), 159–171.
Pensa, S., Masala, E., Lami, I.M., 2013. Supporting planning processes by the use of dynamic visualisation. In: Geertman, S., Toppen, F., Stillwell, J. (Eds.), Planning Support Systems for Sustainable Urban Development. Springer, pp. 451–467.
Petts, J., Leach, B., 2000. Evaluating Methods for Public Participation: Literature Review. Research and Development. Technical Report E135, University of Birmingham, Environment Agency.
Proctor, W., Drechsler, M., 2006. Deliberative multicriteria evaluation. Eviron. Plann. C. Gov. Policy 24 (2), 169–190.
Quinet, E., 2000. Evaluation methodologies of transportation projects in France. Transp. Policy 7 (1), 27–34.
RAC (Resource Assessment Commission), 1992. Multi-Criteria Analysis as a Resource Assessment Tool. Research Paper no. 6, AGPS, Canberra.
Renn, O., 2015. Stakeholder and public involvement in risk governance. Int. J. Disaster Risk Sci. 6, 8–20.
Renn, O., Webler, T., Rakel, H., Dienel, P., Johnson, B., 1993. Public participation in decision making: a three-step procedure. Pol. Sci. 26 (3), 189–214.
Rezaei, J., 2015. Best-worst multi-criteria decision-making method. Omega 53, 49–57.
Rogers, M., Duffy, A., 2012. Engineering Project Appraisal. Blackwell Science.
Rogers, M., Bruen, M., Maystre, L.-Y., 2000. ELECTRE and Decision Support: Methods and Applications in Engineering and Infrastructure Investment. Kluwer Academic Publishers.
Rosenberger, R.S., 2001. An integrative Hierarchical Framework for Environmental Valuation: Value Pluralism, Thresholds, and Deliberation. Research Paper 2001–14, Regional Research Institute and Division of Resource Management West Virginia University.
Roy, B., 1968. Classement et Choix en Présence de Points de Vue Multiples (La Méthode ELECTRE) (Ranking and selection in the presence of multiple points of view—the ELECTRE method). RIRO 8, 57–75. (In French).

Roy, B., 1996. Multicriteria Methodology for Decision Aiding. Kluwer.
Roy, B., Bouyssou, D., 1986. Comparison of two decision-aid models applied to a nuclear power plant siting example. Eur. J. Oper. Res. 25, 200–215.
Saaty, T.L., 1980. The Analytic Hierarchy Process. McGraw Hill.
Saaty, T.L., 1990. An exposition of the AHP in reply to the paper "remarks on the analytic hierarchy process" Manag. Sci. 36, 259–268.
Saaty, T.L., 2001. Decision Making for Leaders: The Analytical Hierarchy Process for Decisions in a Complex World. RWS Publications.
Saaty, T.L., 2003. Decision-making with the AHP: why is the principal eigenvector necessary. Eur. J. Oper. Res. 145, 85–91.
Sager, T., Ravlum, I.A., 2005. The political relevance of planners' analysis: the case of a parliamentary standing committee. Plan. Theory 4 (1), 33–65.
Salling, K.B., 2008. Assessment of Transport Projects: Risk Analysis and Decision Support. Ph.D. Dissertation, Department of Transport, Technical University of Denmark.
Salling, K.B., Jensen, A.V., Leleur, S., 2005. COSIMA-DSS evaluation system: a new decision support system for large-scale transport infrastructure projects. In: Paper presented at 10th Jubilee Meeting of the EURO Working Group on Transportation 'Advances in Modeling, Optimization and Management of Transportation Processes and Systems—Theory and Practice' and 16th Mini-EURO Conference 'Artificial Intelligence in Transportation'. Publishing House of Poznan University of Technology, Poznan, Poland, pp. 601–607.
Salling, K.B., Barfod, M.B., Pryn, M.R., Leleur, S., 2018. Flexible decision support for sustainable development: the SUSTAIN framework model. Eur. J. Transp. Infrastruct. Res. 18 (3), 295–315.
Sayers, T.M., Jessop, A.T., Hills, P.J., 2003. Multi-criteria evaluation of transport options—flexible, transparent and user-friendly? Transp. Policy 10 (1), 95–105.
Schärlig, A., 1985. Décider Sur Plusieurs Critères: Panorama De L'aide à la Décision Multicritère Decide on Several Criteria: Panorama of Multiple-Criteria Decision Analysis Vol. 1. Presses Polytechniques et Universitaires Romandes. (In French).
Söderbaum, P., 1998. Economic and sustainability: an actor-network to evaluation. In: Lichfield, N., Barbanente, A., Borri, D., Khakee, A., Prat, A. (Eds.), Evaluation in Planning: Facing the Challenge of Complexity. Kluwer Academic Publishers, pp. 51–72.
Stagl, S., 2006. Multicriteira evaluation and public participation: the case of UK energy policy. Land Use Policy 23 (1), 53–62.
Stagl, S., 2007. SDRN Rapid Research and Evidence Review on Emerging Methods for Sustainable Valuation and Appraisal. A Report to the Sustainable Development Research Network, Final Report. Policy Studies Institute, London.
Stirling, A., 1998. Risk at a turning point? J. Risk Res. 1 (2), 97–109.
Stirling, A., 2006. Analysis, participation and power: justification and closure in participatory multi-criteria analysis. Land Use Policy 23 (1), 95–107.
Stirling, A., 2008. Opening up or closing down: participation, pluralism and diversity in the social appraisal of technology. J. Sci. Technol. Hum. Values 33 (2), 262–294.
Stirling, A., Mayer, S., 2001. A novel approach to the appraisal of technological risk: a multicriteria mapping study of a genetically modified crop. Eviron. Plann. C. Gov. Policy 19 (4), 529–555.
TFNSW (Transport for New South Wales), 2016. Principles and Guidelines for Economic Appraisal of Transport Investment and Initiatives Transport Economic Appraisal Guidelines. Transport for New South Wales.
Thokala, P., Devlin, N., Marsh, K., Baltussen, R., Boysen, M., Kalo, Z., Longrenn, T., Mussen, F., Peacock, S., Watkins, J., Ijzerman, M., 2016. Multiple criteria decision analysis for health care decision making—an introduction: report 1 of the ISPOR MCDA emerging good practices task force. Value Health 19, 1–13.

Triantaphyllou, E., 2000. Multi-Criteria Decision Making Methods: A Comparative Study. Kluwer Academic Publishers.
Triantphyllou, E., Mann, H., 1989. An examination of the effectiveness of multi-dimensional decision-making methods: a decision-making paradox. Decis. Support. Syst. 5, 303–312.
TS (Transport Scotland), 2008. Scottish Transport Appraisal Guidance. The Scottish Government.
Tsamboulas, D., Yiotis, G.S., Panou, K.D., 1999. Use of multicriteria methods for the assessment of transport projects. J. Transp. Eng. 125 (5), 407.
Van Pelt, M.J.F., 1993. Ecological Sustainability and Project Appraisal. Averbury.
Vanclay, F., 1999. Social impact assessment. In: Petts, J. (Ed.), Handbook of Environmental Impact Assessment Volume 1—Environmental Impact Assessment: Process, Methods and Potential. Blackwell Science Ltd, pp. 301–326.
Vari, A., 1995. Citizens' advisory committee as a model for public participation: a multiple-criteria evaluation. In: Renn, O., Webler, T., Wiedemann, P. (Eds.), Fairness and Competence in Citizen Participation—Evaluation Models for Environmental Discourse. Kluwer Academic Publisher, pp. 103–115.
Véron-Okamoto, A., Sakamoto, K., 2014. Toward a Sustainability Appraisal Framework for Transport. Asian Development Bank Sustainable Development Working Paper Series, No. 31.
Vickerman, R., 2000. Evaluation methodologies for transport projects in the United Kingdom. Transp. Policy 7 (1), 7–16.
Vincke, P., 1992. Multi-criteria Decision-Aid. Wiley.
von Winterfeldt, D., Edwards, W., 1986. Decision Analysis and Behavioural Research. Cambridge University Press.
Voogd, J.H., 1983. Multicriteria Evaluation for Urban and Regional Planning. Pion.
WAG (Welsh Assembly Government), 2008. Welsh Transport Planning and Appraisal Guidance. Welsh Assembly Government.
Wang, J.-J., Jing, J.-J., Zhang, C.-F., Zhao, J.-H., 2009. Review on multi-criteria decision analysis aid in sustainable energy decision-making. Renew. Sustain. Energy Rev. 13 (9), 2263–2278.
Ward, E.J., Dimitriou, H.T., Dean, M., 2016a. Theory and background of multi-criteria analysis: toward a policy-led approach to mega transport infrastructure project appraisal: toward a policy-led approach to mega transport infrastructure project appraisal. Res. Transp. Econ. 58, 21–45. Special Edition.
Ward, E.J., Dimitriou, H.T., Wright, P., Dean, M., 2016b. Application of policy-led multi-criteria analysis to the appraisal of the northern line extension, London. Res. Transp. Econ. 58, 46–80. Special Edition.
Watróbski, J., Jankowski, J., Ziemba, P., Karczmarczyk, A., Ziolo, M., 2018. Generalised framework for multi-criteria method selection. Omega 86, 107–124.
WG (Welsh Government), 2017. WelTAG 2017 Welsh Transport Appraisal Guidance. Welsh Government.
Worsley, T., Mackie, P., 2015. Transport Policy, Appraisal and Decision-Making. RAC Foundation, Institute for Transport Studies, University of Leeds, London.
Zanakis, S.H., Solomon, A., Wishart, N., Dublish, S., 1998. Multi-attribute decision making: a simulation comparison of select methods. Eur. J. Oper. Res. 107, 507–529.
Zardari, N.H., Ahmed, K., Shirazi, S.M., Yusop, Z.B., 2015. Weighting Methods and their Effects on Multi-Criteria Decision Making Model Outcomes in Water Resources Management. Springer.
Zeleny, M., 1982. Multiple Criteria Decision Making. McGraw-Hill.

CHAPTER SEVEN

Comparing cost-benefit analysis and multi-criteria analysis

Niek Mouter[a,*], Marco Dean[b], Carl Koopmans[c,d], and José Manuel Vassallo[e]

[a]Faculty of Technology, Policy and Management, Engineering Systems and Services Department, Transport and Logistics Group, Delft, Netherlands
[b]Bartlett School of Planning, University College London, London, United Kingdom
[c]Department of Spatial Economics, Vrije Universiteit Amsterdam, School of Business and Economics, Amsterdam, Netherlands
[d]SEO Amsterdam Economics, Amsterdam, Netherlands
[e]Professor of Transport Economics and Planning, Transport Research Centre (TRANSyT), Universidad Politécnica de Madrid, Madrid, Spain
*Corresponding author: e-mail address: n.mouter@tudelft.nl

Contents

Abstract

We provide an in-depth comparison of cost-benefit analysis (CBA) and multi-criteria analysis (MCA) by, among other things, reviewing the literature which elaborates on the differences between both methods. The root of all the differences between the two methods is that welfare economics provides strict procedures for conducting a CBA, whereas MCA methods are not based on this theory which gives MCA analysts a relatively large degree of freedom when conducting the appraisal. We identified five inherent differences between the two methods: (1) a CBA investigates how citizens and firms that are affected by a transport project experience the impacts of the project, whereas a MCA is based on the judgments of experts and/or stakeholders who might not experience any impacts of a transport project themselves; (2) a CBA only includes

ISSN 2543-0009
https://doi.org/10.1016/bs.atpp.2020.07.009

the impacts that affect the welfare of individuals, whereas MCA analysts have the full freedom to include every possible impact in their studies; (3) CBA measures a project's societal value by making impacts of transport projects comparable in monetary terms using the notion of individuals' willingness to pay. The aggregation of impacts/criteria in a MCA can be partly based on translating impacts/criteria into monetary terms, but the aggregation is also based on at least one other weighting method (e.g., scoring or ranking); (4) CBA inherently accounts for the fact that social impacts of transport projects occur over a number of periods by discounting future impacts of the project, whereas the time dimension is rarely included in a MCA; (5) the final indicators of a CBA communicate very clearly and are therefore easy to use in the media and the public/political debate. The interpretation of the outcome of a MCA is relatively unclear. This chapter closes with conducting a CBA and a MCA for a fictious transport project to illustrate the differences between the two methods.

Keywords: Cost-benefit analysis, CBA, Benefit-cost analysis, Multi-criteria analysis, Multi-criteria decision-making, MCA transport appraisal, Comparing CBA and MCA

1. Introduction

As stated in previous chapters, cost-benefit analysis (CBA) and multi-criteria analysis (MCA) are widely used appraisal methods in the domain of transport policy and planning. Both methods were described in Koopmans and Mouter (2020) and Dean (2020a) respectively, including a discussion of state-of-the-art developments and remaining research challenges. The purpose of the present chapter is to provide an in-depth comparison of the two methods by, among other things, reviewing the literature which elaborates on the pros and cons of both methods. Before discussing the differences between the methods, it is worth noting that they are also quite similar in several respects. Both appraisal methods aim to provide policy makers with information to assess the desirability of a transport policy option by comparing this option with a reference case. As a result, both methods depend on transportation model results (including their often large uncertainties). Also, both methods may be complementary in some applications. CBA and MCA, however, are based on quite different methodological approaches.

Koopmans and Mouter (2020) explained that CBA measures a project's social desirability by quantifying the project's societal effects by making costs and benefits comparable in monetary terms using the notion of the number of euros individuals are willing to pay from their private income. Subsequently, these monetary impacts are presented as present values using a discount rate which accounts for the effect that people prefer present impacts over future impacts. Finally, present values are aggregated into a final indicator such as the net present value (NPV), the internal rate of return (IRR) or the benefit-cost ratio (BCR). Dean (2020a) explained that a deep variety of MCA methods has been developed over the past decades. MCA typically encompasses the following stages: development of options; identification of objectives and criteria against which to test options; weighting of criteria; and scoring of impacts of options against the different criteria to arrive at a ranking of options. In some MCA procedures the performances of options are not scored or weighted but simply displayed using tables, graphs or diagrams. Such MCA approaches, like the UK Appraisal Summary Table, do not aim to provide a final ranking of the options. Although the variety of MCA methods problematizes the identification of differences between the CBA and MCA appraisal techniques, we identified five inherent differences between the two methods (fundamental differences).

Section 2 will elaborate on the fundamental differences between CBA and MCA. Section 3 describes differences between CBA and MCA which occur in practice. In Section 4, we show that CBA and MCA can be combined in transport project evaluation. Finally, in Section 5, we provide an extensive example in which both a CBA and an MCA are carried out and compared for the same (fictitious) transport project.

2. Fundamental differences between CBA and MCA

This section elucidates the fundamental differences between CBA and MCA. The root of all these differences is that welfare economics provides the theoretical framework underlying CBA, whereas MCA methods are not built on this framework. Welfare economics provides strict procedures for the objects which have standing in the CBA analysis, for the criteria/impacts that are considered in the analysis, for the way different impacts are valued, for the way that intertemporal effects are treated and for the interpretation of the results of the CBA analysis. The strictness of these procedures and instructions result in theoretical unambiguousness which can be seen as a strength of CBA (Beria et al., 2012; Macharis and Bernardini, 2015). This unambiguity makes CBA "a common language, known and used worldwide" (Beria et al., 2012, p. 148).[a] MCA analysts, on the other hand, have a large degree of freedom when selecting criteria and determining the

[a] We note, however, that in applying CBA practical choices are needed (as described below and in Koopmans and Mouter, 2020) which do not necessarily follow from theoretical considerations.

weights. This can be seen as a strength of MCA when benchmarked against CBA, but it can also be seen as a weakness because the ambiguity makes MCA more vulnerable for steering the outcomes of the appraisal in a direction which is favorable for the commissioner of the study.

2.1 Which individuals have standing in the analysis?

A key decision analysts need to make when conducting an appraisal study concerns the individuals that are (not) included in the analysis which is also known as the question of "standing" (Mouter, 2019). Welfare economics starts from the postulation of "individualism" (also called: welfarism), which implies that the welfare of a country consists of the welfare of its individual citizens (Sen, 1979). Moreover, welfare economists in principle adopt the postulation of "non-paternalism" which implies that individuals are conceived to be the best judge of their own welfare. Hence, the citizens and firms that are affected by the policy (either directly or through externalities such as noise pollution) are the sole objects who have standing in a CBA study and their preferences are respected. In principle, preferences of experts, stakeholders and policy makers about the impacts of the transport project do not play any role in the analysis, however, Koopmans and Mouter (2020) showed that there are exceptions in the sense that the valuation of CO_2 emissions is generally rooted in pledges of policy makers instead of stated or revealed preferences of individual citizens.

On the contrary, Dean (2020a) describes in this book that experts are generally the unit of analysis in a MCA study. He distinguishes between non-participatory (i.e., analyst-led) MCAs and participatory MCAs. In non-participatory assessments, the analysis is carried out autonomously by one of more analysts, according to a typical technocratic approach. Participatory MCA techniques adopt a more collaborative and (in principle more democratic) decision-making style, with the direct involvement of the different interested and affected parties (i.e., problem stakeholders) in the analysis. Many MCA experts (e.g., Macharis and Nijkamp, 2011) emphasize that, ideally, in a MCA exercise all the parties that are affected by the issue under discussion should be involved or represented, with no viewpoint excluded a priori. However, Dean (2018) observes that participatory MCA processes rarely involve more than 30 individuals as the practical need for creating a workable and efficient process drastically limits the number of group decision-making participants. Real-world applications whose outcomes are clearly used as input in the decision-making process are generally analyst-led and so far, there have been mainly theoretical applications of participatory MCA, see Dean (2020a).

Both analyst-led and participatory MCA processes do not start from "individualism" and "non-paternalism" as the analysis is not based on the evaluations of all affected citizens, but on the judgments of experts and/or stakeholders who might not experience any impacts of a transport project. To be clear, a MCA analyst might very well approach a few representatives from the citizens that are affected by a specific transport project to evaluate the criteria, but these citizens are then conceived as stakeholders which have the same role as other stakeholders that participate in the weighting procedure. To illustrate the differences between CBA and MCA in terms of the choices that are made regarding standing, let us consider a road project which results in travel time savings for 9,000 citizens and noise pollution for another group of 1,000 citizens. In this case, a CBA aims to evaluate this road project by investigating how the 10,000 affected citizens experience these impacts, whereas in a MCA experts (or stakeholders if the MCA is participatory) evaluate the impacts of the project. A CBA analyst might very well consult academics and policy makers, but she will ask these actors whether they have evidence with regard to the way these impacts are experienced by citizens instead of asking about their opinion of the criteria/impacts on which the project will be evaluated. Instead, a MCA analyst might ask these actors about their own opinion on the weight that should be assigned to the criteria which are part of the analysis.

The most important argument supporting the two postulations underpinning CBA ("individualism" and "non-paternalism") is that a CBA reflects the interests of affected citizens, and not the interests of stakeholders, academics or policy makers, and that in a democracy it makes sense that preferences of citizens are transmitted to elected officials. Mackie et al. (2014) also coin CBA as the "taxpayers only model of representation at the political negotiation table" (Mackie et al., 2014). Following this argument, it makes sense to select citizens as the main unit of analysis of an appraisal study and not stakeholders or experts who are already represented in political negotiations.

The explicit inclusion of stakeholders in a participatory MCA is advocated by Beria et al. (2012) who assert that the consent of stakeholders is often a crucial factor for the successful implementation of a transport project.

Moreover, the involvement of different interests and affected parties in the appraisal exercise is expected to promote mutual learning and build trust among stakeholders (Dimitriou et al., 2016; Macharis et al., 2012) and the participation of stakeholders is also supposed to increase the likelihood of acceptance of the results of the analysis by actors and groups involved in the process (Macharis et al., 2009; Macharis and Nijkamp, 2013; Ward et al., 2016).

The most important argument for grounding the MCA (partly) in expert opinions is that a group of scientists and trained specialists is best suited to make complex technical decisions. That is, a major reason against adopting "non-paternalism" for an appraisal study derives from doubt whether individuals are indeed the best judge of their own welfare. Koopmans and Mouter (2020) in this book already pointed out that this postulation of CBA is criticized because individual citizens might be prone to make erroneous choices and there seems to be consensus among academics that economists should not instruct policy makers to mimic errors made by consumers (Shogren and Thunström, 2016). On the other hand, "experts" are not automatically error-free either.

2.2 Which impacts to consider?

The principles of welfare economics provide CBA researchers and users with a clear frame of reference when selecting the impacts of policy measures that should (not) be included in a CBA, whereas MCA analysts have the full freedom to include every possible impact in their studies (Barfod and Salling, 2015; Barfod et al., 2011; Beria et al., 2012; Macharis and Bernardini, 2015). Welfare economics prescribes that only impacts that affect the welfare of individuals (directly or through externalities) should be included. To give an example of an impact which should not be considered in a CBA (but can be considered in a MCA), let's assume that blue-green algae are only harmful to people's health when the populations of this type of algae are equal to or greater than 20,000 cells per milliliter. When a policy option results in a decrease of blue-green algae in a lake from 10,000 cells per milliliter to 5,000 cells per milliliter this does not affect people's health and therefore this impact should not be considered in a CBA. In a MCA, however, at least in theory, this impact can be included in the evaluation. Moreover, citizens' preferences for the way that the benefits and burdens of a transport policy option are distributed across society are not part of the total net benefits in a CBA (Mouter et al., 2017). In practice, CBA reports may provide information concerning the distributional consequences of specific transport projects/policies by reporting the net present value of the project/policy under scrutiny for specific regions or by providing a "winners and losers" table in the report (e.g., Annema et al., 2007; HEATCO, 2006). Moreover, distinguishing impacts (e.g., transport impacts, environmental impact, wider economic impacts, investment costs) "automatically" gives information on the distribution of impacts (e.g., transport users, people living nearby roads or rail links, companies, workers, taxpayers). However, this information does not affect the final indicators of a CBA (the net present value or the benefit-cost ratio). On the other side, a MCA analysis can include distributional aspects as a separate criterion which affects the final outcome of a MCA (Van Wee, 2012). Another consequence that is excluded from a CBA, but can be included in a MCA, is public support for a transport policy option (Mouter, 2017).

An advantage of MCA is that the appraisal method gives analysts more degrees of freedom regarding their decisions on including or excluding consequences of a transport policy option that are relevant in the decision-making process. On the other hand, MCA has been criticized for the lack of rigor and arbitrariness at the time of selecting the criteria to be considered in the analysis (Barfod et al., 2011; Browne and Ryan, 2011; Hobbs and Horn, 1997). In (non-participatory) analyst-led MCA, the analyst is required to select a list of relevant objectives and criteria to account for the possible impacts of the proposal(s) under study. In doing so, the analyst is likely to adopt (implicitly or explicitly) the client perspective (e.g., the Minister, government department, project promoter, agency or group that has commissioned the analysis) and/or take into account (indirectly) the positions of the most relevant stakeholders (i.e., the most organized, and often most powerful, groups, that have consolidated themselves as a public presence). Also, personal preferences or biases of the analyst may be included, known or unknown by the analyst. In participatory MCA methods, the analyst identifies objectives and criteria based on the direct input of (a few tens of) group decision-making participants (who may comprise project stakeholders, experts, academics, government representatives, etc.). The choice of whom to involve in the process is difficult and largely arbitrary and often risks reinforcing existing patterns of social and political disparities. As a result, it would be possible to argue that in neither case (non-participatory and participatory MCA processes) it is possible to ensure a completely balanced and comprehensive selection of objectives/criteria and impacts. Moreover, Beria et al. (2012) argue that MCA analysts may include an array of criteria other than the welfare effect of transport projects in their appraisal. This might lead to positive recommendations on projects that have a negative impact on the efficiency of public expenditure. Finally, Macharis and Bernardini (2015) observe that in some countries, one example being France, there was a move away from MCA because policy makers thought that the institutionalization of the method led to inefficient spending of government resources (Quinet, 2000; Sayers et al., 2003).

2.3 How to evaluate the impacts?

A third fundamental difference between CBA and MCA concerns the weighting procedure that is used to evaluate the impacts of a transport policy option. As pointed out in Koopmans and Mouter (2020), CBA measures a project's societal value by quantifying the project's societal effects and making these effects comparable in monetary terms using the notion of the amount of money individuals are willing to pay for these effects from their private income. On the other hand, the aggregation of impacts/criteria in a MCA can be partly based on translating impacts/criteria into monetary terms, but the aggregation is also based on at least one other weighting method (e.g., scoring, ranking or weighting of a wide range of qualitative impact categories and criteria).

Several disadvantages of using private willingness to pay for evaluating impacts of transport projects were addressed in this book Mouter et al., (2019). One key concern is that WTP-based valuation is an inappropriate way to evaluate impacts of government projects that are difficult to translate into private income (Aldred, 2006; Clark et al., 2000). For instance, Sunstein (1993) asserts that values which are not traded in a real-life market setting, such as free speech, nature and landscape cannot be valued in terms of private income without somehow corroding or degrading them. As a result, objectives such as preserving landscapes and biodiversity are often examined only in a qualitative manner (i.e., without monetization) in a CBA (e.g., Mackie et al., 2014; Mouter et al., 2015). Hence, they are often not included in either of the indicators that are often decisive in the political process and the media: the benefit-cost ratio and the net present value (e.g., Annema and Koopmans, 2015). Based on an analysis of 67 CBAs performed in the Netherlands between 2000 and 2011, Annema and Koopmans (2015) conclude that in many cases relevant environmental effects are omitted or not monetized in CBAs. Moreover, they observe that non-monetized effects are often excluded from CBA conclusions. Mouter et al. (2015) establish that a result of the relatively weak position of effects that are difficult to monetize is that these can be underweighted in the decision-making process. Nash et al. (1991) argue that computing a net present value which includes a monetary valuation of time and accident savings, but excludes all environmental effects, is seriously misleading.

Beria et al. (2012) and Gühnemann et al. (2012) assert that MCA seems to be better in measuring intangibles and soft impacts than CBA as these effects don't have to be converted into private income. On the other hand, MCA has been criticized for the arbitrariness in the selection of the weights applicable to different criteria (Annema et al., 2015; Barfod et al., 2011; Beria et al., 2012; Browne and Ryan, 2011; Hobbs and Horn, 1997). Qualitative assessment and the imputation of value-laden weightings to different criteria may lead to subjective biasing (Munda, 2004; White and Lee, 2009). This arbitrariness in MCA has often been used by politicians to justify already pre-adopted decisions, which has undermined the rigor of the MCA appraisal method (Dobes and Bennett, 2010). According to Sayers et al. (2003) the lack of procedures for aggregating the evaluations of the individual criteria and unregulated weights that were left to the whim of the decision-takers was another reason why some governments moved away from MCA and returned to the conventional CBA method. Moreover, Dean (2020a) explains that in reality MCA suffers from the same issues as CBA because, due to constraints affecting data collection or the high level of uncertainty surrounding the decision problem, the few most tangible criteria implicitly become the most important parameters for the analysis.

2.4 The use of a discount rate

A fourth difference between the two methods is that CBA inherently accounts for the fact that social impacts of transport projects occur over a number of periods by discounting future impacts of the project. As described in Koopmans and Mouter (2020), there is much discussion on the appropriate choice of the discount rate in CBA. Dean (2020a) explains that the time dimension is rarely included in a MCA. As a result, criteria and impacts are likely to present inconsistencies in temporal scales.

2.5 Clarity of the interpretation of the results of the study

Although Koopmans and Mouter (2020) addressed that one of the main research challenges for CBA concerns pinpointing exactly what a CBA study measures (social welfare, efficiency, or aggregate net willingness to pay for the impacts of the transport policy) there is consensus that the final indicators of a CBA (the net present value and the benefit-cost ratio) communicate very clearly and are therefore easy to use in the media and the public/political debate. Mouter et al. (2013) and Mouter (2017) observe that both key actors in the Dutch CBA practice and Dutch politicians believe that a strength of CBA concerns its ability to provide insights into the order of magnitude of positive and negative welfare effects of a transport project. This can alarm politicians to not support a project that clearly has a detrimental effect on the country's welfare. We note, however, that the impact of CBA on actual decisions does not seem to be strong, as described in Koopmans and Mouter (2020). Mouter (2017) finds that politicians also think it is positive that CBA can enhance the sharpness of political debates and the underpinning of political decisions. Moreover, Dutch politicians and high-level civil servants argue that CBA can act as a filter ("gatekeeper") to prevent weak projects proceeding very far through the planning process (Mouter, 2017).

The strong communicative power of CBA results cannot only be seen as a positive characteristic of the methodology. For instance, Dutch politicians experience that a CBA is regularly used to "kill the political debate" and to terminate a political discussion (Mouter, 2017). They mention spatial equity, public support and welfare effects that are not considered in CBAs as elements in the political trade-off that are not captured in CBA (Mouter, 2017). Moreover, Nyborg (1998) observes that particularly left-wing politicians perceive that CBA does not pay special attention to the interests of the poor in society which is not in line with their political worldview.

The interpretation of the outcome of a MCA study is relatively unclear. Beria et al. (2012) state that MCA methods which weight the different options and provide a final ranking of the options compute the alternative with the "best outcome" or "the most preferable option." Dean (2020a) argues that some MCA methods aim to establish the "best option to address the problem at hand." First of all, it is not really clear what these interpretations exactly mean. On top of that a MCA does not provide any tangible information concerning the extent to which the "best option" outperforms the second best option and the reference case. This is much more clear in a CBA in which the user can find information about the net present value of the various transport policy options that are assessed. However, the relatively unclear interpretation of a MCA cannot only be seen as a weak point of the method. A benefit of the weak communicative power of the method is that the risk that the results will be used to kill the political debate is low.

3. Practical differences between CBA and MCA

Apart from the fundamental differences discussed in the previous section, the literature discusses some practical differences that emerge from various applications of the two methods. For instance, Annema et al. (2015), Beria et al. (2012) and Tudela et al. (2006) assert that in MCA there is a risk of double counting of impacts of transport policy options. Dean (2020a) points out that especially simplified MCA techniques regularly suffer from many inconsistencies and errors such as double counting between criteria. Annema et al. (2015) assert that double counting of project effects would be more difficult to avoid in MCA compared to CBA because strict criteria for the inclusion of effects are lacking. We note that when a MCA is conducted in a comprehensive way and strict guidelines for inclusion of project impacts are developed, this problem may be avoided. Moreover, the problem of double counting can also emerge in poorly conducted CBAs. However, in practice the risk of double counting seems to be more prominent in MCA, because there are less incentives from strict guidelines. Especially if the time and budgets available for the research are limited (which is usually the case), less incentives with respect to applying appropriate methods may induce simplified approaches, including double counting.

On the other hand, a critique regarding the postulation of "individualism" in a CBA is that the analysis generally focuses on the preferences of individuals that can express their preferences. This implies that future generations, animals and nature in general have no standing in the appraisal study (e.g., Baum, 2009). For instance, consequences for animals and future generations only count when humans that are currently living in a certain country value them in the sense that they are willing to pay for these consequences from their private income (Mouter, 2019). A MCA analyst can of course decide to compensate for this by assigning extra weight to the impacts of a policy on nature, animals and future generations, but the critique that future generations and animals are not able to express their preferences cannot be resolved.

Both CBA and MCA are criticized for lack of transparency in the analysis and being a "black box" (e.g., Annema et al., 2015; Beukers et al., 2012). This critique seems to particularly emerge from the way that the impacts are weighed/valued in the two appraisal methods (Annema et al., 2015). Dean (2020a) points out that transparency issues particularly emerge in more sophisticated MCA methods which require complex calculations. In such methods, often the mathematical algorithms at the heart of MCA may even be locked within proprietary software. Simplistic MCA methods in which objectives, appraisal criteria, weights and scores, and impacts are displayed through tables and diagrams, and where some explanations for the scores/weights assigned are offered can, however, be quite transparent. Annema et al. (2015) draw a similar conclusion by arguing that issues with transparency in MCA and CBA can be remedied by providing a trade-off sheet which gives a clear picture of the (unweighted) quantitative and qualitative impacts.

4. Combining CBA and MCA

In the previous century, CBA and MCA were often presented as strictly contrasting and competing approaches (e.g., Voogd, 1983). However, at present the intensity of the discussion has diminished and the focus of the discourse has partially shifted toward the identification of possible complementarities between the two appraisal/evaluation approaches (e.g., Salling et al., 2005; Schutte, 2010; Sijtsma, 2006; Van Pelt, 1993). For instance, in many countries MCA is seen as complementary to CBA and employed to capture impacts which are difficult to translate into monetary terms (Mackie et al., 2014). Mackie et al. (2014) note that all the seven Western countries they assess, include CBA in a more comprehensive framework which includes non-monetized benefits. Gühnemann et al. (2012) present an MCA in which monetized impacts are translated into scores. They use this method to prioritize road infrastructure in Ireland. Sijtsma (2006) describes a combination of CBA and MCA. In his approach, stakeholders play an important role. For instance, the stakeholders decide which impacts are monetized, based on consensus. ECMT (2001) sees CBA as the basis for transport project appraisal but acknowledges that MCA can be used to expand the framework with other effects. Combining both methods apparently has advantages in the appraisal process.

5. Case study of a transport road project

To better illustrate the differences, similarities and complementary aspects of CBA and MCA this section considers the case of a transport project which is appraised by using both methods. Despite the significance of the topic, it appears that only few authors have tried to provide similar practical examples. Tudela et al. (2006) adopt a MCA in the form of the analytic hierarchy process (AHP) to assess a road improvement scheme in Concepcion, Chile and compare the output of the analysis with that of a CBA developed by a public agency. However, their paper focuses almost exclusively on the AHP application. Beria et al. (2012) discuss CBA and MCA in the context of an *ex ante* assessment of a sustainable mobility plan at the neighborhood scale, but without going too much into details. Dean and Hickman (2018) examine different alternative improvements of the South Fylde railway line in North West England through both a standard CBA and a participatory MCA, involving six different stakeholder groups (see also Hickman and Dean, 2018). This comparison is, however, mainly oriented toward the identification of potential strengths and weaknesses of participatory MCA methods.

The (fictious) project used for this example represents a 25 km, 2 × 2 lane, toll-free interurban road to be added to the existing road transport network between two major cities. The main objective of this new road is the provision of additional road capacity along that transport corridor and the alleviation of the local roads, which go through smaller settlements, from transit traffic. Shifting a significant volume of traffic, particularly heavy vehicles, from local roads to the new road would also improve road safety and reduce nuisances (especially in terms of exhaust gases) to local residents.

The hypothetical CBA study of the road project draws extensively on the guidelines developed by the European Commission (EC, 2008, 2015) and the European Investment Bank (EIB, 2013) as well as on other books and manuals, while the list of objectives and appraisal criteria adopted for the theoretical MCA exercise is based on the multi-criteria frameworks presented by Dean (2020a) in this book. We assume a time horizon of 34 years (4-year construction period and 30-year operating life).

5.1 Cost-benefit analysis

As highlighted by Koopmans and Mouter (2020), the purpose of CBA is to estimate the possible social surplus produced by a policy or an investment.

In order to determine this social surplus, CBA measures the economic costs and benefits potentially generated by the proposal in question and compares them to the costs and benefits which are likely to accrue in a "without project" or "do-minimum" situation. The latter represents the scenario which might materialize if the proposal does not obtain approval and constitutes the reference case for the analysis. There is a presumption in CBA that costs and benefits are calculated by taking into account the effects experienced by all members of society. Costs are mainly represented by economic resources needed for the project during its implementation and operational phases.

The main impacts produced by the hypothetical project under examination are travel time savings, reduction in vehicle operating costs, improvement of traffic safety and a slight reduction in CO_2 emissions. Equity considerations are not considered in this CBA.

In a CBA, these costs and benefits first need to be estimated in physical terms (e.g., the number of inputs and activities to build the road, the travel time saved, the number of crashes eliminated) by using different, often rather sophisticated forecasting models. They need then to be monetized through various, sometimes highly controversial techniques and discounted to present values to make them directly comparable.

5.1.1 Construction costs

The construction costs of a project encompass the expenditures for all the economic resources (e.g., purchase of land, workers, equipment and raw material) and activities (e.g., planning, design, construction, mitigation works) necessary to complete the road. The construction costs of a project must be estimated as accurately and possible. The economic value of these items can then be directly estimated through their market price. For the road project under scrutiny total economic costs have been estimated at about € 175 million (2020 price). Preparatory activities are supposed to commence in late 2020, while construction works are planned to be carried out between 2021 and 2023.

5.1.2 Maintenance costs

These costs include all labor, machinery and material costs for routine, periodic and rehabilitation maintenance of the road. These costs can generally be determined by means of an analysis of the historical expenditure levels for similar projects. Annual maintenance costs for the road project have been estimated at € 750,000. This value has been derived on the basis of average costs required for the maintenance of the existing regional road network. Routine maintenance costs for the existing local roads along the transport corridor in question are assumed to be the same in both the "with project" and "without project" scenarios and are thus excluded from the assessment.

5.1.3 Travel time savings

Reductions in journey times are generally considered to be the most significant benefits that arise from the construction of a new transport project or the improvement of existing transport infrastructure. The road project under examination, in particular, is assumed to lower travel time of both its users and the travelers using the existing local roads due to traffic diversion and consequent reduced congestion on these roads as a result of the project. The key parameter to determine travel time saving benefits as well as other economic benefits generated by a transport project are the projections regarding future traffic flows. Current traffic conditions, future traffic demand without the project, and potential additional traffic generated by the new infrastructure are necessary to estimate the potential travel time savings. Note that new travelers are assumed to experience only half of the benefits (the so-called rule of half, see Winkler, 2015 for an in-depth discussion). Transport modeling approaches relate traffic growth to projected changes in GDP, population and other relevant variables.

An important step in valuing a project's travel time saving benefits is then to establish travel time unit costs. Because these values cannot be derived directly from the market some alternative approaches need to be employed. As illustrated by De Jong and Kouwenhoven (2020), different methods, can be used to determine the value of travel time (savings). They show that the value of travel time can differ between the types of trips (e.g., business trips, commuting journeys or leisure trips), types of vehicles (e.g., cars or heavy vehicles) and the length of the journey. Once travel time savings and travel time unit costs have been established for each trip category, the project's total travel time saving benefits can be calculated. For the road project in question, travel time saving benefits are assumed to represent over 80% of the total benefits which is quite in line with the conventional CBA practice (Eliasson and Lundberg, 2012; Mackie et al., 2001).

5.1.4 Vehicle operating cost savings

Vehicle operating costs are defined as the costs borne by owners of road vehicles to operate them and encompass fuel and lubricants, tire deterioration, repair and maintenance and so forth. Such costs are of course correlated with the type of vehicle, the average speed as well as with the geometry, surface conditions of the roads. New transport infrastructure or the rehabilitation and upgrade of existing ones may thus imply a change in the vehicle operating costs. Possible cost savings are calculated taking into account the estimated changes in traffic volumes and travel speed along a given transport corridor, possible improvement in road conditions and their effects on the vehicles, and appropriate values for all the vehicle operating costs. In the example considered, vehicle operating cost savings due to the improved transport corridor constitute almost 15% of the total benefits.

5.1.5 Accident cost savings

Changes in traffic volume, road type, lane width and speed factors can also lead to a change in the expected frequency and/or severity of accidents. In the case of a reduction of the rate and magnitude of accidents, cost savings include avoided medical and rehabilitation expenses; avoided damage to vehicles, properties, and road structure; avoided income loss due to injuries; and avoided deaths. Such costs are typically calculated by multiplying unit cost values per accident and per casualty (obtained through indirect methods based also on the willingness-to-pay concept) by forecast data regarding the change in the number of accidents of each type. The monetization of human life and safety is based on the Value of a Statistical Life (see Andersson, 2020). By diverting a large proportion of the traffic to a safer road with two lanes for each direction, the road project under examination is assumed to reduce the accident rate compared to the existing local road. The level of accident severity in both the "with project" and "without project" scenarios is instead supposed to remain the same. Overall, accident cost saving amounts to almost 4% of the total benefits.

5.1.6 Impacts on climate change/CO_2 savings

The environmental impacts considered in this analysis concern CO_2 emissions avoided by the new road (for simplicity, we abstract from other environmental impacts). In general, the total volume of emissions generated or avoided by a transport project are calculated based on the expected changes in traffic volumes, travel distance and travel speed along a given transport corridor, and emission factors included in specific guidelines and inventories. The total benefits or costs are then determined by applying monetary values per unit of emission reduction or increase. Such unit costs are derived also in this case through a metric prescribed in formal guidelines. The road project under examination is assumed to lower slightly the CO_2

emissions compared to a "without project" scenario, as a result of a more favorable alignment which will reduce the distance traveled for the majority of the traffic. These benefits, however, constitute less than 2% of the total benefits.

5.1.7 Results of the analysis

In Table 1 the expected economic results of the road project are shown in terms of net present value (NPV) and benefits-costs ratio (BCR). The NPV of monetized benefits is € 85.5 million, but there are negative intangible impacts on the landscape. This suggests that society would be better off after the construction of the road if the negative value of the impacts on the landscape is not larger than € 85.5 million. Whether this is the case could be investigated in further research projects which aim to value the negative impact on landscape; and otherwise it is up to elected officials to debate and weigh the importance of the positive NPV and the negative landscape impacts. The BCR indicates that for every euro of costs spent on the project, society gains about € 1.5, again excluding the negative effects on landscapes.

The reliability of these results, however, depends on the quality of the transport models, data and assumptions adopted in the analysis. Because all long-term forecasts and projections are subject to considerable uncertainty and large margins of errors, risk and sensitivity tests are always highly desirable. Sensitivity tests are typically performed by calculating the percentage change of the NPV and BCR as a consequence of changes in some key parameters of the analysis (e.g., investment costs, maintenance costs, traffic on new road, value of time, etc.). If the results of the analysis turn out to be very sensitive to such changes, risk analyses, either qualitative (e.g., risk matrices) or quantitative (e.g., Monte Carlo simulation), need to be performed to estimate the probability of a negative NPV and identify prevention and mitigation measures.

On the one hand, the NPV and BCR indicators provide the decision-makers with a relatively simple criterion for establishing the desirability of the proposal from a societal point of view. Given the use of common and standardized procedures for the calculation of costs and benefits, these indicators can also be useful to compare projects (also in different areas or sectors) which are competing for funds. Through this approach scarce resources can be allocated to their most valued uses, namely projects with the highest BCR. On the other hand, CBA does not offer information regarding the possible contribution of the projects to the achievement of other policy

Table 1 Example of hypothetical CBA for a 25 km, 2 × 2 lane, toll-free interurban road project (differences between investment scenario and reference case).

	Present value (€ M)	Implementation phase				Operational phase											
		2020	2021	2022	2023	2024	2025	2026	2027	2028	2029	2030	2031	2032	2033	2043	2053
(1) Construction costs	−175.3	−3.8	−57.4	−68.6	−63.2	0	0	0	0	0	0	0	0	0	0	0	0
(2) Maintenance costs	−10.0	0	0	0	0	−0.75	−0.75	−0.75	−0.75	−0.75	−0.75	−0.75	−0.75	−0.75	−0.75	−0.75	−0.75
Total costs (PVC) (1) + (2) + (3)	−185.2	−3.8	−57.4	−68.6	−63.2	−0.75	−0.75	−0.75	−0.75	−0.75	−0.75	−0.75	−0.75	−0.75	−0.75	−0.75	−0.75
(4) Travel time savings	217.4	0	0	0	0	7.6	7.7	7.8	8.1	8.4	8.9	9.4	10	10.7	11.4	23.9	48.1
(5) Vehicle operating cost savings	38.7	0	0	0	0	1.6	1.7	1.8	1.9	2	2.1	2.3	2.4	2.5	2.6	4	5.3
(6) Safety benefits	10.5	0	0	0	0	0.5	0.5	0.5	0.5	0.6	0.6	0.7	0.7	0.7	0.7	1	1.4
(7) Impacts on climate change/ CO_2 savings	4.04	0	0	0	0	0.2	0.2	0.2	0.2	0.2	0.2	0.3	0.3	0.3	0.3	0.4	0.5
(8) Impact on landscape	–																

Total benefits (PVB) (4) + (5) + (6) + (7) + (8)	270.7/–	0	0	0	0	9.9	10.1	10.3	10.7	11.2	11.8	12.7	13.4	14.2	15	29.3	55.3
Net present value (NPV) PVB-PVC	€ 85.5 M/–																
Benefit cost ratio (BCR) PVB/PVC	1.5																
Social discount rate	5%																
Sensitivity analysis on social discount rate																	
Social discount rate	4%		→	NPV =		€ 137.6 M/–			BCR =		1.7						

objectives, which cannot be properly measured by consumer preferences. Examples of such objectives are equity and public support.

In this analysis, a 5% social discount rate has been adopted to discount costs and benefits occurring at different points during the economic life of the road back to the current year's price level, in line with what recommended by the European Commission (EC, 2015). However, it is evident that by influencing the speed at which discounted costs and benefits decline into the future, this parameter can have a dramatic effect on the outcome of CBA, determining whether a proposed project is judged to be socially beneficial or not. For instance, as illustrated in Table 1, by repeating the analysis with a 4% social discount rate (the most common values of the social discount rate in Europe range from 3.5% to 4.5%, see Mouter, 2018), the NPV becomes € 137.6 million (an increase of more than 60% compared with the original NPV) and the new BCR becomes 1.7. Indeed, a lower social discount rate preserves the value of the long-term benefits of the project, while it has minor effects on the construction costs of the project.

5.2 Multi-criteria analysis

In a MCA exercise, typically, one or more project options are assessed against a number of different objectives and criteria. In operational terms, the exercise encompasses the following key steps:

- selection of objectives and criteria;
- identification of the impacts of the option(s) against the different criteria;
- scoring of impacts of the option(s) against the different criteria;
- weighting of criteria;
- combination of scores and weights to obtain the global score of the option(s).

Different from CBA, however, MCA does not constitute a single, specific method. Indeed, as highlighted in Dean (2020a), there are hundreds of different multi-criteria techniques, which are based on clashing theories and procedures. To guarantee the possibility of third-party audit on a MCA exercise, transparency over the key parameters and underlying assumptions adopted in the process thus becomes imperative (Dean, 2020a). This principle, however, remains, of course, valid and important also for more regulated appraisal and evaluation methods such as CBA. For the appraisal of the road project a simple additive weighting model has been employed due to the fact that, as shown in Dean (2020a), this represents one of the most widely used MCA approaches in transport appraisal practice.

5.2.1 Selection of objectives and criteria

Due to the absence of strict guidelines, the identification of objectives and criteria for appraising the road project was based on the multi-criteria frameworks conceived by the UK's Department of Transport (see tables 5 and 6 in Dean, 2020a) and the Sustainable Transport Appraisal Rating framework proposed by the Asian Development Bank (ADB) (see table 7 in Dean, 2020a). In the attempt to ensure, to the maximum possible extent, the consistency of the process and the rigor of the analysis, the list of criteria has also been formulated in accordance with some basic logical requirements suggested in the MCA literature (e.g., Belton and Stewart, 2002; Keeney and Gregory, 2005; Roy, 1996):

- *Exhaustiveness*: the set of criteria must cover all important aspects of the problem under consideration.
- *Manageability*: in order to avoid unnecessary analytical effort, the value tree must not be more detailed than necessary, and the total number of criteria must be as limited as possible.
- *Understandability*: analysts, decision-makers and problem stakeholders and all the other parties involved in the process must have a shared understanding of the assumptions and concepts behind each criterion (e.g., whether criteria need to be maximized or minimized to obtain high performance scores).
- *Measurability*: criteria must measure the performances of an option as precisely and clearly as possible, in a quantitative or qualitative way, compatible with the characteristics of the measure under consideration.
- *Non-redundancy*: criteria that have been judged to be excessively similar to others must be excluded from the list to avoid double counting problems (i.e., inclusion of criteria which account for effects already taken into account elsewhere by other criteria).[b]

As illustrated in Table 2, 10 quantitative and qualitative criteria, grouped in four dimensions (i.e., economic, environmental, social, strategic) have been selected. At first glance, this constitutes a more holistic framework than that provided by CBA. However, selecting a comprehensive and balanced multi-criteria framework in the attempt to capture the interests of all the members in society is not a straightforward and easy task. In principle, a different combination of dimensions, objectives and criteria could have been adopted.

[b] In addition to the above requirements, the possibility of effectively employing a simple additive weighted model to aggregate scores and weights into a global score would require the condition of mutual preferential independence between criteria to be satisfied (see Dean, 2020a). To simplify the example, this condition has not been considered.

Table 2 Example of hypothetical MCA for a 25 km, 2 × 2 lane, toll-free interurban road project.

Dimensions	Objectives	Criteria	Criterion weights (0 ÷ 100%)	Project impacts	Scores (−3 ÷ +3)	Weighted scores
Economic	1. To ensure a wise use of economic resources	Project's construction and maintenance costs	10%	• Construction costs: € 175 million (2020 price) • Maintenance costs: € 750,000 per year (2020 price)	−2	−0.2
	2. To provide employment opportunity	Number of jobs created as a result of the project	10%	• About 600 jobs during the construction phase • An average of 15 workers per years required for maintenance works • About 10 permanent jobs created by a small rest area along the road	+2	+0.2
	3. To improve the attractiveness of living areas	Project improves quality of life in the surrounding areas	10%	The new road will result in travel time reductions. As a result of this the area becomes more attractive for companies and households which is reflected in the real estate prices	+1	+0.1
Environmental	4. To minimize adverse effects on local air quality	Reduction in greenhouse gas as a result of the project	10%	Reduction of CO_2 emission by 1500 tons per year	+1	+0.1
	5. To reduce noise	Reduction in the noise level	10%	Some houses will benefit from the scheme, whereas some other houses will experience disbenefits as a result of it. The overall contribution to the reduction of noise in the area will be marginal	−1	−0.1
	6. To protect the landscape	Potential alterations to the landscape	10%	The road will impair the rural character of the landscape	−2	−0.2

Social	7. To improve the transport system	Improved journey time, comfort and convenience	10%	• Private cars using the full length of the new road will save up to 15 min, whereas freight vehicles will save up to 10 min • Driver stress likely to be reduced	+2	+0.2
	8. To improve transport safety	Reduction in car accidents	10%	Overall, 70 car accidents will be prevented over the life cycle of the road (30 years)	+2	+0.2
Strategic	9. To promote integration between policies and strategies at all level	Extent to which the project aligns with wider policy objectives and development strategies	10%	• The project aligns with local and regional transport objectives • Several conflicts with environmental and sustainability objectives at all levels	0	0
	10. Public support	Percentage of citizens who support the project	10%	• There is a large group of citizens who support the project. Mainly people who benefit from it • Group of people who opposes the project is of an equal size	0	0
				Overall weighted score: +0.3		

Although extremely important, the non-redundancy requirement is quite difficult to fulfill, especially when the multi-criteria framework involves a large number of criteria. In the framework adopted to appraise the road, for example, it is possible to notice some overlaps between the objective of improving the transport system of the region and the attractiveness of the living area in the neighborhoods which experience an improvement of accessibility. It has become common practice, particularly in rough MCA applications, to include the NPV and BCR criteria in the multi-criteria framework so as to better account for economic efficiency considerations. This however implies severe double counting problems since the two metrics are highly correlated. In this case, for example, the inclusion of the BCR as additional criterion would have led to double counting problems with several criteria (project costs, CO_2 emissions, improved journey time and safety) which, as illustrated in the previous section, are typically taken into account by CBA.

5.2.2 *Identification of the impacts of the option(s) against the different criteria*

Once the objectives and criteria have been identified, quantitative and/or qualitative data and information regarding the performance of the project option(s) under investigation against the various criteria can be collected. In the case of *ex ante* appraisal exercises, performance metrics are based on forecasts, mathematical models, and predictions, combined with assumptions and expert judgments. Impacts can be derived directly from CBA, economic impact studies, environmental and social impact assessments, life-cycle analyses as well as other studies carried out on the project. On the one hand, MCA can thus be seen as a sort of overarching appraisal framework capable of combining the results of different forms of (economic, environmental and social) appraisal exercises. On the other hand, since different appraisal methods adopt different assumptions and procedures, inconsistencies may arise. In particular, the impacts included in the summary table may refer to very different temporal horizons. In Table 2, for instance, project costs represent the discounted economic costs of the project as obtained from the CBA, while maintenance costs are not discounted. The public support criterion considers mainly aspects related to the decision-making process, whereas other objectives such as safety improvements and employment opportunities refer to the whole operational phase of the road. By comparison, some other objectives such as integration between policies and quality of life benefits do not include a clear and specific time-based period. Moreover, as highlighted in Dean

(2020a), in many MCA applications, objectives and criteria are selected with only scant attention paid to the geographical dimensions of the analysis. In Table 2, for example, it is possible to notice that whereas some criteria, such as journey times and reduction in the number of accidents are referred to a relatively small project area, others, such as quality of life take into account the potential impacts of the road on a much wider area.

5.2.3 Scoring of impacts of the road project against the different criteria

To make the performance of the option(s) against the different criteria comparable, the impacts need to be converted to a common scale by using performance scores (i.e., pure numbers with no physical meaning). Performance scores measure the degree to which the different objectives are met. High-performing options are assigned higher scores, while low-performing options score lower on the scale. Scores can be assigned through different procedures with various degrees of complexity and rigorousness. A very rigorous approach to scoring involves the use of a value function to translate the impacts of the options against the various criteria into the selected measurement scale. More often, however, especially in the case of simplistic MCA applications, where time and resources to undertake the analysis are limited, a direct rating approach to scoring is adopted (Dean, 2020b). This approach simply uses an expert judgment to assign a value on a given scale (typically a Likert-type scale, which is often incorrectly used as an interval scale) to account for the impacts of an option against each criterion. It is not clear whether these judgments are capable of capturing the overall societal point of view or take merely a single perspective on the problem (e.g., that of the evaluator or the project promoter).

Different scales can, in principle, be employed for scoring the performances of the options. For this exercise, in line with the ADB's Sustainable Transport Appraisal Rating framework, a seven-point scale, ranging from "very strongly positive" performances (+3) to "very strongly negative" performances (−3) and where 0 represents a neutral value (i.e., no significant effects), has been adopted. It is evident, however, that the use of a different scale (e.g., a 0–10 scale) could have changed, even substantially, the results of the scoring process.

In this example, scores for the road project are assigned with reference to a do-minimum scenario, which assumes that in absence of this project there will be sufficient investment to keep the existing road network operational in the future.

5.2.4 Weighting of criteria

Dean (2020a) has pointed out that the weighting of criteria constitutes the most controversial aspect of any MCA exercise, given the significant value judgments involved in this step and the strong influence that weights can have on the results of the analysis. A review of the literature highlights the presence of conflicting views and numerous misunderstandings regarding the real meaning of weights, the overarching approach to weighting and the specific techniques to be used for assigning weights to criteria (Dean, 2020a). In this exercise, for reasons of simplicity, all the different criteria are assumed to have an equal weight. Of course, the impact of using a different set of weights can be analyzed using sensitivity analyses.

5.2.5 Aggregation of scores and weights to obtain the global score of the road project

As shown in Table 2, the global performance score of the road project, obtained as weighted sum of the single performance scores against each criterion is +0.3, which, according to the measurement scale adopted ($-3 \div +3$), indicates that overall the project would be capable of producing moderately beneficial impacts. By comparing Tables 1 and 2, it is possible to argue that a simplistic form of MCA provides a clearer and more transparent appraisal and evaluation approach relative to CBA. Indeed, an appraisal summary table such as that displayed in Table 2 can be more easily understood also by non-specialists.

However, the global performance score obtained with MCA does not offer any indications about the possible net social benefits generated by the intervention. It is thus not possible to understand whether the proposal represents the best use of society's limited resources. It would be also difficult (if not impossible) to compare this global score with the one obtained by another competing project, unless all the key parameters of the analysis (i.e., objectives, criteria, scoring and weighting procedures, interval scales adopted for scores and weights, aggregation rules, spatial and temporal dimensions considered) were the same.

6. Concluding remarks

The purpose of the present chapter is to provide an in-depth comparison of cost-benefit analysis (CBA) and multi-criteria analysis (MCA) by, among other things, reviewing the literature which elaborates on the pros and cons of both methods. We identified five inherent differences between the two methods. The root of all these differences is that welfare economics provides the theoretical framework underlying CBA, whereas MCA methods are not built on this framework. Welfare economics provides strict procedures for (1) the objects which have standing in the CBA analysis; (2) for the criteria/impacts that are considered in the analysis; (3) for the way different impacts are valued; (4) for the way that intertemporal effects are treated; (5) and for the interpretation of the results of the CBA analysis. The strictness of these procedures and instructions result in theoretical unambiguousness which can be seen as a strength of CBA. MCA analysts, on the other hand, have a large degree of freedom when selecting criteria and determining the weights. This can be seen as a strength of MCA when benchmarked against CBA, but it can also be seen as a weakness because the ambiguity makes MCA more vulnerable for steering the outcomes of the appraisal in a direction which is favorable for the commissioner of the study. In general, the advantages of CBA are the drawbacks of MCA and vice versa. We establish in this chapter that we see a trend toward combining CBA and MCA in transport appraisal to ensure that each method covers "weak spots" of the other method. Further research may study whether this is indeed a prosperous road ahead. We recommend further research which investigates how important user groups of appraisal studies such as policy makers and politicians evaluate the merits of combining CBA and MCA in one appraisal framework compared to presenting the results of one of these appraisal methods in isolation.

References

Aldred, J., 2006. Incommensurability and monetary valuation. Land Econ. 82 (2), 141–161.

Andersson, H., 2020. The value of statistical life. In: Mouter, N. (Ed.), Standard Transport Appraisal Methods. Advances in Transport Policy and Planning, vol. 6. Elsevier, Amsterdam, pp. 75–99 (Chapter 3).

Annema, J.A., Koopmans, C.C., 2015. The practice of valuing the environment in cost-benefit analysis in transport and spatial projects. J. Environ. Plan. Manag. 58 (9), 1635–1648.

Annema, J.A., Koopmans, C.C., Van Wee, B., 2007. Evaluating transport infrastructure investments: the Dutch experience with a standardised approach. Transp. Rev. 27 (2), 125–150.

Annema, J.A., Mouter, N., Rezaei, J., 2015. Cost-benefit analysis (CBA), or multi-criteria decision-making (MCDM) or both: politicians' perspective in transport policy appraisal. Transp. Res. Proc. 10, 788–797.

Barfod, M.B., Salling, K.B., 2015. A new composite decision support framework for strategic and sustainable transport appraisals. Transp. Res. A 72 (1), 1–15.

Barfod, M.B., Salling, K.B., Leleur, S., 2011. Composite decision support by combining cost-benefit and multi-criteria decision analysis. Decis. Support. Syst. 51 (1), 167–175. https://doi.org/10.1016/j.dss.2010.12.005.

Baum, S.D., 2009. Description, prescription and the choice of discount rates. Ecol. Econ. 69 (1), 197–205.

Belton, V., Stewart, T., 2002. Multiple Criteria Decision Analysis: An Integrated Approach. Kluwer Academic Publisher.

Beria, P., Maltese, I., Mariotti, I., 2012. Multicriteria versus cost benefit analysis: a comparative perspective in the assessment of sustainable mobility. Eur. Transp. Res. Rev. 4 (3), 137–152.

Beukers, E., Bertolini, L., Te Brömmelstroet, M., 2012. Why cost benefit analysis is perceived as a problematic tool for assessment of transport plans: a process perspective. Transp. Res. A Policy Pract. 46 (1), 68–78.

Browne, D., Ryan, L., 2011. Comparative analysis of evaluation techniques for transport policies. Environ. Impact Assess. Rev. 31 (3), 226–233.

Clark, J., Burgess, J., Harrison, C.M., 2000. I struggled with this money business: respondents' perspectives on contingent valuation. Ecol. Econ. 33, 45–62.

De Jong, G., Kouwenhoven, M., 2020. Value of travel time and travel time reliability. In: Mouter, N. (Ed.), Standard Transport Appraisal Methods. Advances in Transport Policy and Planning, vol. 6. Elsevier, Amsterdam, pp. 43–74 (Chapter 2).

Dean, M., 2018. Assessing the Applicability of Participatory Multi-Criteria Analysis Methodologies to the Appraisal of Mega Transport Infrastructure. Ph.D. Dissertation, The Bartlett School of Planning, University College London, United Kingdom. https://www.academia.edu/41754950/Assessing_the_Applicability_of_Participatory_Multi-Criteria_Analysis_Methodologies_to_the_Appraisal_of_Mega_Transport_Infrastructure.

Dean, M., 2020a. Multi-criteria analysis. In: Mouter, N. (Ed.), Standard Transport Appraisal Methods. Advances in Transport Policy and Planning, vol. 6. Elsevier, Amsterdam, pp. 165–224 (Chapter 6).

Dean, M., 2020b. A Practical Guide to Multi-Criteria Analysis. (Forthcoming).

Dean, M., Hickman, R., 2018. Comparing cost-benefit analysis and participatory multi-criteria analysis methodologies. In: Baudry, G., Macharis, C. (Eds.), Decision-Making for Sustainable Transport and Mobility: Multi Actor Multi Criteria Analysis. Edward Elgar, pp. 100–119.

Dimitriou, H.T., Ward, E.J., Dean, M., 2016. Presenting the case for the application of multi-criteria analysis to mega transport infrastructure appraisal. Res. Transp. Econ. 58, 7–20. Special Edition.

Dobes, L., Bennett, J., 2010. Multi-criteria analysis: ignorance or negligence? In: Paper Presented at the 'Australasian Transport Research Forum 2010', Canberra, Australia, 29 September—1 October.

EC (European Commission), 2008. Guide to Cost-Benefit Analysis of Investment Projects. EC (European Commission), Brussels.

EC (European Commission), 2015. Guide to Cost-Benefit Analysis of Investment Projects: Economic Appraisal Tool for Cohesion Policy 2014–2020. EC (European Commission), Brussels.

ECMT, 2001. Assessing the Benefits of Transport. European Conference of Ministers of Transport, Brussels.

EIB (European Investment Bank), 2013. The Economic Appraisal of Investment Projects at the EIB. EIB (European Investment Bank), Luxemburg.

Eliasson, J., Lundberg, M., 2012. Do cost-benefit analyses influence transport investment decisions? Experiences from the Swedish transport investment plan 2010–2021. Transp. Rev. 32 (1), 29–48.

Gühnemann, A., Laird, J.J., Pearman, A.D., 2012. Combining cost-benefit and multi-criteria analysis to prioritise a national road infrastructure programme. Transp. Policy 23, 15–24.

HEATCO, 2006. Developing Harmonised European Approaches for Transport Costing and Project Assessment. Deliverable 5: Proposal for Harmonised Guidelines. HEATCO.

Hickman, R., Dean, M., 2018. Incomplete cost—incomplete benefit analysis in transport appraisal. Transp. Rev. 38 (6), 689–709.

Hobbs, B.F., Horn, G.T., 1997. Building public confidence in energy planning: a multimethod MCDM approach to demand-side planning at BC gas. Energy Policy 25 (3), 357–375. https://doi.org/10.1016/S0301-4215(97)00025-6.

Keeney, R.L., Gregory, R.S., 2005. Selecting attributes to measure the achievement of objectives. Oper. Res. 53 (1), 1–11.

Koopmans, C.C., Mouter, N., 2020. Cost-benefit analysis. In: Standard Transport Appraisal Methods. Advances in Transport Policy and Planning, vol. 6. Elsevier, Amsterdam, pp. 1–42 (Chapter 1).

Macharis, C., Bernardini, A., 2015. Reviewing the use of multi-criteria decision analysis for the evaluation of transport projects: time for a multi-actor approach. Transp. Policy 37, 177–186.

Macharis, C., Nijkamp, P., 2011. Possible Bias in Multi-Actor Multi-Criteria Transportation Evaluation: Issues and Solutions. Research Memorandum 2011-31. Faculty of Economics and Business Administration, VU University Amsterdam.

Macharis, C., Nijkamp, P., 2013. Multi-actor and multi-criteria analysis in evaluating mega-projects. In: Priemus, H., van Wee, B. (Eds.), International Handbook on Mega-Projects. Edward Elgar. ch. 11.

Macharis, C., De Witte, A., Ampe, J., 2009. The multi-actor multi-criteria analysis methodology (MAMCA) for the evaluation of transport projects: theory and practice. J. Adv. Transp. 43 (2), 183–202.

Macharis, C., Turcksin, L., Lebeau, K., 2012. Multi actor multi criteria analysis (MAMCA) as a tool to support sustainable decisions: state of use. Decis. Support. Syst. 54, 610–620.

Mackie, P.J., Jara-Díaz, S., Fowkes, A.S., 2001. The value of travel time savings in evaluation. Transp. Res. E 37, 91–106.

Mackie, P., Worsley, T., Eliasson, J., 2014. Transport appraisal revisited. Res. Transp. Econ. 47, 3–18.

Mouter, N., 2017. Dutch politicians' attitudes towards cost-benefit analysis. Transp. Policy 54, 1–10.

Mouter, N., Ojeda Cabral, M., Dekker, T., van Cranenburgh, S. 2019. The value of travel time, noise pollution, recreation and biodiversity: a social choice valuation perspective. Research in Transportation Economics 76.

Mouter, N., 2018. A critical assessment of discounting policies for transport cost-benefit analysis in five European practices. Eur. J. Transp. Infrastruct. Res. 18 (4), 389–412.

Mouter, N., 2019. The Politics of Cost-Benefit Analysis. Oxford Research Encyclopedia of Politics.

Mouter, N., Annema, J.A., van Wee, B., 2013. Attitudes towards the role of cost-benefit analysis in the decision-making process for spatial-infrastructure projects: a Dutch case study. Transp. Res. A Policy Pract. 58, 1–14.

Mouter, N., Annema, J.A., Van Wee, B., 2015. Managing the insolvable limitations of cost benefit analysis: results of an interview based study. Transportation 42 (2), 277–302.

Mouter, N., van Cranenburgh, S., van Wee., G.P., 2017. An empirical assessment of Dutch citizens' preferences for spatial equality in the context of a national transport investment plan. J. Transp. Geogr. 60, 217–230.

Munda, G., 2004. Social multi-criteria evaluation: methodological foundations and operational consequences. Eur. J. Oper. Res. 158 (3), 662–677.

Nash, C.A., Preston, J.M., Hopkinson, P.G., 1991. Applications of stated preference analysis. In: Rickard, J.H., Larkinson, J. (Eds.), Longer Term Issues in Transport. Avebury Publishing Company, pp. 41–80.

Nyborg, K., 1998. Some Norwegian politicians' use of cost-benefit analysis. Public Choice 95 (3–4), 381–401.

Quinet, E., 2000. Evaluation methodologies of transportation projects in France. Transp. Policy 7 (1), 27–34.
Roy, B., 1996. Multicriteria Methodology for Decision Aiding. Kluwer.
Salling, K.B., Jensen, A.V., Leleur, S., 2005. COSIMA-DSS evaluation system: a new decision support system for large-scale transport infrastructure projects. In: Paper Presented at 10th Jubilee Meeting of the EURO Working Group on Transportation 'Advances in Modeling, Optimization and Management of Transportation Processes and Systems—Theory and Practice' and 16th Mini-EURO Conference 'Artificial Intelligence in Transportation'. Publishing House of Poznan University of Technology, Poznan, Poland, pp. 601–607.
Sayers, T.M., Jessop, A.T., Hills, P.J., 2003. Multi-criteria evaluation of transport options—flexible, transparent and user-friendly? Transp. Policy 10 (1), 95–105.
Schutte, I.C., 2010. The Appraisal of Transport Infrastructure Projects in the Municipal Sphere of Government in South Africa, With Reference to the City of Tshwane. Ph. D. Dissertation, Department of Transport Economics, Logistics and Tourism. University of South Africa.
Sen, A., 1979. Utilitarianism and welfarism. J. Philos. 76, 463–489.
Shogren, J.F., Thunström, L., 2016. Do we need a new behavioral benchmark for BCA? J. Benefit-Cost Anal. 7 (1), 92–106.
Sijtsma, F.J., 2006. Project Evaluation, Sustainability and Accountability: Combining Cost-Benefit Analysis (CBA) and Multi-Criteria Analysis (MCA). Doctoral Dissertation, University of Groningen, Netherlands.
Sunstein, C.R., 1993. Incommensurability and valuation in law. Mich. Law Rev. 92, 779.
Tudela, A., Akiki, N., Cisternas, R., 2006. Comparing the output of cost benefit and multi-criteria analysis. Transp. Res. A Policy Pract. 40 (5), 414–423.
Van Pelt, M.J.F., 1993. Ecological Sustainability and Project Appraisal. Avebury.
Van Wee, B., 2012. How suitable is CBA for the ex-ante evaluation of transport projects and policies? A discussion from the perspective of ethics. Transp. Policy 19 (1), 1–7.
Voogd, J.H., 1983. Multicriteria Evaluation for Urban and Regional Planning. Pion.
Ward, E.J., Dimitriou, H.T., Dean, M., 2016. Theory and background of multi-criteria analysis: toward a policy-led approach to mega transport infrastructure project appraisal. Res. Transp. Econ. 58, 21–45. Special Edition.
White, L., Lee, G.J., 2009. Operational research and sustainable development: tackling the social dimension. Eur. J. Oper. Res. 193 (3), 683–692.
Winkler, C., 2015. Transport user benefits calculation with the "rule of a half" for travel demand models with constraints. Res. Transp. Econ. 49, 36–42.

CHAPTER EIGHT

Environmental Impact Assessment for transport projects: A review of technical and process-related issues

Julio A. Soria-Lara[a,b,*], Rosa M. Arce-Ruiz[a], Aldo Arranz-López[a], and Amor Ariza-Álvarez[a]
[a]Transport Research Centre—TRANSyT—Universidad Politécnica Madrid, Madrid, Spain
[b]Institute of Economics, Geography, and Demography, Spanish National Research Council (CSIC), Madrid, Spain
*Corresponding author: e-mail address: julio.soria-lara@upm.es

Contents

Abstract

Environmental Impact Assessment (EIA) evaluates the likely effects of major transport projects. Since EIA effectiveness in the transport field is determined by a set of technical and process-related aspects, the academic literature has developed promising theories and applications to address these issues. This chapter presents a systematic and comprehensive review of the literature on the application of EIA in transport projects, distilling existing obstacles, new developments and potential research gaps with regard

Advances in Transport Policy and Planning, Volume 6
ISSN 2543-0009
https://doi.org/10.1016/bs.atpp.2020.07.002

to these aforementioned technical and process-related issues. It explores the technical developments in project and baseline information, the identification and evaluation of environmental impacts, the use of impact prediction methods; and techniques to compare project alternatives; it also describes various process-related barriers such as EIA timing, transparency, stakeholders' involvement in early EIA stages, and public participation. Based on this review, a set of further research issues are discussed in the context of EIA for transport projects.

Keywords: Transport, Infrastructure, Stakeholders, Public participation

1. Introduction

The implementation of the National Environmental Policy Act of 1969 (NEPA) in the USA led to a growing interest in incorporating environmental assessment into decision-making. The scientific community was called on to provide efficient evaluation tools, which transformed environmental assessment into a rapidly developing field (Deakin et al., 2007; Gasparatos, 2010). Many environmental assessment methods—with different levels of practical implementability—have thus been developed to evaluate the consequences of policy/program changes and project implementations. Three main areas can be identified to classify these methods (Ness et al., 2007; p. 499). The first concerns indicators/indexes, namely simple measures (indicators) and/or aggregated measures (indexes) that represent a state of economic, social and environmental development in a specific place and for a specific action (project, policy, and/or program implementation). The second focuses on product-related tools that analyze flows in the production and consumption of goods and services (e.g., life cycle assessment, product energy analysis). The third is based on integrated assessment methods used for assessment on the local scale with an ex-ante focus that integrates aspects of both nature and society (e.g., multicriteria analysis; cost benefit analysis). Within this group of integrated assessment methods, one of the most representative is associated with environmental impact instruments, namely the Environmental Impact Assessment (EIA).

EIA essentially refers to the evaluation of the likely effects of major projects (and other actions) that significantly affect the environment. It provides decision-makers with an indication of the environmental consequences of their actions (Jay et al., 2007). EIA was originally firmly rooted in rational planning theory, which was developed in the mid-1950s and widely extended during the 1960s (Fischer, 2003). This rational approach demands a technical evaluation of the projects' impacts as the basis for objective decision-making (Owens et al., 2004). However, in the face of the emergence of communicative planning approaches in the transport field (Innes and Booher, 2018), the EIA role should exceed its traditional focus on evaluation, becoming a learning instrument for consultants, policy-makers, and transport planners that can use EIA to provide inputs for (re) designing project alternatives (Soria-Lara et al., 2016).

Since the 1970s, the role of EIA in planning processes has become increasingly important, and is now incorporated into national legislation worldwide. For example, the National Environmental Policy Act of 1969 (NEPA) implemented EIA for federal agency actions. In the case of the European Union (EU), the EIA Directive 85/337/EEC has been in force since 1985 and applies to a wide range of public and private projects. It was amended in 1997, 2003, 2009 and 2014, and was the first EU Directive to provide details on the nature and scope of the EIA and its use and participation rights in the planning process, including the transport field. Since 1985, EIA has been periodically incorporated into the legislation of European member states. Due to the legal requirements for EIA implementation, there are now strict guidelines for the EIA process for different countries and regions (Cornero, 2010). Since the legal requirements that determine EIA content may vary depending on the country, the usual information contained in the Environmental Impact Assessment report is: (a) project description; (b) significant effects of the project on the environment; (c) measures envisaged to avoid, prevent or reduce the effects on the environment; (d) description of alternatives and the main reasons for the alternative chosen; and (e) a non-technical summary. Taking the example of the EIA legal system in the European Union (Cornero, 2010), Annex I contains a brief summary of the minimum information required for the EIA report in European member states.

The fact that EIA is only applied to certain types of projects (mainly infrastructure projects in the field of transport) was seen as an important limitation for areas where environmental damage is caused by decisions made at a more strategic level (e.g., air emissions produced by sustainable urban mobility plans). This gave rise to the development of the concept and methods of Strategic Environmental Assessment (SEA) in order to evaluate the environmental effects of plans and programs. In the USA, SEA was incorporated into national legislation in the early 1990s, while the European Union adopted the SEA Directive 2001/42 in 2001. It should be noted that this chapter essentially focuses on EIA, and does not cover SEA issues. Our comments, arguments and discussions refer mainly to the evaluation of the environmental impacts of transport infrastructure projects.

The effectiveness of EIA in the transport field is increasingly contested by academics, consultants and policy-makers. Two main groups of reasons can be noted, highlighting the potential gaps to be bridged and further pathways for innovation: technical and process-related aspects. Technical aspects refer to content and methodological developments affecting EIA effectiveness (e.g., methods for forecasting environmental impacts). The academic literature has traditionally tended to focus on improving EIA by addressing technical aspects, which is strongly based on the rational idea that more accurate assessment results can be obtained by increasing the sophistication of the EIA (Folkeson et al., 2013; Zhou and Sheate, 2011). The other group of aspects are process-related and illustrate situations focused on EIA procedure, including the benefits and obstacles originated by the actors involved in the EIA process (Lee, 2006; Soria-Lara et al., 2015, 2016). Unlike the technical issues, these process-related aspects have received limited attention in the academic literature. However, the importance of aspects related to EIA processes is growing thanks to the emergence and implementation of collaborative transport planning approaches (Bertolini, 2007; Willson, 2001), where rational thinking is being called into question and a greater number of stakeholders and professional domains are taking an active part in the EIA.

This chapter aims to provide an insight into the abovementioned issues and to offer an up-to-date and comprehensive overview of EIA literature in the field of transport. The geographical focus is mostly based on the EIA application in the Western world, paying special attention—but not exclusively—to examples and lessons from Europe and USA. The review distils existing obstacles, new developments and potential research gaps for both technical and process-related aspects of the EIA. The SCOPUS database was used to search and filter publications. The review was completed in December 2019. The rest of the chapter is organized as follows. Section 2 shows the research design; Section 3 presents the results focused on technical aspects, and Section 4 illustrates the results for process-related aspects. Finally, Section 5 concludes with some final remarks.

2. Research design

The main aim of this chapter is to provide a review that offers a comprehensive overview of EIA literature in the field of transport. Relevant academic publications on EIA practice were reviewed after conducting abundant searches of the Scopus database during November and

December 2019, resulting in a total of 358 articles without double counting. Two types of filters were used to select the publications. First, abstracts were consulted and the publications were selected that focused on EIA applications in the transport sector. Second, the selected publications were read in-depth, filtering for any that provided specific knowledge of both technical and process-related aspects. The in-depth analyses of the publications were carried out by content analysis according to the main aim of the chapter (Bryman, 2016). Next, the findings were classified into technical and process-related aspects of EIA in transport, providing a comprehensive reflection on the existing gaps and further challenges to be addressed (Sections 3 and 4).

3. Technical aspects

Technical aspects refer to content and methodological developments affecting EIA effectiveness (e.g., improving methods to forecast environmental impacts). Unlike other types of projects, the environmental impacts originated by transport projects are diverse and affect several environmental components (e.g., landscape, air, etc.). Karlson et al. (2014) also point out that only some impacts generated by transport projects are related to the construction itself, while most are indirect and result from the construction and design of the physical structure and from its utilization and management.

The usual EIA procedure establishes that the project developer should submit an EIA report on the environmental viability of major transport projects (e.g., high-speed rail, highways, light rail systems, etc.). The EIA report must contain a brief project description, a baseline description of the environment where the project is located; it must identify and predict potential impacts, assess several project alternatives, and include a set of preventive, corrective or compensatory measures to minimize, correct or offset the predicted impacts. The remainder of this section shows technical developments associated with some content of the EIA report.

3.1 Project and baseline information

The first part of the EIA report describes both the transport project and the baseline scenario. The description of the transport project usually serves to identify potential sources of environmental impacts (project actions), while the baseline scenario includes a description of the site location and the surrounding area. Technical developments have generally been based on geographic information technologies to improve and complement data-gathering and in-depth analysis (Arce et al., 2007). A good example of this is the use of remote sensing techniques (by satellite, airplane, LIDAR, etc.). Other information sources are digital aerial photographs and thematic environmental maps. Photographs and animated 3D designs are particularly useful for describing landscape vulnerability, which is very important in the context of infrastructure projects (Antonson, 2011; Valencia-Sandoval et al., 2010).

It is worth mentioning that the use of Geographic Information Systems (GIS) since the 1980s is one of the most significant technical developments for this stage of the EIA. Sfakianaki and O'Reilly (2002) highlight that in the initial stages of EIA, GIS has been a key instrument for positioning transport infrastructures in their geographical context and describing a project's environment and topography. GIS can also be used to confirm the requirement for EIA in certain transport projects, and can expedite the scoping process by creating a database of local information. These databases may contain information on different areas such as ecology, archeology, noise and air quality. GIS have also been key for developing several models to assess landscape quality in transport projects by mapping physical landscape attributes that are useful for infrastructure planning (Dramstad et al., 2006; Loro et al., 2014; Martín et al., 2016, 2018; Vizzari, 2011; Wu et al., 2006).

3.2 Identification and evaluation of environmental impacts

The identification and evaluation of environmental impacts must be based on the causal relationship between the source of the impacts (specific project actions such as land movement) and their effect on the environment (alteration of environmental factors such as air quality, landscape, etc.). This obvious cause-effect relationship is sometimes overlooked, and the identification of impacts appears to be based on detecting the relationship between the cause of the alteration and the fragility of the environment. However, the cause of the impact is always mobilized by human action, as explored in detail by Joumard and Gudmundsson (2010). Since EIA has been used to assess transport projects for decades, there are several guidelines and handbooks that include examples of impacts and indicators in transport projects.

One crucial step in EIA is how to measure the environmental impacts originated by transport projects, an issue that has been frequently addressed in the academic literature. This is done using the concept of significance (Briggs and Hudson, 2013; Duinker and Beanlands, 1986; Lawrence, 2007; Sadler, 1996), which depends on both the magnitude (degree of environmental change caused) and the scale of the environmental impact. The magnitude is measured in terms of the corresponding indicator of altered environmental quality (Arce Ruiz, 2002, 2013; Joumard and Gudmundsson, 2010). These indicators may be quantitative (e.g., soil surface affected, number of people affected by a specific noise level) or qualitative (e.g., alteration of landscape quality). Antunes et al. (2001) focus on spatial aspects, and GIS can determine the significance of environmental impacts originated by transport projects. Briggs and Hudson (2013) conducted a review of how the determination of significance in ecological impacts has changed over time, what the current practice is, and what would lead to future improvements in measuring the significance of environmental impacts. They conclude that the determination of significance has become more standardized and subjective, and is constrained through a transparent framework. In contrast, Lawrence (2007) offers an overview of good general practices in impact significance and the potential methods for addressing the challenges of determining significance, and notes that tools such as scenarios, models, system maps, network diagrams, schematic trees, life cycle analysis and matrices can enhance the understanding of significant system interactions. The author also points out that the process and methods used to determine significance can be substantially altered when determining the significance of potential cumulative impacts, and when integrating impact significance determination and sustainability. Some authors like Briggs and Hudson (2013) consider that the determination of significance in Environmental Impact Assessment has improved in recent decades, but point to limitations in the accuracy of the studies due to the quality of the baseline survey data, the scientific understanding of ecological processes, and the lack of monitoring and feedback of the results.

In the field of transport, special attention has been paid to cumulative impacts (Burris and Canter, 1997; Smit and Spaling 1995) deriving from multiple activities whose direct individual impacts may be relatively minor but which in combination with others have a significant environmental effect. Cumulative effects can be difficult to predict and assess (Tricker, 2007; Wärnbäck and Hilding-Rydevik, 2009). Pavlickova and Vyskupova (2015) offers insights into methodologies to evaluate cumulative effects and analyses some different approaches to use. Finally, Canter and Ross (2010) summarize the state of the professional practice of the assessment and management of cumulative effects.

The complexity of evaluating a wide range of potential environmental impacts has contributed to the changes in the EIA, including the development of complementary methods which—although undoubtedly inspired by EIA—can be seen as independent assessment methodologies (Costanzo and Sánchez, 2019). One example is social impact assessment, introduced in the late 1970s in the USA due to the perception of EIA as an assessment method with a strong biophysical bias (Morgan, 2012; Taylor et al., 2004). According to Vanclay (2003, p. 6), "social impact assessment includes the processes of analyzing, monitoring and managing the intended and unintended social consequences, both positive and negative, of planned interventions (policies, programs, plans, projects) and any social change processes invoked by those interventions." In this respect, social impacts must be seen much broader than the limited social issues frequently considered in EIA processes. The focus of social impact assessment should be related to those impacts based on people's way of life, their culture, their community, their political system, their personal and property rights, and their fears and aspirations.

A similar reasoning resulted in the emergence of Health Impact Assessment methods, which is based on a combination of methods aimed at evaluating the health impacts on a population of a policy, project, or programmed that does not necessarily have health as its primary priority (Lock, 2000). It is based on a broad model of health, which proposes that political, economic, psychological, and environmental factors can determine population health. Moreover, health impact assessment used to be a multidisciplinary process that takes the opinions and concerns of those who may be affected by a proposed policy. In particular, the Australian HIA guidance recognizes the desirability and efficiency of the interdisciplinary approach offered by integrated HIA/EIA (Wright, 2004). Bhatia and Wernham (2008) notes that countries such as Canada and Australia have developed formal guidelines for integrating HIA into EIA (EnHealth, 2001; Health Canada, 2004).

The consideration of climate change in EIA has been another relevant factor for identifying and evaluating potential impacts, and is even mandatory in the revised EU Directive 2014/52 on EIA. Byer et al. (2012) mention some of the guidelines and best practice documents developed by different organizations to evaluate climate change during EIA processes. Specific models and tools useful for EIA have been developed to increase effectiveness when assessing the carbon footprint effects of transport modes. One example is the HERA tool (Highway EneRgy Assessment), which evaluates the carbon and energy footprint of traffic flows at both a micro (specific stretches of highway) and macro level (highway network)

(Sobrino et al., 2016). The fragmentation of ecosystems and habitats is another important aspect to take into account when evaluating assessment projects (Geneletti, 2003). In particular, Gontier et al. (2010) defend the use of ecological models as tools for predicting habitat loss and fragmentation, compensating for the lack of quantification methods for impact prediction, without considering the spatial and temporal scales of ecological processes. GIS-based ecological models are considered crucial to address spatial analysis related to environmental impacts. However, Scolozzi and Geneletti (2012) claim that the simple application of GIS may be insufficient to evaluate biodiversity impact without the use of other additional methods that integrate different approaches, such as landscape graphs, object-oriented rule-based habitat assessment and expert knowledge. Loro et al. (2015, 2016) include examples of uses of graphs for ecological connectivity analysis and fuzzy set theory and multicriteria analysis for landscape resistance to animal dispersal evaluation. Finally, concepts and tools related to life cycle assessment and building information modeling (BIM) have been used to advance in EIA tools (Li et al., 2019; Marzouk et al., 2017).

3.3 Impact prediction methods

The objective of prediction is to identify the magnitude and other dimensions of a change identified in the environment with a project/action, compared to the situation without the project action. Prediction also serves as a basis for assessing significance. Many scientific models have been developed to predict impacts that are closely related to transport infrastructures. Some relevant examples are the models for estimating traffic noise levels, road traffic emissions, road runoff quality, and train-induced vibration. These models have generally been developed through a statistical analysis of similar situations and require a series of initial variables to predict future impacts.

Several countries have developed their own noise prediction models to predict the noise level caused by road traffic. Some of the first to be developed were the Federal Highway Administration Traffic Noise model (FHWA) in USA (Barry and Reagan, 1978) and the Calculation of Road Traffic Noise (CoRTN) in the United Kingdom (Givargis and Mahmoodi, 2008). Other known models are the ASJ RTN-Model 2008 in Japan (Yamamoto, 2010), the Nord 2000 model in the Nordic countries (Kragh et al., 2002), the NMPB-Routes-2008 model in France (Besnard et al., 2009; Dutilleux et al., 2010), the German model RLS 90 (Quartieri et al., 2009), and the Son Road model (Heutschi, 2004). In the European Union, the

HARMONOISE project developed a model for strategic noise assessment to be used by member states (Defrance et al., 2007; van Maercke and Defrance, 2007; Watts, 2005). Later, the European Commission developed CNOSSOS-EU (Common Noise Assessment Methods in Europe) for noise mapping road traffic, railway traffic, aircraft and industrial noise with the aim of developing a harmonized methodological framework for noise assessment (Kephalopoulos et al., 2012). A review of these main traffic noise models can be found in a study by Steele (2001), and more recently in a study by Garg and Maji (2014). The earlier models applied conventional regression modeling techniques and required a large number of input variables (road gradient, traffic type, traffic volume, speed, environmental data, etc.) to predict noise. More recent models apply other advanced modeling techniques, such as artificial neural networks, support vector machine, generic algorithms and machine learning models (Ahmed and Pradhan, 2019; Ali Khalil et al., 2019; Avşar et al., 2004; Bravo-Moncayo et al., 2019; Cammarata et al., 1995; Genaro et al., 2010; Kumar et al., 2014; Nedic et al., 2014; Nourani et al., 2020). The key advantage of these recent models is their ability to attain high prediction accuracy while requiring fewer input variables. This is important to make them easier to generalize and implement.

Another group of environmental impact prediction models is focused on estimating road traffic emissions, and several models have been developed for different application scales. The vehicular emission modeling software COPERT (COmputer Programme to calculate Emissions from Road Transport) is extensively used for generating emissions levels for the National Emissions Inventory in Europe and internationally (Dey et al., 2019; Gkatzoflias et al., 2007). It is also regularly applied to calculate traffic-related emissions in urban regions and small areas (Smit et al., 2008). This model estimates emissions based on traffic data, and expresses vehicular emissions as a function of average car speed (Gkatzoflias et al., 2007). To assess road traffic emissions and the resulting total air pollution, most studies introduce modeling methods that combine traffic prediction models, emissions calculations and dispersion models (Borrego et al., 2003; Hatzopoulou and Miller, 2010; Yang et al., 2020). In vehicle traffic estimations, agent-based models are also helpful for predicting the impacts of individual decisions and behavior on traffic levels (Van Dam et al., 2012; Waraich et al., 2009; Wise et al., 2016). Among pollution dispersion models, computational fluid dynamic models involving a sophisticated simulation of air turbulence are appropriate for small-scale urban areas (Vardoulakis et al., 2003). Sobrino et al. (2016) also mention different models used worldwide to estimate road traffic emissions and energy consumption, some of which are widely used, as already mentioned: COPERT (Gkatzoflias et al., 2007), MOBILE (United States Environmental Protection Agency, 2002) and its recent version MOVES—Motor Vehicles Emission Simulator—(United States Environmental Protection Agency, 2009), ARTEMIS—Assessment and Reliability of Transport Emission Models and Inventory Systems—(André, 2004), and VERSIT+ (Smit et al., 2007).

Regarding the impacts of the construction of transport infrastructures on water quality, numerous researchers have also highlighted the importance of developing road runoff quality models to predict pollutant concentrations in road runoff (Huber et al., 2016; Luell et al., 2010; McIntyre et al., 2015; Opher and Friedler, 2010; Pan and Miao, 2015; Stagge et al., 2012; Trenouth and Gharabaghi, 2016). Artificial neural networks have been used as a predictive tool to understand water quantity and quality issues; they have been successfully applied to predict flows in watersheds, sediments and other water quality parameters, including nutrient loading, direct runoff volumes and overall water quality (Chebud et al., 2012; Khuan et al., 2002; Kim et al., 2012; Trenouth and Gharabaghi, 2016), and groundwater contamination due to highway construction (El Tabach et al., 2007).

Another interesting aspect is the estimation of vibration levels, particularly for railway infrastructures. A variety of numerical models have been proposed to predict building-induced vibrations due to railway traffic, including comprehensive 3D models with a high computational cost (Fiala et al., 2007; Galvín et al., 2018). Other more simplified vibration prediction tools are commonly used in the early stages of railway projects due to their lower computation times (Connolly et al., 2014, 2015, 2016; López-Mendoza et al., 2017).

3.4 Methods for evaluating and comparing project alternatives

The aim is to systematize the treatment of information and facilitate the aggregation of impacts and the selection of alternatives (Arce Ruiz, 2002). Different approaches and methods have been discussed in the last decades (Arce Ruiz, 2002, 2013; Canter et al., 1997; Clark et al., 1976, 1978, 1979, 1981; Morris and Therivel, 1995; Orea and Villarino, 2013). These types of methods for comparing alternatives may differ in both concept and complexity, and cover descriptive techniques to more complex ones. The latter may include the description of cause-effect interactions, the identification of relationships between different environmental components, and the systematic aggregation of impacts for the various project alternatives under evaluation. In many cases, these assessment methods for comparing project alternatives have evolved in line with major projects requiring ad hoc assessment methods (e.g., high-speed rail projects in Spain).

Two main sequential levels can be identified during the assessment of project alternatives: the evaluation of individual impacts and the comparison of project alternatives. In fact, the EIA always includes both levels, as the environmental evaluation involves not only identifying and quantifying impacts, but also comparing the impacts of project alternatives. Different methods can be identified for each assessment level (Fig. 1). In the first assessment level (evaluation of the individual impacts of each project alternative), the methods used are simpler and more straightforward (e.g., cause-effect matrixes), while the methods in the second level are more complex, to facilitate the comparison of alternatives (e.g., Leopold matrix, RENFE-FAB method) (Arce Ruiz, 2002, 2013).

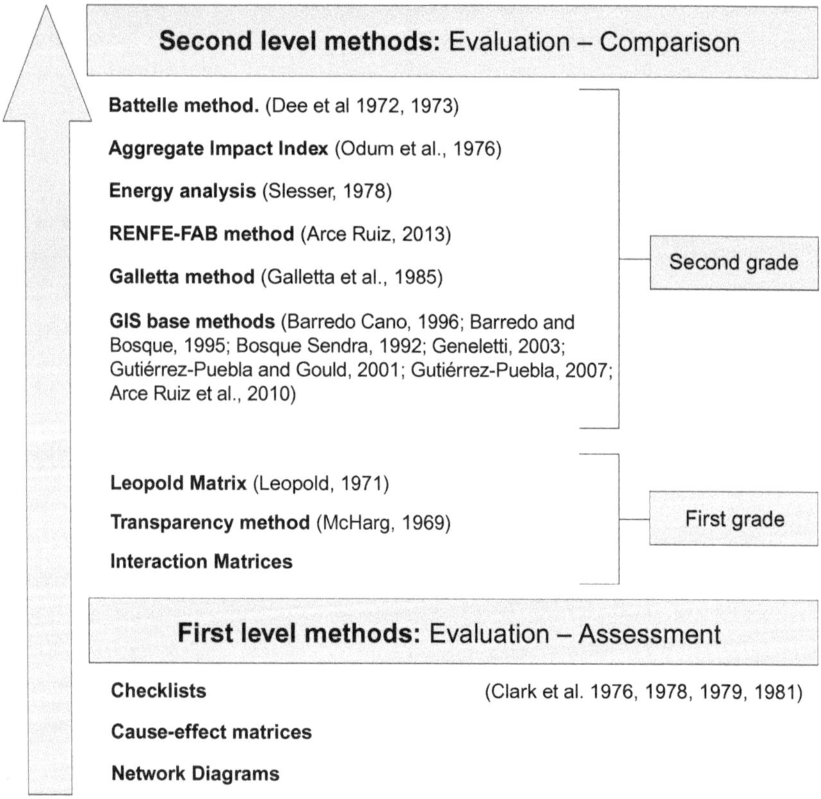

Fig. 1 Classification of Environmental Impact Assessment methods.

The use of GIS has contributed to progress in developing new methods to assess transport project alternatives in EIA. For example, operating thematic maps has made it easier to compare environmental impacts between project alternatives (e.g., comparison of suitable corridors for transport infrastructure projects). Banerjee and Ghose (2016) describe the spatial analysis methods and models implemented by GIS-based EIA for highway projects in mountainous areas. This is a highly developed application (mention), since the configuration of these systems means it is the most immediate. Other examples of the usefulness of GIS concern the analysis of spatial fragility to identify suitable places to locate transport infrastructure projects, understanding the functioning of ecological and socioeconomic systems, and overlapping thematic layers by using Boolean algebra and weighted linear combinations (Cox and Gifford, 1997; Malczewski, 2004). GIS technologies allow more accurate and objective measurements and calculations than could otherwise be achieved (Bishop and Hulse, 1994; Gharehbaghi and Scott-Young, 2018; Loro et al., 2015), and also simplify the application of multicriteria evaluation methods.

After evaluating project alternatives, one key aspect is impact assessment follow-up. This includes monitoring, analysis/interpretation, management, and communication of post approval decision development activity (Marshall et al., 2005, Morrison-Saunders et al., 2007). It is widely recognized that impact assessment follow-up should be framed at three separate tiers (Arts and Morrison-Saunders, 2012): the development of activity level, impact assessment system level, and impact assessment concept level. The main elements of impact assessment follow-up should be (Marshall et al., 2005): (i) monitoring, based on collecting data and comparing with standards, predictions, and expectations. That should include baseline monitoring during pre-decision stages; (ii) evaluation, which means the appraisal of the conformity with standards, predictions, and expectations; (iii) management, based on taking appropriate actions in response to issues arising from monitoring and evaluation; (iv) communication, focused on informing stakeholders about the results of EIA follow-up.

4. Process-related aspects

EIA process-related aspects respond to the significant changes taking place in the transport planning field. Instrumental rationality particularly has been called into question (Bertolini, 2007; te Brömmelstroet and Bertolini, 2011; Willson, 2001), leading to an ever greater relevance of collaborative approaches (Beukers et al., 2014; Curtis, 2011; Pfaffenbichler, 2011).

According to Willson (2001, p. 2), the foregoing implies "interactive processes rather than the deliberative process of a single actor or group of actors, emphasizing the design of planning processes, participation and learning, and a reconciliation of different ways of understanding planning opportunities." From this particular viewpoint, an increasing number of actors and professional domains now participate in EIA processes, making the assessment more complex and resilient to collective views of transport systems (Soria-Lara et al., 2016). The context described substantially limits the applicability of instruments grounded in instrumental rationality, and the EIA is a case in point. Together with technical EIA aspects (Section 3), a wide range of process-related issues (Table 1) (i.e., transparency and stakeholder involvement) appear to have a significant effect on EIA effectiveness in the emerging, more communicative planning context (Hildén et al., 2004; Lidskog and Soneryd, 2000; Mayer et al., 2012; Pinho et al., 2007; Sánchez and Morrison-Saunders, 2011; Tomlinson, 2011; Zhang et al., 2013). If these process-related aspects negatively affect the assessment, the EIA will fail to adequately address the social value of transport projects, and the process may become biased or subverted as a result, with certain forms of knowledge being prioritized unjustifiably (Richardson, 2005; Soria-Lara et al., 2017). However, if those process-related aspects are effectively addressed, EIA could enhance its credibility as a collective process where different actors can discuss and exchange their views on the goals, alternatives and impacts of the proposed projects (Saarikoski, 2000, p. 682).

The remainder of this section describes the main groups of process-related aspects covered by the review, and explores how far they are relevant for the field of transport, their testing and assessment by academic studies, and how they represent further challenges for researchers, practitioners and policy-makers. A total of four groups of process-related aspects are described: (i) the EIA timing; (ii) transparency; (ii) stakeholder involvement in earlier EIA stages; and (iv) public participation.

4.1 EIA timing

One group of publications highlights EIA timing as one of the most important process-related aspects to overcome, essentially when the EIA is seen to be implemented too late in decision-making. This leads to a drastic reduction in EIA effectiveness in transport projects, as EIA is then unable to be part of the process of selecting project alternatives, which has been a persistent problem for decades. For example, Steinemann (2001) presents a two-year

Table 1 Description of EIA process-related barriers in transport projects identified by Soria-Lara et al. (2015).

Process-related barriers	Description
Implemented too late in the planning process	EIA is implemented in decision-making when big decisions on transport projects have been already made
Implemented too early in the planning process	EIA is implemented in decision-making when relevant issues of transport projects are still unknown
Marginal tool in decision-making	EIA is used to support decisions previously made, rather than used it to make those decisions
Insufficient quality	EIA outcomes are inaccurate for taking them into consideration during the evaluation
Insufficient for supporting decisions	EIA outcomes are inconclusive to support decisions during the evaluation
Not transparent	EIA process is unclear regarding the methods used, stakeholders involved, information sources, etc.
Low communication value	EIA outcomes are not understandable for project-developers and policy-makers
Not user friendly	EIA outcomes are too complex and tedious by people not involved in the EIA process
Not interactive enough	EIA process does not facilitate the interaction between stakeholders
Too rigid	EIA process and methods follow strict guidelines without any consideration to project specifications
Evaluation time too long	EIA process is high-time consuming, slowing down the development of transport project in a significant way
Too specific	EIA outcomes are mostly covering specific issues with low general impact on the environment
Too comprehensive	EIA outcomes are mostly covering general issues, and limited attention is paid to impacts originated from project specifications

Continued

Table 1 Description of EIA process-related barriers in transport projects identified by Soria-Lara et al. (2015).—cont'd

Process-related barriers	Description
Outcomes not credible	EIA outcomes are not credible due to methods implemented, stakeholders involved, and sources of information used, etc.
Too expensive	EIA cost is significant in comparison with the cost of the project under evaluation
Not enough collaborative work	Limited interaction between key stakeholders is reached during EIA process
Limited stakeholder involvement	Key stakeholders do not take part during the EIA process
Limited cooperation between public and private sectors	Limited interaction between EIA participants from public and private sectors
Irrelevant alternatives assessment	EIA outcomes are not leading the assessment of project alternatives
Not oriented on refining alternatives	EIA outcomes are not orientated toward refining the selected project alternative to reduce its environmental impact
Assessment methods not suitable	EIA methods are inappropriate to evaluate most of project specifications
Insufficient public participation	EIA process does not involve the public in a significant way
Insufficient consideration of soft impacts	EIA methods are mostly focused on big impacts rather than in soft impacts
Unstructured scoping phase	Scoping phase in early EIA stages is poorly addressed, being unclear how stakeholders take part
Irrelevant monitoring system	EIA outcomes are irrelevant for activating an effective monitoring system
Monitoring system irrelevant for guiding actions	The monitoring system established by EIA is irrelevant to make further decisions on project management

study on the development of alternatives in EIA in the USA, showing that the EIA process often occurs too late to evaluate a full range of project alternatives, limiting its usefulness when making earlier strategic decisions. The author also points out that EIA traditionally starts after an agency has already proposed a particular project alternative. Pediaditi et al. (2018) highlight EIA timing problems in the context of Greece. By using in-depth interviews with key stakeholders, the authors undertake a comprehensive, systematic and multi-scale evaluation of EIA effectiveness. The results show the difficulty of making EIA a part of decision-making as it is implemented too late in the process, when micro-scale project solutions have already been completed. EIA is used to justify decisions rather than to select the best project alternatives and integrate environmental criteria in the earliest phases of decision-making. This affects multiple EIA levels such as the quality of EIA reports, the screening of potential impacts and the design of mitigating actions.

Taking three large-scale transport infrastructure projects (two road tunnels and one light rail) in Sydney, Australia, Harris et al. (2018) study EIA practice within its institutional context, building on "new institutional" approaches to policy analysis that emphasize actors (the stakeholders involved in the EIA), structures (the rules influencing EIA practice in systems) and power. They particularly noted how EIA was undertaken as a compliance process relatively late in the planning process. The purpose of the EIA did not include the consideration of project options. Their findings and other authors (Arce and Gullón, 2000) suggest that the main impacts of transport projects (e.g., health and air quality) should clearly be positioned earlier in the decision-making process, increasing the EIA's capacity to influence the key issues that characterize each project alternative. In another context, Soria-Lara et al. (2015) carried out specific research in Spain to identify process-related barriers linked to EIA application in the transport field. Environmental consultants and transport planners were asked to participate by filling out an online survey, which revealed that one important barrier was that EIA was implemented too late, at a time when key decisions on alternatives had already been made. This view was particularly significant for environmental consultants, who specifically noted how the EIA's relevance and effectiveness is drastically reduced when its implementation comes too late in the decision-making process. In a cross-comparative study in Italy, Portugal, and Spain (Soria-Lara et al., 2020), practitioners also point out that EIA is implemented too late in transport projects, resulting in a limited capacity to take part in the comparison of alternatives.

4.2 Transparency

According to Zhang et al. (2013), who carried out a literature review to determine the critical factors affecting EIA effectiveness, transparency and openness are seen as one of the main barriers in EIA implementation. Transparency is crucial in a context of increasing the involvement of the public, stakeholders, and professional domains under the umbrella of a collaborative planning approach (Weston, 2004). Kruopienė et al. (2009) also emphasize the relevance of transparency problems during the EIA process. Their study focuses on the context of Lithuania, and the authors investigate EIA effectiveness using a combination of archive research and quantitative/qualitative analysis. A lack of information exchange can be observed between authorities, environmental consultants and project-developers, resulting in a situation where individual subjectivity prevails. This produces a systematic non-transparent assessment process and undermines the EIA's capacity to anticipate impacts, compare alternatives and activate mitigating policies. Mottee and Howitt (2018) in Australia underline the need for greater transparency in urban-scale plans and key infrastructure projects, which are highly politicized. In the authors' view, this has reduced the application of EIA processes to a minimum standard and with a low level of transparency regarding their outcomes. The authors call for better management and monitoring of the environmental and social impacts of urban transport infrastructure projects, fostering more robust and transparent assessment processes that effectively involve practitioners, decision-makers and the community.

Nevertheless, transparency—like many other process-related barriers—is significantly affected by the context. For example, Bassi et al. (2012) point out that EIA is seen by participants as a relatively transparent process that provides decision-makers with useful information about potential impacts, and enhances the projects' environmental soundness. The authors compare EIA performance in Italy and the UK by collecting views from key project participants and selecting case studies in the field of transport, renewable energy and tourism development. The findings on transparency in EIA processes are particularly applicable to the UK, where the EIA system tends to be more transparent, integrated and participatory. In this respect, transparency is recognized as a key factor, since most EIA teams in the UK include a broader spread of disciplines and expertise and apply holistic working methodologies.

4.3 Stakeholder involvement in earlier EIA stages

The involvement of stakeholders in earlier EIA stages is key to determine the scope of the assessment process. However, EIA implementation in transport planning is often a series of disconnected steps where experts and stakeholders participate separately with zero feedback between them (Soria-Lara et al., 2017). This especially affects the so-called scoping phase, which occurs early in the EIA and identifies its content, scale and scope. Although this scoping phase may vary depending on legal frameworks and political contexts, it is usually completed in a short period of time using existing information and consultations with stakeholders and the affected community. The aim of the scoping phase is to provide all the relevant information on the impacts to be evaluated and the system boundaries, and to recommend particular assessment methods (Lee, 2006). The traditional list of participants during the scoping phase includes environmental authorities (local and regional governments, air quality agencies, nature associations, spatial planning agencies, etc.), other interested parties (sectorial governments, specific population groups, etc.) and the general public (residents, community figures, etc.).

Some authors note that the effectiveness of the scoping phase to provide meaningful information for later EIA stages is related to how the information is requested and its level of complexity (Balasubramaniam and Voulvoulis, 2005; Kolkman et al., 2007; Sainath and Rajan, 2015; Wood et al., 2007). For example, the way in which authorities request information during the scoping phase is too generic, or the stakeholders' responses are too complex and technical, so their usefulness is limited. Another group of authors signal that stakeholder involvement during the scoping phase can be improved by using EIA as a learning process, creating a different kind of dialog spaces, namely spaces (physically and figuratively) where stakeholders can give their views and discuss transport projects and impacts in a range of different ways (Karjalainen et al., 2013; Liu et al., 2013; Saarikoski, 2000; Soria-Lara et al., 2016). These include interacting bilaterally with decision-makers and other stakeholders and sharing and discussing their views together.

4.4 Public participation

In recent decades the need to enhance public participation in EIA processes has been a central issue in the academic literature. The benefits of public participation are often overlooked, so it is often poorly articulated which makes it difficult to determine how it can effectively be achieved (Lidskog and Soneryd, 2000). The shift toward more collaborative transport planning and decision-making approaches favors the replacement of the language of consultation with the language of deliberation. O'Faircheallaigh (2010) analyses at least four different models to understand and integrate public participation in EIA processes: (i) to provide (new) information; (ii) to fill some information gap; (iii) to contest existing information; and (iv) to solve problems by social learning. Efficient EIA processes should distinguish between participation models that activate efficient methods based on information needs, rather than implementing standard participation processes with no specific targets. Rozema and Bond (2015) also recognize a direct relationship between the arguable effectiveness of EIA in the field of transport and its capacity to accommodate civil society discourse, and call for an assessment process that is more grounded in inclusive democracy. This is analyzed in two different projects and contexts: the HS2 rail network in England and the A4DS motorway in the Netherlands. The authors conclude that EIA is unable to integrate all the possible discourses, especially arguments characterized by opposition, a situation that can seriously limit EIA effectiveness, and pointing to the need to adopt methodologies capable of analyzing and integrating community discourse into the assessment process.

5. Conclusions

This book chapter aimed to show an up-to-date and comprehensive overview of EIA literature in the field of transport, mainly focused on lessons learned from the Western world. The review distils existing obstacles, new developments and potential research gaps for both technical and process-related aspects of the EIA for transport projects. Issues related to Strategic Environmental Assessment have not been covered. The chapter reflects on how the EIA implementation for transport projects is an intrinsically complex multi-dimensional process, considering scientific facts (environmental, ecological and socioeconomic impacts), but also including subjective values from different actors involved (judgment, preference, value and concern).

On the one hand, EIA technical aspects were included in this review. They refer to content and methodological developments affecting EIA effectiveness. In particular, a total of four technical aspects have been covered: (i) project and baseline information; (ii) identification and evaluation of environmental impacts; (iii) impacts prediction methods; (iv) methods for evaluating and comparing project alternatives. Some further issues included here are:

- Geographical Information Technologies (e.g., GIS; remote sensing) have facilitated a more accurate use of spatial information to assess environmental impacts linked to transport projects. That has been particularly relevant for evaluating effects on landscape, protected areas, water resources, etc. However, new challenges in how processing EIA information and estimating impacts can be associated with big data analysis, in particular for calibrating impact prediction models and comparing project alternatives.
- Evaluation methods should progress to integrate more efficiently both natural and socioeconomic aspects related to infrastructure transport projects. Moreover, mixed methodologies that incorporate quantitative and qualitative approaches are required in this respect.

On the other hand, EIA process-related aspects also took part in the chapter. They illustrate situations focused on EIA procedure, including the benefits and obstacles originated by the actors involved in the EIA process. Specifically, four groups of process-related aspects are described: (i) the EIA timing; (ii) transparency; (ii) stakeholder involvement in earlier EIA stages; and (iv) public participation. Some further issues included here are:

- A shift in how EIA actors are involved in EIA for transport projects seems to be needed. This strongly affects the scoping phase, the process of identifying the content and extent of the EIA. Frequently, it is completed in a relatively short period of time using existing information and consultations with stakeholders. Furthermore, the improvement of the public's involvement in EIA processes is also necessary. For this reason, a better integration of knowledge is needed where actors and the public can interact each other in open dialogue processes, discussing on evaluation boundaries and EIA scope.
- The EIA timing is another important aspect to be addresses. A balance between incorporating EIA at strategic levels and in moments when project alternatives are defined is crucial to increase the EIA effectiveness in transport projects.

Future research aiming to provide more robust results could focus on improving both technical and process-related aspects of EIA in transport projects. More rigorously experimental settings could help improve existing problems and stimulate new technical developments. Furthermore, testing the proposed solutions and developments in different geographical and institutional contexts would help harness more insight on the effectiveness of EIA in transport projects.

Acknowledgments

This paper has been developed in the context of the following research projects: (i) "TRANS-URBAN: Simulacio´n de escenarios colaborativos para integrar poli´ticas de transporte urbano sostenible y usos del suelo." The project was funded by the Spanish Government under National R+D Plan (2018–2020) JCR. Grant Agreement no. CSO2017-86914-C2-2-P; (ii) "iCITIES: Efectos urbanos y sociales del uso de internet para compras y trabajo." Accio´n financiada por la Comunidad de Madrid en el marco del Convenio Plurianual con la Universidad Polite´cnica de Madrid en la li´nea de actuacio´n esti´mulo a la investigacio´n de M190020074JASL.

Annex I. Example of content of EIA report established by European Union Directive 2014/52/EU

In particular, the Annex IV of the Directive defines the following information for the Environmental Impact Assessment report (brief summary):

- *Description of the project.*
- *A description of the reasonable alternatives* (for example, in terms of project design, technology, location, size and scale) studied by the developer, which are relevant to the proposed project and its specific characteristics, and an indication of the main reasons for selecting the chosen option, including a comparison of the environmental effects.
- *A description of the relevant aspects of the current state of the environment (baseline scenario) and an outline of the likely evolution* thereof without implementation of the project as far as natural changes from the baseline scenario can be assessed with reasonable effort on the basis of the availability of environmental information and scientific knowledge.
- *A description of the factors likely to be significantly affected by the project*: population, human health, biodiversity (for example, fauna and flora), land (for example, land take), soil (for example, organic matter, erosion, compaction, sealing), water (for example, hydromorphological changes, quantity and quality), air, climate (for example, greenhouse gas emissions, impacts relevant to adaptation), material assets, cultural heritage, including architectural and archeological aspects, and landscape.
- *A description of the likely significant effects of the project on the environment* resulting from the different phases and aspects of the project. The

description of the likely significant effects on the factors affected by the project should cover the direct effects and any indirect, secondary, cumulative, transboundary, short-term, medium-term and long-term, permanent and temporary, positive and negative effects of the project. This description should take into account the environmental protection objectives established at Union or member state level which are relevant to the project.

- *A description of the forecasting methods or evidence, used to identify and assess the significant effects on the environment*, including details of difficulties (for example, technical deficiencies or lack of knowledge) encountered compiling the required information and the main uncertainties involved.
- *A description of the measures envisaged to avoid, prevent, reduce or, if possible, offset any identified significant adverse effects on the environment and, where appropriate, of any proposed monitoring arrangements* (for example, the preparation of a post-project analysis). That description should explain the extent, to which significant adverse effects on the environment are avoided, prevented, reduced or offset, and should cover both the construction and operational phases.
- *A description of the expected significant adverse effects of the project on the environment deriving from the vulnerability of the project to risks of major accidents and/or disasters which are relevant to the project concerned.* Where appropriate, this description should include measures envisaged to prevent or mitigate the significant adverse effects of such events on the environment and details of the preparedness for and proposed response to such emergencies.
- *A non-technical summary.*
- *A reference list* detailing the sources used for the descriptions and assessments included in the report.

References

Ahmed, A.A., Pradhan, B., 2019. Vehicular traffic noise prediction and propagation modelling using neural networks and geospatial information system. Environ. Monit. Assess. 191 (3), 190.

Ali Khalil, M., Hamad, K., Shanableh, A., 2019. Developing machine learning models to predict roadway traffic noise: an opportunity to escape conventional techniques. Transp. Res. Rec. 2673 (4), 158–172.

André, M., 2004. The ARTEMIS European driving cycles for measuring car pollutant emissions. Sci. Total Environ. 334, 73–84.

Antonson, H., 2011. The treatment of landscape in a Swedish EIA process. Environ. Impact Assess. Rev. 31 (3), 195–205.

Antunes, P., Santos, R., Jordao, L., 2001. The application of geographical information systems to determine environmental impact significance. Environ. Impact Assess. Rev. 21 (6), 511–535.
Arce, R., Gullón, N., 2000. The application of strategic environmental assessment to sustainability assessment of infrastructure development. Environ. Impact Assess. Rev. 20 (3), 393–402.
Arce Ruiz, R.M., 2002. La Evaluación de Impacto Ambiental en la Encrucijada. Los Retos del Futuro. Ecoiuris, Madrid.
Arce Ruiz, R.M., 2013. La Evaluación Ambiental en la Ingeniería Civil. Ediciones Mundi Prensa.
Arce Ruiz, R.M., Pérez, E.O., Pastor, I.O., 2010. Los Sistemas de Información Geográfica aplicados a la Evaluación Ambiental en la planificación de infraestructuras de transporte. Ciudad y Territorio Estudios Territoriales 42 (165–166), 513–528.
Arce, R., Aizpurua, N., del Rey, J., González, J., Rojas, G., 2007. Las Tecnologías de la Información y las Comunicaciones y el Medio Ambiente. Fundación Gas Natural, Barcelona, Spain (In Spanish).
Arts, J., Morrison-Saunders, A., 2012. Assessing Impact: Handbook of EIA and SEA Follow-Up. Routledge, p. 167.
Avşar, Y., Saral, A., Gönüllü, M.T., Arslankaya, E., Kurt, U., 2004. Neural network modelling of outdoor noise levels in a pilot area. Turk. J. Eng. Environ. Sci. 28 (3), 149–156.
Balasubramaniam, A., Voulvoulis, N., 2005. The appropriateness of multicriteria analysis in environmental decision-making problems. Environ. Technol. 26 (9), 951–962.
Banerjee, P., Ghose, M.K., 2016. Spatial analysis of environmental impacts of highway projects with special emphasis on mountainous area: an overview. Impact Assess. Proj. Apprais. 34 (4), 279–293.
Barredo, J., Bosque, J., 1995. Integración de evaluación multicriterio y sistemas de información geográfica para la evaluación de la capacidad de acogida del territorio y la asignación de usos del suelo. In: Actas del IV Congreso Español de Sistemas de Información Geográfica. Barcelona, pp. 191–200.
Barredo Cano, J.I., 1996. Sistemas de Información Geográfica y Evaluación Multicriterio. Edit. RA-MA, Madrid, p. 264.
Barry, T.M., Reagan, J.A., 1978. FHWA highway traffic noise prediction model, FHWA-RD-77-108.
Bassi, A., Howard, R., Geneletti, D., Ferrari, S., 2012. UK and Italian EIA systems: a comparative study on management practice and performance in the construction industry. Environ. Impact Assess. Rev. 34, 1–11.
Bertolini, L., 2007. Evolutionary urban transportation planning: an exploration. Environ. Plan. A. 39 (8), 1998–2019.
Besnard, F., Hamet, J.F., Lelong, J., Le Duc, E., Furst, N., Doisy, S., Dutilleux, G., 2009. Road Noise Prediction 1—Calculating Sound Emissions From Road Traffic. SETRA, Bagneux.
Beukers, E., Bertolini, L., Te Brömmelstroet, M., 2014. Using cost benefit analysis as a learning process: identifying interventions for improving communication and trust. Transp. Policy 31, 61–72.
Bhatia, R., Wernham, A., 2008. Integrating human health into environmental impact assessment: an unrealized opportunity for environmental health and justice. Environ. Health Perspect. 116 (8), 991–1000.
Bishop, I.D., Hulse, D.W., 1994. Prediction of scenic beauty using mapped data and geographic information systems. Landsc. Urban Plan. 30 (1–2), 59–70.
Borrego, C., Tchepel, O., Costa, A.M., Amorim, J.H., Miranda, A.I., 2003. Emission and dispersion modelling of Lisbon air quality at local scale. Atmos. Environ. 37 (37), 5197–5205.

Bosque Sendra, J., 1992. Sistemas de Información Geográfica. Edit. Rialp, Madrid.
Bravo-Moncayo, L., Lucio-Naranjo, J., Chávez, M., Pavón-García, I., Garzón, C., 2019. A machine learning approach for traffic-noise annoyance assessment. Appl. Acoust. 156, 262–270.
Briggs, S., Hudson, M.D., 2013. Determination of significance in ecological impact assessment: past change, current practice and future improvements. Environ. Impact Assess. Rev. 38, 16–25.
Bryman, A., 2016. Social Research Methods. Oxford University Press.
Burris, R.K., Canter, L.W., 1997. Cumulative impacts are not properly addressed in environmental assessments. Environ. Impact Assess. Rev. 17 (1), 5–18.
Byer, P., Cestti, R., Croal, P., Fisher, W., Hazell, S., Kolhoff, A., Kørnøv, L., 2012. Climate change in impact assessment: international best practice principles. In: Special Publication Series No. 8. International Association for Impact Assessment.
Cammarata, G., Cavalieri, S., Fichera, A., 1995. A neural network architecture for noise prediction. Neural Netw. 8 (6), 963–973.
Canter, L., Ross, B., 2010. State of practice of cumulative effects assessment and management: the good, the bad and the ugly. Impact Assess. Proj. Apprais. 28 (4), 261–268.
Canter, L., Sadler, B., Lee, N., 1997. A tool kit for effective EIA practice: review of methods and perspectives on their application. Proj. Apprais. 12 (4), 266.
Chebud, Y., Naja, G.M., Rivero, R.G., Melesse, A.M., 2012. Water quality monitoring using remote sensing and an artificial neural network. Water Air Soil Pollut. 223 (8), 4875–4887.
Clark, B.D., Chapman, K., Bisset, R., Wathern, P., 1976. Assessment of major industrial applications. A manual. Research report n 13, Department of the Environment, Londres.
Clark, B.D., Chapman, K., Bisset, R., Wathern, P., 1978. Environmental impact assessment in the USA: a critical review. Research report n 26, 1978, Department of Environment and Department of Transportation, Londres.
Clark, B.D., Chapman, K., Bisset, R., Wathern, P., 1979. Environmental impact analysis. In: Lovejoy, D. (Ed.), Land Use and Landscape Planning, second ed. Leonard Hill, pp. 51–88.
Clark, B.D., Chapman, K., Bisset, R., Wathern, P., 1981. A Manual for the Assessment of Major Development Proposals. Her Majesty's Stationery Office, Londres. 1981.
Connolly, D.P., Kouroussis, G., Woodward, P.K., Giannopoulos, A., Verlinden, O., Forde, M.C., 2014. Scoping prediction of re-radiated ground-borne noise and vibration near high speed rail lines with variable soils. Soil Dyn. Earthq. Eng. 66, 78–88.
Connolly, D.P., Costa, P.A., Kouroussis, G., Galvin, P., Woodward, P.K., Laghrouche, O., 2015. Large scale international testing of railway ground vibrations across Europe. Soil Dyn. Earthq. Eng. 71, 1–12.
Connolly, D.P., Marecki, G.P., Kouroussis, G., Thalassinakis, I., Woodward, P.K., 2016. The growth of railway ground vibration problems a review. Sci. Total Environ. 568, 1276–1282.
Cornero, A., 2010. Improving the implementation of environmental impact assessment. Report, European Environmental Agency.
Costanzo, B.P., Sánchez, L.E., 2019. Innovation in impact assessment theory and practice: how is it captured in the literature? Environ. Impact Assess. Rev. 79, 106289.
Cox, A.B., Gifford, F., 1997. An overview to geographic information systems. J. Acad. Librariansh. 23 (6), 449–461.
Curtis, C., 2011. Integrating land use with public transport: the use of a discursive accessibility tool to inform metropolitan spatial planning in Perth. Transp. Rev. 31 (2), 179–197.

Deakin, M., Mitchell, G., Nijkamp, P., Vreeker, R. (Eds.), 2007. Sustainable Urban Development Volume 2: The Environmental Assessment Methods. Routledge, pp. 492–509.
Dee, N., Baker, J.K., Drobny, N.L., 1972. Environmental Evaluation System for Water Resource Planning. Water Resources Research.
Dee, N., Baker, J., Drobny, N., Duke, K., Whitman, I., Fahringer, D., 1973. An environmental evaluation system for water resource planning. Water Resour. Res. 9 (3), 523–535.
Defrance, J., Salomons, E., Noordhoek, I., Heimann, D., Plovsing, B., Watts, G., Aballea, F., 2007. Outdoor sound propagation reference model developed in the European Harmonoise project. Acta Acust. United Ac. 93 (2), 213–227.
Dey, S., Caulfield, B., Ghosh, B., 2019. Modelling uncertainty of vehicular emissions inventory: a case study of Ireland. J. Clean. Prod. 213, 1115–1126.
Dramstad, W.E., Tveit, M.S., Fjellstad, W.J., Fry, G.L., 2006. Relationships between visual landscape preferences and map-based indicators of landscape structure. Landsc. Urban Plan. 78 (4), 465–474.
Duinker, P.N., Beanlands, G.E., 1986. The significance of environmental impacts: an exploration of the concept. Environ. Manag. 10 (1), 1–10.
Dutilleux, G., Defrance, J., Ecotière, D., Gauvreau, B., Bérengier, M., Besnard, F., Duc, E.L., 2010. NMPB-ROUTES-2008: the revision of the French method for road traffic noise prediction. Acta Acust. United Ac. 96 (3), 452–462.
El Tabach, E., Lancelot, L., Shahrour, I., Najjar, Y., 2007. Use of artificial neural network simulation metamodelling to assess groundwater contamination in a road project. Math. Comput. Model. 45 (7–8), 766–776.
EnHealth, 2001. Health Impact Assessment Guidelines. Commonwealth Department of Health and Aged Care, Canberra, Australia.
Fiala, P., Degrande, G., Augusztinovicz, F., 2007. Numerical modelling of ground-borne noise and vibration in buildings due to surface rail traffic. J. Sound Vib. 301 (3–5), 718–738.
Fischer, T.B., 2003. Strategic environmental assessment in post-modern times. Environ. Impact Assess. Rev. 23 (2), 155–170.
Folkeson, L., Antonson, H., Helldin, J.O., 2013. Planners' views on cumulative effects. A focus-group study concerning transport infrastructure planning in Sweden. Land Use Policy 30 (1), 243–253.
Galletta, B., Gandolfo, M.A., Iannazi, H., Pieri Buti, G., 1985. Valutazione di Impatto Ambientale del Tracciato Autostradale Rieti-Terni-Orte. Tratto: Moggio. Terni.SS. 3 Flaminia. Svincolo E45. Regione dell'Umbria. Dipartimento per l'Assetto del Territorio, Ufficio del Piano Urbanistico Territoriale. 1985.
Galvín, P., Mendoza, D.L., Connolly, D.P., Degrande, G., Lombaert, G., Romero, A., 2018. Scoping assessment of free-field vibrations due to railway traffic. Soil Dyn. Earthq. Eng. 114, 598–614.
Garg, N., Maji, S., 2014. A critical review of principal traffic noise models: strategies and implications. Environ. Impact Assess. Rev. 46, 68–81.
Gasparatos, A., 2010. Embedded value systems in sustainability assessment tools and their implications. J. Environ. Manage. 91 (8), 1613–1622.
Genaro, N., Torija, A., Ramos-Ridao, A., Requena, I., Ruiz, D.P., Zamorano, M., 2010. A neural network based model for urban noise prediction. J. Acoust. Soc. Am. 128 (4), 1738–1746.
Geneletti, D., 2003. Biodiversity impact assessment of roads: an approach based on ecosystem rarity. Environ. Impact Assess. Rev. 23 (3), 343–365.
Gharehbaghi, K., Scott-Young, C., 2018, March. GIS as a vital tool for environmental impact assessment and mitigation. In: IOP Conference Series: Earth and Environmental Science. vol. 127. IOP Publishing, p. 012009. No. 1.

Givargis, S., Mahmoodi, M., 2008. Converting the UK calculation of road traffic noise (CORTN) to a model capable of calculating LAeq, 1h for the Tehran's roads. Appl. Acoust. 69 (11), 1108–1113.

Gkatzoflias, D., Kouridis, C., Ntziachristos, L., Samaras, Z., 2007. COPERT 4: Computer Programme to Calculate Emissions From Road Transport. European Environment Agency.

Gontier, M., Mörtberg, U., Balfors, B., 2010. Comparing GIS-based habitat models for applications in EIA and SEA. Environ. Impact Assess. Rev. 30 (1), 8–18.

Gutiérrez-Puebla, J., 2007. Los Sistemas de Información Geográfica en la Planificación del Transporte, Información espacial y nuevas tendencias en las tecnologías de la información geográfica (TIGs)., ISBN: 978-84-338-4798-0, pp. 67–110.

Gutiérrez-Puebla, J., Gould, M., 2001. SIG: Sistemas de Información Geográfica. Ed. Síntesis, Madrid.

Harris, P., Riley, E., Sainsbury, P., Kent, J., Baum, F., 2018. Including health in environmental impact assessments of three mega transport projects in Sydney, Australia: a critical, institutional, analysis. Environ. Impact Assess. Rev. 68, 109–116.

Hatzopoulou, M., Miller, E.J., 2010. Linking an activity-based travel demand model with traffic emission and dispersion models: transport's contribution to air pollution in Toronto. Transp. Res. Part D: Transp. Environ. 15 (6), 315–325.

Health Canada, 2004. Canadian Handbook on Health Impact Assessment, Vol 1. The Basics. Health Canada, Ottawa.

Heutschi, K., 2004. SonRoad: new Swiss road traffic noise model. Acta Acust. United Ac. 90 (3), 548–554.

Hildén, M., Furman, E., Kaljonen, M., 2004. Views on planning and expectations of SEA: the case of transport planning. Environ. Impact Assess. Rev. 24 (5), 519–536.

Huber, M., Welker, A., Helmreich, B., 2016. Critical review of heavy metal pollution of traffic area runoff: occurrence, influencing factors, and partitioning. Sci. Total Environ. 541, 895–919.

Innes, J.E., Booher, D.E., 2018. Planning With Complexity: An Introduction to Collaborative Rationality for Public Policy. Routledge.

Jay, S., Jones, C., Slinn, P., Wood, C., 2007. Environmental impact assessment: retrospect and prospect. Environ. Impact Assess. Rev. 27 (4), 287–300.

Joumard, R., Gudmundsson, H., 2010. Indicators of Environmental Sustainability in Transport: An Interdisciplinary Approach to Methods. European Commission.

Karjalainen, T.P., Marttunen, M., Sarkki, S., Rytkönen, A.M., 2013. Integrating ecosystem services into environmental impact assessment: an analytic–deliberative approach. Environ. Impact Assess. Rev. 40, 54–64.

Karlson, M., Mörtberg, U., Balfors, B., 2014. Road ecology in environmental impact assessment. Environ. Impact Assess. Rev. 48, 10–19.

Kephalopoulos, S., Paviotti, M., Anfosso-Lédée, F., 2012. Common Noise Assessment Methods in Europe (CNOSSOS-EU). European Union.

Khuan, L.Y., Hamzah, N., Jailani, R., 2002, July. Prediction of water quality index (WQI) based on artificial neural network (ANN). In: Student Conference on Research and Development. IEEE, pp. 157–161.

Kim, R.J., Loucks, D.P., Stedinger, J.R., 2012. Artificial neural network models of watershed nutrient loading. Water Resour. Manag. 26 (10), 2781–2797.

Kolkman, M.J., van der Veen, A., Geurts, P.A., 2007. Controversies in water management: frames and mental models. Environ. Impact Assess. Rev. 27 (7), 685–706.

Kragh, J., Plovsing, B., Storeheier, S., Taraldsen, G., Jonasson, H.G., 2002. Nordic environmental noise prediction methods. In: Nord2000 summary report: Danish electronics light & acoustics.

Kruopienė, J., Židonienė, S., Dvarionienė, J., 2009. Current practice and shortcomings of EIA in Lithuania. Environ. Impact Assess. Rev. 29 (5), 305–309.

Kumar, P., Nigam, S.P., Kumar, N., 2014. Vehicular traffic noise modeling using artificial neural network approach. Transp. Res. Part C Emerg. Technol. 40, 111–122.
Lawrence, D.P., 2007. Impact significance determination—back to basics. Environ. Impact Assess. Rev. 27 (8), 755–769.
Lee, N., 2006. Bridging the gap between theory and practice in integrated assessment. Environ. Impact Assess. Rev. 26 (1), 57–78.
Leopold, L.B., 1971. A Procedure for Evaluating Environmental Impact. vol. 28 US Department of the Interior. No. 2.
Li, H., Deng, Q., Zhang, J., Olubunmi Olanipekun, A., Lyu, S., 2019. Environmental impact assessment of transportation infrastructure in the life cycle: case study of a fast track transportation project in China. Energies 12 (6), 1015.
Lidskog, R., Soneryd, L., 2000. Transport infrastructure investment and environmental impact assessment in Sweden: public involvement or exclusion? Environ. Plan. A. 32 (8), 1465–1479.
Liu, T.K., Sheu, H.Y., Tseng, C.N., 2013. Environmental impact assessment of seawater desalination plant under the framework of integrated coastal management. Desalination 326, 10–18.
Lock, K., 2000. Health impact assessment. BMJ 320 (7246), 1395–1398.
López-Mendoza, D., Romero, A., Connolly, D.P., Galvín, P., 2017. Scoping assessment of building vibration induced by railway traffic. Soil Dyn. Earthq. Eng. 93, 147–161.
Loro, M., Arce, R.M., Ortega, E., Martín, B., 2014. Road-corridor planning in the EIA procedure in Spain. A review of case studies. Environ. Impact Assess. Rev. 44, 11–21.
Loro, M., Ortega, E., Arce, R.M., Geneletti, D., 2015. Ecological connectivity analysis to reduce the barrier effect of roads. An innovative graph-theory approach to define wildlife corridors with multiple paths and without bottlenecks. Landsc. Urban Plan. 139, 149–162.
Loro, M., Ortega, E., Arce, R.M., Geneletti, D., 2016. Assessing landscape resistance to roe deer dispersal using fuzzy set theory and multicriteria analysis: a case study in Central Spain. Landsc. Ecol. Eng. 12 (1), 41–60.
Luell, S.K., Hunt, W.F., Winston, R.J., 2010. Improving Water Quality and Hydrology Associated With Highway Bridge Deck Runoff Using Bioretention and a Swale. 2010 Pittsburgh, Pennsylvania, June 20-June 23, 2010, American Society of Agricultural and Biological Engineers, p. 1.
Malczewski, J., 2004. GIS-based land-use suitability analysis: a critical overview. Prog. Plan. 62 (1), 3–65.
Marshall, R., Arts, J., Morrison-Saunders, A., 2005. International principles for best practice EIA follow-up. Impact Assess. Proj. Apprais. 23 (3), 175–181.
Martín, B., Ortega, E., Otero, I., Arce, R.M., 2016. Landscape character assessment with GIS using map-based indicators and photographs in the relationship between landscape and roads. J. Environ. Manage. 180, 324–334.
Martín, B., Arce, R., Otero, I., Loro, M., 2018. Visual landscape quality as viewed from motorways in Spain. Sustainability 10 (8), 2592.
Marzouk, M., Abdelkader, E.M., El-zayat, M., Aboushady, A., 2017. Assessing environmental impact indicators in road construction projects in developing countries. Sustainability 9 (5), 843.
Mayer, R.M., Poulikakos, L.D., Lees, A.R., Heutschi, K., Kalivoda, M.T., Soltic, P., 2012. Reducing the environmental impact of road and rail vehicles. Environ. Impact Assess. Rev. 32 (1), 25–32.
McHarg, I.L., 1969. Design with Nature. American Museum of Natural History by the Natural History Press, Garden City, NY.

McIntyre, J.K., Davis, J.W., Hinman, C., Macneale, K.H., Anulacion, B.F., Scholz, N.L., Stark, J.D., 2015. Soil bioretention protects juvenile salmon and their prey from the toxic impacts of urban stormwater runoff. Chemosphere 132, 213–219.

Morgan, R.K., 2012. Environmental impact assessment: the state of the art. Impact Assess. Proj. Apprais. 30 (1), 5–14.

Morris, P., Therivel, R. (Eds.), 1995. Methods of Environmental Impact Assessment. UBC Press, p. 124.

Morrison-Saunders, A., Marshall, R., Arts, J., 2007. EIA Follow-Up: International Best Practice Principles. International Association for Impact Assessment.

Mottee, L.K., Howitt, R., 2018. Follow-up and social impact assessment (SIA) in urban transport-infrastructure projects: insights from the parramatta rail link. Aust. Plan. 55 (1), 46–56.

Nedic, V., Despotovic, D., Cvetanovic, S., Despotovic, M., Babic, S., 2014. Comparison of classical statistical methods and artificial neural network in traffic noise prediction. Environ. Impact Assess. Rev. 49, 24–30.

Ness, B., Urbel-Piirsalu, E., Anderberg, S., Olsson, L., 2007. Categorising tools for sustainability assessment. Ecol. Econ. 60 (3), 498–508.

Nourani, V., Gökçekuş, H., Umar, I.K., 2020. Artificial intelligence based ensemble model for prediction of vehicular traffic noise. Environ. Res. 180, 108852.

Odum, E.P., Bramlett, G.A., Ike, A., Champlin, J.R., Zieman, J.C., Shugart, H.H., 1976. Totality indexes for evaluating environmental impacts of highway alternatives. Transp. Res. Rec. (561), 57–67.

O'Faircheallaigh, C., 2010. Public participation and environmental impact assessment: purposes, implications, and lessons for public policy making. Environ. Impact Assess. Rev. 30 (1), 19–27.

Opher, T., Friedler, E., 2010. Factors affecting highway runoff quality. Urban Water J. 7 (3), 155–172.

Orea, D.G., Villarino, M.T.G., 2013. Evaluación de Impacto Ambiental. Mundi-Prensa Libros.

Owens, S., Rayner, T., Bina, O., 2004. New agendas for appraisal: reflections on theory, practice, and research. Environ. Plan. A. 36 (11), 1943–1959.

Pan, T., Miao, T., 2015. Contamination of roadside soils by runoff pollutants: a numerical study. Transp. Geotech. 2, 1–9.

Pavlickova, K., Vyskupova, M., 2015. A method proposal for cumulative environmental impact assessment based on the landscape vulnerability evaluation. Environ. Impact Assess. Rev. 50, 74–84.

Pediaditi, K., Banias, G., Sartzetakis, E., Lampridi, M., 2018. Greece's reformed EIA system: evaluating its implementation and potential. Environ. Impact Assess. Rev. 73, 90–103.

Pfaffenbichler, P., 2011. Modelling with systems dynamics as a method to bridge the gap between politics, planning and science? Lessons learnt from the development of the land use and transport model MARS. Transp. Rev. 31 (2), 267–289.

Pinho, P., Maia, R., Monterroso, A., 2007. The quality of Portuguese environmental impact studies: the case of small hydropower projects. Environ. Impact Assess. Rev. 27 (3), 189–205.

Quartieri, J., Mastorakis, N.E., Iannone, G., Guarnaccia, C., D'ambrosio, S., Troisi, A., Lenza, T.L.L., 2009, December. A review of traffic noise predictive models. In: Recent Advances in Applied and Theoretical Mechanics, 5th WSEAS International Conference on Applied and Theoretical Mechanics (MECHANICS'09) Puerto De La Cruz, Tenerife, Canary Islands, Spain December, pp. 14–16.

Richardson, T., 2005. Environmental assessment and planning theory: four short stories about power, multiple rationality, and ethics. Environ. Impact Assess. Rev. 25 (4), 341–365.

Rozema, J.G., Bond, A.J., 2015. Framing effectiveness in impact assessment: discourse accommodation in controversial infrastructure development. Environ. Impact Assess. Rev. 50, 66–73.
Saarikoski, H., 2000. Environmental impact assessment (EIA) as collaborative learning process. Environ. Impact Assess. Rev. 20 (6), 681–700.
Sadler, B., 1996. Environmental assessment in a changing world. In: Evaluating practice to improve performance-final report.
Sainath, N.V., Rajan, K.S., 2015. Meta-analysis of EIA public hearings in the state of Gujarat, India: its role versus the goal of environmental management. Impact Assess. Proj. Apprais. 33 (2), 148–153.
Sánchez, L.E., Morrison-Saunders, A., 2011. Learning about knowledge management for improving environmental impact assessment in a government agency: the Western Australian experience. J. Environ. Manage. 92 (9), 2260–2271.
Scolozzi, R., Geneletti, D., 2012. A multi-scale qualitative approach to assess the impact of urbanization on natural habitats and their connectivity. Environ. Impact Assess. Rev. 36, 9–22.
Sfakianaki, E., O'Reilly, M., 2002. GIS in road environmental planning and management. WIT Trans. Built Environ. 60, 10.
Slesser, M., 1978. Energy Analysis: Its Utility and Limits. International Institute for Applied System Analysis.
Smit, B., Spaling, H., 1995. Methods for cumulative effects assessment. Environ. Impact Assess. Rev. 15 (1), 81–106.
Smit, R., Smokers, R., Rabé, E., 2007. A new modelling approach for road traffic emissions: VERSIT+. Transp. Res. Part D: Transp. Environ. 12 (6), 414–422.
Smit, R., Brown, A.L., Chan, Y.C., 2008. Do air pollution emissions and fuel consumption models for roadways include the effects of congestion in the roadway traffic flow? Environ. Model. Software 23 (10–11), 1262–1270.
Sobrino, N., Monzon, A., Hernandez, S., 2016. Reduced carbon and energy footprint in highway operations: the highway energy assessment (HERA) methodology. Netw. Spat. Econ. 16 (1), 395–414.
Soria-Lara, J.A., Bertolini, L., te Brömmelstroet, M., 2015. Environmental impact assessment in urban transport planning: exploring process-related barriers in Spanish practice. Environ. Impact Assess. Rev. 50, 95–104.
Soria-Lara, J.A., Bertolini, L., te Brömmelstroet, M., 2016. An experiential approach to improving the integration of knowledge during EIA in transport planning. Environ. Impact Assess. Rev. 56, 188–199.
Soria-Lara, J.A., Bertolini, L., Te Brömmelstroet, M., 2017. Towards a more effective EIA in transport planning: a literature review to derive interventions and mechanisms to improve knowledge integration. J. Environ. Plan. Manag. 60 (5), 755–772.
Soria-Lara, J.A., Batista, L., Le Pira, M., Arce-Ruiz, R., Inturri, G., Pinho, P., 2020. Revealing EIA process-related barriers in transport projects: the cases of Italy, Portugal, and Spain. Environ. Impact Assess. Rev. 83, 106402.
Stagge, J.H., Davis, A.P., Jamil, E., Kim, H., 2012. Performance of grass swales for improving water quality from highway runoff. Water Res. 46 (20), 6731–6742.
Steele, C., 2001. A critical review of some traffic noise prediction models. Appl. Acoust. 62 (3), 271–287.
Steinemann, A., 2001. Improving alternatives for environmental impact assessment. Environ. Impact Assess. Rev. 21 (1), 3–21.
Taylor, C.N., Bryan, C.H., Goodrich, C., 2004. Social Assessment: Theory, Process and Techniques. Centre for Resource Management.
te Brömmelstroet, M., Bertolini, L., 2011. A transition towards sustainable strategy making: integrating land use and transport knowledge types. In: Transitions Towards Sustainable Mobility. Springer, Berlin, Heidelberg, pp. 19–40.

Tomlinson, P., 2011. SEA and Transport Planning. Earthscan Publications Ltd, London and Washington, DC, pp. 177–189.
Trenouth, W.R., Gharabaghi, B., 2016. Highway runoff quality models for the protection of environmentally sensitive areas. J. Hydrol. 542, 143–155.
Tricker, R.C., 2007. Assessing cumulative environmental effects from major public transport projects. Transp. Policy 14 (4), 293–305.
United States Environmental Protection Agency, 2002. MOBILE6 Vehicle Emission Modelling Software, EPA-420-R-02-001, United States.
United States Environmental Protection Agency, 2009. MOVES2010a Mobile Source Emissions Model Update, EPA-420-B-09-041, United States.
Valencia-Sandoval, C., Flanders, D.N., Kozak, R.A., 2010. Participatory landscape planning and sustainable community development: methodological observations from a case study in rural Mexico. Landsc. Urban Plan. 94 (1), 63–70.
Van Dam, K.H., Nikolic, I., Lukszo, Z. (Eds.), 2012. Agent-Based Modelling of Socio-Technical Systems. vol. 9. Springer Science & Business Media, p. 238.
van Maercke, D., Defrance, J., 2007. Development of an analytical model for outdoor sound propagation within the Harmonoise project. Acta Acust. United Ac. 93 (2), 201–212.
Vanclay, F., 2003. SIA principles. Impact Assess. Proj. Apprais. 21 (1), 5–11.
Vardoulakis, S., Fisher, B.E., Pericleous, K., Gonzalez-Flesca, N., 2003. Modelling air quality in street canyons: a review. Atmos. Environ. 37 (2), 155–182.
Vizzari, M., 2011. Spatial modelling of potential landscape quality. Appl. Geogr. 31 (1), 108–118.
Waraich, R.A., Charypar, D., Balmer, M., Axhausen, K.W., 2009. Performance improvements for large scale traffic simulation in MATSim. In: 9th STRC Swiss Transport Research Conference: Proceedings (Vol. 565). Swiss Transport Research Conference.
Wärnbäck, A., Hilding-Rydevik, T., 2009. Cumulative effects in Swedish EIA practice—difficulties and obstacles. Environ. Impact Assess. Rev. 29 (2), 107–115.
Watts, G.R., 2005. Harmonoise prediction model for road traffic noise, published project report PPR034. Transport Research Laboratory, Wokingham, UK.
Weston, J., 2004. EIA in a risk society. J. Environ. Plan. Manag. 47 (2), 313–325.
Willson, R., 2001. Assessing communicative rationality as a transportation planning paradigm. Transportation 28 (1), 1–31.
Wise, S., Crooks, A., Batty, M., 2016, May. Transportation in agent-based urban modelling. In: International Workshop on Agent Based Modelling of Urban Systems. Springer, Cham, pp. 129–148.
Wood, G., Rodriguez-Bachiller, A., Becker, J., 2007. Fuzzy sets and simulated environmental change: evaluating and communicating impact significance in environmental impact assessment. Environ. Plan. A. 39 (4), 810–829.
Wright, J.S.F., 2004. HIA in Australia. In: Kemm, J., Parry, J. (Eds.), Health Impact Assessment: Concepts, Techniques and Applications. Oxford University Press, Oxford, UK, pp. 223–233.
Wu, Y., Bishop, I., Hossain, H., Sposito, V., 2006. Using GIS in landscape visual quality assessment. Appl. GIS 2 (3), 18.1.
Yamamoto, K., 2010. Road traffic noise prediction model "ASJ R TN-Model 2008": report of the research committee on road traffic noise. Acoust. Sci. Technol. 31 (1), 2–55.
Yang, L., Zhang, L., Stettler, M.E., Sukitpaneenit, M., Xiao, D., van Dam, K.H., 2020. Supporting an integrated transportation infrastructure and public space design: a coupled simulation method for evaluating traffic pollution and microclimate. Sustain. Cities Soc. 52, 101796.
Zhang, J., Kørnøv, L., Christensen, P., 2013. Critical factors for EIA implementation: literature review and research options. J. Environ. Manage. 114, 148–157.
Zhou, K.Y., Sheate, W.R., 2011. EIA application in China's expressway infrastructure: clarifying the decision-making hierarchy. J. Environ. Manage. 92 (6), 1471–1483.

CHAPTER NINE

Project appraisal methods: Tools for optimizing or for informed political debate?

Petter Næss*
Department of Urban and Regional Planning, Norwegian University of Life Sciences, Ås, Norway
*Corresponding author: e-mail address: petter.nass@nmbu.no

Contents

Abstract

In this chapter, I discuss points of criticism raised against the appraisal methods most commonly used within the transportation sector, and possible remedies to reduce these flaws. Since cost-benefit analysis is the dominant method of transportation project appraisal and the one against which most points of criticism can be raised, discussion of this method will cover a major part of the text. Merits and shortcomings of multicriteria analysis will also be discussed, although more briefly. Based on the points of criticism raised and the prospects for addressing them within the framework of each method, I then suggest what could be done to avoid the shortcomings identified, recognizing that the criteria for project evaluation should be explicit rather than concealed in the minds of the individual planners and decision-makers. The decisions on proposed projects should be informed by impact analyses that do not give privilege to those effects that can be quantified. The impact analyses should illuminate environmental, social, economic and psychological effects as well as impacts of proposed projects on the direction in which society at large develops. The political nature of decisions on transport infrastructure should be recognized. These political decisions involve tough choices and prioritizations between conflicting values and interests that are irreducible to mathematical optimization.

Keywords: Cost-benefit analysis, Inaccuracy, Bias, Multicriteria analysis, Impact analysis, Improvements

ISSN 2543-0009
https://doi.org/10.1016/bs.atpp.2020.07.007

1. Introduction

Assessing anticipated impacts of a proposed intervention is an indispensable element in planning. In his seminal article about ends and means in planning, Banfield (1959) identified comparative evaluation of consequences as one of the key steps of a rational planning procedure, defined as a procedure for selecting a course of action likely to attain the objectives of the planning subject or maximize the chances of their attainment. Although Banfield's model for rational planning has been heavily attacked since its publication more than six decades ago, the later developments in procedural planning theory still implicitly assume that the likely impacts of proposed solutions must in some ways be judged. Otherwise, there would not be any point for the different stakeholders in incremental planning processes (Lindblom, 1959) to fight for or against specific proposed projects, or for the participants in deliberative processes to argue that one proposed solution is better than an alternative one (Forester, 1999; Innes, 1996). Without assessment of likely consequences, actors—be they public authorities or private agents—could as well roll dice about what solutions to choose.

In many fields of planning in the public domain, impact assessments of alternative solutions do not follow predefined, quantitative procedures. This applies to urban land use planning, nature conservation planning, and planning within the educational, cultural and law enforcement sectors, just to mention a few examples. In particular, the most strongly formalized appraisal method, cost-benefit analysis (CBA), is virtually non-existing within these sectors. For example, apart from the Netherlands (Van Zutphen Economisch Advies, 2020), which appears as a clear exception in this matter, most countries have until now managed to do land use planning without having to rely on cost-benefit analyses, and there is little evidence of any proliferation of such analyses in land use planning.[a] Public authorities have been able to make decisions for a long period through history applying neither cost-benefit analyses nor sophisticated multicriteria analyses (MCA). Buildings have been erected, electricity supply has been provided, transport infrastructure has been constructed and educational programs have been

[a] A search on the Internet in the summer of 2020 showed one academic book on the topic and a couple of articles, but hardly any other hits for the search "cost-benefit analysis" "urban planning."

established long before anyone knew the meaning of acronyms such as CBA or MCA. The decisions to build these material structures and to establish the public services can hardly be characterized as generally ill-informed (although they may often have promoted to the interests of privileged elites to the detriment of less well-off groups). Anyway, planning and decision-making in the public domain is evidently possible regardless of the availability of results from sophisticated appraisal methods. Moreover, studies show that actual decisions on project implementation often deviate substantially from the recommendations based on formal appraisal methods (Annema et al., 2017; Eliasson and Lundberg, 2012; Eliasson et al., 2015; Mouter, 2017; Nyborg, 1998; Odeck, 2010; Sager and Ravlum, 2005; Sager and Sørensen, 2011).

Within the transportation sector, there is a long tradition of using cost-benefit analyses to inform decision-makers about the value for money of infrastructure investments. In many countries, this method is codified in official guidelines. Over the recent decades, appraisal guidelines require an increasing number of impacts to be monetized and included in the calculations of costs and benefits. Proponents of the method claim that the use of cost-benefit analysis is necessary to avoid subjectivity and arbitrariness, but is this method objective? Several critics have argued the opposite (e.g., Ackerman and Heinzerling, 2004; Metz, 2008; Næss, 2006; Orland, 1998; Sagoff, 1981).

Several critics of the cost-benefit analysis method have pointed at multicriteria analysis as an alternative approach (e.g., Dimitriou et al., 2016; Hill, 1985; Keeney and Raiffa, 1976; Munda, 1995). Although this approach avoids some of the shortcomings of cost-benefit analysis, many of the variants covered under the multicriteria analysis umbrella have their own weaknesses (e.g., Dean et al., 2018; Miller, 1985; Richardson, 2005; Voogd, 1983).

In the remainder of this chapter, I will first discuss various points of criticism raised against cost-benefit analyses (Section 2). Since this is the dominant method of transport project appraisal and the one against which most points of criticism can be raised, this section will cover a major part of the text. Thereupon, Section 3 discusses merits and shortcomings of multicriteria analyses. In Section 4, I will suggest what could be done to avoid the shortcomings identified, recognizing that the criteria for project evaluation should be explicit rather than concealed in the minds of the individual planners and decision-makers. A few brief concluding remarks round off the chapter (Section 5).

2. Critique of the cost-benefit analysis method

2.1 Inaccuracy

Proponents of cost-benefit analysis often argue that this method offers more exact information on which decisions can be based, compared to other project appraisal methods. By applying the same measurement unit (Euro or other monetary currency) to the different types of positive and negative impacts, the inexactness pertaining to subjective assessments of the importance of different impact categories can be avoided, according to CBA proponents (Sunstein, 2000). The discounting rules are also said to offer a more exact assessment of how much value is to be attached to long-term impacts compared to short-term impacts. Other methods leave this assessment to qualitative judgments based on decision-makers' ethical prioritizations in each specific case. Moreover, due to its requirement for monetized assessment of each impact included in the analysis, cost-benefit analysis implies a quest for quantifying as many impacts as possible. Such quantified impact estimates (measured at a scale level) are widely held to be more exact than rank-ordered (ordinal) or purely qualitative (nominal) estimates.

But how exact are cost-benefit-analyses in transportation planning practice? Let us first consider the translation of quantified impacts into monetary values. On the benefit side, travel time savings is normally the dominant item, often accounting for 80–90% of the calculated benefit of a road investment project (Eliasson and Lundberg, 2012; Mackie et al., 2001). However, in a study published in 2005, the valuation of time savings per minute for journeys to work varied by a factor of 10 between the two EU neighbor countries of Austria and Hungary (Odgaard et al., 2005). If we only include more recent figures (covering the Netherlands, Germany, France and the United Kingdom, with data from the years 2011–14), there is a factor 3 variation in the value of travel time for car commuting below 50 km between the highest value (12.5 Euro in the United Kingdom versus 4.2 Euro in Germany), measured per hour income and prices (De Jong and Kouwenhoven, 2020). For long (above 100 km) business trips by train, the variation is even larger between the highest (Germany, 45.3 Euro) and the lowest value (United Kingdom, 11.2 Euro), i.e., a factor of 4 (ibid.). Updated international comparisons of the prices for greenhouse gas emissions in cost-benefit analyses are not available, but according to the above-mentioned study by Odgaard et al. (2005), the valuation of CO_2 emissions varied by a factor of 5 between the neighboring EU countries of Sweden and Finland. Regarding traffic fatalities, the official value of a statistical life in cost-benefit analyses was more than twice as high in 2018 in Denmark and Sweden (41 and 40 million NOK, respectively) as in the United Kingdom (18 million NOK), with Norway in-between with 34 million NOK (Bjånesøy, 2019). However, a decade and a half earlier, the value of a Danish statistical life was set to be only a half of the Norwegian value (Odgaard et al., 2005). As the examples above show, the translation of quantified effect sizes into monetized values is by no means an exact science. The large variations in the price per minute of travel time, ton of greenhouse gas emissions, statistical life, etc., imply that there must be a large scope for subjective judgment when deciding the assumptions on which the calculations of unit prices are to be based (Mouter, 2016).

The estimated sizes of the various kinds of (non-monetized) impacts of transportation projects are also not necessarily very accurate. As mentioned above, the dominant impact category on the benefit side is travel time savings. These savings depend on the change in travel speed and in the number of travelers that experience travel time savings. The estimations of traffic volumes and travel speeds are based on traffic forecasts normally generated by means of transport models. However, although such forecasts may seem very accurate, with numbers of vehicles quantified in precise numbers, comparisons of forecasted traffic volumes with the amount of traffic actually occurring in the relevant transport corridors after project implementation show considerable deviations. For example, a study of 146 road projects and 31 rail projects in Scandinavia and the United Kingdom showed standard deviations of 33% and 35% inaccuracy for the completed road and rail projects, respectively (Nicolaisen and Driscoll, 2014; Nicolaisen and Næss, 2015). Inaccuracy here refers to the percentage that the actual traffic volume exceeded or was below the forecasted traffic volume. In an older study of 183 road and 27 rail projects in 14 countries on 5 continents, Flyvbjerg et al. (2005) found standard deviations of 44% and 52% forecasting inaccuracy, respectively, for road and rail projects. In a study of 50 road projects in Norway, Welde and Odeck (2011) found lower, but still considerable forecasting inaccuracies with standard deviations of 22% and 20% for tolled and non-tolled roads, respectively.

Inaccurate traffic forecasts affect the estimates of how many travelers will experience the travel speed improvement (if any) resulting from the projects. But estimated travel speed changes per traveler will also be affected if traffic volumes are inaccurately forecasted, especially in situations where congestion relief is among the purposes for road construction. If the actual traffic turns out to be higher than forecasted, the new road may be filled up with so many vehicles that congestion builds up anew. This adds to the uncertainty of the calculations of travel time savings, as illustrated in a study of a road project in Copenhagen (Næss et al., 2012).

The largest item on the cost side of cost-benefit analyses of transportation projects is normally the construction costs. Here, too, large forecasting inaccuracies appear to be the rule rather than the exception. In a study of 258 infrastructure projects worldwide, Flyvbjerg et al. (2002) found a standard deviation of 39% inaccuracy for forecasted construction costs of the whole sample, with 30% for roads, 38% for rail and as much as 62% for fixed links. In a similar vein, Nicolaisen (2012) found forecasted construction costs of 105 infrastructure projects in Scandinavia and the United Kingdom to be inaccurate with standard deviations of 36% (roads) and 33% (rail).

The large uncertainty margins resulting from the high inaccuracy levels of future traffic volumes and speeds as well as construction costs translate into even bigger uncertainties for the key performance indicators of cost-benefit analyses, namely the benefit/cost ratio and the net present value. Add to this the uncertainties evident from the large variation in the assigned monetary value per unit for important impact categories such as travel time savings and traffic fatalities.

According to Asplund and Eliasson (2016), although there is a lot of uncertainty in cost-benefit analyses, this does not matter for the rankings of projects. However, given the large standard deviations of forecasts, the error margins around the estimates are wide, and a project where traffic and costs are inaccurately forecasted in a way unfavorable for its realization (i.e., too pessimistic) may then be ranked too low compared to a project where the forecasts are too optimistic.

In addition, there is a large variation between countries in discounting policies. In the Netherlands, the risk-adjusted discount rate is 5.5%. Sweden and the United Kingdom both apply 3.5% as the discount rate, whereas a rate of 4% is used in Norway as well as Denmark (Mouter, 2018).[b] In the USA, the

[b] In Norway, Denmark and the United Kingdom, discount rates are lower for effects occurring in a long-term than for short- and medium-term effects. In the United Kingdom, a 3.5% rate has since 2003 been applied for impacts occurring during the first 30 years, 3% for impacts occurring between 30 and 75 years, and thereafter gradual reduction down to 1% for impacts occurring more than 300 years after implementation. In Norway, the discount rate has since 2014 been 4% for impacts occurring during the first 40 years, 3% for impacts occurring between 40 and 75 years, and 2% for later impacts. In Denmark, the discount rate was until recently 6% but was reduced to 4% in 2017, declining to 3% for impacts occurring in more than 35 years and 2% for impacts after 70 years.

most recent federal practice is to calculate the present value of future long-term environmental impacts as the midpoint of estimates based on 3% and 7% discount rates (Lee and Pizer, 2019). Although these differences may appear small, they add up to large differences over time. After 40 years, the present value of an impact will be 2.15 times smaller in the Netherlands than in Sweden and the UK, and 9.1 times smaller in the USA than in these two European countries.

2.2 Bias in cost-benefit analyses

The results of cost-benefit analyses of transportation projects are not only encumbered with uncertainty but are often also biased. Partly, such bias stems from underestimation of induced car traffic (or overestimation of traffic in case an increase in road capacity is not built), which may lead to skewed estimation of travel time savings, environmental impacts and traffic accidents. Another source of bias is underestimated land use impacts of infrastructure development, notably in the form of a higher land consumption and fragmentation of landscapes due to urban sprawl facilitated by the construction of infrastructure. Disadvantages pertaining to the construction period are also in many cases neglected or substantially underestimated (Næss et al., 2017). Further examples are the underestimated pricing of greenhouse gas emissions in most of the countries where such impacts are monetized at all, and the neglect of other important impact categories. Finally, discounting of environmental impacts implies bias against future generations, whereas the willingness-to-pay principle implies a bias against the poor.

Below, each of these sources of bias will be discussed.

2.2.1 Biased traffic forecasts

Several studies have shown on average higher actual traffic volumes than forecasted on new road infrastructure. Flyvbjerg et al. (2005) and Næss et al. (2006) found that forecasts underestimated the actual traffic on 16 investigated Danish roads completed between 1962 and 1988 by as much as 50% (but with no similar underestimation for the part of the sample of investigated roads located in other countries). Interestingly, there was on average no underestimation for the Danish projects completed until 1976, while the mean underestimation was as large as 96% among the nine projects completed later (i.e., 1980–88).

Road improvements generally tend to induce additional traffic due to less time spent to reach a given destination.[c] According to Andersen (2013:300, 303), the traffic-generating effects of improved and widened roads (induced traffic) were included in Danish transport project evaluation practice until the early 1970s, whereas the subsequent regional transport models ignored induced traffic. This can be part of the explanation why forecasted traffic volumes of Danish road projects completed in the 1980s were underestimated, but not those completed in the previous two decades. Moreover, increased environmental awareness influenced the prevailing political attitudes in Denmark in the 1970s and early 1980s, which might form an incentive for road planners to produce underestimated traffic forecasts[d] (Næss et al., 2006).

Given the very low size of the above-mentioned sample of Danish projects, one should be cautious of drawing too firm conclusions from that study. However, in a study of 146 major road projects in Scandinavia and the United Kingdom (Nicolaisen, 2012), traffic forecasts were also found to underestimate the actual traffic volumes. In this case, the underestimation was much more moderate (11.2%), but still statistically significant. A review of international studies published in 1988–2012 on forecasting inaccuracy for road projects found underestimations ranging from 3% to 21% (Nicolaisen and Driscoll, 2014).[e] One reason for these relatively moderate levels of underestimation could be that induced traffic was already being somehow included in some of the forecasts, based on projections of past growth trends—trends that were partly the result of traffic growth induced by earlier road constructions (Andersen, 2013; Næss, 2011). However, while such forecasts of the general traffic development may reduce the forecasting inaccuracy of the "build" alternatives, new bias will then be introduced for the "build nothing" alternatives. With common traffic

[c] In line with Schmidt and Campbell (1956, cited in Cervero, 2001, p. 4), induced traffic is here understood as "the added component of traffic volume which did not previously exist in any form, but which results when new or improved transport facilities are provided." This includes vehicle traffic resulting from increased distances between origins and destinations, changes in travel routes, changes in travel modes, and changes in trip frequencies (Hills, 1996). The effect of induced traffic is now widely accepted among transport researchers (American Association of State Highway Officials, 1957; Downs, 1962; Duranton and Turner, 2011; Goodwin, 1996; Litman and Colman, 2001; Mogridge, 1990; Næss et al., 2001; Noland and Lem, 2002; SACTRA, 1994; Thomson, 1977).

[d] This hints at "strategic misrepresentation" (Flyvbjerg, 2007) as one of the causes of forecast inaccuracies. Substantially overestimated passenger forecasts for new rail lines (Flyvbjerg et al., 2005; Nicolaisen and Driscoll, 2014) point in the same direction, see also Næss et al. (2015).

[e] In addition, one study published in 1981 found forecasts to overestimate traffic volumes by 7%, but this study was methodically less sophisticated than the remaining studies.

growth trajectories for the "build" and "build nothing" alternatives, the deterrent effect of congestion on further traffic growth will be neglected in the latter alternatives (Næss, 2011). Interviews with planners show that the practice of using common traffic growth projections for both the "build" and "build nothing" alternatives is, or has at least been until relatively recently, standard practice in Denmark (Andersen, 2013; Næss et al., 2014, 2015). This tends to result in overestimated traffic forecasts for the "build nothing" alternatives, termed by Næss (2011) as "pessimism bias" against the zero-alternatives due to the depiction of the "build nothing" scenarios as resulting in traffic growth beyond the capacity of the road network and hence intolerable congestion levels.

An analysis of the 36 projects of Nicolaisen's sample for which traffic forecasts for the "build nothing" alternative as well as actual traffic volumes on the non-expanded road network were available for the planned (but delayed) year of opening of the new road, shows that traffic in the "build nothing" alternative was overestimated by on average 7% (Nicolaisen and Næss, 2015). The overestimation was statistically significant at the 0.001 level. This study suggests that biased forecasts for the "build nothing" alternative are not restricted to the few cases where such mechanisms have been demonstrated through qualitative interviews with transport modelers and planners (Andersen, 2013; Næss, 2011). Together, the 11% average underestimation of traffic in the "build" alternatives and the 7% overestimation of traffic in the "build nothing" alternatives in Nicolaisen's sample represent a combined bias of 15–20%, most likely reflecting neglect or underestimation of the traffic-increasing effects of road capacity increases.

In a wider European context, MOTOS (2007) pointed at neglect of induced traffic as a common phenomenon, reflecting that many of the transport models in use did not include this effect. In a similar vein, a more recent study of a sample of 120 Scandinavian researchers and consultants dealing with transport modeling showed that traffic models were often considered as poor at estimating the additional traffic induced when infrastructure is being built, if at all taken into consideration (Næss et al., 2014). Although transport models in some countries have been improved, the forecasts actually used in transportation planning still often do not take induced traffic into account. For example, the climate impact report for a recently planned new motorway connecting the western part of Oslo with a town at the fringe of the metropolitan area showed only microscopic difference (0.1%) in forecasted traffic volumes in 2044 between the "build" and "build nothing" alternatives (Bane NOR, 2018:19). This was despite the fact that Norwegian traffic models have since the early 2000s been able to model short-term induced traffic.

All the above comparisons of forecasted and actual traffic volumes cover only the short-term forecasting inaccuracies (i.e., in the first year after project opening). However, higher travel speeds allow for longer journeys to be undertaken within the same time budget as earlier. Improvements in the accessibility of outskirt locations enable households and businesses to move to locations that are more car-based and at longer distances from the city center. This increases the market demand for dwellings and commercial buildings at such locations, which makes construction of housing, workplaces, retail and other activities in peripheral, car-dependent and traffic-generating areas more attractive. These land use impacts occur in a longer time-perspective than the initial induced traffic and comprise chains of mechanisms where road capacity expansions affect land use developments that in turn contribute to increased traffic volumes (Kasraian et al., 2016; Litman, 2016; Noland and Lem, 2002). The sprawling urban development facilitated by infrastructure development reducing the "friction of distance" within an urban region does not just induce more traffic in the corridor connecting the new peripheral housing or commercial areas with the central city. Due to the generally poorer public transport provision in the outer areas and the easier conditions for local car driving (with uncongested local roads and ample parking possibilities), sprawl also contributes to increased car traffic to local destinations such as stores for daily necessities purchases, preschools, and schools to which children are escorted (Dovre and TØI, 2012).

Additional traffic increase may also appear due to reductions in the quality of public transport resulting from the initial loss of passengers triggered by road development itself (Mogridge, 1997) as well as by subsequent more dispersed land use. This reduced quality will in turn make car travel even more competitive compared with public transport.

Such longer-term effects due to changes in location patterns, land use, and the service level of public transport are very difficult to model[f] and therefore,

[f] So-called land use and transport interaction (LUTI) models aim to iteratively predict land use changes resulting from transport infrastructure development, and the subsequent effects of these land use changes on travel. However, there is great uncertainty in these forecasts (Pogonyi, 2020). Moreover, the models presuppose that land use responds to the attractiveness for development that new infrastructure offers to surrounding areas, regardless of any land use regulations to prevent a merely market-based development. Such models thus basically assume that there is no public land use planning.

to my knowledge, they are not included in any existing transport models in use in transportation planning in European countries. The long-term induced traffic can be substantial, typically around twice as large after 3–5 years or more as in the first year after opening (Litman, 2019; Noland and Lem, 2002; Twitchett and Nicolaisen, 2013). The actual forecasting bias due to underestimation or neglect of induced traffic is therefore likely to be considerably larger than the 15–20% indicated by Nicolaisen's above-mentioned studies.

2.2.2 Biased assessment of traffic-related impacts

Neglect of induced traffic and ignoring the deterrent effect of congestion on future traffic growth can render the cost-benefit analysis highly misleading. Some researchers (e.g., Welde and Odeck, 2011) and transport planning practitioners (see Andersen, 2013; Næss et al., 2014) have depicted omission of induced traffic as a sort of precaution in order to avoid exaggerating the benefits from travel time savings in the economic project evaluation. While it may be the case in uncongested rural areas that the benefits of the increased number of travelers using an improved road will outweigh any reduction in travel speed on these roads due to induced traffic, this is clearly not the case in urban regions. This may lead to skewed ranking of road projects in rural areas versus road projects in urban regions where congestion occurs. As shown by Næss et al. (2012), neglect of induced traffic in the cost-benefit analyses of a proposed road scheme in a congested area can lead to severely biased estimates of the economic performance of the project. Using a traffic model that neglected induced traffic, the net present value of a planned new urban highway in Copenhagen (Nordhavnsvej) was calculated to be 2.16 billion DKK, compared with only 0.40 billion DKK if induced traffic was taken into consideration. In the latter case, the initial congestion relief, and hence travel time savings, would be substantially reduced as the new road filled up with additional cars. In the case of the moderately congested Frederikssund motorway in the outer parts of Copenhagen metropolitan area too, the inclusion of induced traffic resulted in a lower net present value than if induced traffic was omitted (Næss et al., 2012).

Moreover, induced traffic on new rural roads may, even if it does not lead to congestion on the new piece of infrastructure, lead to "downstream" congestion in the cities and urban regions they lead to. This is, for example, likely to be the case for the planned new E18 and E16 road schemes in the western part of the Oslo region.

Effects on health, safety and the environment included in the cost-benefit analysis will be affected too if induced traffic is neglected or underestimated. Such negative effects will be systematically underestimated when traffic is underestimated, regardless of whether induced traffic contributes positively or negatively to travel time savings in the specific geographical context. Conversely, any calculated improvements in terms of health, safety or environment will be overestimated if traffic is underestimated. In some cases, a seemingly positive effect in this area may turn out to be negative when taking short-term and long-term induced traffic into consideration. Usually, the impact of new road schemes on traffic accidents is shown as having a positive economic value, reflecting a predicted decrease in traffic accidents due to, for example, the lower number of crossings when driving on a motorway. However, induced road traffic implies that more people will be exposed to the risks of traffic accidents. Moreover, since trips do not start and end on the slip roads of the motorway, but go from origins to destinations all over the city and the region, the increasing traffic caused by a new motorway will expose a larger number of people to the risk of accidents along local roads. These effects may well outweigh the lower safety risk per vehicle kilometer of motorways compared with other roads.

Similar bias will occur for the calculations regarding exposure to noise and local air pollution if induced traffic is underestimated or ignored. The same applies to greenhouse gas emissions. For example, in the 2006 environmental impact assessment of the proposed Third Limfjord Crossing near Aalborg, the analysis predicted that the construction of a new motorway bypass road would reduce energy consumption and greenhouse gas emissions, alleviate noise, and help to reduce the numbers of traffic injuries and deaths (Næss, 2011). Regarding CO_2 emissions, additional skewness occurs if, as is often the case, the impact of increased driving speeds beyond the fuel-economic optimum level is disregarded. In Scandinavian countries, at least, it has been common practice to include the effect of congestion relief on fuel economy, but not to take into account the reduced fuel economy of facilitating increase in driving speeds beyond 80–90 km/h (Næss, 2011; Strand et al., 2009).

Some of the above-mentioned biases are not inherent shortcomings of the cost-benefit method as such but hold for all appraisal methods that rely on transport models. However, when it comes to induced traffic, methods other than cost-benefit analysis can apply locally adapted interpretations of theoretical knowledge and elasticities found in empirical research for similar contexts, also taking long-term induced traffic into consideration. Cost-benefit analysis needs (pseudo)accurate point estimates and thus has to rely on transport models.[g] It is possible to develop and use transport models taking short-term induced traffic into account. It is also possible, for example, to take the increased CO_2 emissions from high-speed driving into regard. However, the long-term induced traffic is difficult, if at all possible, to predict by means of transport modeling.

At the same time, because cost-benefit analyses require precise, quantitative input data about, for example, traffic volumes and travel speed levels, the cost-benefit analysis regime in transport planning and decision-making depends on forecasting methods that can seemingly produce exact point estimates of effects. Cost-benefit analysis thus prioritizes effects that can be modeled quantitatively and tends to disregard effects that the forecasting models are not able to capture (Annema and Koopmans, 2015; Mouter et al., 2015). As we have seen, this creates serious bias, and when it comes to the long-term induced traffic, there does not seem to be any remedy in sight.

Through their sophisticated calculations and complicated equation structures, the models obtain credibility, and a model-based point estimate becomes more easily "reified" than a rough estimate based on theoretical judgment (Porter, 1995; Roeh and Feldman, 1984)—no matter whether the latter is actually closer to reality. This has to do with the fact that most people are not able to judge critically the credibility of the model results presented in a cost-benefit analysis. This, in its turn, has to do with the "black box" (Hajer, 1995:272) nature of the transport models as well as of the cost-benefit analysis method itself. Cost-benefit analysis therefore arguably transforms transport modeling into a "truth-producing technology" (Ackerman, 2008; Henman, 2002) rather than a tool for planners to explore possible impacts of different combinations of infrastructure solutions and other policy measures during the process of plan-making. At least regarding long-term induced traffic, the "truths" thus produced are actually false, and there does not seem to be any remedy in sight.

2.2.3 Underestimation of land use impacts

As mentioned above, the long-term induced traffic resulting from transport infrastructure construction leads to land use changes, particularly in the form

[g] One could of course imagine that elasticities of induced traffic and scenarios for the "background" traffic development were applied in cost-benefit analysis instead of using forecasts based on transport models. Such estimates would necessarily be rough, and although they might less biased than model-based forecast, such a change of practice would be a radical deviation from the methodological ideology (Lawson, 2016) of the disciplinary tradition to which the method of cost-benefit analysis belongs.

of urban sprawl, i.e., urban spatial expansion characterized by low population density, inefficient use of land and fragmented patterns of development (European Environmental Agency, 2006). Because of the many negative environmental (Næss et al., 2020) as well as economic (Burchell et al., 1998; Mønnesland, 1991) impacts of such urban development, many European cities and national governments have over recent decades aimed at a more compact urban development. Such urban development, characterized by a high share of densification rather than outward expansion, is today widely considered a desirable tool to deliver positive environmental, economic and social outcomes (OECD, 2012; UN Habitat, 2014).

Highway development in urban regions tends to facilitate and encourage urban sprawl. It will be a tougher task for planning authorities to counteract sprawl if much highway development takes place than if there were no road capacity increase (Litman, 2016). Infrastructure-induced urban sprawl is an effect not only of road construction, but also of public transport investments (notably high-speed rail), making it faster and more convenient to travel from the outskirts of a metropolitan area to the city center.

Since building densities are normally lower on the outskirts of an urban region than in its inner parts, and inner-city construction of dwellings and commercial buildings often takes place in areas that are already dominated by technical encroachments, such sprawl will entail a higher consumption of natural areas and/or farmland than would otherwise be the case. Apart from the land taken for constructing a sprawl-inducing highway or rail line, decentralized and low-density urban development will require the construction of more access roads and usually more parking space than if urban development were to take place as densification within existing urban areas. Such development entails direct economic as well as ecological costs, but is rarely, if ever, taken into consideration in cost-benefit analyses of transportation projects.

2.2.4 Disadvantages pertaining to the construction period

Most transport infrastructure projects take years to implement. Difficulties in and around the construction period can include consequences for traffic on existing networks, local noise and pollution due to construction activities, temporary landscape impacts, disadvantages for local businesses, and social disruption of neighborhoods due to the influx of a temporary population of people working on the projects (Næss et al., 2017). Of these, the consequences for traffic (in terms of negative time savings, or time losses) are assumed to have the largest economic impact on the project's net present value. More generally, any disadvantages that occur early in the lifecycle of a project could have a major impact on the estimated net present value due to the effect of discounting. However, these consequences are disregarded altogether in the current Norwegian framework for cost-benefit analyses, where they are not even mentioned among the non-monetary set of impacts (Hagen et al., 2012), and they are not mentioned in the EU guide to cost-benefit analysis regarding road projects (Sartori et al., 2015).[h]

Disruptions in the traffic system might occur for road projects, rail projects, and other transport infrastructure projects. Insofar as the capacity of the existing infrastructure of a category is affected (e.g., due to temporary lane closure on a road), such disruptions can lead to changes in people's choices of travel modes, and to "disappearing traffic" (Cairns et al., 2002), in a way similar to the induced traffic resulting from capacity increase after the opening of a project. In many cases, disruption during the construction process has resulted in lower-than-expected congestion (Cairns et al., 2002; Tennøy et al., 2016). However, this depends on whether alternative routes and travel modes are available, and on the extent to which it is possible for those who travel to make their trips at a different time of the day (i.e., outside the peak period) or simply drop some trips. The movement of bulldozers, tractors, excavators, and other contractor's vehicles on the roads during the construction process represents an additional source of disruption. For public transport projects, disruption during the construction period (e.g., the construction of an additional track on a railway) can make some passengers shift to using cars or to other public transport connections, similar to the changes that may appear among car travelers during road construction. Remaining passengers who must rely on alternative, temporary public transport services such as "bus for train" often experience increased travel times.

The construction process also entails energy use and related greenhouse gas emissions. Such energy use and emissions can be quite substantial, depending on the geographical context of the project. For intercity two-lane roads and other types of road building schemes in rural areas, the contribution to CO_2

[h] The EU guidelines include case examples of how to calculate the benefits and costs of a motorway and an urban tram line. Here, time savings, fewer accidents and reduced levels of CO_2 and VOC emissions are all assumed to contribute positively during the operation of the new infrastructure, whereas these impacts are all set to zero during the three-year construction periods (Sartori et al., 2015:108, 141). For a third example, a railway line, it is acknowledged that the construction period will generate some service disruptions, and resulting cost estimates are included in the calculation example, but with very small values.

I do not have information on whether cost-benefit analysis practice in individual EU countries include negative impacts pertaining to the construction period, but lack of hits when searching for the keywords cost-benefit and construction period suggest that this may not be common practice.

emissions and energy use stems mainly from the construction process. This is especially the case if long tunnels must be constructed. For two-lane roads in smaller towns and urban settlements, the construction process also accounts for a substantial part. For new and expanded highways in a metropolitan area, the contribution of the road project to energy use and CO_2 emissions is mainly due to induced traffic, whereas the construction process itself accounts for a much more moderate proportion (Strand et al., 2009). For railway projects, the construction process can account for a very high share of the lifetime energy use and CO_2 emissions (NRA/Jernbaneverket, 2012).

By neglecting or underestimating negative impacts pertaining to the construction period, cost-benefit analyses present projects in a more flattering light than what should realistically be the case. On the other hand, the impacts occurring during the construction period are probably difficult to quantify, and they will hence add to the uncertainties of the results if included in the cost-benefit analysis. Neglect of negative impacts in the construction period can of course occur also if other project evaluation methods are used. However, since other methods do not depend on the same degree of quantification as cost-benefit analysis does, it may be easier to take impacts pertaining to the construction period into regard when using these methods.

2.2.5 Biased pricing

The economic valuation of environmental consequences of transport investment projects is problematic. For some impacts, the valuation is based on willingness-to-pay investigations. However, people often do not have sufficient knowledge about the impact of a project to be able to state in a meaningful way how much they are willing to pay in order to make a contribution to avoid an impact. Willingness-to-pay investigations are hardly able to account for the multi-faceted social value of (changes in) environmental qualities such as clean air or the combined function of a particular area as a beautiful landscape, an outdoor recreation area, a rich ecosystem, and the habitat of particular species. As a result, conservation of an ecosystem, for example, the territory of a species threatened by extinction, is highly unlikely to obtain a sufficient monetary price in a cost-benefit analysis to render an otherwise profitable infrastructure project unprofitable.

The pricing of carbon emissions in cost-benefit analyses is also unlikely to prevent infrastructure projects contributing to increased greenhouse gas emissions from being built. In Norway, the price per ton of CO_2 emissions was on average set to 35 USD in the cost-benefit analyses of 111 large public works projects performed in the period 2005–13 (Volden, 2013). In

Denmark, the unit price to be used in cost-benefit analyses is currently 23 USD per ton (Center for Transport Analytics, 2019). The World Bank (2017) has recently recommended to apply a "shadow price" for carbon emissions rising from 40 to 80 USD per ton in 2020 to 78–156 USD per ton in 2050. Even these somewhat higher prices are unlikely to make much difference to the net present value of transport infrastructure projects.

On the other hand, the pricing of time savings has been criticized for being exaggerated. For one thing, the option to work while traveling, for example, on a train journey, may strongly influence whether or not travel time savings equate to increases in productivity. There is little evidence that this has impacted the value of travel time savings so far (Halse, 2020). Slow adaptation of unit prices for travel time savings in cost-benefit analyses to the increasing possibilities of combining travel with other meaningful activities results in exaggerated estimates of time benefits. More fundamentally, people tend to expand their radius of action rather than using travel time savings from higher travel speed for non-travel purposes (Metz, 2008). In the short-term, this may give accessibility benefits (but also negative environmental and safety impacts due to increased traffic volumes). In a longer-term, shorter travel times within a region tend, as mentioned above, to contribute to urban sprawl, and the increased access to distant jobs that local residents may experience is counterweighed by higher competition for locally available jobs from non-local residents. Increased travel speeds thus tend to not only make it possible, but also necessary for people to transport themselves longer distances to reach daily and weekly activities.

2.2.6 Bias against future generations and the poor

Although increasingly debated, it is still common practice in cost-benefit analyses to discount future effects at the same rate across impact categories, regardless of whether the impacts are travel time savings or irreversible environmental damages. Apart from the subjectivity in setting the discount rates, the discounting practice can represent severe bias against future generations. Some academics (such as Chichilnisky, 1997; Gowdy et al., 2010; Stern, 2007) have asserted that discount rates should be based on ethical considerations instead of market interest rates. However, this is almost never done in practice, and several other cost-benefit scholars have explicitly argued against including ethical considerations (Nordhaus, 2007; Purves, 2016). Discounting long-term and irreversible environmental impacts implies a "short-termism" where consequences to future generations are considered insignificant. Such discounting represents serious bias against future generations, playing hazard with their basic life conditions. Even with the reduced discounting rate of 2% recently proposed in Norway for impacts occurring after more than 75 years, a climate disaster occurring in 150 years has a discounted cost today 20 times smaller than if it occurred next week. The discounting of future impacts of global warming places alternatives generating high greenhouse gas emissions in a much more favorable light than what would otherwise be the case and may lead to the preference of such solutions rather than lower-emission alternatives.

The principle of willingness-to-pay gives the highest influence on decisions to those whose ability to pay is highest. Failure to distinguish between on the one hand human needs and on the other hand wants and market demand (Assiter and Noonan, 2007; Dean, 2007) legitimizes a utilitarian focus only on the total amount of demand satisfaction. While democratic majority decisions are based on the principle of one vote per person, the number of "votes" available for each person to influence which alternative will obtain the highest willingness-to-pay is determined by his/her level of affluence.[i] If a majority prefers alternative A to alternative B, but the minority has a high willingness to pay for alternative B, the latter project may well be the one which obtains the highest total willingness-to-pay. Considering the sum of the individual's willingness to pay as an adequate indicator of the need among the population thus implies an underestimation of the needs among low-income groups.

In order to avoid this bias, some theorists have proposed to replace private willingness-to-pay with collective willingness to pay or willingness to allocate public budget (Mouter et al., 2020). The one-Euro-one-vote principle would then be replaced by one-person-one-vote. This would be a progressive reform of existing cost-benefit analysis practice, but there are problems with this approach as well. People cannot be expected to be fully informed about the impacts of an infrastructure project on the environmental or other goods

[i] In practice, the same value is used many countries across population groups for impact categories such as traffic fatalities and travel time (Mouter, 2019). However, for other impact categories, such as local air pollution and noise in the residential neighborhood, or the loss of a local park or other outdoor recreation area, standard numbers do not apply. Willingness-to-pay investigations might then show a higher benefit from building a proposed road as an underground tunnel instead of as a surface road through a rich than a poor neighborhood. Maybe compensation demand would be less biased in favor of the rich than willingness to pay, since a poor person may just as much as a rich person demand a high compensation for an environmental damage. But people's frames of reference will still reflect their economic situations. Therefore, it seems likely that millionaires will on average demand higher compensations than low-income people for a given kind of negative impact (for example, the loss of a local outdoor recreation area in their residential neighborhood).

affected, nor about the social and ecological ramifications of these impacts. How would they then be able to state how much public money to spend to obtain or prevent those impacts? People are also hardly fully informed about the consequences of taking money from other sectors' budgets to enable the spending of public money on project-related mitigations.

3. Multicriteria analysis—A more adequate alternative?

As noted by several authors, including Dean (2020) in this volume, the branch of methods referred to as multicriteria analysis avoids some of the most problematic aspects pertaining to cost-benefit analyses, since it depends neither on monetizing of all impacts nor on discounting environmental impacts. Common to these methods is that they are based on assessing a score for each investigated alternative indicating its performance against each impact category, resembling the way students' performances are graded at an exam. The impact categories should in principle cover all kinds of impacts that affected stakeholders consider important. Similar to a simple impact analysis (environmental or social), the anticipated impacts of a project alternative must first be described as precisely as possible, verbally and if relevant also quantitatively. Since both verbally described and quantified impacts can be translated into scores, multicriteria analyses can include a wider range of impact categories in the formal analysis than for cost-benefit analysis. In the latter case, non-quantifiable and non-monetized impacts are relegated to a separate analysis of "non-priced impacts" usually receiving less attention by decision-makers than the main performance indicators (net present value and benefit/cost ratio). Because of this, and that the importance of long-term environmental impacts such as greenhouse gas emissions are not "discounted away," multicriteria analyses are more favorable than cost-benefit analyses from a sustainability point of view, especially when comparing different "build" alternatives with the "build nothing" alternative.

There are still several problems pertaining to multicriteria analyses. Most such methods imply that a weight is to be attached to each impact category to account for differences in their mutual importance. Several more or less sophisticated methods have been developed to elicit such weights from stakeholders' priorities. Most often, the weighting process is aimed at obtaining a single set of weights to be used in the project appraisal. A question immediately arises: how legitimate will these weights be? Because of the substantial disagreement in society on the importance of different normative values, such weighting techniques are only suitable for consensus-building within relatively homogeneous groups (such as an environmentalist group, an organization of local residents, or the chamber of commerce), and not for arriving at conclusions about the "optimal" solution for society as a whole. Regardless of whether the stakeholder representatives involved in the weighting process are able to arrive at some sort of consensus about the weights (which appears rather unlikely) or the weights are calculated as an average of the stakeholder representatives' individual weights, the question still remains: how representative are the persons involved in the weighting process for the population at large, or for the elected politicians?

Theoretically, a solution could be to include all members of the relevant political decision-making body (e.g., all members of the national parliament if the project is of a kind that will ultimately be decided at that level), but in practice it has proven difficult to involve the elected members of a political decision-making body, or a representative panel of its politicians, in such processes (Dean, 2018, 2020). To my knowledge, no example of such a study exists in the literature on multicriteria analyses. This leaves us with the questionable legitimacy of the weights as well as the project alternatives' aggregate scores based on these weights. On the other hand, merely adding the scores of each impact category without any weighting implies the highly subjective assumption that each kind of impact is equally important.

As noted by several methodologists (see Dean, 2020), the overall score of an alternative may be affected by the number of detailed criteria each main value dimension includes. This can be solved by organizing the criteria hierarchically, where the sum of weights at a lower level correspond to the weight of the dimension in question at a higher level in the hierarchy. It can still be a tricky task to avoid "double-counting" while at the same time acknowledging that one measurable criterion can affect two or more normative concerns belonging to different value dimensions. Choosing an adequate description of the outcomes corresponding to the various levels of the scoring scale for each impact category is another challenging task. Ideally, the highest score should be for the best possible outcome and the lowest for the worst possible outcome (Edwards and Newman, 1982), but what is to be considered as "possible" here? This will depend on the actual context—geographically, socially, technically, economically and, not the least, politically. If the span between the best and worst outcome of the evaluation scale is narrow, a small impact difference can result in a large difference in scores. In order not to attach too high importance to such small outcome differences, the weights should, other things being equal, be lower in such cases than for impact categories where the span between the highest and lowest score corresponds to a large difference in outcomes. Although this can in theory be solved, it may be difficult to ensure in practice that the range of outcomes, scores, number of criteria and weights is made consistent. For example, stakeholders may attach weights to impact categories based on how important they consider the issue as such to be, without taking into consideration how narrow or broad the difference in outcomes defining the highest and lowest scores of each impact type is described.

Yet another problem is rarely mentioned in the literature but may still be an important one. Some concerns (and their associated impact categories) may in practice be very important to decision-makers without being articulated (for example, because they are not "politically correct", are ethically difficult to defend, or might scare away voters). In such cases, an alternative that obtains the best score in the multicriteria analysis may still be considered politically unacceptable if it conflicts with such non-articulated, but de facto important concerns. The assessment of three different strategic alternatives for land use and transport infrastructure development in the 10 largest Norwegian urban regions three decades ago may serve as an example. Alternatives based on a combination of compact urban development, reduced road building, restrictions on car driving and improved transit provision obtained the clearly highest scores but were not chosen as the base for follow-up planning. Instead, strategies including substantial road development were chosen. In the multicriteria analysis, the politically important criterion "car drivers' satisfaction" was evidently missing. The researchers evaluating the assessment process concluded that the environmental alternatives were best, but the road plans won (Strand, 1992). On the other hand, by showing discrepancies between strategies favorable for reaching the official political goals and the strategies actually chosen, multicriteria analyses can be helpful in revealing hidden agendas (Barfod, 2012).

4. What should be done (instead)?

As argued in the preceding sections, both cost-benefit analyses and weight-based multicriteria analyses have serious shortcomings. The reliance of the cost-benefit analyses on exact, quantified predictions of future situations ignores measurement problems and inevitable forecasting uncertainty (Næss and Strand, 2012). For instance, the method requires precise input data, but in practice traffic forecasts are inaccurate and often also biased. The valuation of many impact categories is contestable and inconsistent across countries, and the discounting rules entail an untenable diminishing of long-term and irreversible negative environmental impacts. These biases can legitimate too much infrastructure construction and disarm environmental opponents of the projects. The willingness-to-pay principle on which the method is based represents ethical bias against the poor, future generations and affected parties outside the local context. It is also based on the neoclassical ontological assumption of fully informed, selfish and utility-maximizing humans, which is a highly unrealistic understanding of human nature (Næss, 2006).

In my view, cost-benefit analysis is therefore not appropriate for assessing whether or not to build a proposed project of a particular category (e.g., a road project) in a specific geographical context. The above-mentioned negative impacts neglected or underestimated in cost-benefit analyses may also well outweigh any wider economic benefits (cf. Pogonyi, 2020) referred to in the literature (Næss et al., 2017).

Cost-benefit analysis may be less inappropriate if the task is to compare different alternative ways of designing an adopted project (e.g., layout A, layout B or layout C for a proposed new road). This is because the main uncertainties and biases occur when comparing building a proposed project with the "build nothing" alternative. When comparing different layouts of such a project, many of the uncertainties and biases will be relatively similar for all alternatives and thus be less important for the mutual comparison of alternatives. However, due to the uncertainties mentioned in Section 2, the cost-benefit analysis should then only be used to assess the marginal differences between different variants of the project, not its absolute economic value.

As mentioned in Section 2.1, Asplund and Eliasson (2016) claim that the ranking of projects will not be affected by the uncertainties of cost-benefit analyses, since many uncertainties point in the same direction. However, as shown in Section 2.2, the shortcomings of cost-benefit analysis include not only uncertainties but also biases. Although these biases are particularly severe for comparisons of "build" with "build nothing" alternatives, they also tend to skew rankings between different projects. Because induced traffic tends to affect travel time savings negatively in urban regions and positively in rural areas, cost-benefit analyses based on model-based traffic forecasts will tend to give road projects in urban areas too high rankings and roads in rural areas too low rankings. In addition, the discounting of long-term negative environmental impacts implies that projects resulting in high greenhouse gas emissions or extinction of species will obtain a too high ranking, compared to projects with smaller such impacts. The same applies to comparisons between investments in road capacity and transit improvements.

While multicriteria analysis avoids some of the problematic epistemological and ontological assumptions of cost-benefit analysis, it has its own shortcomings. Many of these shortcomings can in principle be remedied, for example, through careful processes to ensure consistency between the range of defined outcomes, scores, number of criteria and weights, and by including all relevant assessment criteria, based on inputs from a wide range of stakeholder groups and interdisciplinary experts. However, establishing weights "on behalf of society" remains an unsolvable problem. At the same time, such a single set of weights is necessary if the multicriteria analysis is to be able to tell which alternatives are better or worse. Since transport infrastructure projects subject to formal appraisal are usually decided by the political bodies at national or regional level, establishing a set of weights representing the decision-maker's priorities would require that the members of these political assemblies got involved in the weight-eliciting process. Since this appears highly unrealistic, it would be better to let go with the ambition of using multicriteria analyses to determine the "best" or "optimal" alternatives, which can simply not be identified in the absence of society-representative weights.

If a weight-based multicriteria approach is to be pursued, separate processes of weighting, evaluation and discussion of the alternatives should instead be carried out among each group of stakeholders, based on the importance attached by each group to different impact categories. The relevant consequence categories should be identified on the basis of a broad hearing among experts from different disciplines and representatives of different stakeholder and population groups. The goal hierarchy, representing desirable outcomes for each impact category, should include all the concerns mentioned by any of the participating stakeholder groups, and would thus be a "gross" compilation of goals. The various impacts would be indicated by experts according to a goal achievement scale (e.g., a five- or ten-level scale) for each impact category. The total, weighted score of each alternative for non-monetized dimensions could then be compared to each alternative's economic score (construction costs and possible other items that may be valorized in an appropriate way). This could make up a basis for an interactive discussion within each stakeholder group of the mutual ranking of the alternatives.

While separate weight-eliciting processes have been recommended by several multicriteria analysis experts (e.g., Edwards and Newman, 1982; Quereshi and Harrison, 2006), these processes are usually considered only as a step on the way toward arriving at common, cross-stakeholder weights. Distinct from using multicriteria analysis as another "truth-producing tool" (Henman, 2002), my recommendation is to use the multicriteria analysis as a "backstage" dialogical tool for helping a relatively homogeneous stakeholder group (for example, an environmental organization, or a regional development council) in identifying the alternative that best meets the group's values and interests. The planning authorities should offer help to facilitate such processes among interested stakeholder groups.

Even for such relatively homogeneous groups, the synthesizing method would only be suitable as an interactive tool for arriving at a more reasoned opinion of the merits of the project alternatives and the "build nothing" alternative, and not for arriving at firm conclusions. One must be aware that such group processes are time-consuming. On the other hand, the processes could contribute to more vivid stakeholder participation in the planning and decision-making process. The costs of carrying out the processes should also be compared to the substantial costs associated with obtaining the data required for a cost-benefit analysis.

The approach outlined above implies that the weight-based multicriteria analysis would not be part of the official project appraisal. The latter should instead be conducted as an ordinary impact analysis covering impact categories identified by multi-disciplinary experts and representatives of different stakeholder and population groups as outlined above.

Due to the inherent and high uncertainty of forecasts of the general (background) traffic growth and the context-dependency of each particular planning situation, traffic forecasting should be differentiated reflecting the degrees of openness/closure of the systems at hand: Scenario analyses exploring different alternative futures at the strategic level where the general, nation-scale traffic development is assessed; theory-informed, rough estimates at the tactical level where the difference between building or not building a project is assessed; whereas more traditional micro-simulations should be used only at a detailed operational level, e.g., for comparison between different layouts of a proposed project (Næss and Strand, 2012).

In the impact analysis, direct construction costs (costs for land purchases, materials, construction work, financing costs, etc.) should of course be estimated as accurately as possible in monetary terms.[j] The same applies to

[j] Empirically, construction costs have often been found to be considerably biased (on average underestimated). According to Flyvbjerg et al. (2002) this is largely due to strategic misrepresentation, and I do think this is part of the explanation. However, recent studies from Norway (Odeck and Kjerkreit, 2019) show that Norwegian road projects are now completed with construction costs matching the budgeted amounts quite well (yet with a small average underestimation of 5%). Anyway, construction cost budgets obviously need to be made for projects, so it would be ridiculous not to include them in the appraisal. Reducing these costs to a score on a grade scale would imply unnecessary loss of information. However, tough measures to counteract "strategically misrepresented" construction cost budgets should be institutionalized.

expenses such as maintenance of the infrastructure and compensation for demolished buildings. All other impacts should be expressed in non-monetary terms and given a score similar to the grades at exams. They should all be qualitatively described, supplemented with quantifications only when appropriate. This implies that travel time savings, which is currently the main item on the benefit side of cost-benefit analyses of transportation projects, would not be included among the monetized impacts. Due to the inability of transport models to forecast future traffic volumes and travel speeds (especially long-term) in a reasonably accurate way and the contested nature of travel time valuation, I consider such estimates to be far too uncertain to warrant this exercise. Some other effects (e.g., the amount of conversion of different types of natural areas and farmland, or the size of noise zones and number of dwellings within these areas) may be quantified without monetarization. Effects that are difficult to measure should be made subject to qualitative descriptions or be assessed from a combination of qualitative and quantitative indicators.

Proponents of cost-benefit analysis and common-weight multicriteria analysis may argue that the approach proposed above does not provide decision-makers with the answer about whether or not a project should be implemented, or how to rank several implementation-worthy projects. However, the belief that it is possible to give a technical answer to these questions is trying to do the impossible: to reconcile incommensurable values in one quantitative and objective indicator. Political issues should not be reduced to technocratic calculations.

5. Concluding remarks

The recommendations above may appear unrealistic and naïve, given the hegemonic position of cost-benefit analysis in transportation planning. Why is this method still holding the hegemony, despite its documented shortcomings? According to Lawson (2016), an over-reliance on mathematical methods of analysis has caused widespread and long-lived failings of the discipline of mainstream economics. This methodological ideology (ibid.) may be some of the reason for the strong belief in the possibility of identifying socially optimal solutions through calculations. However, as shown in Section 2, cost-benefit analyses tend to be not only inaccurate but also biased. Some of these biases could be reduced without rejecting the method of cost-benefit analysis as such (for example, by using traffic forecasts taking induced traffic fully into account, or using zero or negative interest rate for greenhouse gas emissions), although the inherent uncertainty of such calculations would still persist. Theoretically, the cost-benefit analysis can also be carried out under environmental constraints (Minken and Samstad, 2003).[k] Moreover, it is possible to avoid the substitution of votes with purchasing power implicit in the private willingness-to-pay principle by valuing impacts based on collective willingness to pay or willingness to allocate public budget, as suggested by Mouter et al., 2019. However, amending the practice of cost-benefit analysis along the lines suggested above would probably render the process considerably more data-hungry and complicated. Some of the reforms might also not sit well with existing power relations within the transportation sector, and the ministries responsible for project appraisals might be unwilling to adopt these reforms for political reasons.

According to Ackerman and Heinzerling (2004), the method of cost-benefit analysis promotes a deregulatory agenda under the cover of scientific objectivity. Cost-benefit analysis is well suited to neoliberal growth policies, whereas it depicts policies prioritizing environmental protection or a higher degree of equality in society above growth as being economically irrational. In a situation where sustainable mobility is on the agenda and an increasing number of countries have adopted political objectives of curbing the growth in car traffic,[l] leaning on an appraisal method favoring satisfaction of the demand for higher car mobility appears contradictory.

Although differing in important ways from cost-benefit analysis, common-weight multicriteria analysis shares the technocratic belief in identifying optimal solutions through calculation and is arguably rooted in the same methodological ideology emphasizing mathematical methods of analysis.

[k] According to Minken and Samstad (2003), the bias toward future generation could theoretically be solved by carrying out the cost-benefit analysis subject to constraints regarding non-renewable resources, notably "land" and "climate," following an approach inspired by Chichilnisky (1996) and Heal (2000). Discounting would then only be made for impacts not included in these constraints. The method recommended by Minken and Samstad (ibid.:22) differs from an ordinary cost-benefit analysis in the following ways: (1) the application of a parameter for equitable intergenerational distribution, e.g., a discount rate decreasing over time; (2) a shadow price of unused areas and of CO_2 emissions; and (3) the rejection of strategies that do not reach certain environmental objectives, objectives concerning public budgets and other political goals at the end of the evaluation period.

[l] For example, according to an agreement on climate policy in, 2012 among six of the by then seven parties represented in the Norwegian parliament, all growth in the amount of traveling in the largest Norwegian urban regions is to take place as public and non-motorized transport, with no growth in car driving despite high forecasted population growth. This goal is included in National Transport Plans adopted in the 2013 and 2017.

Instead, the political nature of decisions on transport infrastructure should be recognized. These political decisions involve tough choices and prioritizations between conflicting values and interests that are irreducible to mathematical optimization. The decisions on proposed projects should be informed by impact analyses that do not give privilege to those effects that can be quantified. The impact analyses should illuminate environmental, social, economic and psychological effects as well as impacts of proposed projects on the direction in which society at large develops, and they should clarify how well different alternatives meet adopted political objectives. In this way, project appraisals could inform politicians as well as civil society and enrich public debates on transportation policy.

References

Ackerman, F., 2008. Critique of Cost-Benefit Analysis, and Alternative Approaches to Decision-Making. Friends of the Earth England, Wales and Northern Ireland, London.

Ackerman, F., Heinzerling, L., 2004. Priceless: On Knowing the Price of Everything and the Value of Nothing. New Press, New York.

American Association of State Highway Officials, 1957. A Policy on Arterial Highways in Urban Areas. American Association of State Highway Officials, Washington.

Andersen, J.A., 2013. The Shaping of Transport Model Based Knowledge Production: An Embedded Case Study of Danish Transport Modeling Practice in a Contemporary and Historical Perspective. PhD thesis, Aalborg University, Aalborg.

Annema, J.A., Koopmans, C.C., 2015. The practice of valuing the environment in cost-benefit analysis in transport and spatial projects. J. Environ. Plan. Manag. 58 (9), 1635–1648.

Annema, J.A., Frenken, K., Koopmans, C.C., Kroesen, M., 2017. Relating cost-benefit analysis results with transport project decisions in the Netherlands. Lett. Spat. Resour. Sci. 10 (1), 109–127.

Asplund, D., Eliasson, J., 2016. Does uncertainty make cost-benefit analyses pointless? Transp. Res. A 92, 195–205.

Assiter, A., Noonan, J., 2007. Human needs: a realist perspective. J. Crit. Realism 6 (2), 173–198.

Bane NOR, 2018. Klimabudsjett for infrastruktur og transport. Reguleringsplan med konsekvensutredning (KU), Fellesprosjektet Ringeriksbanen og E16 Høgkastet—Hønefoss. Document FRE-00-A-25300. https://www.banenor.no/globalassets/documents/prosjekter/ringeriksbanen-og-e16/reguleringsplan/horingsdokumenter-reguleringsplan/klimabudsjett-for-infrastruktur-og-transport.pdf.

Banfield, E.C., 1959. Ends and means in planning. Int. Soc. Sci. J. 9 (3), 361–368.

Barfod, M.B., 2012. Optimising Transport Decision Making Using Customised Decision Models and Decision Conferences. PhD thesis, Technical University of Denmark, Kgs. Lyngby.

Bjånesøy, V., 2019. Verdi av statistisk liv i samfunnsøkonomiske analyser. [Value of Statistical Life in Socio-Economic Analyses.]. Master thesis, University of Bergen, Department of Economics, Bergen.

Burchell, R.W., Shad, N.A., Listokin, D., Phillips, H., Downs, A., Seskin, S., Davis, J.S., Moore, T., Helton, D., Gall, M., 1998. The Costs of Sprawl—Revisited. National Academy Press, Washington, DC.

Cairns, C., Atkins, S., Goodwin, P., 2002. Disappearing traffic? The story so far. Proc. Inst. Civ. Eng. Munic. Eng. 151 (1), 13–22.
Center for Transport Analytics, 2019. Transportøkonomiske enhedspriser til brug for samfundsøkonomiske analyser. Technical University of Denmark, Kgs. Lyngby.
Cervero, R., 2001. Induced Demand: An Urban and Metropolitan Perspective. University of California, Department of City and Regional Planning, Berkeley. Accessed December 1, 2013 at http://www.uctc.net/papers/648.pdf.
Chichilnisky, G., 1996. An axiomatic approach to sustainable development. Soc. Choice Welf. 13 (2), 231–257.
Chichilnisky, G., 1997. What is sustainable development? Land Econ. 73, 467–491.
De Jong, G., Kouwenhoven, M., 2020. Value of travel time and travel time reliability. In: Mouter, N. (Ed.), Standard Transport Appraisal Methods. Advances in Transport Policy and Planning, vol. 6. Elsevier, Amsterdam, pp. 43–74 (Chapter 2).
Dean, K., 2007. Needs. In: Hartwig, M. (Ed.), Dictionary of Critical Realism. Routledge, London/New York, pp. 323–324.
Dean, M., 2018. Assessing the Applicability of Participatory Multicriteria Analysis Methodologies to the Appraisal of Mega Transport Infrastructure. Ph.D. Dissertation, The Bartlett School of Planning, University College, London.
Dean, M., 2020. Multi-criteria analysis. In: Mouter, N. (Ed.), Standard Transport Appraisal Methods. Advances in Transport Policy and Planning, vol. 6. Elsevier, Amsterdam, pp. 165–224 (Chapter 6).
Dean, M., Hickman, R., Chen, C.-L., 2018. Testing the application of participatory MCA: the case of the south Fylde line. Transp. Policy 73, 62–70.
Dimitriou, H.T., Ward, E.J., Dean, M., 2016. Presenting the case for the application of multicriteria analysis to mega transport infrastructure appraisal. Res. Transp. Econ. 58, 7–20.
Dovre & TØI, 2012. Kvalitetssikring av konseptvalg (KS2): Intercitystrekningene. https://www.regjeringen.no/nb/dokumenter/kvalitetssikring-ks1-avkonseptvalgutr2/id712738/?regj_oss=90.
Downs, A., 1962. The law of peak-hour expressway congestion. Traffic Q. 16 (3), 393–409.
Duranton, G., Turner, M.A., 2011. The fundamental law of road congestion. Evidence from US cities. Am. Econ. Rev. 101 (6), 2616–2652.
Edwards, W., Newman, J.R., 1982. Multiattribute Evaluation. Sage Publications, Thousand Oaks.
Eliasson, J., Lundberg, M., 2012. Do cost-benefit analyses influence transport investment decisions? Experiences from the Swedish Transport Investment Plan 2010–21. Transplant. Rev. 32, 29–48.
Eliasson, J., Börjesson, M., Odeck, J., Welde, M., 2015. Does benefit-cost efficiency influencetransport investment decisions? J. Transp. Econ. Policy 49, 377–396.
European Environmental Agency, 2006. Urban Sprawl in Europe: The Ignored Challenge. EEA, Copenhagen.
Flyvbjerg, B., 2007. Policy and planning for large-infrastructure projects: problems, causes, cures. Environ. Plann. B. Plann. Des. 34, 578–597.
Flyvbjerg, B., Holm, M.S., Buhl, S., 2002. Underestimating costs in public works projects: error or lie? J. Am. Plann. Assoc. 68 (3), 279–295.
Flyvbjerg, B., Holm, M.S., Buhl, S., 2005. How (in)accurate are demand forecasts in public works projects? The case of transportation. J. Am. Plann. Assoc. 71 (2), 131–146.
Forester, J., 1999. The Deliberative Practitioner. M.I.T. Press, Cambridge.
Goodwin, P., 1996. Empirical evidence on induced traffic. A review and synthesis. Transportation 23 (1), 35–54.
Gowdy, J., Howarth, J.B., Tisdell, C., 2010. Discounting, ethics, and options for maintaining biodiversity and ecosystem integrity. In: Kumar, P. (Ed.), The Economics of Ecosystems and Biodiversity: The Ecological and Economic Foundations. UNEP/Earthprint, Nairobi and Stevenage.

Hagen, K.P., Berntsen, S., Bye, B., Hultkrantz, L., Nyborg, K., Pedersen, K.R., Sandsmark, M., Volden, G.H., Avitsland, G., 2012. Cost-Benefit Analysis. 2012 Official Norwegian Report NOU, p. 16.
Hajer, M.A., 1995. The Politics of Environmental Discourse: Ecological Modernisation and the Policy Process. Oxford University Press, Oxford.
Halse, A.H., 2020. Cost benefit analysis (CBA) of infrastructure projects: strengths and weaknesses. In: Presentation at the Norwegian University of Life Sciences, March 10, 2020.
Heal, G., 2000. Valuing the Future. Economic Theory and Sustainability, Economics for Sustainable Earth. Columbia University Press, New York.
Henman, P., 2002. Computer modelling and the politics of greenhouse gas policy in Australia. Soc. Sci. Comput. Rev. 20, 161–173.
Hill, M., 1985. Can multiple-objective evaluation methods enhance rationality in planning? In: Breheny, M., Hooper, A. (Eds.), Rationality in Planning—Critical Essay on the Role of the Rationality in Urban and Regional Planning. Pion Limited, London, pp. 166–182.
Hills, P.J., 1996. What is induced traffic? Transportation 23 (1), 5–16.
Innes, J., 1996. Planning through consensus building. A new view of the comprehensive planning ideal. J. Am. Plann. Assoc. 62, 460–472.
Kasraian, D., Maat, K., Stead, D., van Wee, B., 2016. Long-term impacts of transport infrastructure networks on land-use change: an international review of empirical studies. Transplant. Rev. 36 (6), 772–792.
Keeney, R., Raiffa, H., 1976. Decision With Multiple Objectives. John Wiley & Sons, New York.
Lawson, T., 2016. Ideology and economics. In: Næss, P., Price, L. (Eds.), Crisis System: A Critical Realist and Environmental Critique of Economics and the Economy. Routledge, London and New York, pp. 8–29.
Lee, Q., Pizer, W.A., 2019. Discounting for Public Cost-Benefit Analysis. Resources for the future, Washington, DC. Working Paper 19–02, Accessed July 2020 from https://media.rff.org/documents/WP-19-02-Li-Pizer-f.pdf.
Lindblom, C., 1959. The science of "muddling through". Public Adm. Rev. 19 (2), 79–88.
Litman, T., 2016. Evaluating Transportation Land Use Impacts. Considering the Impacts, Benefits and Costs of Different Land Use Development Patterns. Victoria Transport Policy Institute, Victoria. http://www.vtpi.org/landuse.pdf.
Litman, T., 2019. Generated Traffic and Induced Travel. Implications for Transport Planning. Victoria Transport Policy Institute, Victoria. http://www.vtpi.org/gentraf.pdf.
Litman, T., Colman, S.B., 2001. Generated traffic. Implications for transport planning. ITE J 71 (4), 38–47.
Mackie, P.J., Jara-Díaz, S., Fowkes, A.S., 2001. The value of travel time savings in evaluation. Transp. Res. E 37, 91–106.
Metz, D., 2008. The myth of travel time saving. Transplant. Rev. 28 (3), 321–336.
Miller, D.H., 1985. Equity and efficiency effects of investment decisions: multicriteria methods for assessing distributional implications. In: Faludi, A., Voogd, H. (Eds.), Evaluation of Complex Policy Problems. Delftsche Uitgevers Maatschappij B.V., pp. 35–50.
Minken, H., Samstad, H., 2003. Evaluering av samordnet arealbruks- og transportplanlegging med bærekraft som mål. TØI report 686/2003, Institute of Transport Economics, Oslo.
Mogridge, M.J.H., 1990. Travel in Towns. Jam Yesterday, Jam Today and Jam Tomorrow? Macmillan Press, London.
Mogridge, M.H.J., 1997. The self-defeating nature of urban road capacity policy: a review of theories, disputes and available evidence. Transp. Policy 4 (1), 5–23.
Mønnesland, J., 1991. Natur- og miljøvennlig tettstedsutvikling—en vurdering av økonomiske hindringer. NIBR Working Paper 1991:114, Norwegian Institute for Urban and Regional research, Oslo.

MOTOS, 2007. Transport Modelling: Towards Operational Standards in Europe. Accessed 12 June 2010 from http://www.motosproject.eu/?po_id=handbook.
Mouter, N., 2016. Value of travel time: to differentiate or not to differentiate? Transp. Res. Rec. 2597 (1), 82–89.
Mouter, N., 2017. Dutch politicians' use of cost-benefit analysis. Transportation 44 (5), 1127–1145.
Mouter, N., 2018. A critical assessment of discounting policies for transport Cost Benefit Analysis in five European practices. Eur. J. Transp. Infrastruct. Res. 18 (4), 389–412.
Mouter, N., Ojeda Cabral, M., Dekker, T., van Cranenburgh, S., 2019. The value of travel time, noise pollution, recreation and biodiversity: a social choice valuation perspective. Research in Transportation Economics 76.
Mouter, N., Koster, P.R., Dekker, T., 2020. Contrasting the recommendations of Participatory Value Evaluation and Cost-Benefit Analysis in the context of urban mobility investments. Tinbergen Institute Working Paper.
Mouter, N., Annema, J.A., Van Wee, B., 2015. Managing the insolvable limitations of cost-benefit analysis: results of an interview based study. Transportation 42 (2), 277–302.
Munda, G., 1995. Multicriteria Evaluation in a Fuzzy Environment—Theory and Applications in Ecological Economics. Springer, Switzerland.
Næss, P., 2006. Cost-benefit analyses of transportation investments: neither critical nor realistic. J. Crit. Realism 5 (1), 32–60.
Næss, P., 2011. The Third Limfjord Crossing—a case of pessimism bias and knowledge filtering. Transplant. Rev. 31 (2), 231–249.
Næss, P., Strand, A., 2012. What kinds of traffic forecasts are possible? J. Crit. Realism 11 (3), 277–295.
Næss, P., Mogridge, M.J.H., Sandberg, S.L., 2001. Wider roads, more cars. Nat. Res. Forum 25, 147–155.
Næss, P., Flyvbjerg, B., Buhl, S., 2006. Do road planners produce more 'honest numbers' than rail planners? An analysis of accuracy in road-traffic forecasts in cities versus peripheral regions. Transplant. Rev. 26 (5), 537–555.
Næss, P., Nicolaisen, M.S., Strand, A., 2012. Traffic forecasts ignoring induced demand: a shaky fundament for cost-benefit analyses. Eur. J. Transp. Infrastruct. Res. 12 (3), 291–309.
Næss, P., Andersen, J., Nicolaisen, M.S., Strand, A., 2014. Transport modelling in the context of the 'predict and provide' paradigm. Eur. J. Transp. Infrastruct. Res. 14 (2), 102–121.
Næss, P., Andersen, J., Nicolaisen, M.S., Strand, A., 2015. Forecasting inaccuracies: a result of unexpected events, optimism bias, technical problems, or strategic misrepresentation? J. Transp. Land Use 8 (3), 39–55.
Næss, P., Volden, G.H., Odeck, J., Richardson, T., 2017. Neglected and Underestimated Negative Impacts of Transport Investments. Concept report no. 54, Trondheim: Ex Ante Academic Publisher, Trondheim.
Næss, P., Saglie, I.-L., Richardson, T., 2020. Urban sustainability: is densification sufficient? Eur. Plan. Stud. 28 (1), 146–165. https://doi.org/10.1080/09654313.2019.1604633.
Nicolaisen, M.S., 2012. Forecasts: Fact or Fiction? Uncertainty and Inaccuracy in Transport Project Evaluation. PhD thesis, Aalborg University, Aalborg.
Nicolaisen, M.S., Driscoll, P., 2014. Ex-post evaluations of demand forecast accuracy: a literature review. Transp. Rev. 34, 540–557.
Nicolaisen, M.S., Næss, P., 2015. Roads to nowhere: the accuracy of travel demand forecasts for do-nothing alternatives. Transp. Policy 37, 57–63.
Noland, R.B., Lem, L.L., 2002. A review of the evidence for induced travel and changes in transportation and environmental policy in the US and the UK. Transp. Res. D 7 (1), 1–26.

Nordhaus, W., 2007. Critical assumptions in the stern review on climate change. Science 317 (5835), 201–202.
NRA/Jernbaneverket, 2012. Høyhastighetsutredningen 2010–2012 Konklusjoner og oppsummering av arbeidet i Fase 3. Del 1. National Roads Authority and the Norwegian National Rail Administration, Oslo.
Nyborg, K., 1998. Some Norwegian politicians' use of cost-benefit analysis. Public Choice 95 (3–4), 381–401.
Odeck, J., 2010. What determines decision-makers' preferences for road investments? Evidence from the Norwegian road sector. Transplant. Rev. 30, 473–494.
Odeck, J., Kjerkreit, A., 2019. The accuracy of benefit-cost analyses (BCAs) in transportation: an ex-post evaluation of road projects. Transp. Res. A 120 (C), 277–294.
Odgaard, T., Kelly, C., Laird, J., 2005. Current practice in project appraisals in Europe. In: Paper for the Conference Trafikdage på Aalborg Universitet, Aalborg, August 2005.
OECD, 2012. Compact City Policies: A Comparative Assessment. OECD Publishing, Paris.
Orland, B., 1998. Economic Evaluation: Cost-Benefit Analysis. East St. Louis Action Research Project, St. Louis.
Pogonyi, C.G., 2020. The wider economic benefits of transportation. In: Mouter, N. (Ed.), Standard Transport Appraisal Methods. Advances in Transport Policy and Planning, vol. 6. Elsevier, Amsterdam, pp. 129–164 (Chapter 5).
Porter, T.M., 1995. Trust in Numbers: The Pursuit of Objectivity in Science and Public Life. Princeton University Press, Princeton.
Purves, D., 2016. The case for discounting the future. Ethics Policy Environ. 19 (2), 213–230.
Quereshi, M.E., Harrison, S.R., 2006. Process. In: Herath, G., Prato, T. (Eds.), Using Multicriteria Decision Analysis in Natural Resource Management. Ashgate, Farnham, pp. 41–59.
Richardson, T., 2005. Environmental assessment and planning theory: four short stories about power, multiple rationalities and the need for situated ethical judgement. Environ. Impact Assess. Rev. 25 (4), 341–365.
Roeh, I., Feldman, S., 1984. The rhetoric of numbers in front-page journalism: how numbers contribute to the melodramatic in the popular press. Text Talk 4 (4), 347–368.
SACTRA, 1994. Trunk Roads and the Generation of Traffic. Standing Advisory Committee on Trunk Road Assessment, London.
Sager, T., Ravlum, I.A., 2005. The political relevance of planners' analysis. The case of a parliamentary standing committee. Plan. Theory 4 (1), 33–65.
Sager, T., Sørensen, C.H., 2011. Planning analysis and political steering with New Public Management. Eur. Plan. Stud. 19 (2), 217–241.
Sagoff, M., 1981. The limits of cost-benefit analysis. Philos. Public Policy Q. 1 (3), 9–11.
Sartori, D., Catalano, G., Genco, M., Pancotti, C., Sirtori, E., Vignetti, S., Bo, S.D., 2015. Guide to Cost-Benefit Analysis of Investment Projects. Economic Appraisal Tool for Cohesion Policy 2014–2020. European Commission, Directorate-General for Regional and Urban Policy, Brussels.
Schmidt, R.E., Campbell, E.M., 1956. Highway Traffic Estimation. Eno Foundation for Highway Traffic Control, Saugatuck, CT.
Stern, N., 2007. The Economics of Climate Change. Cambridge University Press, Cambridge and New York.
Strand, A., 1992. Evaluering av TP10-arbeidet: Miljøalternativene var best, men vegplanene vant!. *Samferdsel*, 8/92.
Strand, A., Næss, P., Tennøy, A., Steinsland, C., 2009. Gir bedre veger mindre klimagassutslipp? TØI report 1027/2009, Institute of Transport Economics, Oslo.
Sunstein, C.R., 2000. Cognition and cost-benefit analysis. J. Leg. Stud. 29 (52), 1059–1103.

Tennøy, A., Wangsness, P.B., Aarhaug, J., Gregersen, F.A., 2016. Experiences with capacity reductions on urban main roads—rethinking allocation of urban road capacity? Transp. Res. Proc. 19, 4–17.

Thomson, J.M., 1977. Great Cities and Their Traffic. Gollancz, London.

Twitchett, C., Nicolaisen, M.S., 2013. Trafikspring [induced traffic]. Trafik og Veje 8, 7–9.

UN Habitat, 2014. Urban Patterns for a Green Economy Leveraging Density. UNON Publishing Services, Nairobi.

Van Zutphen Economisch Advies, 2020. MKBA Database. Accessed June 2020 from http://www.vanzutpheneconomischadvies.nl/index.php/mkba-database.

Volden, G.H., 2013. Use of carbon prices in cost-benefit analysis practices in project appraisals of major public investment projects under the Norwegian state project model. Concept report no. 37, Norwegian University of Science and Technology, Trondheim.

Voogd, J.H., 1983. Multicriteria Evaluation for Urban and Regional Planning. Pion Limited, London.

Welde, M., Odeck, J., 2011. Do planners get it right? The accuracy of travel demand forecasting in Norway. Eur. J. Transp. Infrastruct. Res. 11 (1), 80–105.

World Bank, 2017. Shadow Price of Carbon in Economic Analysis. Guidance Note. http://pubdocs.worldbank.org/en/911381516303509498/2017-Shadow-Price-of-Carbon-Guidance-Note-FINAL-CLEARED.pdf.

FSC
www.fsc.org
MIX
Papier | Fördert gute Waldnutzung
FSC® C083411

Kolibri 360 GmbH
Ferdinand-Jühlke-Straße 7
99095 Erfurt, Deutschland
produktsicherheit@kolibri360.de